THE ECONOMICS OF DISAPPEARING DISTANCE

In honor of T.R. Lakshmanan, gentleman and scholar

The Economics of Disappearing Distance

Edited by

ÅKE E. ANDERSSON
Royal Institute of Technology, Sweden

BÖRJE JOHANSSON
Jönköping International Business School, Sweden

WILLIAM P. ANDERSON
Boston University, USA

ASHGATE

Published by
Ashgate Publishing Limited
Gower House
Croft Road
Aldershot
Hampshire GU11 3HR
England

Ashgate Publishing Company
Suite 420
101 Cherry Street
Burlington, VT 05401-4405
USA

Ashgate website: http://www.ashgate.com

British Library Cataloguing in Publication Data
The economics of disappearing distance
1.Space in economics 2.Economic development
I.Andersson, Åke E., 1936- II.Johansson, B. (Börje)
III.Anderson, William P.
338'.09

Library of Congress Cataloging-in-Publication Data
The economics of disappearing distance / edited by Åke E. Andersson, Börje Johansson and William P. Anderson.
p. cm.
Includes bibliographical references and index.
ISBN 0-7546-3273-3
1. Regional economics. 2. Space in economics. 3. Urban economics. 4. Transportation.
I. Andersson, Åke E., 1936- II. Johansson, B. (Börje) III. Anderson, William P.

HT388 .E382 2002
330.9--dc21

2002028168

ISBN 0 7546 3273 3

Printed and bound in Great Britain by MPG Books Ltd, Bodmin, Cornwall

Contents

List of Figures

List of Tables

List of Contributors

Nuzul Achjar, Doctoral candidate in the Department of Geography at the University of Illinois, USA.

William P. Anderson, Professor of Geography at Boston University, and a faculty member of the Boston University Center for Transportation Studies, Boston, USA.

Åke E. Andersson, Professor of Infrastructural Economics at the Royal Institute of Technology, Stockholm, Sweden.

David E. Andersson, Ph. D., senior research fellow at Inregia, Sweden.

Roger E. Bolton, Professor of Economics at Williams College in Williamstown, Massachusetts, USA.

Mustafa Dinc, Global Trust Fund Manager at the Development Economics Data Group at the World Bank.

William L. Garrison, Professor Emeritus of Civil and Environmental Engineering and Emeritus Research Engineer in the Institute of Transportation Studies at the University of California, Berkeley, USA.

David Gillen, Adjunct Professor of Civil and Environmental Engineering and Research Economist at the Institute of Transportation Studies, University of California, Berkeley. He is also Professor of Business and Economics at the Wilfrid Laurier University, Waterloo, Canada.

David L. Greene, Corporate Fellow of Oak Ridge National Laboratory, Oak Ridge, Tennessee, USA.

Kingsley E. Haynes, Dean of the School of Public Policy at George Mason University, Fairfax, Virginia where he is also Professor of Public Policy.

Geoffrey J.D. Hewings, Director of the Regional Economics Applications Laboratory at the University of Illinois, Urbana, Illinois, USA.

Ingvar Holmberg, Associate Professor at the Department of Statistics, School of Business and Commercial Law, Göteborg University, Sweden.

Börje Johansson, Professor of Economics, Head of Section for Economics, Statistics and Geography at the Jönköping International Business School, Sweden.

Kiyoshi Kobayashi, Professor at the Graduate School of Civil Engineering, Kyoto University, Kyoto, Japan.

T.R. Lakshmanan, Professor and Director of the Center for Energy and Environmental Studies, Boston University, Boston, USA.

Makoto Okumura, Professor at the Department of Civil and Environmental Engineering, Hiroshima University, Higashi-Hiroshima, Japan.

Jean H.P. Paelinck, Professor of Theoretical Spatial Economics at Erasmus University, Rotterdam, The Netherlands. He is now an emeritus professor of that institution.

Robert E. Skinner, Jr., Executive Director of the Transportation Research Board (TRB), a unit of the non-profit National Academies of Sciences and Engineering.

Michael Sonis, Professor at the Department of Geography, Bar-Ilan University (Israel) and a Research Professor in the Regional Economic Applications Laboratory, University of Illinois.

Wilbur A. Steger, President and founder of Consad Research Corporation, Pittsburgh, PA, is the author of more than 50 published articles at the intersection of comprehensive planning, policy analysis and regional economics. His Ph.D. in Economics is from Harvard University, 1956.

Ulf Strömquist, Chairman and Senior Consultant at Temaplan, Stockholm, Sweden.

Christopher R. Williges, an Analyst at Booz-Allen & Hamilton in San Francisco, California, USA.

Wei-Bin Zhang, Professor at Ritsumeikan Asia Pacific University, College of Asia Pacific Management, Beppu-Shi, Japan.

Preface

This Festschrift honors T.R. Lakshmanan as he enters his fifth decade of active research. It is offered in recognition of the lasting influence he has had on the field of spatial analysis and as an expression of the high esteem in which he is held by the many friends and colleagues who know him simply as 'Laksh'.

A native of Madras, India, T.R. Lakshmanan came to the USA to complete his doctorate in Geography at the Ohio State University. During the early 1960s he was one of a small group of pioneers who applied statistical models to problems in spatial planning and policy. He later extended his analytical skills to the environment as one of the principal architects of the first comprehensive environmental analysis system used by the US Environmental Protection Agency. After a decade of leadership in the consulting industry, he joined the academic world in the 1970s, first as Professor of Geography and Environmental Engineering at Johns Hopkins University and later at Boston University, where he founded America's first energy and environmental studies program in 1979. He answered the call of President Bill Clinton in 1994 to become the founding Director of the Bureau of Transportation Statistics in the US Department of Transportation. In five years at this post he created one of the most research-supportive government agencies in the world by making huge volumes of critical data available at no cost. In 1999 he returned to Boston University to found the Center for Transportation Studies, where he currently serves as Director. He is a life member of Clare Hall College, Cambridge, has been fellow of the Netherlands Institute for Advanced Studies, and Visiting Scholar at the International Institute for Applied Systems Analysis, MIT Center for International Studies and the Institute for Futures Studies, Stockholm.

Along the way he has written or edited many books on subjects ranging from environmental policy analysis to international trade facilitation and served as editor of the Annals of Regional Science. His numerous papers make important contributions to economic theory, operational modeling and institutional analysis – always with an originality and breadth of thought that has distinguished him from his peers. A theme that unites his diversified legacy of publication is spatial interdependency and how it evolves over time due to new technologies, new modes of knowledge, new normative orientations, and new patterns of economic and institutional investment. It is our hope that this theme resonates throughout the chapters of the book.

The contributors to this book have all been touched by 'Laksh' in some way – some as students, many as collaborators, and all as partners in spirited, thought-provoking and humorous conversation. Most of all, we have all been inspired and sustained by the unmistakable joy he derives from his ongoing intellectual journey.

Åke E. Andersson   Börje Johansson   William P. Anderson

Chapter 1

Introduction: Interdependencies of Spatial Development

Åke E. Andersson, William P. Anderson and Börje Johansson

Introduction

The subsequent chapters of this book are focussed on the role of tangible and intangible networks that affect spatial interdependencies in economic and social life. Interaction across geographical space is made possible and facilitated by different categories of interdependent networks, in urban regions and between regions. Some of these networks are based on or characterized by new technologies for communication, economic decisions and governance. In this evolving regime of information technology with mobile communication the role of distance seems to be changing and even disappearing. For certain types of interaction these changes have a capacity to bring about a globalization of markets as well as social life in general. Hence the question posed in the title of the book, is distance disappearing or should we expect new forms of distance phenomena? Moreover, what is the future role of distance in the creation and exchange of knowledge and ideas?

Distortions of distance patterns can be examined for interaction in a city system, interaction between local communities of an urban region, traffic flows with congestion, migration between functional regions, transportation of goods and distribution of energy. Changes in the pertinent spatial interdependencies will have consequences for spatial equilibrium patterns of urban regions and systems of regions, for the distribution of economic activities and population, for productivity change and growth, the size of urban regions and a series of social conditions. In this context one may ask, does the importance of urban size change when interregional links for interaction are improved? Are the networks inside a region evolving into a bottleneck problem for future development?

Networking and Networks – Interaction and Infrastructure

A social system is characterized by interaction between actors. The set of actors comprises individuals, households, firms, public authorities and other organizations. When pairs and groups of such actors interact with a certain frequency, this phenomenon may be thought of as a 'networking activity'. This term often refers to contacts, which are not scheduled or pre-organized, but occur in a seemingly random fashion only governed by self-organization mechanisms.

Random or unplanned interplay of this kind can be efficient if there is an arena on which contacts and communication can be carried out. In other words, networking and interaction requires an infrastructure that can facilitate the interplay processes. We may separate this infrastructure into tangible and intangible networks. The former concept comprises physical networks for interaction, whereas the latter refers to established links for communication and transactions between economic agents. Both forms of networks are spatially dependent. In view of the economic geography they represent transaction links between nodes (sinks, sources and saddle points). In micro contexts a node may represent an individual or an organization and links may be thought of as social ties, mutual trust and smooth codes of communication. In more aggregate analyses the nodes can represent regions or countries. Moreover, transaction links are associated with trade relations, transport paths, networks for information transmission and communication channels.

Physical (tangible) networks for interaction change on a slow time scale. Intangible networks are based on investments that people and organizations make in order to facilitate exchange of information, negotiation and joint decision making. These networks also change at a relatively slow pace. In other words, the use of existing networks may vary and adjust with moderate or little delay. But the networks are rigid and adjust with considerable delays, when the demand for new links and new link capacity develops. All this explains our distinction between networks and networking. Links and networks may be thought of as flow channels, which are characterized by inertia. Networking corresponds to flows, which make use of the flow channels.

In conclusion, the described interdependence between fast and slow adjustments concern the development of new networks for capital markets, stock exchange organizations, mobile phone and Internet systems. The relatively slow process of network enhancement comprises not only physical but also organizational investments.

Networks, Distance and Economic Links

The period 1200–1800 can be seen as a period of experimentation and improvement of the transaction systems in primarily the European economies. Early in this period regions south and north of the Alps became commercially connected. The associated trade was supported by commercial and legal innovations, giving rise to new techniques and methods for formulating contracts and agreements, regulating payments by means of bills of exchange and instruments of debts, controlling debts and loans by means of guarantees and other instruments of credit. In this context transaction systems comprise transport, payment and bank systems. This long period has been characterized as an epoch of broker capitalism, in which production technologies of supplier and customer regions were taken for granted. In the following period, up to the end of the second millennium, the industrial revolution brought about a manufacturing system with radically new logistical solutions. A lot of attention has been paid to the period 1870–1914, during which international trade grew fast, accompanied by increasing capital and labor migration flows (Kenwood and Lougheed, 1971). A corresponding picture is now being painted for the period 1970–2000 (Welfens, 1999).

Globalization of the world economy is reflected by rising international trade and transnational investments. Falling transport and communication costs support this development. In addition, during the 1990s a number of countries have been transformed from planned to market economies, which means that new markets for global trade have emerged. In this group of transitional countries we find Eastern Europe, the former Soviet Union and PR China. The consequences of this change process are obvious. For the OECD countries the growth in both export and import intensity has been considerable, which is illustrated in Table 1.1. The trade intensity has more than doubled in the US between 1970 and 1990. For the Netherlands we can observe an increase by more than 20 per cent.

Table 1.1 Growth of import and export intensity, 1970–1991

	Imports in % of total domestic demand		Exports in % of production	
	1970	1991	1970	1991
United States	5.1	14.0*	5.3	11.0*
Germany	13.3	27.3	18.4	30.0
Sweden	29.5	40.6	29.6	45.0
Netherlands	42.0	66.4	40.9	68.3

* For the US, observations refer to 1990.

Source: OECD (1997).

Functional Regions as Network Systems

Functional region is a crucial concept. The theme in this book has two focal points: interaction inside and interaction between functional (urban) regions. Such regions may be characterized by a set of attributes. In this overview it is defined as a geographic area with concentration of economic activities and with an infrastructure which allows for intense factor mobility inside the region. The region has an internal market potential (home market) that provides opportunities for increasing returns and external economies. At the same time, a functional region gets an individual profile from its slowly changing resources in the form of installed production capital, physical infrastructure and its internal supply of labor categories, which embody different types of knowledge and competence. In this way a functional region has a partly independent economy with the capacity to generate its own economic growth.

Internal Market Potential

Do urban regions vary in any essential ways with regard interurban distances and accessibility patterns? Is there any meaningful classification of urban spatial structure? The latter may be divided into urban form and urban spatial interaction, where form is reflected by the distribution of densities and the associated infrastructure. Although there is a lack of any systematic research in this field, many observers would agree that cities in North America and in Europe represent two archetypes of urban form. The qualitative differences can be identified with regard to both spatial structure and spatial interaction. And these differences can be found for the core and CBD of the cities as well as for the nature of urban sprawl (DiPasquale and Wheaton, 1996; Johansson, 1986).

Although the outward expansion of the boundaries of metropolitan and medium-sized regions is a phenomenon on both sides of the Atlantic Ocean, urban sprawl is much more pronounced in America or Australia than in Europe or parts of Asia. This may, of course, reflect that America and Australia have a much shorter urban history than Europe. However, if we change the perspective slightly and discuss polycentric cities, Europe may not be so different from the US. Recently the notion of edge cities has been introduced to describe urban centers in 'outer rings' of a metropolitan region (Garreau, 1991). This phenomenon suggests that the distance inside an urban region plays a role that is partly at odds with the monocentric model of new urban economics. Mobility is higher and distributed in more dispersed patterns (Darovny and Anderson, 1998).

The internal market potential may be thought of as a region's purchasing power. In a very simplified way this refers to the size of the demand in the region. The latter could also be represented by the gross regional product (GRP). However, one may also conceive that the market potential in addition should reflect GRP per inhabitant. In an urban system with roughly the same income level, the population size of each urban region would function as a reasonable proxy for the internal market potential with regard to household commodities. If we instead consider the demand for intermediary deliveries to producing firms, it becomes relevant to consider the demand pattern for each industry and its size in each region.

Why and how is the size of the internal market potential important? For one thing, the firms inside the region has greater accessibility to customers in the region and in a large region this can provide them with a large 'home market' that facilitates the exploitation of internal and external scale economies. This is an important feature in particular for sales of distance-sensitive products such as many services to households as well as firms. A large market potential would with the same type of argument stimulate a more diversified supply pattern in a region (Henderson, 1986; Andersson, 1985). At this stage we may remark that the features of a region vary also for regions of similar size as observed in Bolton (1992), where notions of 'place' and social capital are employed.

Knowledge interaction and knowledge creation processes are related to density and size phenomena. In the past thirty years the share of knowledge-handling workers have increased at a fast rate all over the OECD countries. And this has not been an a-spatial process. On the contrary, R&D and cultural activities have continued to be concentrated in a selective way on particular urban regions, even if there is an overall increase in the total economy (Andersson et al., 1993). Knowledge-creation activities are indeed dependent on factors such as density and accessibility. In this context we may observe that accessibility in an urban region requires both density and a matching infrastructure. Without a proper infrastructure, density results in congestion and friction and this reduces accessibility.

A Region's External Markets

In a superficial discussion one would definitely argue that globalization of markets is an issue that refers to a region's external markets. When the importance of distance is reduced and transaction costs diminish, then firms and individuals in a region get improved accessibility to the internal markets of other regions. This is a crucial phenomenon to investigate and it is focused on the very core of the concept global – and globalization for that matter.

It is evident that when two different regions have equally large internal markets, then the one with the best accessibility to other markets will have the largest total accessibility to potential customers. Short distance to external markets is of course not completely independent of geographical distance. However, accessibility to customers and suppliers is today strongly associated with networks for air transport and all the new technologies for communication, such as mobile phones and computers, computer networks and other merging forms for mediated contacts.

Given these observations one may contemplate the nature of the heartland of the globalization processes, i.e., the financial markets. It may seem as a paradox that for these markets one can observe both a gradual establishment of extended (transnational) networks, while at the same time stock exchange activities and other financial operations are becoming concentrated to a small set of geographical places. Both these trends seem to develop in an accelerated way.

The contributions in the book have implications for the questions raised above. In particular, there is one important distinction to make. We should observe that different markets and submarkets will have products that differ considerably with respect to their distance sensitivity. In some markets the production, purchasing of inputs or selling of outputs require frequent interface meetings between transactors and such products will generically be distance sensitive. In other markets only a limited amount of contacts is necessary and deliveries may be executed with low movement costs. From this one can conclude that the character of future products will influence the relative importance of internal and external markets. There is also a dual statement. The relative size of distance costs inside a region compared to the distance costs for interregional deliveries will influence which types of products that we should expect in the future.

Networks and Regional Interdependencies

What does it mean to identify a system of urban regions? One may point at two things. First, when focusing on an urban system it becomes relevant to investigate under which conditions such a system can be in equilibrium. Second, dynamic analysis of an urban system is something different from a partial dynamic analysis of individual functional regions.

The contributions in this book imply that one has to distinguish between medium-term and long-term equilibrium of an urban system. With a temporal distinction, a short-term equilibrium is characterized by prices that make demand and supply equal, for a given location of demand potentials and supply sources. In a medium-term perspective, short-term equilibrium is embedded in equilibrium conditions that concerns the location of supply and demand, given the existing properties of the built environment. The latter includes transport and communication networks, production facilities and housing infrastructure. These patterns change as the result of infrastructure investments and interregional mobility of households and represent very slow adjustment processes. Distance and accessibility phenomena have strong impacts on these processes.

What more can we say about the medium-term adjustments? The location of supply and demand across regions also implies a particular sectoral composition in each functional region. In a dynamic analysis one would assume that the medium-term adjustments provide stimuli to long-term adjustments of the urban and interurban infrastructure (Fujita, Krugman and Mori, 1995). However, there are examples of contributions in which the sector composition of regions are taken as given in analyses of impacts of interregional transport investments on inter-city equilibrium (e.g. Kanemoto and Mera, 1985).

The relation between economic structure and slowly changing variables such as infrastructure and population can also be put into another perspective. When urban regions grow as a consequence of agglomeration economies and other self-organization processes, the slow adjustments generate lock-in effects, which bring about lasting regional advantages. In this way a region can continue to benefit from its history also if interregional friction is reduced and accessibility advantages disappear. Hence, path-dependent structures play a partly independent role in the development of interregional equilibrium patterns. At the same time such developments operate under conditions of multiple equilibria.

Globalization and Localization

We have already portrayed globalization as the consequence of a system with reduced interaction friction. Such a reduction is frequently assumed to prevail both inside a country and across country borders. It implies intensified price competition with regard to established and standardized products but also a more widespread global R&D competition. Another feature in the globalized world economy is the role of transnationals with establishments in many countries, and this phenomenon would indicate that globalization has two faces. On the one hand, we can observe extensive and far-reaching networks between establishments belonging to the same firm or concern. On the other hand, the multilocational pattern of a firm reveals the advantages that a firm can achieve by having establishments in many places. Otherwise the wide spread networks would not make sense. Specific locations may have accessibility to customers, to R&D resources, to sectoral clusters and to many other attributes attached to a region.

Another feature in the so called 'new economy' is a continuing process of outsourcing, in which firm activities are decomposed into groups that are allocated to different individual firms. Also in this case one may identify how networks are formed and extended, but now with a higher degree of flexible adjustments.

According to the above picture we should expect the economic evolution to generate an ever-richer pattern of concrete economic links between economic units (firms and establishments). On an aggregate level this is reflected in abstract networks between regions and across sectors. Several modeling issues arise in economic systems with these properties. How can we trace the generation of value added in complex production chains? Can we trust how profit and losses are recorded by firms and in public statistics? How do delivery-flows between sectors in different regions influence the growth of productivity across sectors and regions? One may ask a similar question with regard to employment changes.

Several contributions in this book contemplate the associated complexities. These become obvious in the linkages between sectors, in the increasing variety of goods and services and in the interface between the local and the global.

Outline of the Chapters

The subsequent chapters of this book are arranged in a sequence of thematic perspectives. Chapters 2–5 form the first group which contains multiregional models and analyses, focusing on spatial equilibrium and interregional externalities and influence. In Chapters 6–8 the authors examine the structure of an individual region, its internal networks and interaction patterns. Going from the first to the second group is a shift from interregional to intraregional accessibility and distance.

Chapters 9–12 represent the third group. Here the emphasis is on dynamics and growth. This comprises long-term population and infrastructure dynamics, economic-demographic evolution and development policies under conditions of economic globalization. In the final group of chapters, the authors investigate transport systems and analyze impacts of transport improvements, transport and energy consumption and methods to assess infrastructure plans.

In Chapter 2, Okumura and Kobayashi investigate disappearing distance in city systems. They develop a computable general equilibrium model, based on assumptions about agglomeration economies and monopolistic competition. They trace impacts of disappearing distance and reveal multiple equilibria and path-dependence in their simulations. Effects of transportation hubs play an essential role in the analysis.

Chapter 3, by Zhang presents an equilibrium model with two cities and one rural or farming area. There are two industries and one farming sector. Amenities and technology are assumed to be different in the rural area and in the cities. The major question posed is: which are the equilibrium conditions? Moreover, how will labor be divided between the three sectors of the economy? Under certain conditions the system has a unique equilibrium. Amenity differences between the two cities will have an impact on the spatial structure. At the same time, the location behavior of producers and consumers are complicated to derive.

In Chapter 4, Sonis, Hewings and Achjar examine spatial exchange in a multiregional system. They identify hierarchical fields of influence. A distinction is made between a region's internal and external sources of change and their impacts are investigated in detail. In this effort the authors manage to make precise the implicit network properties that are inherent in the exchange of products (goods and services).

In Chapter 5, Haynes, Dinc and Paelinck extend the classic shift-share method in order to analyze productivity development in a multiregional system. In the 1980s and 1990s researcher could witness a remarkable process of structural change in the US economy, accompanied by fast growth in the 1990s, and this forms the background of this chapter. The process of changing productivity is related to increased competition in an increasingly open and globalized market place. The authors investigate productivity changes across sectors in a set of regions and study the interplay between changes in productivity and employment. In order to carry out this analysis the authors develop a new shift-share model, and apply it to the development of manufacturing industries with a special focus on production workers.

In Chapter 6, Bolton claims that a functioning local community can be modeled as a network of social interactions. This is expressed in the pronounced title "'Place' as 'Network'". The author develops a framework that allows him to describe planning as the partial 'ownership' of a network. By management of the network, benefits are produced in such a way that it accrues to the community as a whole. Networks of this kind are shown to be able to generate a sense of place, which may have both good and bad points. In particular we may observe that the sense of place can promote cooperation with insiders and inhibits collaboration with outsiders and newcomers. In another terminology, the network develops and maintains the social capital of a place, and this creates incentives for participants to contribute socially valuable interactions. As such it is an intangible, location-specific asset.

In North America the process of urban sprawl has been a prevailing trend for a long time. A related and more recent phenomenon is reflected by the concept of edge cities. With this background, Anderson investigates the structure of an urban region in Chapter 7. He observes a rapid expansion of the metropolitan boundary, a general decline in the density of both population and employment, a high density of roads providing good accessibility to a dispersed set of points, and a segregation of residential and other land uses, where the residential growth occurs primarily in peripheral suburbs. Associated with these processes new phenomena such as multinucleated and polycentric cities seem to emerge. In his broad review of the changing urban structure, Anderson concludes that journey-to-work trips become a less central variable and that more complex externalities become more important. In view of all this, traditional urban economics models have to be interpreted with more care, if not skepticism?

The author deliberates upon the associated policy issues. In this context he also questions some recent ideas about spatial structure and suggests that they may be wrong. From an incremental point of view, a new road increases the accessibility of land around it. But a sequence of incremental steps does something more, it creates a network and produces a structure. At the same time, the nature of urban spatial interaction may change due to new technologies for communication. In this evolution the role of distance may very well change but Anderson declares that it does not disappear.

Transport flows have been increasing over time in many regions across the world. One driving force behind this process is the geographical expansion of urban regions with sprawl phenomena and the emergence of edge cities. Such growth in travel demand tends to reduce the service level of the corresponding transport systems, since the growth is not matched by commensurate increases in supply. In Chapter 8, Skinner examines how society adapts to modify its behavior to mitigate the impacts of congestion and delays. Such adaptations involve tradeoffs that individual travelers, households and employers make in the face of travel congestion. Among other things, the tradeoffs comprise travel schedule, mode, trip destination and residential location. These adjustments are not always in society's interest, although they are rational on the individual level.

Over time population and jobs in urban regions develop in an interdependent dynamic process. In Chapter 9, Holmberg, Johansson and Strömquist present a model for a simultaneous estimation of long-term regional job and population changes in a Swedish context. Which variables influence this kind of evolution and how fast does the process converge to the immanent equilibrium attractor of the change process? The change involves the attraction of firms and households to each urban region, and to the municipalities in each region. By selection variables that can describe each region's economic milieu and household milieu the change process is specified by structural equations. Important variables that characterize the regional milieu comprise the size of the market potential, attractiveness of the housing market, commuting conditions, existence of university education. Some of these variables also reflect infrastructure properties of each region. The process is shown to be slow and the estimated model indicates that the development of population has a stronger impact on the development of jobs than vice versa.

In Chapter 10, we learn that each stage of economic development can be associated with a typical morbidity and mortality profile. With this observation as a starting point, Andersson provides a historical – not to say evolutionary – perspective of the relation between health conditions and economic development. First the author outlines the broad determinants of economic development and how different steps in the development change the behavior of the individuals in society. One associated distinction is between entrepreneurial and rent-seeking behavior.

The overview of economic evolution includes the Egyptian civilization as described by Pirenne, the rise of urban capitalism in Europe more than 800 years ago as discussed by, e.g. Hayek, and Sub-Saharan societies in contemporary Africa. By analyzing health data from 1990 for different parts of the world, a pattern of death causes and factors determining years of life lost is identified. This analysis is categorized into tribal, industrial and post-industrial societies. Observations comprise countries in Africa, India, China and established market economies.

Chapter 11, by Andersson presents an analysis of how growth and development policy has to adjust in an era of economic globalization. This new economic regime is described as the result of a phase transition during the late 1980s and the early 1990s. One aspect of this transition is a doubling of world trade, which also implies that trade grows at a much faster pace in comparison with the growth of GDP. The background is reduced global transaction costs and integrated financial markets. As a consequence we can observe a pattern where real rates of interest (after risk compensation) are equalized. This brings regional and national policy makers to consider risk-reducing policy measures. At the same time regions of the advanced countries redefine traditional policies to include strategies that help to increase the attractiveness in view qualified labor and multi-location companies. These conclusions are based on growth theory as developed by von Neumann and Morishima, in combination with corporate finance ideas.

In Chapter 12, Garrison, Gillen and Williges investigate how impacts from transport improvements are generated. The authors ask if transport service enhancements result in the disappearance of distance. Their answer to this question implies that changing friction of distance affects the interdependent evolution of both supply and demand. Rather than examining how transport improvements affects the transport-relevant variables and behavior, the authors focus off-system affect. That includes impacts on production and consumption activities throughout the economy. The ambition is to make clear the ways in which transport improvements increase choices and the economic welfare gains from increased choices. In this way they can focus on both doing old things in new ways and doing new things. This includes innovations in the ways people produce and consume. From this point of view the contribution is characterized by a Schumpeterian spirit.

In Chapter 13, transportation and its energy use is at the forefront. Greene recognizes that transport remains a growing user of fossil fuels, and in this way transport is a significant source of environmental pollution. The author asks whether things have become better or worse? What lessons can be learned from the recent past 25 years of struggling with transportation energy issues?

With this background the analysis focuses on sustainability, clarified as a development that meets the needs of the present without compromising the needs of future generations to meet their own needs. In this context market failure is recognized. It is observed that even if all environmental externalities could be internalized, markets may still fail to produce a sustainable development. Four basic strategies are identified in the form of 1. regulation, 2. government investment in R&D, 3. creation of market incentives and 4. education and development of institutional capital.

In the final chapter of the book Steger and Lakshmanan present plan evaluation methodologies. A primary focus is urban developmental and transportation planning. The authors pose the question: what are the issues in current urban and regional planning? What are the emerging concerns and which are the dimensions? The ambition of the study is an assessment of methodology – of what it is and what it could be.

In this context many questions arise. One may study how control or policy variables are identified and expressed, how the effects or impacts are specified and estimated and how sophisticated expressions of plan evaluation technology differ from generally prevalent practices. Three dimensions are examined: 1. public investment and geographic hierarchy, 2. public versus private and 3. incidence phenomena. The discussion ends with suggestions about how to close the gap between practice and what is possible.

References

Andersson, Å.E. (1985), 'Creativity and Regional Development', *Papers of the Regional Science Association*, vol. 56, pp. 5–20.

Andersson, Å.E., Batten, D.F., Kobayashi, K. and Yoshikawa, K. (1993), 'Logistical Dynamics, Creativity and Infrastructure', in Å.E. Andersson, D.F. Batten, K. Kobayashi and K. Yoshikawa (eds), *The Cosmo-Creative Society – Logistical Networks in a Dynamic Economy*, Springer-Verlag, Berlin.

Bolton, R. (1992), 'Place Prosperity vs. People Prosperity Revisited', *Urban Studies*, vol. 29, pp. 185–203.

Darovny, M. and Anderson, W.P. (1998), 'Location Choice for New Housing Subdivisions in Hamilton-Wentworth: The Influence of Roads and Other Factors', mimeo, McMaster University.

DiPasquale, D. and Wheaton, W.C. (1996), *Urban Economics and Real Estate Markets*, Prentice Hall, Englewoods Cliffs, New York.

Fujita, M., Krugman, P. and Mori, T. (1995), *On the Evolution of Hierarchical Urban Systems*, Discussion Paper 419, Institute of Economic Research, Kyoto University.

Garreau, J. (1991), *Edge City: Life on the New Frontier*, Anchor, New York.

Hayek, F.A. (1988), *The Fatal Conceit: The Errors of Socialism*, Routledge, London.

Henderson, J.V. (1986), 'Efficiency of Resource Usage and City Size', *Journal of Urban Economics*, vol. 19, pp. 47–70.

Johansson, B. (ed.) (1986), *Dynamics in Metropolitan Processes and Policies*, RR-86–8, International Institute for Applied Systems Analysis, Laxenburg, Austria.

Kanemoto, Y. and Mera, K. (1985), 'General Equilibrium Analysis of the Benefits of Large Transportation Improvements', *Regional Science and Urban Economics*, vol. 15, pp. 343–63.

Kenwood, A.G. and Lougheed, A.L. (1971), *The Growth of the International Economy 1820–1960*, George Allen & Unwin, London.

Morishima, M. (1964), *Theory of Economic Growth*, Clarendon Press, Oxford.

von Neumann, J. (1937), 'A Model of General Economic Equilibrium' (translated from German 1945), *Review of Economic Studies*, vol. 33, pp. 1–9.

OECD (1997), *Sustainable Consumption and Production*, OECD, Paris.

Pirenne, H. (1934), *Histoire des institutions et du droit privé de l'anscienne Egypte*, Edition del la Fondation Egyptologique Reine Elisabeth, Bruxelles.

Welfens, P.J.J. (1999), 'Globalization of the Economy', *Unemployment and Innovation*, Springer-Verlag, Berlin.

Chapter 2

Disappearing Distance in City Systems

Makoto Okumura and Kiyoshi Kobayashi

Introduction

Many authors (e.g. Kanemoto and Mera, 1985; Sasaki, 1992) have analyzed the general equilibrium effects of inter-city transportation investment. These studies *a priori* specified the industrial structure of each city and its trading patterns, which is a restrictive assumption for city size distribution. This study will address this restriction as one of its objectives. Urban economists have developed models explaining how the size of each city can be determined in a system of cities (e.g. Henderson, 1985, 1988; Abdel-Rahman, 1990). However, these models did not consider spatial factors at the inter-city level, such as location of cities, distances, or transport costs between them. Krugman (1991a, 1991b, 1993) analyzed industrial location by incorporating transport costs into the multi-region model of interregional trade with scale economies. He found that there may be a concentration of production activities even when all the regions are homogeneous and no comparative advantage exists. Fujita (1993) and Fujita et al. (1995) further developed models to incorporate an economy with multiple industrial sectors and also analyzed the dynamic process of city formation and development. They demonstrated that as an economy's population size increases, the urban system organizes itself into a Christaller-type hierarchical system. Mun (1997) also discussed interactions between agglomeration economies and transport network structure in three-city system. Kobayashi and Okumura (1997) then investigated a dynamic multi-regional growth model with spatial agglomeration, concentrating on interregional knowledge spillovers.

Given that cities grow largely due to the self-reinforcing advantages of agglomeration economies, their very presence generates a lock-in effect in the location space. The lock-in effect is the reason why a city can still prosper even after the disappearance of the friction of distance. The structure of urban systems is not determined freely; rather it is due to the lock-in effect of an urban system as a whole and how its structure tends to follow the power of inertia. However, the strong presence of inertia in the structure of the urban system does not necessarily preclude the chance of structural change in the long run. Agglomeration economies introduce indeterminacy when agents want to congregate where others are. The agglomeration, once the positive feedback has been geared, takes on the nature of a cumulative self-reinforcing process. This is because the emergence of a particular city as a major agglomeration does not only depend upon the intrinsic nature of the city. Historical matters such as political initiatives also appear to be critical in the selection of a particular equilibrium. It is now a well-known fact that minor changes made to the socio-economic environment at a crucial period may result in very different geographical configurations (Batten et al., 1989; Kobayashi et al., 1991; Krugman, 1991a, 1993; Arthur, 1994; Fujita and Krugman, 1995; Matsuyama, 1995).

Path-dependency is omnipresent in the evolutional patterns of urban activities. More and more populations want to agglomerate because of various factors that allow for more diversity and a higher degree of specialization in production, as well as the wide variety of goods and services that are available for consumption. Cities are typically associated with a wide range of products and a wide spectrum of public services allowing consumers to achieve higher utility levels. This provides greater incentives to the non-urban population to migrate to large cities. There is circular causation for the agglomeration of firms and population through forward linkages (an increase in population enhances individual amenity) and backward linkages (a greater number of services attract a larger population) (Fujita, 1993). Through these linkage effects, scale economies at the individual level are transformed into increasing-returns at the level of the city as a whole.

The purpose of this study is to propose a computable general equilibrium model that will provide some insights on the impact of decreasing distances between cities upon economic geography. The interactions among production, consumption, land use, trade and interurban network structure are examined. There is an extensive literature on computable general equilibrium modeling (e.g. Shoven and Whalley, 1972, 1992; McKibbin and Sachs, 1991). The model presented in this paper considers two sources of increasing returns which appear in production as well as in consumption. The first basic force is spatial agglomeration generated through technological externalities in production, e.g. interactions among agents. The other basic source is monopolistic competition that is based on product variety in consumption. The scale economies in production, combined with monopolistic competition, have very complex influences upon the formation of city systems. The model presented in this paper is designed to simulate how these scale economies work within the system of the city and to investigate how the system structure will change in response to inter-city transportation improvement.

Despite the inherent analytical complexity, economies of three or more cities are considered. This assumption comes mainly from the analytical premise that explains the endogenous formation of economic hub cities given the inter-urban transportation system. One cannot have a hub with only two locations. Transportation hubs are especially desirable places to locate the production of goods and services subject to increasing returns. It is the interactions between these increasing returns in production as well as in consumption that leads to the endogenous formation of such transportation hubs. The transportation hub effects can be viewed as an alternative explanation to regional differentiation (Krugman, 1993). This complication can only be made at the sacrifice of analytical tractability of the model. Instead of the rigor of analytical solution, the model simulates the endogenous formation of transportation hubs in the networks of three cities.

The remainder of the paper is organized as follows. In 'The Model', a computable general equilibrium model is presented to describe city system economies with free trade and migration. In 'Computer Simulation', simulation experiments are carried out to illustrate how transportation improvements affect the economic geography of city systems.

The Model

We consider an economic system consisting of K cities, indexed by $k=1,...,K$, where cities are interconnected by a transportation network. In each city, firms produce n_k kinds of differentiated manufactured (tradable) goods and m_k types of (non tradable) services. All manufactured goods are available throughout all cities by means of trade, while services are only available within the city where they are produced. Monopolistic competition is assumed to prevail in the global goods market and in the local services markets of the respective cities. The population is homogeneous and the total population of the economy is fixed exogenously. People can move freely between cities, but can live in only one city at any one time; multi-habitation as well as inter-city commuting are prohibited. The households achieve the same utility levels regardless of the location in which they live.

Each city is geographically mono-centric, and consists of two parts: the CBD and the residential area. The city residents are fully employed and commute to the single CBD via intra-city transportation systems. All production activities are concentrated in the CBD of the respective cities. Production agents make use of the local labor force and the fixed amount of land in the CBD. Economy-wide markets for manufactured goods are monopolistically competitive. On the other hand, labor markets are localized in each city, and the local labor forces are fully employed in their respective markets. Products and population are freely mobile between cities. The inter-urban transportation system is the means for trade among cities. It is endowed upon the economy without any costs (e.g. gifts from foreign countries).

The general equilibrium model describes a static system of cities where all goods are traded in monopolistically competitive markets. Cities in the economy are situated on a flat plain where there is no agriculture. First, we describe the respective city economy *à la* Alonso.

Assume temporarily that the population of each city is predetermined in some manner. In each city, land is owned collectively by city residents through shares in a local land bank. The local land banks pay out dividends to local residents which normally equal the per capita land rent.

For simplicity, the following set of assumptions (Henderson, 1985) are also adopted:

1. The CBD occupies the central area of the respective cities. Each firm is endowed with a fixed amount of land, thus the total area of the CBD is endogenously determined dependant upon the number of firms located in the CBD. The land at the CBD is characterized by homogeneous geographic

attributes, and transportation costs within the CBD are neglected. Hence, all land lots in the CBD are lent to all firms for the same land rent.

2. The residential area around the CBD is divided into land lots, whose areas are fixed at the same size regardless of location.
3. Some parts of the residential area are reserved for public use such as open spaces and rivers, such that the residential use occupies $2\pi\ t$ length out of each circle that extends a distance t beyond the CBD edge.
4. There is no land dedicated to agricultural use. The price of land at the edge of the city is zero. These assumptions are useful in order to eliminate unnecessary model complexity without loss of generality in the following discussions.

Consider a representative household at a distance t from the CBD edge of city k $(k=1,\ldots,K)$. The utility function $(U_k(t))$ for a particular household depends on its consumption of manufactured goods $x_{kil}\ (t)$, its consumption of services $y_{kj}\ (t)$, and the housing lot size $h_k(t)=h_k$. In these terms, i_l $(i = 1,\ldots,n_l)$ denotes the consumed good, which was produced in city l $(l=1,\ldots,K)$, and j $(j=1,\ldots,m_k)$ represents the consumed service, which must be produced in the same city in which it is consumed. The housing lot size is fixed such that $h_k=1$.

The Dixit-Stiglitz function for household utility is thus defined as:

$$U_k(t) = \left(\sum_{l=1}^{K}\sum_{i_l=1}^{n_l} x_{ki_l}(t)^{\sigma}\right)^{\frac{a}{\sigma}} \left(\sum_{j=1}^{m_k} y_{kj}(t)^{\rho}\right)^{\frac{b}{\rho}} h_k^c, \tag{1}$$

where parameters a,b,c are the respective proportions of income spent on manufactured goods, services, and land. The parameters σ and ρ must satisfy $0< \sigma$ *and* $\rho < 1$.

The budget constraint is

$$I_k - c_k w_k t = \sum_{l=1}^{K}\sum_{i_l=1}^{n_l} p_{ki_l} x_{ki_l} + \sum_{j=1}^{m_k} q_{kj} y_{kj} + \zeta_k(t), \tag{2}$$

where I_k is income, w_k is the wage rate, c_k is cost of commuting a unit distance, q_{kj} is the price of service j provided in city k, and $\zeta_k(t)$ is the land rent per fixed lot size at a point t. Let the wage rate of city 1 be fixed to unity. Further, let us assume that the c.i.f. price of manufactured good i_l in city k is given by

$$p_{ki_l} = (1 + \tau_{kl})\hat{p}_{i_l}, \tag{3}$$

where p_{kil} is the c.i.f. price of manufactured good i_l in city k, τ_{kl} is the transportation cost between cities k and l, and $\hat{p}_{il}$ is the f.o.b. price of manufactured good i_l in city l.

The demand functions for manufactured goods and services are given by

$$x_{ki_l}(t) = \frac{a}{a+b}(I_k - c_k w_k t - \zeta_k(t)) \frac{p_{ki_l}^{-\frac{1}{1-\sigma}}}{\sum_{l=1}^{K}\sum_{i_l=1}^{n_l} p_{ki_l}^{-\frac{\sigma}{1-\sigma}}} \tag{4}$$

$$y_{kj}(t) = \frac{b}{a+b}(I_k - c_k w_k t - \zeta_k(t)) \frac{q_{kj}^{-\frac{1}{1-\rho}}}{\sum_{j=1}^{m_k} q_{kj}^{-\frac{\rho}{1-\rho}}} \tag{5}$$

respectively. If all manufacturing firms and service agents have identical technology, the demand functions can be simplified to

$$x_{kl}(t) = \frac{a}{a+b}(I_k - c_k w_k t - \zeta_k(t)) P_k^{\frac{\sigma}{1-\sigma}} p_{kl}^{\frac{-1}{1-\sigma}} \tag{6}$$

$$y_k(t) = \frac{b}{a+b}(I_k - c_k w_k t - \zeta_k(t)) Q_k^{\frac{\rho}{1-\rho}} q_k^{\frac{-1}{1-\rho}}, \tag{7}$$

where $P_k = \left(\sum_{l=1}^{K} nlp_{kl}^{\frac{-\sigma}{1-\sigma}}\right)^{\frac{1-\sigma}{\sigma}}$ and $Q_k = m_k^{-\frac{1-\rho}{\rho}}$ are the price indices of manufactured goods and services, respectively. The indirect utility function is:

$$V_k(t) = AP_k^{-a} Q_k^{-b} (I_k - c_k w_k t - \zeta_k(t))^{a+b}, \tag{8}$$

where, $A = a^a b^b / (a+b)^{a+b}$.

Spatial equilibrium for identical households is characterized by $\partial V_k(t) / \partial t = 0$. From equation (8), it can be seen that the transportation costs, which increase with commuting distance, are offset by reduced rents; thus we have $\partial \zeta_k(t) / \partial t = - c_k w_k$. Integrating this equation, we have

$$\zeta_k(t) = Z_k - c_k w_k t, \tag{9}$$

where Z_k is the maximum residential land rent (the CBD land rent) of city k. At the edge of the city where $t = T_k$, holds $\zeta(T_k)=0$. Now, we have the land rent gradient:

$$\zeta_k(t) = c_k w_k (T_k - t). \tag{10}$$

The utility level of the household at the city edge, $t = T_k$ is

$$V_k(T_k) = AP_k^{-a} Q_k^{-b} (I_k - c_k w_k T_k)^{a+b}. \tag{11}$$

Spatial equilibrium ensures that every household in the city can obtain the same utility levels as in eq.(11), regardless of their location within the city.

Given the fixed lot size over the economy, the size of city k, N_k, can be defined by the area of urban land use. Thus,

$$N_k = 2\pi \int_0^{T_k} t\mathrm{d}t = \pi T_k^2. \tag{12}$$

From eq.(12), the radius of residential land T_k is given as a function of N_k:

$$T_k = \pi^{-\frac{1}{2}} N_k^{\frac{1}{2}}. \tag{13}$$

Rent for residential lots take their highest value at the edge of the CBD ($t = 0$), such that:

$$Z_k = c_k w_k \pi^{-\frac{1}{2}} N_k^{\frac{1}{2}}. \tag{14}$$

Within the CBD, each manufacturing firm uses a fixed area of land given by f, while the service firms each occupy a fixed area of land g. Given the number of manufacturing firms n_k and service firms m_k, the total area of the CBD is $n_k f + m_k g$. The total rental income of the local land bank of city k is given by

$$\begin{aligned} R_k &= 2\pi \int_0^{T_k} t\zeta_k(t)\mathrm{d}t + (n_k f + m_k g) Z_k \\ &= \frac{1}{3} c_k w_k \pi^{-\frac{1}{2}} N_k^{\frac{3}{2}} + (n_k f + m_k g) c_k w_k \pi^{-\frac{1}{2}} N_k^{\frac{1}{2}}. \end{aligned} \tag{15}$$

The total cost associated with commuting within city k is given by

$$TC_k = 2\pi c_k w_k \int_0^{T_k} t^2 \mathrm{d}t = \frac{2}{3} c_k w_k \pi^{-\frac{1}{2}} N_k^{\frac{3}{2}}. \tag{16}$$

By summing individual consumption for the respective manufactured goods and services, the aggregate demand functions can be described as

$$X_{kl} = \frac{a}{a+b} \Xi_k P_k^{\frac{\sigma}{1-\sigma}} p_{kl}^{\frac{-1}{1-\sigma}} \cdot N_k \ , \tag{17}$$

$$Y_k = \frac{b}{a+b} \Xi_k m_k^{-1} q_k^{-1} \cdot N_k \ , \tag{18}$$

where $\Xi_k = I_k - c_k w_k \pi^{(-1\ 2)} N_k^{(1\ 2)}$ is the aggregate household expenditure for manufactured goods and services available in city k. The equilibrium utility levels of a representative household can be fully characterized by the parameters:

$$V_k = A P_k^{-a} Q_k^{-b} \left(I_k - c_k w_k \pi^{-\frac{1}{2}} N_k^{\frac{1}{2}} \right)^{a+b}. \tag{19}$$

To determine income levels in this equation, the production sector of the city's economy is examined.

By the convention adopted in the literature, production technology explicitly includes the agglomeration economies as one of its components (Mun, 1997). The production of city k is described by the Cobb-Douglas production function:

$$X_k = L_k^{\alpha} f_k^{\phi} N_k^{\gamma}, \tag{20}$$

where X_k is the output of a representative manufacturing firm in city k, L_k is the labor input of the firm, f_k is the land area, which is assumed to be fixed at f, α and ϕ are parameters satisfying $\alpha+\phi=1$, and N_k^{γ} describes the local agglomeration effect of city k. The firms control L_k to maximize their profits, while the agglomeration economies N_k^{γ} are exogenous to the firms' decision making powers. The parameters are assumed to satisfy $\alpha+\phi+\gamma>1$ in order to exhibit agglomeration economy. The aggregated demand function of the manufactured goods of a particular manufacturing firm located in city k is given by

$$\begin{aligned} X_k &= \sum_l X_{lk} \\ &= \sum_l \frac{a}{a+b} \Xi_l P_l^{\frac{\sigma}{1-\sigma}} p_{lk}^{\frac{-1}{1-\sigma}} \cdot N_l. \end{aligned} \tag{21}$$

Substituting (3) into (21), we have the price functions:

$$\hat{p}_k(X_k) = \Omega_k X_k^{\sigma-1} \tag{22}$$

$$\Omega_k = \left(\sum_l \frac{a}{a+b} \Xi_l P_l^{\frac{\sigma}{1-\sigma}} (1+\tau_{kl})^{\frac{-1}{1-\sigma}} N_l \right)^{1-\sigma}. \tag{23}$$

The manufacturing firms in city k maximize their profits,

$$\pi_k^g = \hat{p}_k(X_k) X_k - w_k L_k - f Z_k, \tag{24}$$

where w_k is wage rate, $\hat{p}_k(X_k)$ is the f.o.b. price given by eq.(22), and $f\,Z_k$ is payment for the land lots. Assume that the monopolistic powers of the respective firms are sufficiently small and exhibit no significant effects on price indices, i.e., $\partial P_l/\partial X_k=0$. Then, the firms' behavior can be characterized by the first order optimal condition:

$$L_k = \sigma\alpha X_k \frac{\hat{p}_k}{w_k}. \tag{25}$$

Through use of the demand function (21), the profit function is given by

$$\Pi_k^g = \frac{a\beta}{a+b} \hat{p}_k^{-\frac{\sigma}{1-\sigma}} \sum_l \Xi_l P_l^{\frac{\sigma}{1-\sigma}} (1+\tau_{lk})^{\frac{-1}{1-\sigma}} N_l - f c_k w_k \pi^{-\frac{1}{2}} N_k^{\frac{1}{2}}, \tag{26}$$

where $\beta = 1 - \sigma\alpha$. As long as the firms can earn positive profits, new firms will enter the market. In the limit, no firm will be able to earn a profit. Thus, the equilibrium number of manufacturing firms in the cities can be defined by $\boldsymbol{n} = (n_1, \ldots, n_K)$. which simultaneously satisfies the following conditions:

$$\Pi_k^g(\mathrm{n}) = 0 \ (k = 1, \cdots, K). \tag{27}$$

Then, the output and the f.o.b. price of the representative manufacturing firm in city k are respectively given by

$$X_k = \left(\frac{\alpha\sigma f c_k}{\beta}\right)^{\alpha} \pi^{-\frac{\alpha}{2}} N_k^{\left(\frac{\alpha}{2}+\gamma\right)} f^{\phi}, \tag{28}$$

$$\hat{p}_k = f^{-\phi}\left(\frac{f c_k}{\beta}\right)^{1-\alpha} (\alpha\sigma)^{-\alpha} \pi^{-\frac{1-\alpha}{2}} w_k N_k^{\left(\frac{1-\alpha}{2}-\gamma\right)}. \tag{29}$$

With regard to the service sector of the city's economy, firms are assumed to be monopolistically competing with each other, given the identical technology:

$$Y_k = E_k^{\varepsilon} g_k^{\psi} N_k^{\eta}, \tag{30}$$

where parameters ϵ, ψ are such that $\epsilon + \psi = 1$ and $\eta > 0$, Y_k is the output of the respective service firm, E_k is the amount of employment at the firm, and g_k is land area, which is assumed to be fixed at g. Let m_k be the number of service firms in city k. The profit of each respective firm is defined by

$$\Pi_k^s = \hat{q}_k(Y_k) Y_k - w_k E_k - g Z_k \tag{31}$$

where $\hat{q}_k(Y_k)$ is the price function, which is given by

$$\hat{q}_k(Y_k) = \frac{b}{a+b} \Xi_k m_k^{-1} Y_k^{-1} \cdot N_k. \tag{32}$$

The agglomeration economies N_k^{η} are also assumed to be exogenous of all service firms. From the firms' profit maximization strategy, we have

$$E_k = \rho \varepsilon Y_k \frac{\hat{q}k(Y_k)}{w_k} \tag{33}$$

The profit functions of the service firms are also given by functions of the number of service firms m_k:

$$\Pi_k^s = \xi \hat{q}_k(Y_k) Y_k - g c_k w_k \pi^{-\frac{1}{2}} N_k^{\frac{1}{2}}. \tag{34}$$

In the long run equilibrium, the number of service firms is endogenously determined to satisfy the non-zero profit conditions:

$$\Pi_k^s(m_k) = 0 \tag{35}$$

Thus, in the long run, we have

$$Y_k = \left(\frac{\varepsilon \rho g c_k}{\xi}\right)^{\varepsilon} \pi^{-\frac{\varepsilon}{2}} N_k^{\left(\frac{\varepsilon}{2}+\eta\right)} g^{\psi}, \tag{36}$$

$$\hat{q}_k = g^{-\psi} \left(\frac{g c_k}{\xi}\right)^{1-\varepsilon} (\varepsilon \rho)^{-\varepsilon} \pi^{-\frac{1-\varepsilon}{2}} w_k N_k^{\left(\frac{1-\varepsilon}{2}-\eta\right)}. \tag{37}$$

From these equations, the equilibrium number of service firms is explicitly given by

$$m_k = \frac{\xi}{g}(c_k w_k)^{-1} \pi^{\frac{1}{2}} \frac{b}{a+b} \Xi_k N_k^{\frac{1}{2}}. \tag{38}$$

Transportation services are provided by transportation firms with constant-return-to-scale technology, given the historically developed transportation network. No payment is made for the usage of the network. Intra-urban commuting services are provided by the transportation sectors of the respective cities. All transportation firms are regulated by the government such that they make no profits. The profit of commuting service companies Π^t_k is a function of the total employment of the firms F_k:

$$\Pi_k^t = TC_k - w_k F_k. \tag{39}$$

The amount of employment is

$$F_k = TC_k {w_k}^{-1} = \frac{2}{3} c_k \pi^{-\frac{1}{2}} N_k^{\frac{3}{2}}. \tag{40}$$

Transportation of manufactured goods is exclusively supplied by the transportation firms located in the destination cities. The total revenue of the transportation firms in city *k* can be given by

$$D_k = \sum_{l=1}^{K} n_l \tau_{kl} \hat{p}_l X_{lk}. \tag{41}$$

Given the constant-return-to-scale transportation technology, the amount of employment within the transportation firms is

$$G_k = \frac{D_k}{w_k} = \frac{\sum_{l=1}^{K} n_l \tau_{kl} \hat{p}_l X_{lk}}{\delta w_k}. \tag{42}$$

It is assumed that local labor markets are perfectly competitive, and that the economy has reached full employment. Thus, the following holds:

$$N_k = n_k L_k + m_k E_k + F_k + G_k. \tag{43}$$

Eventually, wage rates are regionally differentiated, reflecting the geographic conditions of local labor markets. We have assumed local public ownership of land. The revenue from land ownership is equally shared among the individuals within each city. The net income per household consists of two parts: wage income and income from land ownership. When land rents are divided equally among residents, then the per capita income in city *k* is given by

$$I_k = w_k + \frac{R_k}{N_k}. \tag{44}$$

The population can move freely among cities. The population distribution among cities can be brought into equilibrium when no households have an incentive to move. Thus, the population distribution equilibrium can be characterized as

$$\sum_{k=1}^{K} N_k = N, \tag{45}$$

$$V_1 = V_2 = \cdots = V_k = V. \tag{46}$$

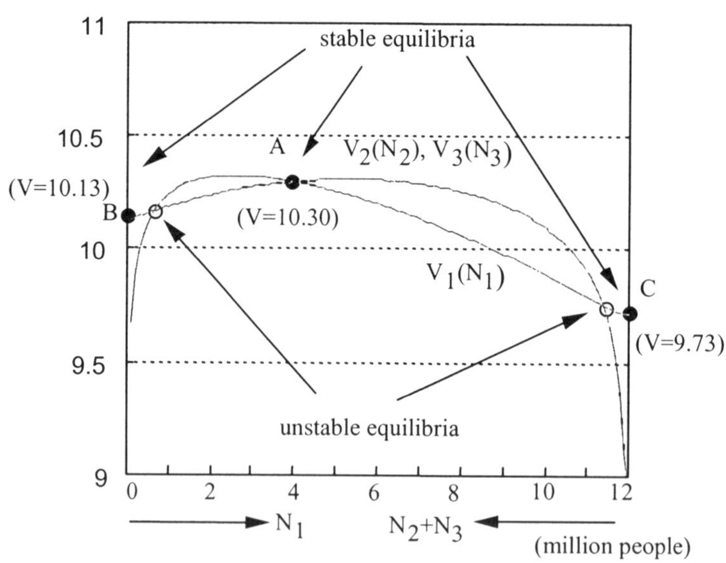

Figure 2.1 Multiple equilibrium patterns in Case 1

The equilibrium utility levels V are endogenously determined in the closed economy. In the limit, all firms' profits will vanish, and all benefits of transportation improvement accrue to the households, due to the public ownership of land. Thus, the benefit to be derived from improvement of the transportation system can be evaluated using the equilibrium utility level V.

Computer Simulation

Despite the inherent analytical complexity, the economy consisting of three cities is considered. Transportation hubs are especially desirable places to locate the production of goods and services subject to increasing returns. The interactions between increasing returns in production and increasing returns in consumption are essential to the endogenous formation of transportation hubs. This complication can only be made at the sacrifice of the analytical tractability of the model.

The total population is set at $N = 12$ (million). The shared consumption of manufactured goods, services and land are assumed to be $a=0.49$, $b=0.32$, $c=0.19$ respectively, reflecting Japanese statistics in 1990. The size of a residential land lot is fixed to unity. Based upon Japanese statistics, the relative size of manufacturing firms and that of service firms are fixed to $f=600$, $g=50$, respectively. To reflect the average railway fare of the Japanese private railway companies, the commuting cost per unit length is fixed to $c_k=0.00015$, which is measured in terms of the wage rate.

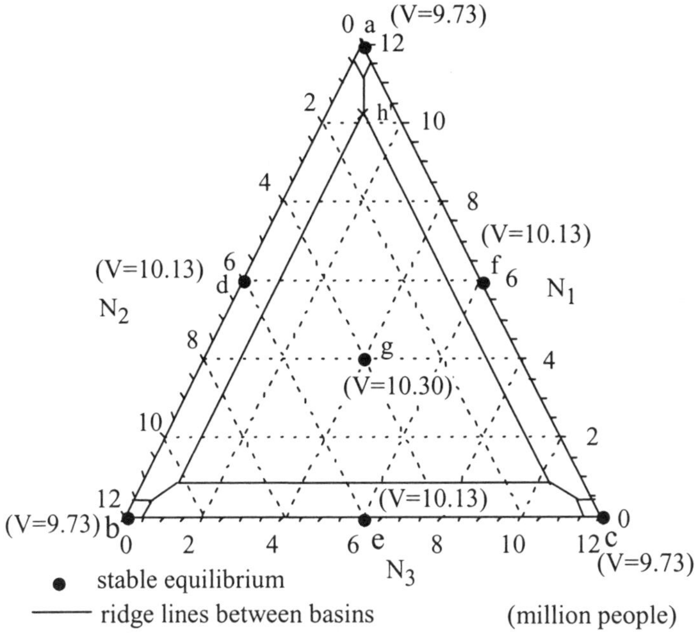

Figure 2.2 Relationship between equilibrium patterns and initial conditions (Case 1)

Exogenous variables of the model are the total population and transportation conditions, while w_k, N_k, m_k, n_k are endogenous variables. The computational procedures are designed to calculate the endogenous variables w_k, N_k, m_k, n_k such that they simultaneously satisfy all equilibrium conditions. Calculations are made in the following manner: 1) assume initial values of w_k, N_k, m_k, n_k, respectively; 2) given these values, all other endogenous variables are numerically solved by the Newton-Raphson Method. These values satisfy (3) (13) (14) (15) (16) (17) (21) (25) (28) (29) (33) (36) (37) (38) (40) (41) (42) (44) (45), and (46). The wage rate of city *1* is selected as a numéraire.

a) The Benchmark Case (Case 1)

In the benchmark case, assume a symmetrical setting where all cities are identical. All intercity transportation costs are assumed to be identical: i.e, $\tau_{kl}=0.04$, *for all* $\{k,l\}$. The parameters σ and ρ of utility function indicate the elasticities for a variety of consumption menus. Smaller values of these parameters imply that the consumers have stronger preferences towards a variety of consumption menus. When $\sigma=1$, $\rho=1$, all products are homogeneous in terms of consumers' preferences. Then, all firms inevitably lose their monopolistic powers. In the benchmark case, we consider an economy with weaker rates of increasing returns both in production and consumption, assuming $\gamma=\eta=0.1$ and $\sigma=\rho=0.8$.

In the benchmark case, seven different equilibria exist: 1) an equilibrium where all three cities share the same population size of *N/3* (call it symmetric equilibrium); 2) three equilibria where population concentrates on two cities with equal shares (polarized equilibria); 3) three equilibria where all population exclusively concentrates on only one city (centralized equilibria). Without loss of generality, let us focus on the equilibrium where cities 2 and 3 share the same population size. In Figure 2.1, the population of city 1 is scaled from the left edge, while the sum of the populations of cities 2 and 3 are scaled in reverse from the right. The indirect utility levels of city 1 as well as those of cities 2 and 3 are plotted on the figure.

As shown in Figure 2.1, the symmetric equilibrium (point A) enjoys the highest utility level ($V=10.30$), while the centralized equilibrium (point C) gives the lowest utility level ($V=9.73$) among the three different types of stable equilibria. In simulation, the initial distribution of population is crucial in determining which equilibrium pattern finally emerges. Figure 2.2 shows the relationship between the initial population configuration and the resulting stable equilibria to which the city system eventually evolves.

b) More Increasing Returns in Production (Case 2)

When agglomeration economies in production become stronger, one cannot expect the symmetric equilibrium to survive. For example, Figure 2.3 illustrates the possible equilibrium patterns when $\eta=0.15$. In this case, there appears to be only polarized equilibria (point B) with a higher utility level ($V=13.04$) and centralized equilibrium (point C) with a lower utility level ($V=12.65$).

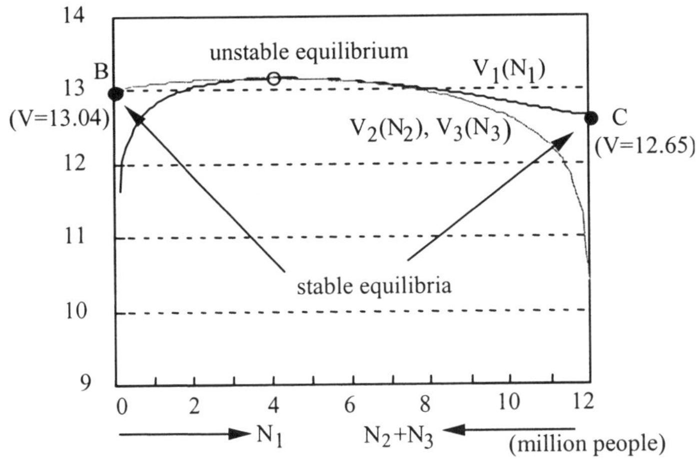

Figure 2.3 Multiple equilibrium patterns (when *η=0.15*)

c) More Increasing Returns in Consumption (Case 3)

When people prefer a wider variety of choice (*ρ=0.70*), the symmetrical equilibrium also disappears and only polarized and centralized equilibrium patterns can be realized as shown in Figure 2.4. As in Case 2, people can enjoy a higher utility level of *V=20.65* in a polarized equilibrium (point B), than in a centralized equilibrium (point C). These two cases illustrate that the symmetric equilibrium pattern may vanish from a city system when increasing returns either work in favor of consumption, production, or both. Only polarized and centralized equilibria can survive in a world of strong increasing returns.

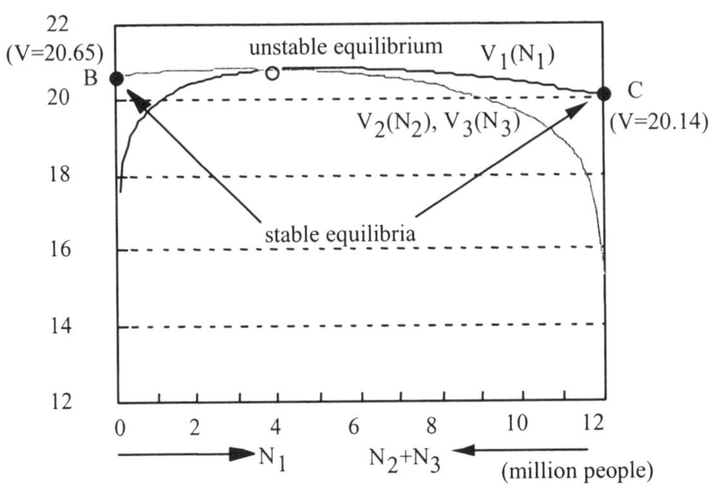

Figure 2.4 Multiple equilibrium patterns (when *ρ=0.70*)

d) Uniform Improvement of Transportation Network (Case 4)

Assume all transportation links of the network are uniformly improved in quality; transportation costs between two nodes decrease to $\tau_{kl}=0.02$ for all node pairs (k,l). Figure 2.5 shows new equilibria when the network is uniformly and simultaneously improved. Through network improvements, the equilibrium utility levels increase both in the symmetric equilibrium (point *g*), and in the polarized equilibria (points *d,e,f*), while utility levels remain unchanged in the centralized equilibria (points *a,b,c*). It must be noted that the range of the initial population distributions that allow system convergence at the symmetric equilibrium is enlarged by the uniform network improvement.

However, once the system reaches one of the equilibria other than the symmetric one by chance, the system remains locked-in at the equilibrium position. Any transition among the equilibrium positions then cannot be made through network improvements. The relocation of a population center by the government, e.g. the relocation of the capital, is then be required to progress from one equilibrium position to another. This type of policy implementation is achieved by moving point *a* to point *h* in Figure 2.5. The relocation of small amounts of the population suffices to realize the transition from the centralized equilibrium (point *a* in Figure 2.5) to the symmetric equilibrium (point *g*).

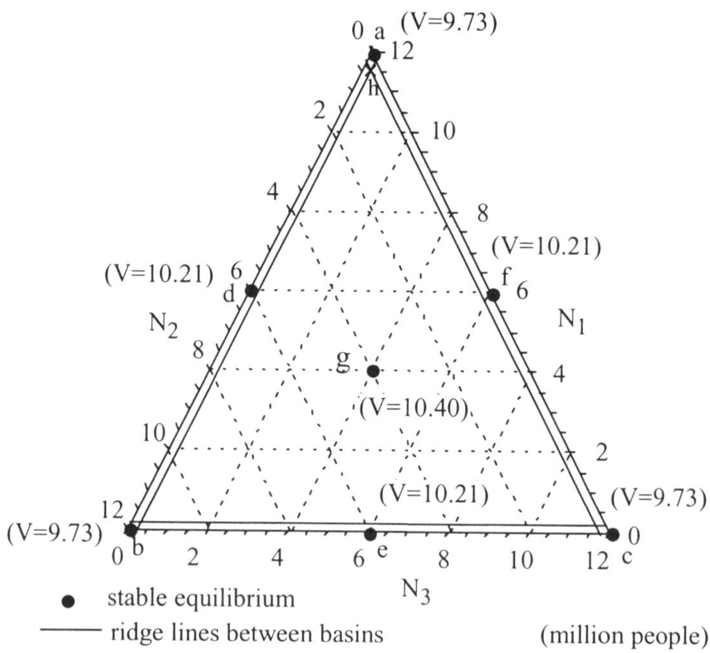

Figure 2.5 Equilibria with uniform network improvement

e) Non-Uniform Network Improvement (Case 5)

Consider the case where non-uniform network improvements are made. Assume that the transportation cost between city 2 and city 3 is exclusively reduced to $\tau_{23}=\tau_{32}=0.02$. In this case, the symmetric equilibrium is eliminated, and only centralized and polarized equilibrium patterns can survive. Figure 2.6 shows the new equilibrium pattern and the basins of the initial population distributions from which the system will converge upon the respective equilibria. Assume the system is initially positioned at the symmetric equilibrium in the benchmark case (designated by point *g* in Figure 2.6.) After the network improvement, point *g* is no longer the equilibrium state, and the system will arrive at a new equilibrium at point *e* in Figure 2.6. Here, city 1 completely loses its entire population. Only centralized and polarized equilibrium patterns (represented by points *a* to *f*) can survive as locally stable equilibria. The polarized equilibrium represented by point *e* in Figure 2.6 gains the large population basin while the other equilibrium points lose basins. Here, consider again the political replacement of the population in this figure. Look at point *d* which is a stable equilibrium point with no population in city 3. Assume that the political replacement of the population from city 2 to city 3 is made, exemplified by a movement from point *d* to point *i*. Then, city 3 autonomously grows through in-migration from cities 1 and 3, and eventually, the system reaches the polarized equilibrium *e*, where cities 2 and 3 share the same population size.

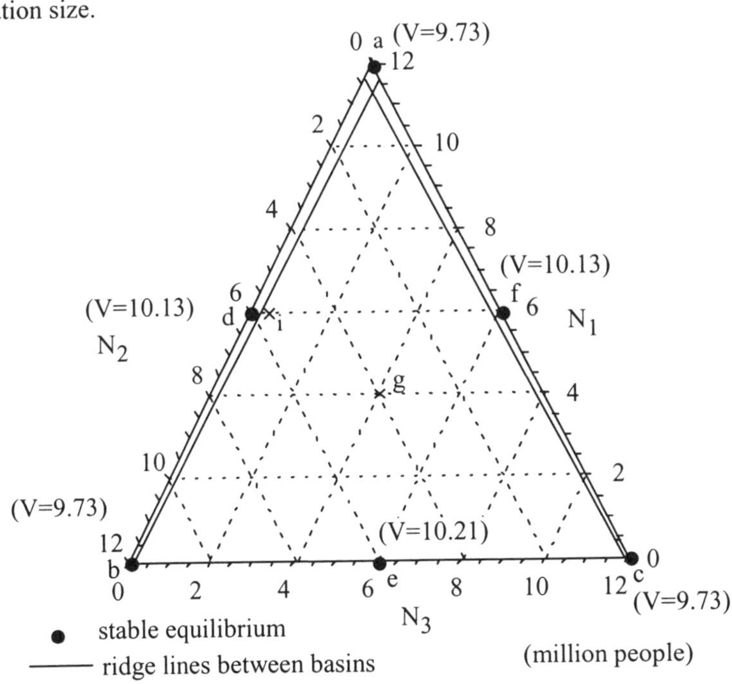

Figure 2.6 Equilibria with non-uniform network improvement

f) Multi-Stage Network Improvement

Assume that a network improvement has been made in the multi-stage fashion starting from the benchmark case: (1) in the first period, the link between city 2 and city 3 is improved; (2) at the second stage, transportation costs between cities 1 and 2 are reduced; (3) finally, the last link between city 3 and city 1 is improved. After all links are improved, the uniformly improved network, identical to Case 4, can be obtained. Figure 2.7 compares the utility levels in the respective equilibrium positions. These utility levels will change as the network improvement processes cause changes in the different values of travel costs.

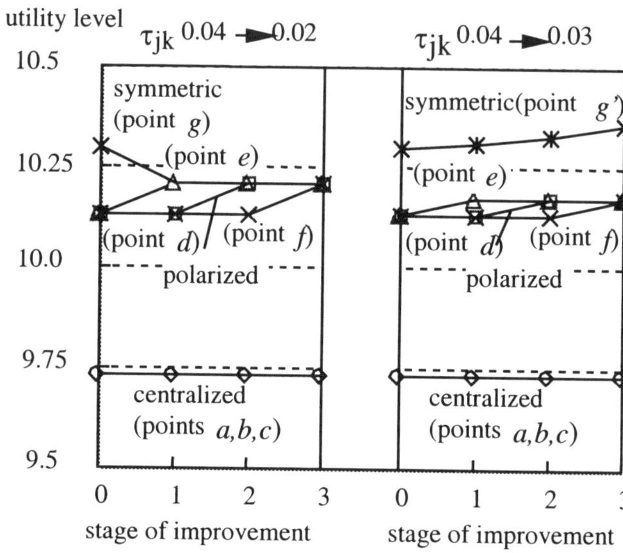

Figure 2.7 Equilibria with multi-stage network improvement

Through all the stages of network improvements, all of the centralized and polarized equilibrium patterns (depicted by points *a* to *f* in Figure 2.2) will always be able to survive. But, the symmetric equilibrium (denoted by point *g'*) can vanish in the first period in the case where τ_{23} is sufficiently small, e.g. $\tau_{23}=0.02$. If a city vanishes from the system during the improvement processes, the city never reappears given that no policy interventions occur in the evolutionary process. This is the case even though the symmetric equilibrium position guarantees the highest utility level at the end of the third period when the network is uniformly improved from the original one.

This analysis illustrates how path-dependency regulates the evolutionary processes of the city system. The sequence of investment decisions is crucial in determining economic geography. Once a small number of agglomerated economies (like polarized and centralized equilibria) are formed by chance, it becomes very difficult to relocate the population to more sparsely populated cities by improving transportation networks.

Conclusion

This chapter has proposed a computable general equilibrium model to investigate the impacts of transportation improvements upon the economic geography of city systems. The model includes two different sources of increasing returns; technological and pecuniary externalities. The former comes from the agglomeration economies in production, while the latter is caused by an increasing diversity in consumption.

As far as these externalities are concerned, there exist multiple stable equilibria in the system. The selection of an equilibrium point is crucial to historical events and policy decisions. The computer simulation in this paper has illustrated that when distance barriers disappear or are largely reduced by the advent of new transport technology, both the population and industries are expected to distribute themselves more evenly across the system. However, as long as distance barriers remain, and increasing-return-to-scale economies work in the system, there will exist a multitude of equilibria. Once the hub-city or -cities are formed in the system, they will exhibit the lock-in effect. The relocation of the population from the larger cities to the smaller ones cannot be made solely through transportation improvements; appropriate regional development policies will be necessary in order to realize an even distribution of population.

The model can still be extended in many different ways. First, it is important to examine the impact of international trade upon economic geography. Second, dynamic models may be able to simulate the knowledge and capital accumulation (Kobayashi and Okumura, 1997). The financial aspect needed to provide infrastructure should also be incorporated in order to simulate the dynamic features of budgetary balance. Third, the proposed model can also be simulated with various combinations of policy parameters.

References

Abdel-Rahman, H.M. (1990), 'Agglomeration Economies, Types, and Sizes of Cities', *Journal of Urban Economics*, vol. 27, pp. 25–45.

Abdel-Rahman, H.M. (1996), 'When do Cities Specialize in Production?', *Regional Science and Urban Economics*, vol. 26, pp. 1–22.

Arthur, B. (1994), *Increasing Returns and Path Dependence in the Economy*, The University of Michigan Press, Ann Arbor.

Batten, D.F., Kobayashi, K. and Andersson, Å.E. (1989), 'Knowledge, Nodes and Networks: An Analytical Perspective', in Å.E. Andersson, D.F. Batten and C. Karlsson. (eds), *Knowledge and Industrial Organization*, Springer-Verlag, Berlin.

Fujita, M. (1993), 'Monopolistic Competition and Urban Systems', *European Economic Review*, vol. 37, pp. 308–15.

Fujita, M., Krugman, P. and Mori, T. (1995), 'On the Evolution of Hierarchical Urban Systems', Discussion Paper 419, *Institute of Economic Research*, Kyoto University.

Henderson, J.V. (1985), *Economic Theory and The Cities*, Academic Press, London.

Henderson, J.V. (1988), *Urban Development, Theory, Fact and Illusion*, Oxford University Press.

Kanemoto, Y. and Mera, K. (1985), 'General Equilibrium Analysis of the Benefits of Large Transportation Improvements', *Regional Science and Urban Economics*, vol. 15, pp. 343–63.

Kobayashi, K., Batten, D.F. and Andersson, Å.E. (1991), 'The Sequential Location of Knowledge-Oriented Firms over Time and Space', *Paper of Regional Science*, vol. 70, pp. 381–97.

Kobayashi, K. and Okumura, M. (1997), 'The Growth of City Systems with High-Speed Railway Systems', *Annals of Regional Science*, vol. 31, pp. 39–56.

Krugman, P. (1991a), *Geography and Trade*, The MIT Press, Cambridge, MA.

Krugman, P. (1991b), 'Increasing Returns and Economic Geography', *Journal of Political Economy*, vol. 99, pp. 483–99.

Krugman, P. (1993), 'On the Number and Location of Cities', *European Economic Review*, vol. 37, pp. 293–8.

McKibbin, W.J. and Sachs, J.D. (1991), *Global Linkages: Macroeconomic Interdependence and Cooperation in the World Economy*, Brookings Institution.

Matsuyama, K. (1995), 'Complementarities and Cumulative Process in Models of Monopolistic Competition', *Journal of Economic Literature*, vol. 33, pp. 701–29.

Mun, S.-I. (1997), 'Transport Network and System of Cities', *Journal of Urban Economics*, vol. 42, pp. 205–21.

Sasaki, K. (1992), 'Trade and Migration in a Two-City Model of Transportation Investments', *Annals of Regional Science*, vol. 26, pp. 305–17.

Shoven, J.B. and Whalley, J. (1972), 'A General Equilibrium Calculation of the Effects of Differential Taxation on Income from Capital', U.S., *Journal of Public Economics*, vol. 1, pp. 281–322.

Shoven, J.B. and Whalley, J. (1992), *Applying General Equilibrium*, Cambridge University Press, New York.

Chapter 3

Spatial Equilibrium with Cities and Rural Areas

Wei-Bin Zhang

Introduction

This chapter proposes an equilibrium model of economic geography with two cities and one farm. The model provides equilibrium conditions of a perfectly competitive spatial economy. The economic system consists of one agricultural and two industrial sectors. It is assumed that all the households have identical preferences and that any possible costs for occupational changes and people movement among cities and countryside are omitted. Cities and countryside are different in amenity level and technology. This chapter examines how the division of labor and differences in amenity levels among the urban and rural areas may affect the spatial distribution of economic variables. The model is an extension of the model on the spatial division of labor and economic geography by Zhang (1993).

The Model

The economic system consisting of two cities, indexed by 1 and 2 respectively and one farm. Each city consists of two parts – the CBD and a residential area. The locations of the CBDs are pre-specified points and all industrial activities are concentrated at the CBDs. Similar to Zhang (1993), this chapter features a linear two-city system on a homogeneous plain whose width is unity. For simplicity, it is assumed that the two CBDs are one-side edged as shown in Figure 3.1. This implies that the workers of each city can travel only in one direction. As shown in Figure 3.1, the agricultural sector is assumed to be located between the two urban areas.

The system produces agricultural goods and two industrial commodities. The two commodities are respectively indexed by 1 and 2. The economic system exhibits a strict spatial division of labor. For simplicity, transportation costs of commodities are neglected. It is assumed that labor markets are characterized by perfect competition and that people are freely mobile among three occupations.

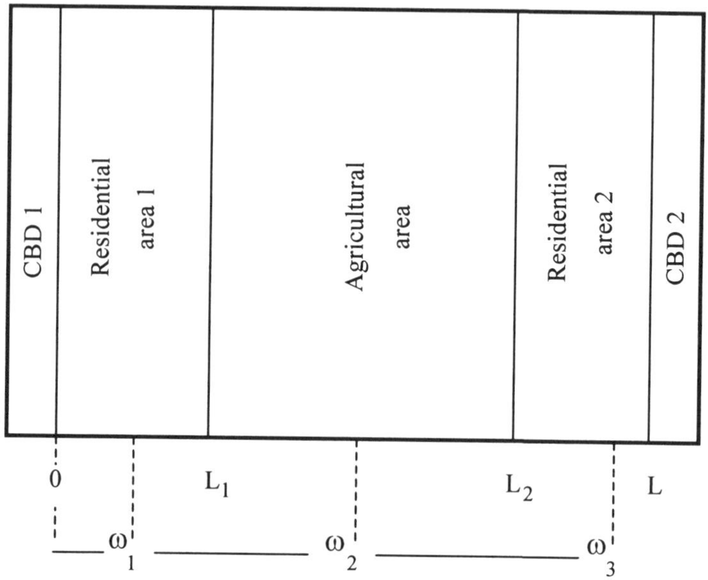

Figure 3.1 The two-city and one-farm system

The labor force is homogeneous and the agricultural good is selected to serve as numeraire, with all other prices being measured relative to its price. Wage rates may be different among different occupations but identical within the same occupation. The equilibrium of labor markets is guaranteed by the conditions that the household gets the same level of utility, irrespective of its location and occupation. We define the following variables:

L and N -	the given labor force and territory size, respectively;
L_1 -	the distance from CBD 1 to the boundary between residential area 1 and the agricultural area;
L_2 -	the distance from CBD 1 to the boundary between the agricultural area and residential area 2;
ω_1, ω_2 and ω_3 -	the dwelling location of city 1's residents, farmers and city 2's residents, respectively, $0 \leq \omega_1 < L_1$, $L_1 \leq \omega_2 < L_2$ and $L_2 \leq \omega_3 \leq L$;
$R(\omega_j)$ -	the land rent at location ω_j, $j = 1, 3$;
R_a -	the land rent of the agricultural area;
N_j and N_a -	city j's employment and the number of farmers, respectively;
F_j and F_a -	the output of city j and the agricultural sector, respectively;
p_j -	the price of commodity j; and
w_j and w_a -	the wage rate in city j and wage rate of farmers, respectively.

Agricultural Production

It is assumed that agricultural production is carried out by a combination of labor force and land in the following way

$$F_a = L_a^{\alpha} N_a^{1-\alpha}, \quad 0 < \alpha < 1, \tag{1}$$

where L_a is land employed by the agricultural sector and α is a parameter. Profit maximization yields

$$R_a = \alpha F_a / L_a, \quad w_a = (1 - \alpha) F_a / N_a. \tag{2}$$

Let C_j and C_a denote total consumption of agricultural product by city j and farmers, respectively. The balance of demand for and supply of agricultural product is given by

$$C_1 + C_2 + C_a = F_a. \tag{3}$$

Industrial Production

It is assumed that industrial commodities are produced with only one input, labor. Other possible inputs such as capital and land are neglected. Linear production functions of the two industrial sectors are specified as follows:

$$F_1 = z_1 N_1, \quad F_2 = z_2 N_2, \tag{4}$$

where z_j is city j's production efficiency parameter. The parameter, z_j, measures economic efficiency and technology levels of city j in aggregated terms.

As there is only one input factor in each production sector, one always has $w_1 N_1 = p_1 F_1$ and $w_2 N_2 = p_2 F_2$, i.e.,

$$w_1 = p_1 z_1, \quad w_2 = p_2 z_2. \tag{5}$$

City j's wage rate is equal to industry j's product value per labor input. As the labor markets are perfectly competitive and production functions are linear with a single input, the equations, (5), consist of two 'accounting relations'.

Let C_{ij} and C_{aj} denote total consumption of city j's product by city i and by the farmers, respectively. The balances between demand for and supply of industrial commodities are given by

$$C_{11} + C_{21} + C_{a1} = F_1, \quad C_{12} + C_{22} + C_{a2} = F_2. \tag{6}$$

Behavior of Consumers

It is assumed that the utility level of a household depends on four variables, consumption levels of the three commodities and of housing. Here, housing consumption is measured by the household's dwelling size. A typical household's utility function is specified as follows:

$$U(\omega_j)=\theta_j c_1(\omega_j)^{\xi_1}\ c_2(\omega_j)^{\xi_2}\ c_a(\omega_j)^{\xi_a}\ c_h(\omega\ \ )^{\xi_h}\ ,\ \xi_1,\xi_2,\xi_a,\xi_h>0, j=1,2,3,$$

$$0 \le \omega_1 < L_1,\quad L_1 \le \omega_2 < L_2,\quad L_2 \le \omega_3 \le L, \tag{7}$$

where $c_1(\omega_j)$, $c_2(\omega_j)$, $c_a(\omega_j)$ and $c_h(\omega_j)$ are, respectively, the consumption levels of commodity 1, commodity 2, agricultural good and housing of a household at location ω_j. The three parameters, θ_1, θ_2 and θ_3, are called, respectively, amenity levels of city 1, the countryside and city 2.

The consumer problem is defined by

$$\max U(\omega_j)\ ,\ \text{s.t.:}$$

$$p_1c_1(\omega_j) + p_2c_2(\omega_j) + p_ac_a(\omega_j) + R(\omega_j)c_h(\omega_j) = y(\omega_j),\quad j = 1, 2, 3, \tag{8}$$

in which

$$y(\omega_1) = w_1 - \tau\omega_1,\ \ 0 \le \omega_1 < L_1,\ \ y(\omega_2) = w_a,\ \ L_1 \le \omega_2 < L_2,$$

$$y(\omega_3) = w_2 - \tau(L - \omega_3),\quad L_2 \le \omega_3 \le L,$$

where τ is travel cost per unit of distance. Here, $\tau\omega_1$ and $\tau(L - \omega_3)$ are the total traveling cost per household between the dwelling site and the CBDs in urban area 1 and 2, respectively. As wages are only source of income and savings are omitted, a household's wage is distributed among travel cost, industrial goods purchases and land rent.

The optimal problem has the following unique solution

$$c_1 = \xi\xi_1y(\omega_j)/p_1,\ \ c_2 = \xi\xi_2y(\omega_j)/p_2,\ \ c_a = \xi\xi_ay(\omega_j),\ \ c_h = \xi\xi_hy(\omega_j)/R(\omega_j), \tag{9}$$

where $\xi \equiv 1/(\xi_1 + \xi_2 + \xi_a + \xi_h)$. Let $n(\omega_j)$ denote the residential density at dwelling site ω_j. According to the definitions of n and c_h, we have:

$$n(\omega_1) = 1/c_h(\omega_1),\ \ 0 \le \omega_1 < L_1,\quad n(\omega_3) = 1/c_h(\omega_3),\ \ L_2 \le \omega_3 \le L. \tag{10}$$

The population of each city is equal to the sum of its residents, i.e.,

$$\int_0^{L_1} n(\omega_1)\,d\omega_1 = N_1,\ \int_{L_2}^{L} n(\omega_3)\,d\omega_3 = N_2. \tag{11}$$

The agricultural land, which is equal to the territory size minus the total land used by the two cities, is distributed between agricultural production and farmers' housing, i.e.,

$$L_a + c_h(\omega_2)N_a = L_2 - L_1. \tag{12}$$

The conditions, (3) and (6), are rewritten as follows:

$$\int_0^{L_1} n(\omega_1)c_1(\omega_1)d\omega_1 + \int_{L_2}^{L} n(\omega_3)c_1(\omega_3)d\omega_3 + (L_2 - L_1)c_1(\omega_2) = F_1,$$

$$\int_0^{L_1} n(\omega_1)c_2(\omega_1)d\omega_1 + \int_{L_2}^{L} n(\omega_3)c_2(\omega_3)d\omega_3 + (L_2 - L_1)c_2(\omega_2) = F_2,$$

$$\int_0^{L_1} n(\omega_1)c_a(\omega_1)d\omega_1 + \int_{L_2}^{L} n(\omega_3)c_a(\omega_3)d\omega_3 + (L_2 - L_1)c_a(\omega_2) = F_a. \tag{13}$$

The spatial equilibrium system is thus complete. The system consists of 22 variables, N_j, F_j, c_j, w_j, p_j, N_j, L_j ($j = 1, 2$), F_a, N_a, w_a, R, c_h, c_a, n, U. It contains the same number of equations.

The Unique Equilibrium

This section proves that the 22 variables can be expressed as functions of z_1, z_2, L, N and the other parameters in the system. First, we note that the utility level of households is identical, irrespective of their dwelling location and occupations. Using (7), (9), $U(\omega_1) = U(0)$ for $0 \le \omega_1 < L_1$ and $U(\omega_3) = U(L)$ for $L_2 \le \omega_3 \le L$, we have:

$$R(\omega_1)/R_a = \{y(\omega_1)/y(L_1)\}^{1/\xi\xi_h} < 1, \quad 0 \le \omega_1 < L_1,$$

$$R(\omega_3)/R_a = \{y(\omega_3)/y(L_2)\}^{1/\xi\xi_h} < 1, L_2 < \omega_3 < L, \tag{14}$$

where $y(L_1) = w_1 - \tau L_1$ and $y(L_2) = w_2 - \tau(L - L_2)$. Each urban area's land rent declines with distance from its CBD. This conclusion is reasonable since households from the same city have identical wage rates.

Using (7), (9), $U(\omega_1) = U(\omega_2)$ at $\omega_1 = \omega_2 = L_1$ and $U(\omega_2) = U(\omega_3)$ at $\omega_2 = \omega_3 = L_2$, we obtain

$$w_1 - \tau L_1 = (\theta_2/\theta_1)^{\xi} w_a, \quad w_2 - \tau(L - L_2) = (\theta_2/\theta_3)^{\xi} w_a. \tag{15}$$

Thus, if the amenity level in farming is much lower than in cities, the farmers' wage rate may be higher than the workers' in the cities in a competitive equilibrium. In reality one may find that urban workers may enjoy higher amenities and earn higher wage rates than farmers. This is due, among other things, to the fact that the urban and rural labor forces have different human capital. In particular, highly educated people tend to be concentrated in cities. This suggests that in order to explain the well-observed difference in wages and amenities between urban workers and farmers it is necessary to further classify the labor force according to education and human capital.

The following proposition shows that the system has a unique equilibrium under certain conditions.

Proposition 1

If $\theta_3 > \theta_1$ and $\xi_1 < \xi_2$, the system has a unique equilibrium. The above proposition is proved in the appendix. The requirement, $\theta_3 > \theta_1$, implies that city 2's amenity level is higher than that of city 1. The condition $\xi_1 < \xi_2$ states that the propensity to consume city 1's product is lower than the propensity to consume city 2's product. One can see that proposition 1 holds for the case of $\theta_3 < \theta_1$ and $\xi_1 > \xi_2$. It should be remarked that the existence of a unique equilibrium is generally not guaranteed in the case of $\theta_3 < \theta_1$ and $\xi_1 < \xi_2$ (or $\theta_3 > \theta_1$ and $\xi_1 > \xi_2$). In the remainder of this chapter, $q_3 > q_1$ and $x_1 < x_2$ are assumed to hold.

Let us examine a special case of $\theta_1 = \theta_3$, $\xi_1 = \xi_2$ and $\xi_a = 0$. The two cities have identical amenity level, the propensities to consume the two industrial commodities are identical and there is no demand for the agricultural product. It is easy to show that $L_1 = L_2 = L/2$ and $N_1 = N_2 = N/2$ is the equilibrium solution. At this equilibrium the agricultural sector disappears from the system, the boundary between the two urban areas is located at the middle point of the two cities and the two cities employ the same amount of labor.

Corollary 1

If $\xi_1 = \xi_2$, $\xi_a = 0$ and $\theta_1 = \theta_3$, then the agricultural sector disappears in the system and the two urban areas have the identical structure at equilibrium. That is, $L_1 = L_2 = L/2$, $N_1 = N_2 = N/2$, $\omega_1 = \omega_2$, $c_1(\omega_1) = c_1(\omega_2)$, $c_2(\omega_1) = c_2(\omega_2)$, $c_h(\omega_1) = c_h(\omega_2)$, and $R(\omega_1) = R(\omega_2)$ for any ω_1 and ω_2, $0 \leq \omega_1 = \omega_2 - L \leq L/2$.

The Impact of City 1's Amenity Level

This section examines effects of changes in city 1's amenity level, θ_1, on the equilibrium structure of the spatial economy. Taking derivatives of (36) with respect to θ_1, together with (35) and (15), we obtain

$$M' dW_2/d\theta_1 = \xi\xi_2\alpha_1\tau\xi_h^2 L_1/\xi_a\theta_1\omega_2 > 0, \qquad (16)$$

where $W_2 = w_2/w_a$ and $M' > 0$ is defined in (A.13). As city 1's amenity level increases, the ratio of city 1's and farmers' wage rates also increases. From (34) we obtain:

$$dW_1/d\theta_1 = -W_1/\xi_h\theta_1 + \left\{\xi_1 (\theta_1/\theta_2)^{1/\varsigma_h} (W_2/W_1)^{1/\xi\xi_h - 1} / \xi\xi_h\xi_2\right\} dW_2/d\theta_1, \qquad (17)$$

where $W_1 = w_1/w_a$. In general, $dW_1/d\theta_1$ may be either positive or negative. If $dW_2/d\theta_1$ is very small, then $dW_1/d\theta_1$ tends to be negative. As an increases in city 1's amenity level makes city 1 more attractive in comparison to the rural area and city 2, city 1's wage rate tends to decline relative to the wage rate in the agricultural sector.

Taking derivatives of (33) with respect to θ_1 yields

$$\{(1-\alpha)W/\alpha w_a\}dw_a/d\theta_1 = \{\xi_1/W_1 + \xi_2/W_2 + \xi_a(1 - \alpha)\}(dW_1/d\theta_1 - dW_2/d\theta_1 + \xi\theta_2^{\xi}/\theta_1^{\xi+1})$$

$$+ (W_2 - W_1 + \Theta)\{(\xi_1/W_1^2)dW_1/d\theta_1 + (\xi_2/W_2^2)dW_2/d\theta_1\}, \qquad (18)$$

where $W \equiv (W_2 - W_1 + \theta)\{\xi_1/W_1 + \xi_2/W_2 + \xi_a(1 - \alpha)\} > 0$. From (4.2) and (3.2) we have:

$$dW_1/d\theta_1 - dW_2/d\theta_1 + \xi\theta_2^{\xi}/\theta_1^{\xi+1} = - \{(1 - \xi_h)\xi\theta_2^{\xi}/\theta_1^{\xi} - \tau L_1\}/\xi_h\theta_1$$

$$+ \left\{\xi_1 (\theta_1/\theta_2)^{1/\xi_h} (W_2/w_1)^{1/\xi\xi_h - 1} / \xi\xi_a\xi_2 - 1\right\} dW_2/d\theta_1. \qquad (19)$$

The right-hand side of (19) is negative when $dW_2/d\theta_1$ is small. Examining each term in the right-hand side in (18), one may conclude that when $dW_2/d\theta_1$ is small, $dw_a/d\theta_1$ may be negative. Otherwise, $dw_a/d\theta_1$ may be either positive or negative. Summarizing the above discussion, one sees that only when $dW_2/d\theta_1$ is very small is it possible to explicitly judge the signs of $dW_1/d\theta_1$ and $dw_a/d\theta_1$.

For convenience of explanation, in the remainder of this section we assume that $dW_2/d\theta_1$ is so small that $dW_1/d\theta_1 < 0$ and $dw_a/d\theta_1 < 0$. When this requirement is not satisfied, it is difficult to explicitly judge effects of changes in the parameter. From $W_1 = w_1/w_a$, $W_2 = w_2/w_a$ and (5), we obtain

$$dw_1/d\theta_1 < 0, \; dw_2/d\theta_1 < 0, \; dp_1/d\theta_1 < 0, \; dp_2/d\theta_1 < 0. \qquad (20)$$

An improvement in city 1's amenity reduces wage rates (in the terms of agricultural product) in the three sectors and reduces the prices of the two industrial commodities.

Taking derivatives of (37) with respect to θ_1 together with (15) and (17) yields:

$$dL_1/d\theta_1 = - \{\tau L_1 + w_a(1 - \xi\xi_h)\theta_2^{\xi}/\theta_1^{\xi}\}/\tau\xi_h\theta_1 + (L_1/w_a)dw_a/d\theta_1$$

$$+\left\{\xi_1 w_a \left(\theta_1/\theta_2\right)^{1/\xi_h} \left(W_2/W_1\right)^{1/\xi\xi_h -1} /\tau\xi\xi_h\xi_2\right\} dW_2/d\theta_1,$$

$$dL_2/d\theta_1 = (w_a/\tau)dW_2/d\theta_1 + (L_2/w_a)dw_a/d\theta_1. \tag{21}$$

City 1's urban area is decreased but city 2's urban area, $L - L_2$, is expanded as city 1's amenity is increased. From (24) and (21)

$$(1/R_a)dR_a/d\theta_1 = -\{(1-\alpha)/\alpha w_a\}dw_a/d\theta_1 > 0,\ (1/\alpha\alpha_1)dL_a/d\theta_1 = dL_2/d\theta_1 - dL_1/d\theta_1,$$

$$(1/N_a)dN_a/d\theta_1 = \{1/(1-\alpha)R_a\}dR_a/d\theta_1 + (1/L_a)dL_a/d\theta_1,$$

$$\{1/c_h(\xi_2)\}dc_h(\xi_2)/d\theta_1 = -\{1/R_a(1-\alpha)\}dR_a/d\theta_1 < 0. \tag{22}$$

The land rent in the agricultural area is increased. The land and labor force employed by the agricultural sector may be either increased or decreased. The last equation in (22) implies that an increase in city 1's amenity level reduces the dwelling size of the farmers.

From (26) we have:

$$dN_1/d\theta_1 = \left(N_1/R_a\right)dR_a/d\theta_1 - \left(R_a/\tau\xi\xi_h\right)^3 \left\{w_1/y\left(L_1\right)^{1/\xi\xi_h}\right.$$
$$\left.\left\{\tau L_1/w_1 y\left(L_1\right)\right\} dw_1/d\theta_1 - \left\{\tau/y\left(L_1\right)dL_1/d\theta_1\right\}\right\},$$
$$dN_2/d\theta_1 = \left(N_2/R_a\right)dR_a/d\theta_1 - \left(R_a/\tau\xi\xi_h\right)^3 \left\{w_2/y\left(L_2\right)^{1/\xi\xi_h}\right.$$
$$\left.\left\{\tau L_2/w_2 y\left(L_2\right)\right\} dw_2/d\theta_1 - \left\{\tau/y\left(L_2\right)dL_2/d\theta_1\right\}\right\}. \tag{23}$$

From (1), (4) and the above analytical results we obtain the effects of a change in θ_1 on the output, $dF_a/d\theta_1$, $dF_1/d\theta_1$ and $dF_2/d\theta_1$, of the three sectors. From (14) we obtain $R(\omega_1)$ for $0 \leq \omega_1 < L_1$ and $R(\omega_3)$ for $L_2 \leq \omega_3 \leq L$. From (9) and (10) we may obtain the effects on the consumption components of all the households and the residential densities in the two urban areas. As these derivations are quite easy and the economic conditions are difficult to interpret, the results will not be presented.

Concluding Remarks

This chapter proposed an economic geographic model of two cities and one farm. Each city produces only one commodity and the farm supplies agricultural goods. Amenity levels are spatially different among the cities and farming area. We demonstrated that the system has a unique equilibrium under certain conditions. We also examined the impact of changes in city 1's amenity level on the spatial economic structure.

Appendix: Proving Proposition 1

The appendix proves Proposition 1. First, from (12), and

$$c_h(\omega_2) = \xi\xi_h w_a/R_a, \quad R_a = \alpha F_a/L_a, \quad w_a = (1 - \alpha)F_a/N_a,$$

we get

$$L_a = \alpha\alpha_1(L_2 - L_1), \quad N_a = (R_a/\alpha)^{1/(1-\alpha)}L_a, \quad w_a = \sigma_0 R_a^{-\alpha/(1-\alpha)},$$

$$c_h(\omega_2) = \xi\xi_h(1 - \alpha)L_a/\alpha N_a, \quad L_1 < \omega_2 \le L_2, \tag{24}$$

where $\alpha_0 \equiv (1 - \alpha)\alpha^{\alpha/(1-\alpha)}$ and $\alpha_1 \equiv 1/\{\alpha + \xi\xi_h(1 - \alpha)\}$. We see that the variables, L_a, N_a, $c_h(\omega_2)$ and w_a, of the agricultural sector can be expressed as functions of the variables, L_1, L_2 and R_a. From (9), (10) and (14), we obtain

$$n(\omega_1) = R_a\{y(\omega_1)/(L_1)\}^{1/\xi\xi_h}/\xi\xi_h y(\omega_1), 0£\omega_1 < L_1,$$

$$n(\omega_3) = R_a\{y(\omega_3)/(L_2)\}^{1/\xi\xi_h}/\xi\xi_h y(\omega_3), L_2 < \omega_3 < L. \tag{25}$$

Substituting (25) into (11) yields

$$N_j = R_a\left[\{w_j/yL_j\}^{1/\xi\xi_h} - 1\right]\Big/\tau\xi_h^2. \tag{26}$$

Substituting (29) and (25) into (13) together with (4) and (5) yields

$$G_1 + G_2 + \xi w_a(L_2 - L_1) = z_j p_j N_j/\xi_j, \quad j = 1, 2, \quad G_1 + G_2 + \xi w_a(L_2 - L_1) = F_a/\xi_a, \tag{27}$$

where

$$G_j = \left\{\xi R_a/\tau\xi_h\,(\xi+\xi_h)\,y(L_j)^{1/\xi\xi_h}\right\}\left\{w_j^{1+1/\xi\xi_h} - y(L_j)^{1+1/\xi\xi_h}\right\}, \tag{28}$$

From (25) we have, $w_1N_1/\xi_1 = w_2N_2/\xi_2 = F_a/\xi_a$, or

$$N_1 = \xi_1 F_a/\xi_a w_1, \quad N_2 = \xi_2 F_a/\xi_a w_2. \tag{29}$$

From (24) one gets $F_a = \alpha_1 R_a(L_2 - L_1)$. With this equation, (29) and (26) we obtain:

$$\{w_j/y(L_j)\}^{1/\xi\xi_h} = \xi_j\alpha_1\tau\xi_h^2(L_2 - L_1)/\xi_a w_j + 1. \tag{30}$$

Substituting $N_a = (1 - \alpha)F_a/w_a$ and (A.6) into $N_1 + N_2 + N_a = N$ yields

$$\alpha_1 R_a(L_2 - L_1)\{\xi_1/\xi_a w_1 + \xi_2/\xi_a w_2 + (1 - \alpha)/w_a\} = N. \tag{31}$$

Substituting $y(L_1) = (\theta_2/\theta_1)^{\xi}w_a$, $y(L_2) = (\theta_2/\theta_3)^{\xi}w_a$, and $w_a = \sigma_0 R_a^{-\alpha/(1-\alpha)}$, into (A.7) and (A.8) yields

$$\begin{aligned}&(\theta_1/\theta_2)^{1/\xi_h} W_1^{1/\xi\xi_h} = \xi_1\alpha_1\tau\xi_h^{\ 2}(W_2/W_1 - 1 + \theta/W_1)/\tau\xi_a + 1,\\ &(\theta_3/\theta_2)^{1/\xi_h} W_2^{1/\xi\xi_h} = \xi_2\alpha_1\tau\xi_h^{\ 2}(1 - W_1/W_2 + \theta/W_2)/\tau\xi_a + 1,\end{aligned} \tag{32}$$

$$w_a^{(1-\alpha)/\alpha} = \tau N\alpha_0^{(1-\alpha)/\alpha}/[\alpha_1(W_2 - W_1 + \theta)\{\xi_1/\xi_a W_1 + \xi_2/\xi_a W_2 + (1 - \alpha)\}], \tag{33}$$

where $W_1 \equiv w_1/w_a$, $W_2 \equiv w_2/w_a$, and $\theta \equiv (\theta_2/\theta_1)^{\xi} - (\theta_2/\theta_3)^{\xi}$. The two equations in (32) have only two independent variables W_1 and W_2. From (32) we solve:

$$\left\{(\theta_1/\theta_2)^{1/\xi_h} W_1^{1/\xi\xi_h} - 1\right\} / \left\{(\theta_3/\theta_2)^{1/\xi_h} W_2^{1/\xi\xi_h} - 1\right\} = \xi_1/\xi_2. \tag{34}$$

It is important to note that (33) is independent of the technological parameters. In the case of $\xi_1 = \xi_2$, $w_1 = (\theta_3/\theta_1)^{\xi}w_2$ holds. This means that if the marginal utility levels of the two industrial commodities are equal, then the sign of the difference in wage rates between the two cities is the opposite to that in amenity levels between the two cities. The city with higher amenity will have lower wage rate than the other one with low amenity. Moreover, in the case of $\xi_1 = \xi_2$ and $\theta_1 = \theta_3$, the wage rates in the two cities are identical, i.e., $w_1 = w_2$.

From (34) we obtain:

$$W_1/W_2 = f(W_2) \equiv (\theta_2/\theta_1)^{\xi}\left\{\xi_1(\theta_3/\theta_2)^{1/\xi_h}/\xi_2 + (1 - \xi_1/\xi_2)/W_2^{1/\xi\xi_h}\right\}^{\xi\xi_h}. \tag{35}$$

Substituting (35) into the second equation in (32) yields

$$M(W_2) \equiv (\theta_3/\theta_2)^{1/\xi_h} W_2^{1/\xi\xi_h} - \xi_2\alpha_1\tau\xi_\eta^{\ 2}(1 - f(W_2) + \theta/W_2)/\tau\xi_a + 1 = 0. \tag{36}$$

It is not difficult to see that whether $M(W_2) = 0$ has a unique positive solution is dependent on the signs of θ and $1 - \xi_1/\xi_2$. It should be remarked that $\theta_3 > \theta_1$ implies $\theta > 0$. Under the requirement of $\theta > 0$ and $\xi_1 < \xi_2$ one has $M(0) < 0$, $M(\infty) > 0$ and $M'(W_2) > 0$ for $0 < W_2 < \infty$. Hence, $M(W_2) = 0$ has a unique positive solution. One may thus express W_2 as a function of the parameters in the system. It is now shown how all other variables in the system can be solved as functions of the system parameters.

The two variables, W_1 and w_a, are determined by $W_1 = W_2f(W_2)$ and (35), respectively. The wage rates, w_1 and w_2, in the two cities are given by $w_1 = w_aW_1$

and $w_2 = w_a W_2$. We thus determined the wage rates, w_a, w_1 and w_2, as functions of the parameters. The two boundaries, L_1 and L_2, are, respectively, given by

$$L_1 = \{w_1 - (\theta_2/\theta_1)^{\xi} w_a\}/\tau, \quad L_2 = \{w_2 - (\theta_2/\theta_3)^{\xi} w_a\}/\tau. \tag{37}$$

The land rent of the agricultural area is given by

$$R_a = (\sigma_0/w_a)^{1/\alpha - 1}.$$

The employment, N_1 and N_2, of the two cities are given by (26). The residential density, $n(\omega_1)$ and $n(\omega_2)$, in the two urban areas are determined by (10). The land and labor force, L_a and N_a, employed the by agricultural sector are given by:

$$L_a = \alpha\alpha_1(L_2 - L_1), \quad N_a = (R_a/\alpha)^{1/(1-\alpha)} L_a.$$

The land rent distribution, $R(\omega_1)$ and $R(\omega_2)$, in the two urban areas are given by (14). The output, F_a, F_1 and F_2, of agricultural and industrial production are given by (1) and (4), respectively. The prices, p_1 and p_2, of the two industrial commodities are solved as $p_1 = w_1/z_1$ and $p_2 = w_2/z_2$. The consumption components of the households in the agricultural area and the two urban areas are obtained by (9).

Summarizing the above discussion, we proved Proposition 1.

Reference

Zhang, W.B. (1993), 'Wages, Service Prices and Rent – Urban Division of Labor and Amenities', *Seoul Journal of Economics*, vol. 6.

Chapter 4

Hierarchical Fields of Influence of Spatial Exchange

Michael Sonis, Geoffrey J.D. Hewings and Nuzul Achjar

Introduction

Interest in the role and impact of international trade has been significantly heightened by the recent developments in multinational trade agreements and the various rounds of GATT and now WTO. Far less attention has been directed to issues surrounding interregional trade within a single economy; this is surprising in view of the importance of this trade. For example, recent estimates suggest that interstate trade in manufacturing and agriculture among the states of Wisconsin, Illinois, Indiana, Ohio and Michigan amounted to $270 billion in 1992; in contrast, US-Canada trade at that time was a little over $100 billion in each direction (see Hewings et al., 1997). Unfortunately, research focusing on the nature and strength of interregional trade has not been anywhere near as prevalent as the concomitant attention focused on international trade. As a result, little progress has been made in identifying expected patterns in the development of interregional trade, its link to overall national development.

Drawing on research conducted on the Indonesian economy, some initial explorations are provided about the nature of interregional trade and the role that linkages with the rest of the economy play in changing the nature and strength of linkages and the importance of sectors. In attempting to measure the role that trade may play in an economy's economic health, several new measures have been proposed; a series of papers (Sonis et al., 1993; 1996, 1997) examined the role of feedback loops and the underlying ideas from this methodology will be employed in this exploration but with a greater focus on notions of hierarchical inclusion.

Feedback Loops, Trade and Development

Elsewhere, Hewings et al. (1998a) have suggested that during the development of an economy, a process of increasing complication (or complexity) may be observed in the linkages between industrial sectors. This process reflects the influence of a variety of factors; increases in per capita income generate demands for greater variety and thus a broadening of the range of products produced. Increases in the size of the national market may create possibilities for the introduction of new suppliers of intermediate goods, thus increasing the degree of intra-national intermediation (the satisfying of demands on the commodity chain of production from domestic sources). In fact, the process may mirror a logistic curve, with a slow period of linkage development followed by relatively rapid deepening and extension of the linkage space. Okazaki (1989) was the first to propose a further development stage, namely one of hollowing out. In this stage, associated with a mature economy, the degree of intermediation actually decreases, while the level of output may not be affected (it may increase, decrease or stay the same). What is happening here is that local suppliers are replaced by less expensive inputs from other international markets. One of the major changes that might be expected would be in the network of international exchanges with more complex patterns of transactions replacing simple bilateral exchange.

Now consider that this national economy is divided into r mutually exclusive regions; what can one suggest about the pattern of interregional trade as the national economy matures? Thompson's (1965) development path suggests a pattern that is not too dissimilar from that described earlier with deepening of the intraregional linkage network and an increase in the variety of products produced and exported. Hence, during this period, one might expect intraregional flows to grow more rapidly than interregional transactions. Furthermore, it is likely that the interregional transactions will be essentially interindustry flows. Unfortunately, there is very little empirical evidence upon which to draw in developing the expected pattern of interregional flows for a mature economy. Evidence for the Chicago metropolitan region highlights a hollowing-out process, especially in the manufacturing sector; in this case, the volume of output in real terms actually increased (see Hewings et al., 1998a). A complementary study found that most of this spatial exchange (with interregional replacing intraregional flows) occurred with other midwestern states (Hewings et al., 1998b); further, these flows were dominated by *intra*industry flows.

This sketchy empirical evidence suggests a need for analytical tools that can help open up new perspectives on the changing nature of these trade patterns. For this reason, feedback loop analysis has been proposed as one of several techniques that might be employed. While attention to analytical explanation of flows is important, there is a complementary need to examine and explain the geographic structure of these flows. Are they concentrated in subsets of regions; are they dominated by certain industries and to what degree has the pattern of the flows become more complicated over time? Complication can be interpreted by feedback loop analysis through the identification of shifts in the dominance of bilateral feedback loops (an essential part of exchange in early economic development) to trilateral and multilateral loops.

What has yet to be explored is the identification of a *spatial hierarchy* of trade flows and it is here that feedback loop analysis provides the potential for uncovering the nature, strength and spatial linkages of trade flows. While the present chapter explores the hierarchy of trade flows at only one spatial level (between regions within a country), other applications have explored the hierarchy across spatial levels (see, for example, Sonis et al., 1994).

One other advantage of employing feedback loop analysis is that it occupies a position midway between the very detailed path-by-path analysis associated with structural path analysis (see, for example, Defourny and Thorbeck, 1984) and the more macro analysis that characterizes computable general equilibrium models. Furthermore, as Sonis and Hewings (1998) have shown, feedback loop analysis shares a great deal in common with the interest in the size and importance of multiregional feedback effects initially associated with the work of Miller (1966, 1969, 1986); In addition, the methodologies share the property that each path in a structural path is part of a global feedback loop that includes the transactions between all sectors (see Sonis et al., 1996).

In this chapter, the underlying perspectives offered by feedback loop analysis are complemented by attention to the process of hierarchical inclusion of linkages within a region, considered first in isolation from the rest of the economy and then in terms of its connections with the national economy in which it is located. In order to provide the basis for this new analytical approach, the following two sections will review two fundamental concepts – the fields of influence of change and the Schur-Banachiewicz ideas for the inversion of block matrices. The next section provides the analytical basis for the hierarchical inclusion of fields of influence while the section thereafter extends these ideas to consider the changes in gross output that are caused by the propagation of intraregional changes. The presentation of results is considered in the context of economic landscapes; the fundamental idea is described, and applied, hierarchically in the last two sections. Application to Indonesia follows and the chapter concludes with some summary remarks.

Fields of Influence of Changes

Consider the economic system that includes a region, *r,* and the rest of economy, *R*. The corresponding input-output system can be represented by the block matrix:

$$A = \begin{pmatrix} A_{rr} & A_{rR} \\ A_{Rr} & A_{RR} \end{pmatrix} \tag{1}$$

where A_{rr}, and A_{RR} are matrix of intra-regional inputs for the two regions, and A_{rR}, A_{Rr} are the inter-regional matrices representing direct input connections between region *r* and the rest of the economy. Assume that an incremental change, E_{rr}, in direct inputs in region *r* is presented by the matrix:

$$E = \begin{pmatrix} E_{rr} & 0 \\ 0 & 0 \end{pmatrix} \tag{2}$$

and the final demand and gross output vectors may be presented as:

$$f = \begin{pmatrix} f_r \\ f_R \end{pmatrix}; \quad X = \begin{pmatrix} X_r \\ X_R \end{pmatrix} \tag{3}$$

further indicating the separation of the region r from the rest of the economy.

If region r is isolated from the rest of economy, the increment changes influence the regional Leontief inverse $B_r = (I - A_{rr})^{-1}$ through the fields of influence of intraregional changes that are the *addita*[1] of the regional Leontief inverse $B_r(E_{rr}) = (I - A_{rr} - E_{rr})^{-1}$.

The following fundamental decomposition holds (Sonis and Hewings, 1989):

$$B_r(E_{rr}) = B_r + D(B_r, E_{rr}) \tag{4}$$

where

$$D(B_r, E_{rr}) = \frac{1}{Q_r(E_{rr})}\left[\sum_{k=1}^{n}\sum_{\substack{i_r < i_{r+1} \\ j_r \neq j_s}}{}' F_r(i_1, i_2, \ldots, i_k; j_1, j_2, \ldots, j_k) e_{j_1 i_1} e_{j_2 i_2} \ldots e_{j_k i_k}\right] \tag{5}$$

Here $F_r(i_1, i_2, \ldots, i_k; j_1, j_2, \ldots, j_k)$ are the matrices of the fields of influence of incremental changes $e_{j_1 i_1}, e_{j_2 i_2}, \ldots, e_{j_k i_k}$ occurring in the places $(j_1, i_1), (j_2, i_2), \ldots, (j_k, i_k)$ of the matrix of direct inputs A_{rr} . The components of these matrices have a form:

$$f_{ij}^r(i_1, i_2, \ldots i_k; j_1, j_2, \ldots, j_k) =$$

$$= (-1)^k \begin{vmatrix} b_{i_1 j_1}^r & b_{i_1 j_2}^r & \ldots & b_{i_1 j_k}^r & b_{i_1 j}^r \\ b_{i_2 j_1}^r & b_{i_2 j_2}^r & \ldots & b_{i_2 j_k}^r & b_{i_2 j}^r \\ \vdots & \vdots & \ldots & \vdots & \vdots \\ b_{i_k j_1}^r & b_{i_k j_2}^r & \ldots & b_{i_k j_k}^r & b_{i_k j}^r \\ b_{i j_1}^r & b_{i j_2}^r & \ldots & b_{i j_k}^r & 0 \end{vmatrix}, \qquad i, j = 1, 2, \ldots, n \tag{6}$$

where b_{ij}^r are the components of the regional Leontief inverse B_r .

Further,

$$Q_r(E_{rr}) = \frac{\det B_r}{\det B_r(E_{rr})} = 1 - \sum_{i_1 j_1} b_{j_1 i_1}^r e_{i_1 j_1} + \sum_{k=2}^{n} (-1)^k \sum_{\substack{i_r < i_{r+1} \\ j_r \neq j_s}}{}' B_{or}^r$$

$$(j_1, j_2, \ldots, j_k; i_1, i_2, \ldots, i_k) e_{i_1 j_1} e_{i_2 j_2} \ldots e_{i_k j_k} \tag{7}$$

where $B_{or}^r\ (j_1, j_2, \ldots, j_k; i_1, i_2, \ldots, i_k)$ is a determinant of order k that includes the components of the Leontief inverse B_r from the ordered set of columns,

$i_1, i_2, \ldots i_k$, and rows, $j_1, j_2, \ldots, j_k$; furthermore, in the sum $\sum'$, the products of changes $e_{i_1 j_1} e_{i_2 j_2} \ldots e_{i_k j_k}$, that differ only by the order of multiplication, are counted only once.

The first order field of influence, $F_r(i_1, j_1)$ associated with the increment, $e_{j_1 i_1}$ is the matrix generated by the multiplication of the j_1^{th} column of the Leontief inverse B_r with its i_1^{th} row:

$$F(i_1, j_1) = \begin{pmatrix} b_{1j_1}^r \\ b_{2j_1}^r \\ \vdots \\ b_{nj_1}^r \end{pmatrix} \begin{pmatrix} b_{i_1 1}^r & b_{i_1 2}^r & \cdots & b_{i_1 n}^r \end{pmatrix} \tag{8}$$

If the change, $e_{j_1 i_1}$, occurs in only one place, then the Leontief inverse, *B(e)*, has the form (c.f. Sherman and Morrison, 1950):

$$B\left(e_{j_1 i_1}\right) = B + \frac{e_{j_1 i_1}}{1 - b_{j_1 i_1} e} F[i_1, j_1] \tag{9}$$

In the next section, attention will be directed to block representation of economic structure drawing on the work of Schur, Banachiewicz and Miyazawa.

The Schur-Banachiewicz Formula

The Leontief inverse B can be formally presented in the following block:

$$B = \begin{bmatrix} B_{rr} & B_{rR} \\ B_{Rr} & B_{RR} \end{bmatrix} \tag{10}$$

and this can be further elaborated with the help of the Schur-Banachiewicz formula (Schur, 1917; Banachiewicz, 1937; Miyazawa, 1960; Sonis and Hewings, 1993):

$$B = \begin{bmatrix} B_{rr} & B_{rr} A_{rR} B_R \\ B_{RR} A_{Rr} B_r & B_{RR} \end{bmatrix} = \begin{bmatrix} B_{rr} & B_r A_{rR} B_{RR} \\ B_R A_{Rr} B_{rr} & B_{RR} \end{bmatrix} \tag{11}$$

where the matrices $B_r = (I - A_{rr})^{-1}$ and $B_R = (I - A_{RR})^{-1}$ represent the Miyazawa internal matrix multipliers for the region r and the rest of economy (revealing the interindustry propagation effects within the isolated region and isolated rest of economy) while the matrices $A_{Rr} B_r$, $B_r A_{rR}$, $A_{rR} B_R$, and $B_R A_{Rr}$ show the induced effects on output or input between the two parts of input-output system (Miyazawa, 1966).

Further:

$$B_{rr} = \left(I - A_{rr} - A_{rR}B_R A_{Rr}\right)^{-1}$$
$$B_{RR} = \left(I - A_{RR} - A_{Rr}B_r A_{rR}\right)^{-1} \tag{12}$$

are the extended Leontief multipliers for the region r and the rest of economy. The connections between these extended Leontief multipliers are:

$$B_{rr} = B_r + B_r A_{rR} B_{RR} A_{Rr} B_r$$
$$B_{RR} = B_R + B_R A_{Rr} B_{rr} A_{rR} B_R \tag{13}$$

By using the Miyazawa decomposition, the extended Leontief inverses can be decomposed into the products of internal and external multipliers describing direct and induced self-influences (Miyazawa, 1966, 1976):

$$B_{rr} = B_r B_{rr}^R = B_{rr}^L B_r$$
$$B_{RR} = B_R B_{RR}^R = B_{RR}^L B_R \tag{14}$$

where

$$B_{rr}^L = \left(I - B_r A_{rR} B_R A_{Rr}\right)^{-1}; \; B_{rr}^R = \left(I - A_{rR} B_R A_{Rr} B_r\right)^{-1}$$
$$B_{RR}^L = \left(I - B_R A_{Rr} B_r A_{rR}\right)^{-1}; \; B_{RR}^R = \left(I - A_{Rr} B_r A_{rR} B_R\right)^{-1} \tag{15}$$

are the left and right Miyazawa external multipliers for the region r and the rest of economy.

The analytical formulations of the last two sections now provide the basis for interpretation of hierarchical fields of influence.

Hierarchical Inclusion of Fields of Influence

The purpose of this section is to describe the hierarchical inclusion of fields of influence of the isolated region associated with the regional Leontief inverse B_r and the fields of influence of Leontief inverse, $B = \left(I - A\right)^{-1}$, associated with the economic system including the region in the rest of economy. It will be shown that the fields of influences of changes of the overall economic system caused by the matrix of incremental changes of direct inputs $E = \begin{pmatrix} E_{rr} & 0 \\ 0 & 0 \end{pmatrix}$ of the region *r* include the fields of influences of changes in the region *r* enveloped by the block matrices of the form (8).

For the construction of the enveloping fields of influences of changes let us consider the block matrix

$$A(E) = \begin{pmatrix} A_{rr} + E_{rr} & A_{rR} \\ A_{Rr} & A_{RR} \end{pmatrix} \tag{16}$$

and the corresponding Leontief inverse:

$$B(E)=\left[I-A(E)\right]^{-1}=\begin{pmatrix} B_{rr}(E_{rr}) & B_{rR}(E_{rr}) \\ B_{Rr}(E_{rr}) & B_{RR}(E_{rr}) \end{pmatrix} \tag{17}$$

Using the general formulae (11) through , one obtains:

$$\begin{aligned} & B_r(E_{rr})=(I-A_{rr}-E_{rr})^{-1}; \quad B_R(E_{rr})=(I-A_{RR}-E_{rr})^{-1}=B_R \\ & B_{rr}(E_{rr})=(I-A_{rr}-E_{rr}-A_{rR}B_RA_{Rr})^{-1} \\ & B_{RR}(E_{rr})=(I-A_{RR}-A_{Rr}B_r(E_{rr})A_{rR})^{-1}=B_R+B_RA_{Rr}B_{rr}(E_{rr})A_{rR}B_R \\ & B_{rR}(E_{rr})=B_{rr}(E_{rr})A_{rR}B_R; \quad B_{Rr}(E_{rr})=B_RA_{Rr}B_{rr}(E_{rr}) \end{aligned} \tag{18}$$

Using the general formulas (4) through (7) one obtains:

$$B_{rr}(E_{rr})=B_{rr}+D(B_{rr},E_{rr}) \tag{19}$$

where

$$D(B_{rr},E_{rr})=\frac{1}{Q_{rr}(E_{rr})}\left[\sum_{k=1}^{n}\sum_{\substack{i_r<i_{r+1}\\ j_r\neq j_s}}{}' F_{rr}(i_1,i_2,\ldots,i_k;j_1,j_2,\ldots,j_k)e_{j_1i_1}e_{j_2i_2}\ldots e_{j_ki_k}\right] \tag{20}$$

and

$$Q_{rr}(E_{rr})=\frac{\det B_{rr}}{\det B_{rr}(E_{rr})}=1-\sum_{i_1j_1}b^{rr}_{j_1i_1}e_{i_1j_1}+\sum_{k=2}^{n}(-1)^k\sum_{\substack{i_r<i_{r+1}\\ j_r\neq j_s}}{}' B^{rr}_{or}$$
$$(j_1,j_2,\ldots,j_k,i_1,i_2,\ldots,i_k)e_{i_1j_1}e_{i_2j_2}\ldots e_{i_kj_k} \tag{21}$$

Therefore, introducing (19) into (18) one obtains:

$$\begin{aligned} & B_{RR}(E_{rr})=B_{RR}+B_RA_{Rr}D(B_{rr},E_{rr})A_{rR}B_R \\ & B_{rR}(E_{rr})=B_{rR}+D(B_{rr},E_{rr})A_{rR}B_R \\ & B_{Rr}(E_{rr})=B_{Rr}+B_RA_{Rr}D(B_{rr},E_{rr}) \end{aligned} \tag{22}$$

In block-matrix form, this implies:

$$\begin{aligned} B(E) &= B+\begin{bmatrix} D_{rr}(B_{rr},E_{rr}) & D_{rr}(B_{rr},E_{rr})A_{rR}B_R \\ B_RA_{Rr}D_{rr}(B_{rr},E_{rr}) & B_RA_{Rr}D_{rr}(B_{rr},E_{rr})A_{rR}B_R \end{bmatrix}= \\ &= B+\begin{bmatrix} I \\ B_RA_{Rr} \end{bmatrix}D_{rr}(B_{rr},E_{rr})\left[I \quad A_{rR}B_R\right] \end{aligned} \tag{23}$$

Consider further a matrix $S_{rr}=I-A_{rr}-A_{rR}B_RA_{Rr}$; obviously,

$S_{rr}B_{rr}=B_{rr}S_{rr}=I$.

Thus,

$$B_{rr}(E_{rr}) = (I - A_{rr} - E_{rr} - A_{rR}B_R A_{Rr})^{-1} = \\ = [(I - E_{rr}B_{rr})(I - A_{rr} - E_{rr} - A_{rR}B_R A_{Rr})]^{-1} = B_{rr}D^L_{rr}(E_{rr}) \quad (24)$$

where

$D^L_{rr}(E_{rr}) = (I - E_{rr}B_{rr})^{-1}$ with the property

$D^L_{rr}(E_{rr}) - I = D^L_{rr}(E_{rr})E_{rr}B_{rr}$.

Therefore, from (19)

$$D(B_{rr}, E_{rr}) = B_{rr}(E_{rr}) - B_{rr} = B_{rr}(D^L_{rr}(E_{rr}) - I) = B_{rr}D^L_{rr}(E_{rr})E_{rr}B_{rr} \quad (25)$$

Introducing (24) into (23) one obtains

$$B(E) = B + \begin{bmatrix} B_{rr} \\ B_R A_{Rr} \end{bmatrix} (I - E_{rr}B_{rr})^{-1} E_{rr} \begin{bmatrix} B_{rr} & A_{rR}B_R \end{bmatrix} \quad (26)$$

which presents the block-matrix analogue of the Sherman-Morrison formula (9). Indeed, the comparison of (25) with (8) provides the basis for the interpretation of the rectangular block matrices $\begin{bmatrix} B_{rr} \\ B_R A_{Rr} \end{bmatrix}$, $\begin{bmatrix} B_{rr} & A_{rR}B_R \end{bmatrix}$ as representing the block-column and block-row of the disintegrated block field of influence enveloping the inner intraregional fields of influence of changes in region *r*.

The expression (23) also yields the possibility for describing the analytical connection between the intraregional fields of influence and the fields of influence of the overall economic system. Through substitution into (23) the expression of the increment $D(B_{rr}, E_{rr})$ from (20), one obtains:

$$B(E) = B + \frac{1}{Q_{rr}(E_{rr})} \sum_{k=1}^{n} \sum_{\substack{i_r < i_{r+1} \\ j_r \neq j_s}} \left\{ \begin{bmatrix} I \\ B_R A_{Rr} \end{bmatrix} F_{rr}(i_1, i_2, \ldots, i_k; j_1, j_2, \ldots, j_k) \begin{bmatrix} I & A_{rR}B_r \end{bmatrix} \right\} e_{j_1 i_1} e_{j_2 i_2} \ldots e_{j_k i_k} \quad (27)$$

This implies that fields of influences of changes for the overall economic system can be expressed in the following block matrix form:

$$F(i_1, i_2, \ldots, i_k; j_1, j_2, \ldots, j_k) = \begin{bmatrix} I \\ B_R A_{Rr} \end{bmatrix} F_{rr}(i_1, i_2, \ldots, i_k; j_1, j_2, \ldots, j_k) \begin{bmatrix} I & A_{rR}B_r \end{bmatrix} \quad (28)$$

reflecting the explicit hierarchy of the *region within the economy*.

This presentation of the hierarchical inclusion of fields of influence describes, at the level of the region, the changes in the internal regional fields of influence caused by the interaction of the region with the rest of economy. When attention is directed to the level of the whole economy, the changes are spread through the rest of economy with the help of the external enveloping fields of influence characterized by the block matrices, $\begin{bmatrix} I \\ B_R A_{Rr} \end{bmatrix}$, $\begin{bmatrix} I & A_{rR} B_R \end{bmatrix}$. By using these expressions, it is now possible to consider changes in output that are generated within the region on the region itself and on the rest of the economy.

Changes in Gross Output Caused by Propagation of Intraregional Changes

Using the structure of incremental change (23), it will be possible now to measure the changes in the components of the gross output $X = \begin{pmatrix} X_r \\ X_R \end{pmatrix}$, where, $\begin{cases} X_r = B_{rr} f_r + B_{rR} f_R \\ X_R = B_{Rr} f_r + B_{RR} f_R \end{cases}$. By applying (23) and (25) one has:

$$\Delta X = \begin{bmatrix} \Delta X_r \\ \Delta X_R \end{bmatrix} = \begin{bmatrix} B(E) - B \end{bmatrix} \begin{bmatrix} f_r \\ f_R \end{bmatrix} =$$

$$\begin{bmatrix} D_{rr}\left(B_{rr}, E_{rr}\right) & D_{rr}\left(B_{rr}, E_{rr}\right) A_{rR} B_R \\ B_R A_{Rr} D_{rr}\left(B_{rr}, E_{rr}\right) & B_R A_{Rr} D_{rr}\left(B_{rr}, E_{rr}\right) A_{rR} B_R \end{bmatrix} \begin{bmatrix} f_r \\ f_R \end{bmatrix} \tag{29}$$

Using (24), this implies that:

$$\begin{aligned} \Delta X_r &= B_{rr} D_{rr}^L(E_{rr}) E_{rr} B_{rr} f_r + B_{rr} D_{rr}^L(E_{rr}) E_{rr} B_{rR} f_R = \\ &= B_{rr} D_{rr}^L(E_{rr}) E_{rr} (B_{rr} f_r + B_{rR} f_R) = B_{rr} D_{rr}^L(E_{rr}) E_{rr} X_r \end{aligned} \tag{30}$$

and

$$\begin{aligned} \Delta X_R &= B_{Rr} D_{rr}^L(E_{rr}) E_{rr} B_{rr} f_r + B_{Rr} D_{rr}^L(E_{rr}) E_{rr} B_{rR} f_R = \\ &= B_{Rr} D_{rr}^L(E_{rr}) E_{rr} (B_{rr} f_r + B_{rR} f_R) = B_{Rr} D_{rr}^L(E_{rr}) E_{rr} X_r \end{aligned} \tag{31}$$

Using (18) and (24), these formulae generate the fundamental relationships between the changes in the components of the gross outputs through the action of the matrix multipliers:

$$\begin{cases} \Delta X_r = B_{rr}(E_{rr})E_{rr}X_r \\ \Delta X_R = B_R A_{Rj} \Delta X_r \end{cases} \tag{32}$$

Economic Landscapes[2]

The interpretation of these changes can be presented in a visual form through the use of artificial *economic landscapes* that incorporate the fundamental properties of key sector analysis. Let $A_{rr} = \left\| a_{ij}^r \right\|$ be a matrix of direct inputs of the region *r* and $B_r = (I - A_{rr})^{-1} = \left\| b_{ij}^r \right\|$ be the associated Leontief inverse matrix. Further, let $B_{\bullet j}^r$ and $B_{i\bullet}^r$ be the column and row multipliers of this Leontief inverse, defined as:

$$B_{\bullet j}^r = \sum_{i=1}^{n} b_{ij}^r, \quad B_{i\bullet}^r = \sum_{j=1}^{n} b_{ij}^r \tag{33}$$

Let V_r be the global intensity of the Leontief inverse matrix B_r :

$$V_r = \sum_{i=1}^{n} \sum_{j=1}^{n} b_{ij}^r \tag{34}$$

Rasmussen (1956) proposed two types of indices drawing on entries in the Leontief inverse:

1. Power of dispersion for the backward linkages, BL_j , as follows:

$$\begin{aligned} BL_j &= \frac{1}{n}\sum_{i=1}^{n} b_{ij}^r \Big/ \frac{1}{n^2}\sum_{i,j=1}^{n} b_{ij}^r = \\ &= \frac{1}{n} B_{\bullet j}^r \Big/ \frac{1}{n^2} V_r = B_{\bullet j}^r \Big/ \frac{1}{n} V_r \end{aligned} \tag{35}$$

and

2. The indices of the sensitivity of dispersion for forward linkages, FL_i , as follows:

$$\begin{aligned} FL_i &= \frac{1}{n}\sum_{j=1}^{n} b_{ij}^r \Big/ \frac{1}{n^2}\sum_{i,j=1}^{n} b_{ij}^r = \\ &= \frac{1}{n} B_{i\bullet}^r \Big/ \frac{1}{n^2} V_r = B_{i\bullet}^r \Big/ \frac{1}{n} V_r \end{aligned} \tag{36}$$

The usual interpretation is to propose that $BL_j > 1$ indicates that a unit change in final demand in sector *j* will create an above average increase in activity in the economy; similarly, for $FL_i > 1$, it is asserted that a unit change in all sectors' final demand would create an above average increase in sector *i*. A key sector, *K*, is usually defined as one in which both indices are greater than 1. The definitions of backward and forward linkages provided by (35) and (36) imply that the rank-size hierarchies (rank-size ordering) of these indices coincide with the rank-size hierarchies of the column and row multipliers.

The input-output multiplier product matrix (MPM) is defined as:

$$M_r = \frac{1}{V_r}\left\| B^r_{i\bullet} B^r_{\bullet j} \right\| = \frac{1}{V_r}\begin{pmatrix} B^r_{1\bullet} \\ B^r_{2\bullet} \\ \vdots \\ B^r_{n\bullet} \end{pmatrix}\begin{pmatrix} B^r_{\bullet 1} & B^r_{\bullet 2} & \cdots & B^r_{\bullet n} \end{pmatrix} = \left\| m^r_{ij} \right\| \tag{37}$$

It is important to underline that the column and row multipliers for the MPM are the same as those for the Leontief inverse matrix B_r. Thus, the structure of the MPM is essentially connected with the properties of sectoral backward and forward linkages.

The structure of the matrix, M_r, can be ascertained in the following fashion: consider the largest column multiplier, $B^r_{\bullet j_o}$ and the largest row multiplier, $B^r_{i_o \bullet}$ of the Leontief inverse B_r. Then, the element , $m^r_{i_o j_o} = \frac{1}{V_r} B^r_{i_o \bullet} B^r_{\bullet j_o}$, located in the place (i_0, j_0) of the matrix, M_r. Moreover, all rows of the matrix, M_r, are proportional to the i_0^{th} row, and the elements of this row are larger than the corresponding elements of all other rows. The same property applies to the j_0^{th} column of the same matrix. Hence, the element located in (i_0, j_0) defines the center of the largest *cross* within the matrix, M_r. If this cross is excluded from M_r, then the second largest cross can be identified and so on. Thus, the matrix M_r, contains the rank-size sequence of crosses. One can reorganize the locations of rows and columns of M_r in such a way that the centers of the corresponding crosses appear on the main diagonal. In this fashion, the matrix will be reorganized in such a way that a descending *economic landscape* will be apparent.

This rearrangement also reveals the descending rank-size hierarchies of the Rasmussen-Hirschman indices for forward and backward linkages. Inspection of that part of the landscape with indices > 1 (the usual criterion for specification of key sectors) will enable the identification of the key sectors. Moreover, the superposition of the hierarchy of one region on the landscape of another region provides a clear visual representation of the similarities and differences in the linkage structure of these regions; these perspectives will be illustrated in the section following the one below.

Hierarchical Inclusion of Economic Landscapes

The direct implication of the formula (28) is that there is the possibility of multiple shifts occurring in the hierarchy of intraregional backward and forward linkages and changes in the position of key sectors under the influence of interaction with the rest of economy. In addition, it will also be possible to evaluate immediately when economic sectors became more important for the regional economy under the influence of synergetic interactions with the rest of economy. The main analytical tool of the hierarchical inclusion of the economic landscapes is the following proposition:

Consider the product $B = B^{/}B^{//}$ of two matrices, $B^{/}$, and $B^{//}$, of dimension, $n \times m$, $m \times p$ correspondingly. Let

$$B_{\bullet j} = \sum_{i=1}^{n} b_{ij}, \quad B_{i\bullet} = \sum_{j=1}^{p} b_{ij}$$

$$B^{/}_{\bullet j} = \sum_{i=1}^{n} b^{/}_{ij} \quad B^{/}_{i\bullet} = \sum_{j=1}^{m} b^{/}_{ij} \tag{38}$$

$$B^{//}_{\bullet j} = \sum_{i=1}^{m} b^{//}_{ij} \quad B^{//}_{i\bullet} = \sum_{j=1}^{p} b^{//}_{ij}$$

be the column and row multipliers of these matrices. Let $V = \sum_{i=1}^{n}\sum_{j=1}^{p} b_{ij}$ be the global intensity of the matrix B. The following multiplicative connections between the vectors of column and row multipliers of these matrices exist:

$$\begin{bmatrix} B_{\bullet 1} & B_{\bullet 2} & \dots & B_{\bullet p} \end{bmatrix} = \begin{bmatrix} B'_{\bullet 1} & B'_{\bullet 2} & \dots & B'_{\bullet m} \end{bmatrix} \times B''; \begin{bmatrix} B_{1\bullet} \\ B_{\bullet 2} \\ \vdots \\ B_{n\bullet} \end{bmatrix} = B' \times \begin{bmatrix} B''_{1\bullet} \\ B''_{2\bullet} \\ \vdots \\ B''_{m\bullet} \end{bmatrix};$$

$$V(B) = \begin{bmatrix} B'_{\bullet 1} & B'_{\bullet 2} & \dots & B'_{\bullet m} \end{bmatrix} \times \begin{bmatrix} B''_{1\bullet} \\ B''_{2\bullet} \\ \vdots \\ B''_{m\bullet} \end{bmatrix} \tag{39}$$

With these definitions, it is now possible to compare the economic landscapes generated by the intraregional Leontief inverse $B_r = (I - A_{rr})^{-1}$ of the isolated region r and the extended regional Leontief inverse

$B_{rr} = (I - A_{rr} - A_{rR} B_R A_{Rr})^{-1}$.

The extended Leontief inverse (see p. 46, The Schur-Banachiewicz Formula) can be decomposed into the products of internal and external multipliers describing direct and induced self-influences (Miyazawa, 1966, 1976):

$$B_{rr} = B_r B^R_{rr} = B^L_{rr} B_r \tag{40}$$

where

$B^L_{rr} = (I - B_r A_{rR} B_R A_{Rr})^{-1}$; $\quad B^R_{rr} = (I - A_{rR} B_R A_{Rr} B_r)^{-1}$

are the left and right Miyazawa external multipliers for the region r.

For the intraregional Leontief inverse, B_r, the economic landscape of the isolated region r corresponds to the following MPM:

$$M_r = \frac{1}{V_r} \begin{pmatrix} B^r_{1\bullet} \\ B^r_{2\bullet} \\ \vdots \\ B^r_{n\bullet} \end{pmatrix} \begin{pmatrix} B^r_{\bullet 1} & B^r_{\bullet 2} & \cdots & B^r_{\bullet n} \end{pmatrix} \tag{41}$$

where

$$V_r = \begin{pmatrix} B^r_{\bullet 1} & B^r_{\bullet 2} & \dots & B^r_{\bullet n} \end{pmatrix} \begin{bmatrix} 1 \\ 1 \\ \vdots \\ 1 \end{bmatrix} = \begin{bmatrix} 1 & 1 & \dots & 1 \end{bmatrix} \begin{pmatrix} B^r_{1\bullet} \\ B^r_{2\bullet} \\ \\ B^r_{n\bullet} \end{pmatrix}$$

Applying the previous proposition to the product (39) one obtains:

$$M_{rr} = \frac{1}{V_{rr}} \begin{pmatrix} B_{1\bullet}^{rr} \\ B_{2\bullet}^{rr} \\ \\ B_{n\bullet}^{rr} \end{pmatrix} \begin{pmatrix} B_{\bullet 1}^{rr} & B_{\bullet 2}^{rr} & \dots & B_{\bullet n}^{rr} \end{pmatrix} = \frac{1}{V_{rr}} B_{rr}^{L} \begin{pmatrix} B_{1\bullet}^{rr} \\ B_{2\bullet}^{rr} \\ \\ B_{n\bullet}^{rr} \end{pmatrix} \tag{42}$$

$$\begin{pmatrix} B_{\bullet 1}^{rr} & B_{\bullet 2}^{rr} & \dots & B_{\bullet n}^{rr} \end{pmatrix} B_{rr}^{R} = \frac{V_r}{V_{rr}} B_{rr}^{L} M_r B_{rr}^{R}$$

where

$$V_{rr} = \begin{pmatrix} B_{\bullet 1}^{r} & B_{\bullet 2}^{r} & \dots & B_{\bullet n}^{r} \end{pmatrix} B_{rr}^{R} \begin{bmatrix} 1 \\ 1 \\ \vdots \\ 1 \end{bmatrix} = \begin{bmatrix} 1 & 1 & \dots & 1 \end{bmatrix} B_{rr}^{L} \begin{pmatrix} B_{1\bullet}^{r} \\ B_{2\bullet}^{r} \\ \\ B_{n\bullet}^{r} \end{pmatrix}$$

Application to Indonesia

The Indonesian economy presents a valuable case study for exploration of these ideas and methods. Using a set of interregional input-output tables constructed for 1993, analysis focused on changes in the hierarchy of sectors caused by viewing first the region within the context of the rest of the economy and then as an isolated region. The first set of visual presentations (Figures 4.1 through 4.10, see pp. 58–67) should be viewed as a set of five pairs of figures; in the first figure of each set (Figures 4.1, 4.3, 4.5, 4.7, 4.9), the economic landscape (as developed in the section Economic Landscapes, p. 51) is portrayed for the region within the national economy. The hierarchy of sectors is then used to develop the economic landscape for the isolated region (Figures 4.2, 4.4, 4.6, 4.8, and 4.10); hence, the hierarchical ordering is only used in the transfer from the first to the second figure in each pair. Since the structures of the regions are different, differences will be revealed in the hierarchical ordering of sectors across regions (compare the hierarchy in Figure 4.1 with that in Figure 4.3 for example).

What types of differences might one expect? For regions whose structure is very similar to the nation (i.e., the rest of the economy), the differences between the two landscapes (the isolated region and the region within the context of the rest of the economy) should be minimal – perhaps with some greater highlighting of some of the more important sectors in the isolated region context. However, one would not expect significant distortions to the hierarchical ordering of sectors. On the other hand, for regions with rather different economic structures than that for the economy as a whole, one might anticipate changes in the hierarchical ordering (that will be reflected in a non-monotonically descending landscape from the northwest corner). There is one complication in the Indonesian case, namely the hegemonic position occupied by Java. Recall that in the methodology proposed, the Rest of the Economy region excludes the region under consideration so that the comparison of a region is not with the national economy that includes the economic structure of the region as part of the nation. Java contains 63 per cent of Indonesia's Gross Domestic Income (1993) and thus when it is compared to the region defined as the Rest of the Economy, there are likely to be some distortions.

For Sumatra, the a priori expectations seem be have been realized; the hierarchy in Figure 4.2 generates a landscape that bears a reasonable relationship with the one shown in Figure 4.1. However, there are some important differences; these are summarized in Table 4.1 (see p. 68). In this table (and for Tables 4.2 through 4.5, see pp. 69–72), the change in the rankings are shown from the isolated region to the region within the rest of the economy. For forward linkages (portrayed along the *x*-axis in each figure), there is reasonable stability for the first six and the last five sectors. In between, there are some major re-orderings; for example, sector 15 (non-ferrous metal) jumps from rank 23 (within the rest of the economy) to 7 (isolated region). For the forward linkages (the *y*-axis in each figure), there is considerable exchange in the hierarchical orderings for the first 23 (of the 28) sectors.

The pattern for Java is rather similar to that for Sumatra; one sector, 7 (non crude oil and gas) moves from rank 5 in terms of backward linkages for the isolated region to rank 26 when the region is placed within the rest of the economy. Sector 15 (non-ferrous metals) also exhibits a similar decrease in importance to the one observed for Sumatra for forward linkages. For both regions, with the exception of those sectors highlighted, the exchanges in rankings were relatively modest in size.

The picture for Kalimantan is different; as Figure 4.6 reveals, the isolated region presents a decidedly non-monotonic landscape in contrast to the one that appears in Figure 4.5. However, the differences reflect a combination of two tendencies. The first tendency is for a sector in which the region is specialized to assume greater importance in terms of say backward linkages but without changing rank (for example, crude oil and gas, sector 6). The second tendency is for a sector that is not very highly ranked in the context of the national economy to assume a more dominant position in the isolated region context. Here, for example, sector 11 (paper and printing) jumps from rank 19 to rank 2 in the isolated region in terms of backward linkages and from rank 19 to rank 1 in terms of forward linkages and presents a significant *uplift* in the economic landscape (in both backward and forward linkages) that contributes to the disruption in the monotonicity of the landscape decline from the northwest corner. Overall, the exchanges in the rankings are larger than for either Sumatra or Java.

A similar pattern emerges for Sulawesi although here the sector exhibiting the largest change in ranking is 14 (iron and steel). In addition, the changes in forward linkage rankings are concentrated in the top 10-12 sectors (see Table 4.4) in contrast to Kalimantan, where the exchange occurred over the top 20 sectors (Table 4.3).

Finally, Figures 4.9 and 4.10 and Table 4.5 reveal the different pattern that emerges for the Eastern Islands. The disruptions to the landscape are much more heavily concentrated – sector 12 (chemical and rubber) dominates the isolated regional economy. With the exception of sectors 9 (textiles) and 11 (paper and printing), the exchanges in rankings are modest (Table 4.5). This regional economy is the most open of all five regions; hence, small changes in structure (generated by including the economy with the rest of Indonesia) can generate changes in the ranking of sectors that are themselves not very large in absolute terms.

Table 4.6 (p. 73) provides a summary of the changes in terms of key sector analysis (see the section Economic landscapes, p. 51). Overall, the identification reveals some of the important insights that the two ways of describing the regional economy provide. For Sumatra, 3 of the 6 key sectors identified in the isolated region disappear when the region is placed in the context of the rest of the economy. In Java's case, none is lost; in fact, two additional sectors are added. Kalimantan also gains two key sectors in the broader context but also loses two while Sulawesi loses only one but does not gain any others. For the Eastern Islands, there is a loss of two sectors and a gain of one. In all cases, the losses are in manufacturing sectors and the gains in services, indicating that the interregional impacts of these sectors are probably more influential.

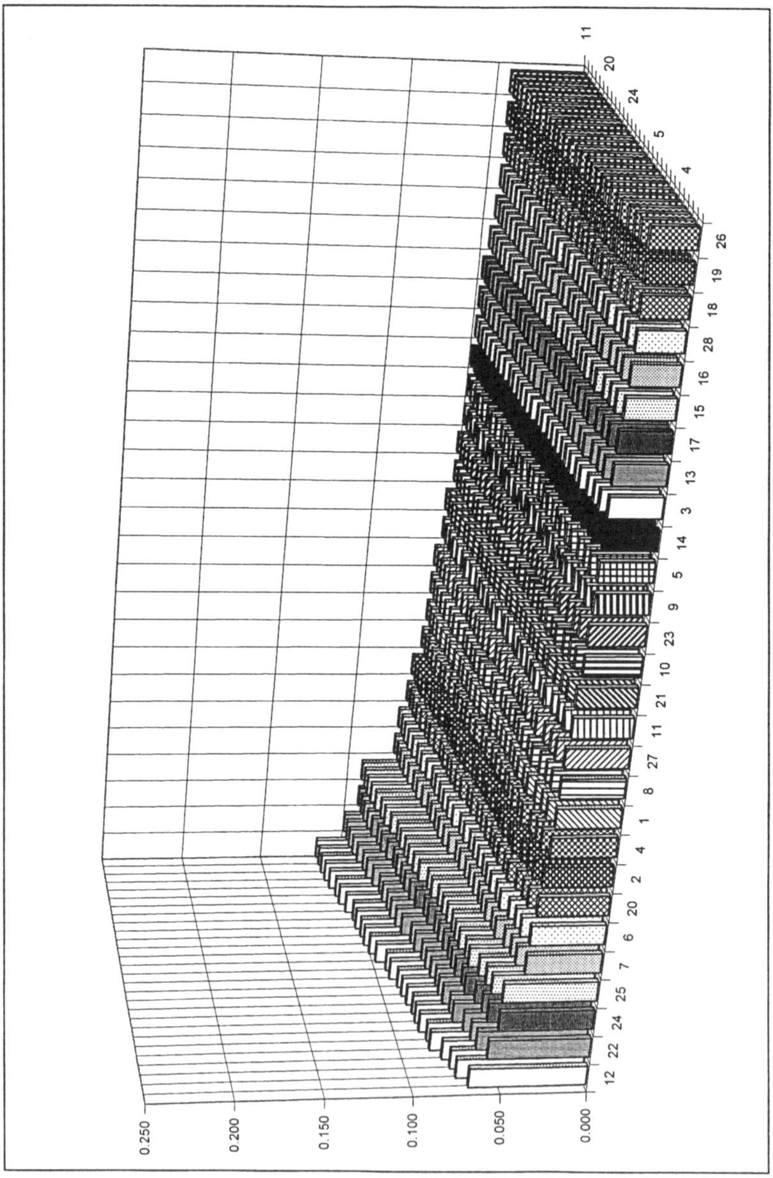

Figure 4.1 SUMATERA: Economic landscape within the national economy

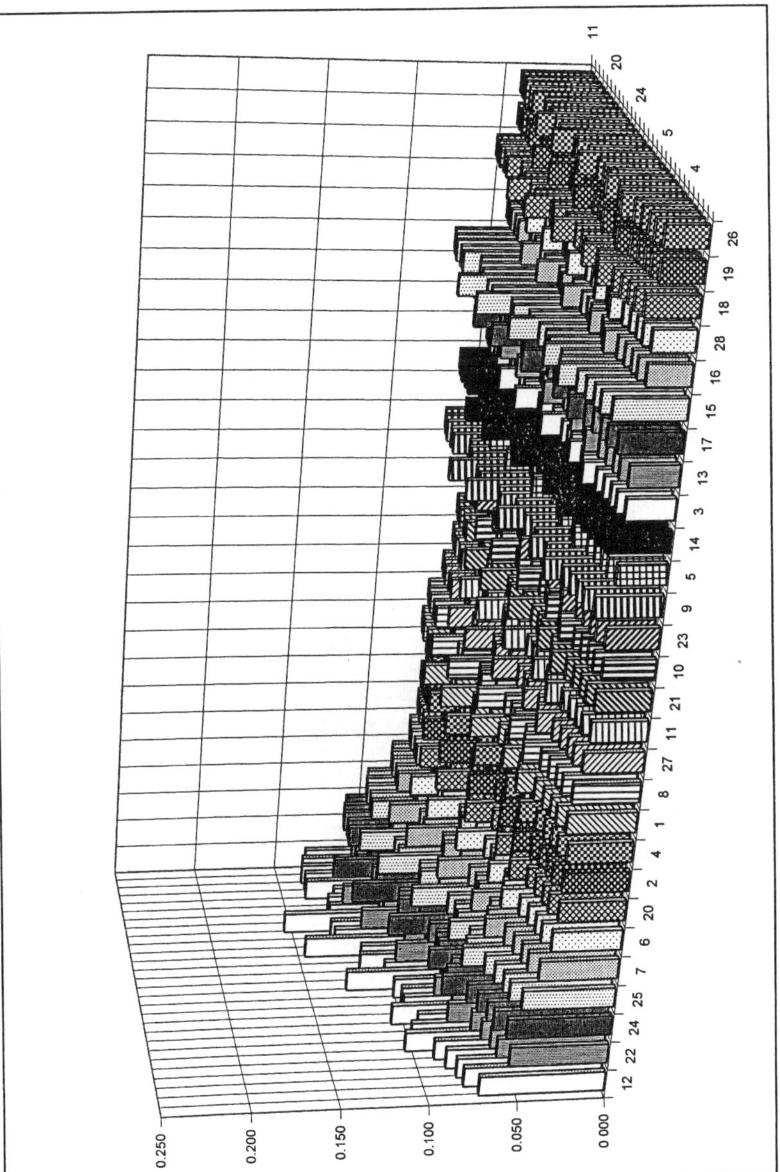

Figure 4.2 SUMATERA: Economic landscape of Sumatera as an isolated region with respect of hierarchies of linkages induced by the national economy

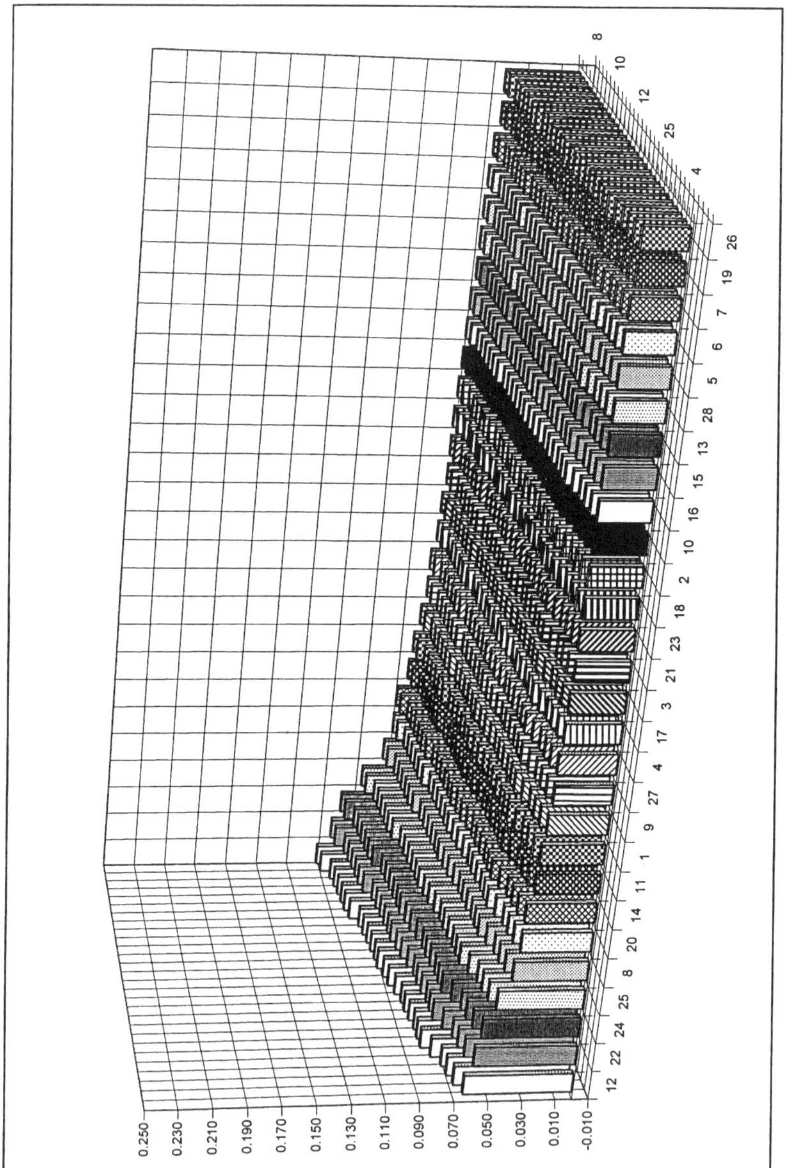

Figure 4.3 JAWA: Economic landscape within the national economy

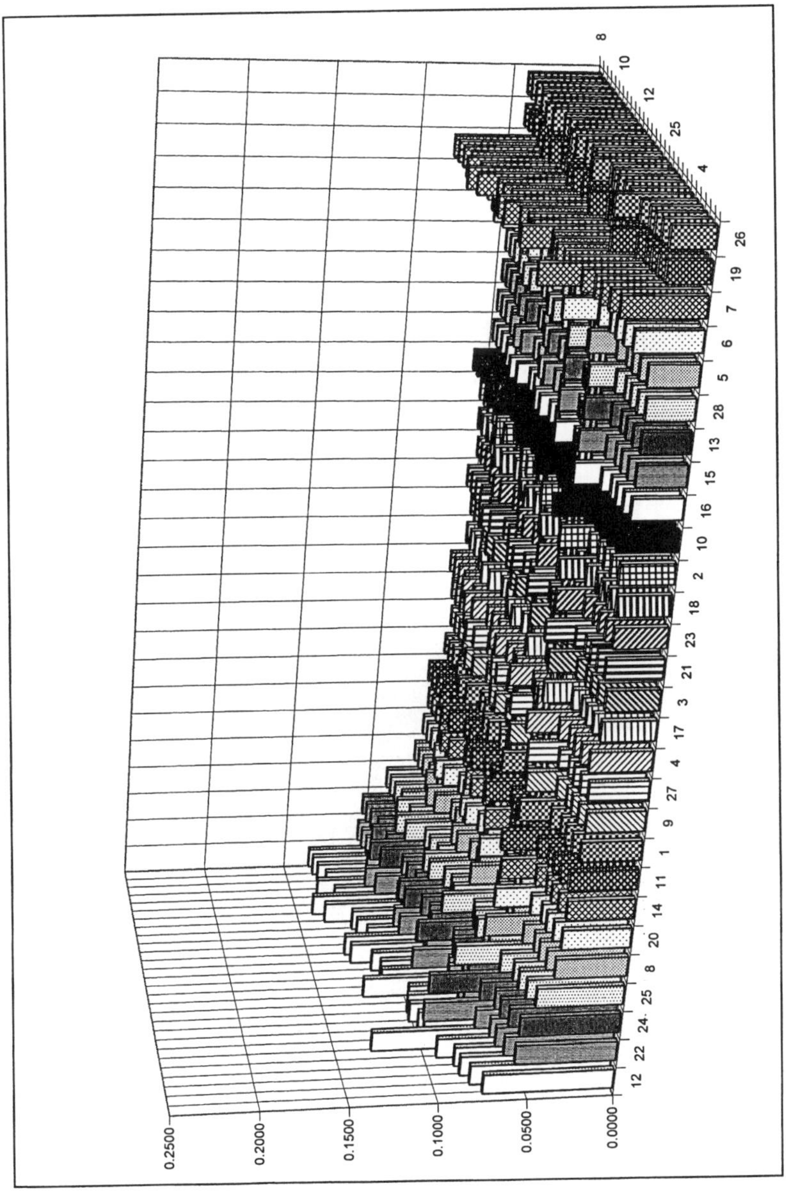

Figure 4.4 JAWA: Economic landscape of Jawa as an isolated region with respect of hierarchies of linkages induced by the national economy

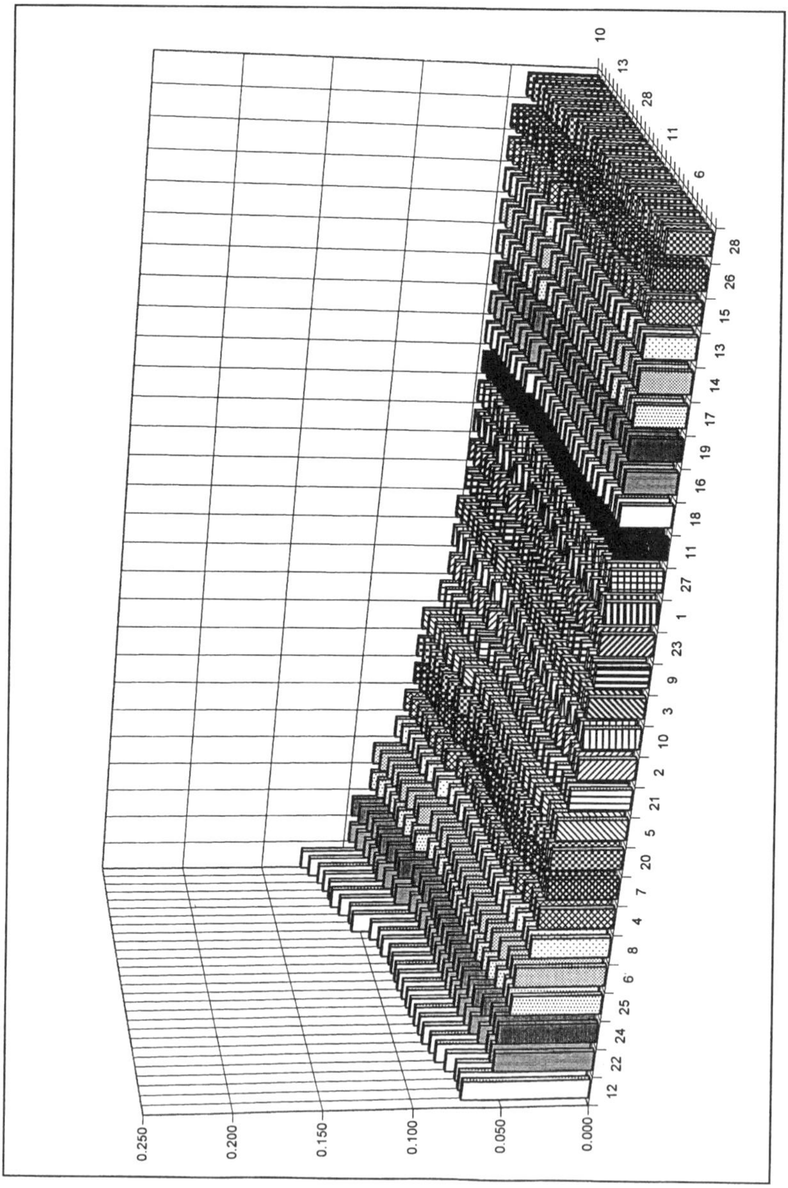

Figure 4.5 KALIMANTAN: Economic landscape within the national economy

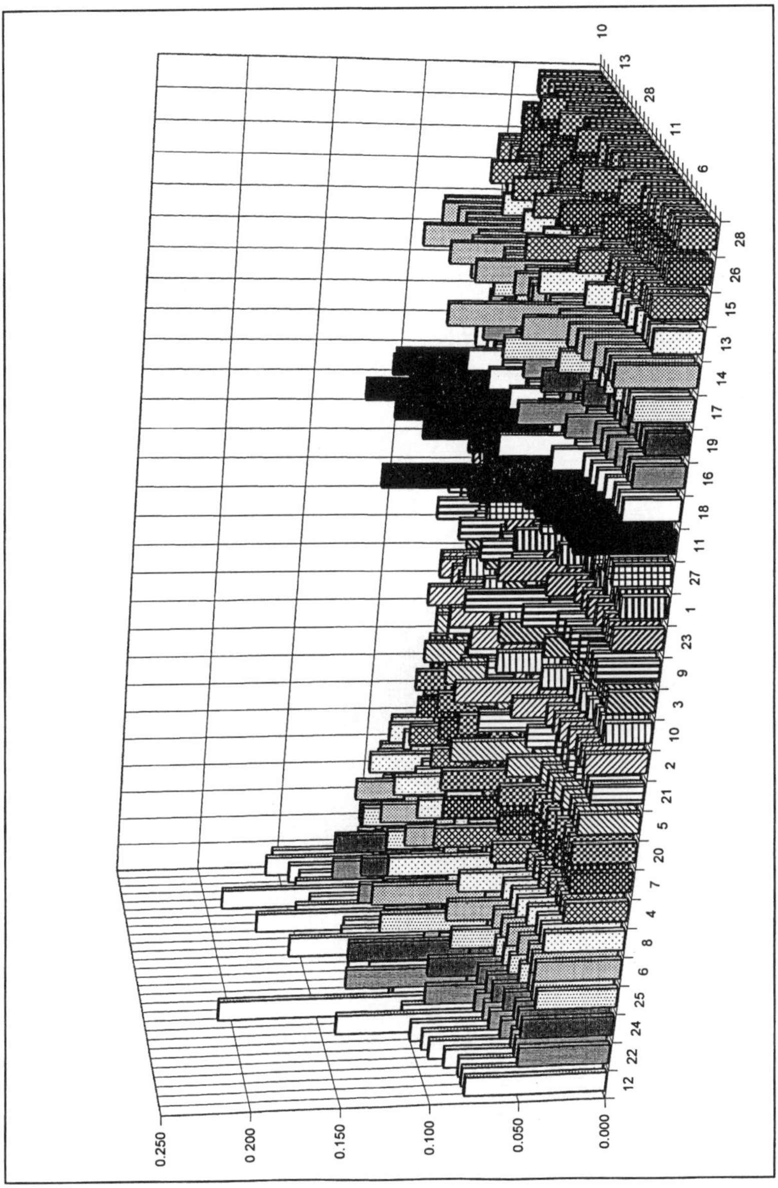

Figure 4.6 KALIMANTAN: Economic landscape of Kalimantan as an isolated region with respect of hierarchies of linkages induced by the national economy

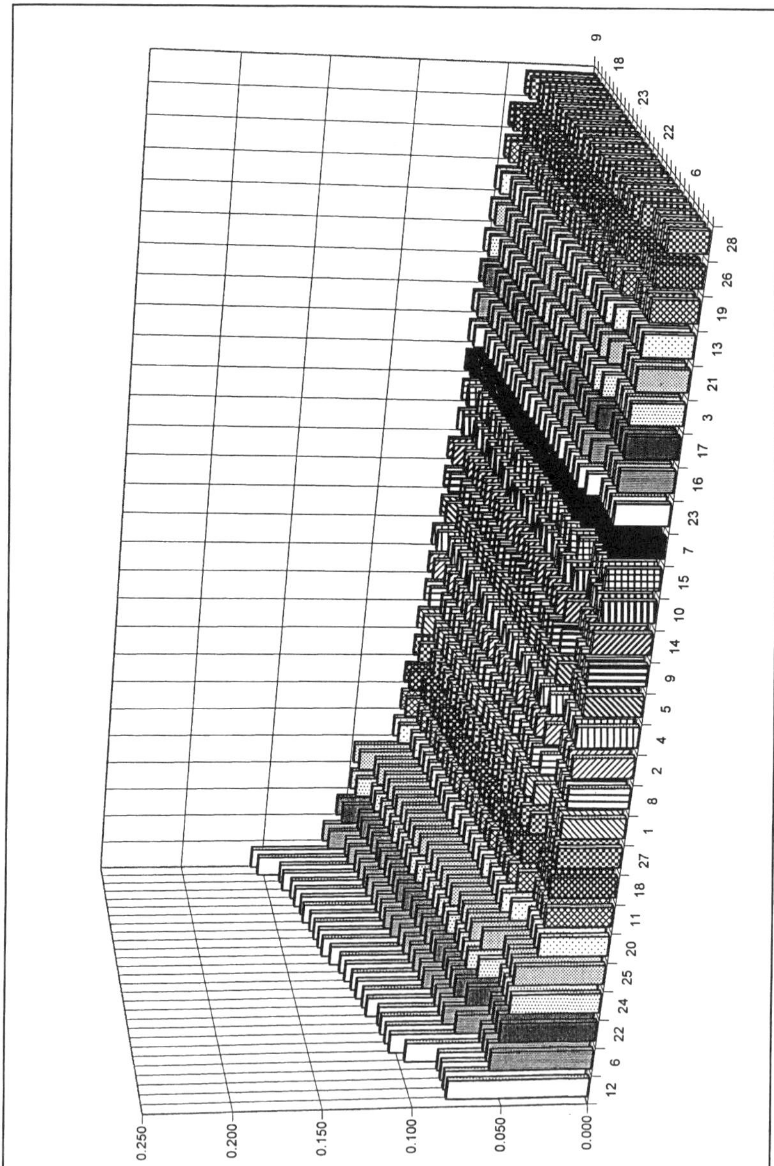

Figure 4.7 SULAWESI: Economic landscape within the national economy

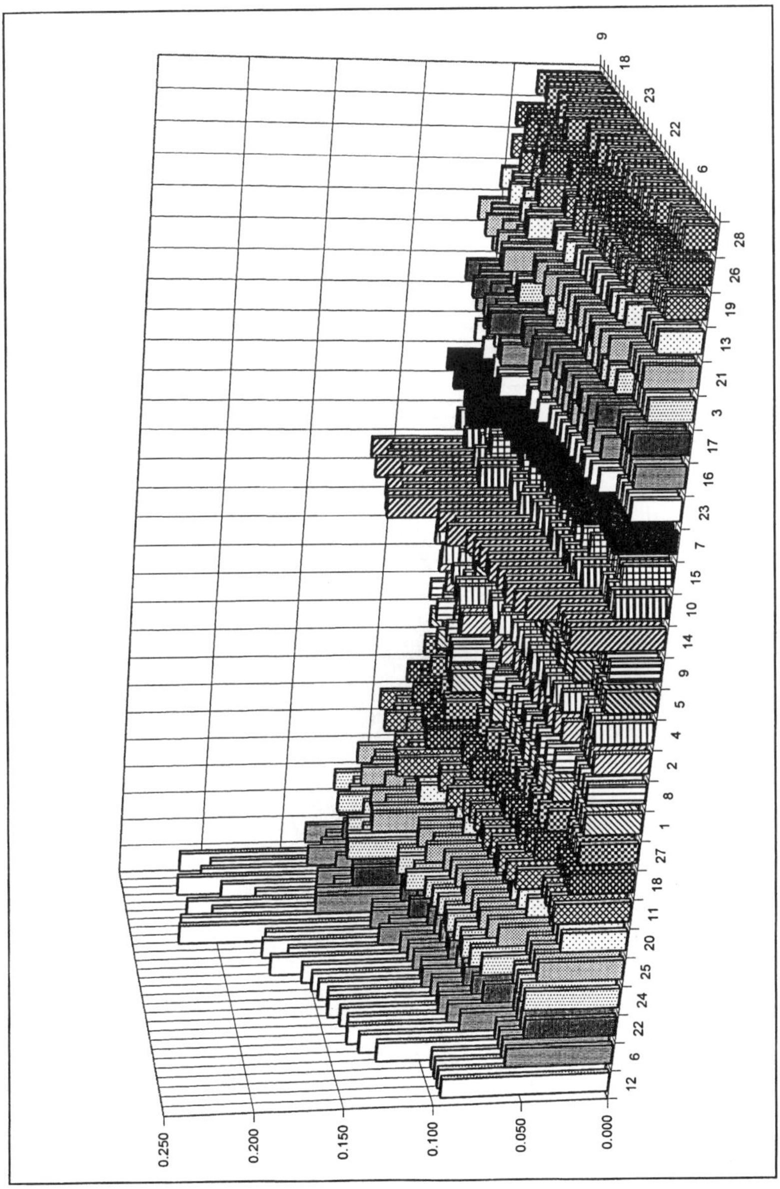

Figure 4.8 SULAWESI: Economic landscape of Sulawesi as an isolated region with respect of hierarchies of linkages induced by the national economy

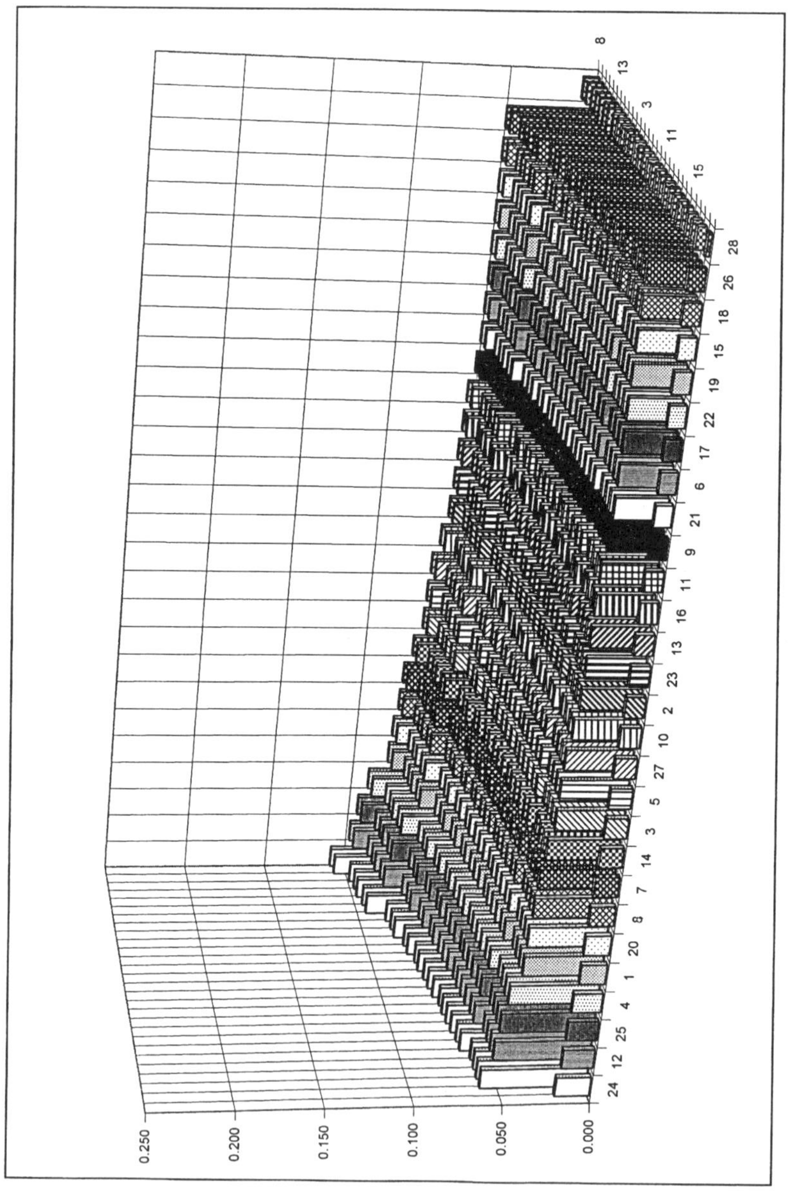

Figure 4.9 EASTERN ISLANDS: Economic landscape within the national economy

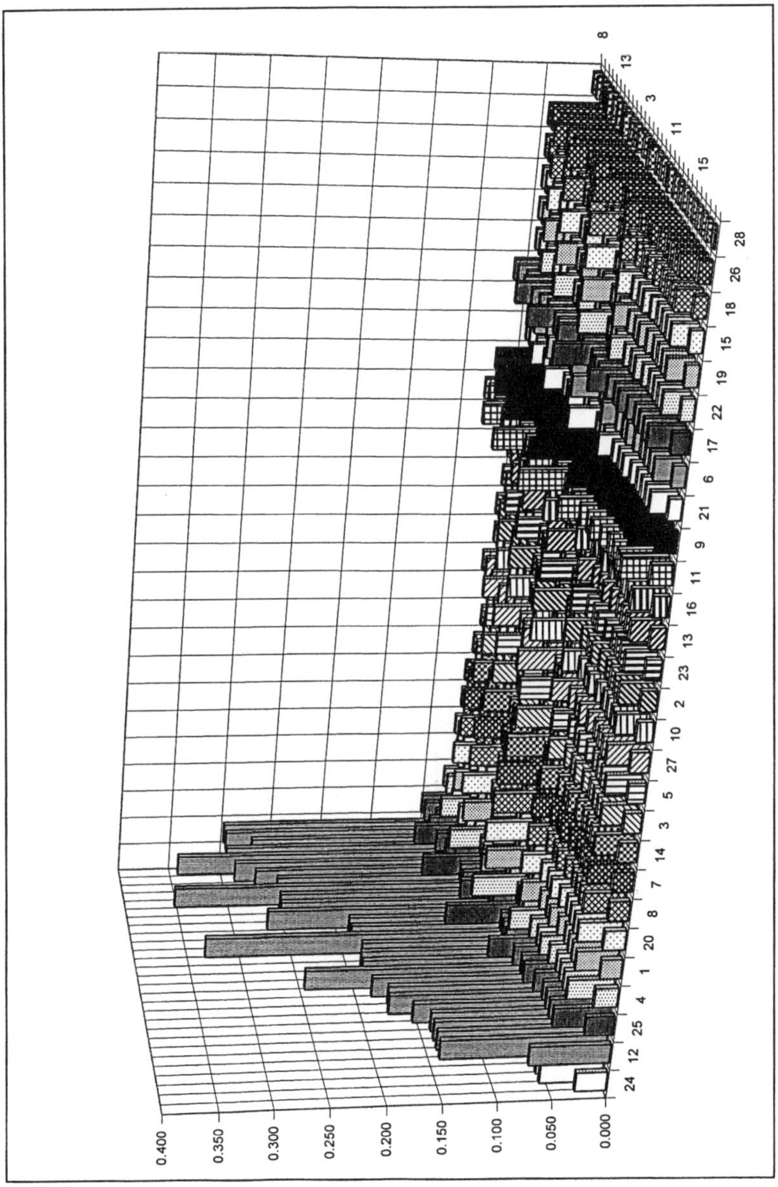

Figure 4.10 EASTERN ISLANDS: Economic landscape of others as an isolated region with respect of hierarchies of linkages induced by the national economy

Table 4.1 SUMATERA: The change of hierarchy of forward and backward linkages caused by the rest of economy, 1993

FORWARD LINKAGES			BACKWARD LINKAGES		
ISOLATED REGION		REGION WITHIN THE ECONOMY	ISOLATED REGION		REGION WITHIN THE ECONOMY
12		12	15		11
24		22	9		10
22		24	23		8
25		25	8		13
7		7	13		23
6		6	10		12
15		20	11		20
1		2	19		21
20		4	18		15
2		1	14		19
8		8	21		14
9		27	20		9
4		11	12		24
17		21	3		3
14		10	24		28
27		23	16		18
11		9	17		7
21		5	28		22
23		14	7		5
18		3	27		16
10		13	5		25
5		17	22		27
13		15	25		17
3		16	2		2
16		28	4		4
28		18	1		1
19		19	6		6
26		26	26		26

1. Farm food crops
2. Estate crops
3. Livestocks
4. Forestry
5. Fishery
6. Crude oil & gas
7. Non-crude oil & gas
8. Food processing
9. Textile
10. Wood processing
11. Paper & printing
12. Chemical & rubber
13. Non-metallic minr.
14. Iron & steel
15. Non-ferrous metal
16. Fabricated metals
17. Machine. & elec. eq.
18. Transport equip.
19. Other manufact.
20. Elect., gas & water
21. Construction
22. Wholesale & retail tr.
23. Restaurant & hotels
24. Transport services
25. Financial services
26. Gov. & public services
27. Other services
28. Non-specified sectors

Table 4.2 JAWA: The change of hierarchy of forward and backward linkages caused by the rest of economy, 1993

FORWARD LINKAGES			BACKWARD LINKAGES		
ISOLATED REGION		REGION WITHIN THE ECONOMY	ISOLATED REGION		REGION WITHIN THE ECONOMY
12		12	10		8
22		22	11		23
24		24	8		14
25		25	21		9
7		8	23		11
8		20	14		16
20		14	15		10
11		11	9		21
14		1	20		18
6		9	12		24
4		27	16		3
1		4	13		20
27		17	18		12
10		3	24		19
9		21	19		27
21		23	3		28
17		18	28		13
2		2	27		17
18		10	7		25
3		16	25		7
23		15	17		5
16		13	5		22
5		28	22		15
15		5	2		2
13		6	4		4
28		7	1		1
19		19	6		6
26		26	26		26

1. Farm food crops
2. Estate crops
3. Livestocks
4. Forestry
5. Fishery
6. Crude oil & gas
7. Non-crude oil & gas
8. Food processing
9. Textile
10. Wood processing
11. Paper & printing
12. Chemical & rubber
13. Non-metallic minr.
14. Iron & steel
15. Non-ferrous metal
16. Fabricated metals
17. Machine. & elec. eq.
18. Transport equip.
19. Other manufact.
20. Elect., gas & water
21. Construction
22. Wholesale & retail tr.
23. Restaurant & hotels
24. Transport services
25. Financial services
26. Gov. & public services
27. Other services
28. Non-specified sectors

Table 4.3 KALIMANTAN: The change of hierarchy of forward and backward linkages caused by the rest of economy, 1993

FORWARD LINKAGES		BACKWARD LINKAGES	
ISOLATED REGION	REGION WITHIN THE ECONOMY	ISOLATED REGION	REGION WITHIN THE ECONOMY
12	12	11	10
11	22	9	8
22	24	14	20
24	25	8	12
6	6	16	23
25	8	10	9
8	4	21	13
14	7	20	21
4	20	23	14
20	5	18	24
2	21	12	27
7	2	13	16
9	10	27	28
5	3	19	19
17	9	24	4
27	23	2	2
18	1	4	5
15	27	28	3
21	11	5	11
23	18	3	22
16	16	22	18
3	19	25	25
10	17	1	1
13	14	7	7
1	13	6	6
19	15	15	15
26	26	26	17
28	28	17	26

1. Farm food crops
2. Estate crops
3. Livestocks
4. Forestry
5. Fishery
6. Crude oil & gas
7. Non-crude oil & gas
8. Food processing
9. Textile
10. Wood processing
11. Paper & printing
12. Chemical & rubber
13. Non-metallic minr.
14. Iron & steel
15. Non-ferrous metal
16. Fabricated metals
17. Machine. & elec. eq.
18. Transport equip.
19. Other manufact.
20. Elect., gas & water
21. Construction
22. Wholesale & retail tr.
23. Restaurant & hotels
24. Transport services
25. Financial services
26. Gov. & public services
27. Other services
28. Non-specified sectors

Table 4.4 SULAWESI: The change of hierarchy of forward and backward linkages caused by the rest of economy, 1993

FORWARD LINKAGES			BACKWARD LINKAGES		
ISOLATED REGION		REGION WITHIN THE ECONOMY	ISOLATED REGION		REGION WITHIN THE ECONOMY
12		12	14		9
6		6	16		8
24		22	11		10
22		24	18		11
14		25	9		20
25		20	10		12
11		11	21		18
20		18	8		21
18		27	20		16
7		1	27		14
27		8	13		24
4		2	12		27
8		4	24		23
1		5	23		13
17		9	19		19
2		14	2		2
10		10	3		3
21		15	22		5
5		7	5		22
9		23	4		4
15		16	25		28
16		17	28		25
23		3	1		1
3		21	7		7
13		13	15		6
19		19	26		15
26		26	17		17
28		28	6		26

1. Farm food crops
2. Estate crops
3. Livestocks
4. Forestry
5. Fishery
6. Crude oil & gas
7. Non-crude oil & gas
8. Food processing
9. Textile
10. Wood processing
11. Paper & printing
12. Chemical & rubber
13. Non-metallic minr.
14. Iron & steel
15. Non-ferrous metal
16. Fabricated metals
17. Machine. & elec. eq.
18. Transport equip.
19. Other manufact.
20. Elect., gas & water
21. Construction
22. Wholesale & retail tr.
23. Restaurant & hotels
24. Transport services
25. Financial services
26. Gov. & public services
27. Other services
28. Non-specified sectors

Table 4.5 Others: The change of hierarchy of forward and backward linkages caused by the rest of economy, 1993

FORWARD LINKAGES		BACKWARD LINKAGES	
ISOLATED REGION	REGION WITHIN THE ECONOMY	ISOLATED REGION	REGION WITHIN THE ECONOMY
12	24	12	8
24	12	20	23
25	25	9	10
4	4	21	21
11	1	8	20
20	20	23	16
1	8	16	13
9	7	13	24
8	14	19	12
7	3	10	18
14	5	27	27
27	27	18	19
17	10	24	3
3	2	11	25
5	23	25	9
2	13	3	22
16	16	2	5
10	11	5	2
23	9	22	11
13	21	7	7
19	6	1	4
21	17	4	1
22	22	6	6
6	19	14	14
15	15	26	15
26	18	15	17
18	26	17	26
28	28	28	28

1. Farm food crops
2. Estate crops
3. Livestocks
4. Forestry
5. Fishery
6. Crude oil & gas
7. Non-crude oil & gas
8. Food processing
9. Textile
10. Wood processing
11. Paper & printing
12. Chemical & rubber
13. Non-metallic minr.
14. Iron & steel
15. Non-ferrous metal
16. Fabricated metals
17. Machine. & elec. eq.
18. Transport equip.
19. Other manufact.
20. Elect., gas & water
21. Construction
22. Wholesale & retail tr.
23. Restaurant & hotels
24. Transport services
25. Financial services
26. Gov. & public services
27. Other services
28. Non-specified sectors

Table 4.6 Comparison of key sectors of the isolated region and the same region within the economy of Indonesia, 1993

Sumatera		Jawa		Kalimantan		Sulawesi		Eastern Islands	
Isolated region	Reg. within the economy	Isolated region	Reg. within the economy	Isolated region	Reg. within the economy	Isolated region	Reg. within the economy	Isolated region	Reg. within the economy
8	-	8	8	8	8	-	-	8	8
9	-	-	-	-	-	-	-	9	-
-	-	11	11	11	-	11	11	11	-
12	12	12	12	12	12	12	12	12	12
-	-	14	14	14	-	14	-	-	-
15	-	-	-	-	-	-	-	-	-
-	-	-	-	-	-	18	18	-	-
20	20	-	20	-	20	20	20	20	20
-	-	-	22	-	-	-	-	-	-
24	24	24	24	-	24	24	24	24	24
-	-	-	-	-	-	-	-	-	27

Note: 8 Food processing
9 Textile
11 Paper & printing
12 Chemical & rubber
14 Iron & steel
15 Non-ferrous metals
18 Transport equipments
20 Electricity, gas & water
22 Wholesale & retail trade
24 Transport services
27 Other services

Conclusions

The findings presented in this chapter complement those in earlier work (Sonis et al., 1997) that focused on interregional structure interpreted by feedback loop analysis. The presentation of a region in the context of the rest of the economy offers an alternative perspective on the role of extra-regional linkages. It is clear that consideration of a region's role in isolation in comparison to that in a broader interregional/national context leads to important differences in the interpretation of the region's economic structure. Neither perspective is necessarily superior to the other; presenting both views of the region's economy enables an analyst to gain some heightened perspective of the role of extra-regional linkages and thus provides a deeper appreciation of the potential intra-regional impact of region-specific policies.

In a country with a very open economy, and with constituent regional economies that exhibit significant variations in openness within the national economy, these additional perspectives may prove to be very valuable. However, it should be acknowledged that Lakshmanan (1982) drew attention to these issues almost two decades ago; however, it would be appropriate to note that, until recently, methodological development has lagged behind the increasing needs for more sophisticated and timely information about the structure of regional and interregional economies.

Notes

1 See Sonis et al. (1994) for definitions.
2 This section draws on Sonis, Hewings and Guo (2000).

References

Banachiewicz, T. (1937), 'Zum Berechung der Determinanten, wie auch der Inversen, und zur daraut basierten Auflosung der systeme linearer Gleichungen', *Acta Astronomica*, ser. C.3, pp. 41–67.

Defourny, J. and Thorbeck, E. (1984), 'Structural Path Analysis and Multiplier Decomposition within a Social Accounting Framework', *Economic Journal,* vol. 94, pp. 111–36.

Hewings, G.J.D., Israilevich, P.R., Sonis, M. and Schindler, G.R. (1997), 'Structural Change in a Metropolitan Economy: The Chicago Region, 1975–2010', in S. Bertuglia, S. Lombardo and P. Nijkamp, (eds), *Spatial Effects of Innovative Behaviour*, Springer-Verlag, Heidelberg.

Hewings, G.J.D., Sonis, M, Guo, J, Israilevich, P.R. and Schindler, G.R. (1998a), 'The Hollowing Out Process in the Chicago Economy 1975–2015', *Geographical Analysis*, vol. 30, pp. 217–33.

Hewings, G.J.D., Israilevich, P.R., Okuyama, Y., Anderson, D.K., Foulkes, M. and Sonis, M. (1998b), *Returns to Scope, Returns to Trade and the Structure of Spatial Interaction in the US Midwest*, Discussion Paper 98–P–3, Regional Economics Applications Laboratory, University of Illinois, Urbana.

Lakshmanan, T.R. (1982), 'Integrated Multiregional Economic Modeling for the USA', in B. Issaev (ed.), *Multiregional Economic Modeling: Practice and Prospects*, North-Holland, Amsterdam.

Miller, R.E. (1966), 'Interregional Feedbacks in Input-output Models: Some Preliminary Results', *Papers Regional Science Association*, vol. 17, pp. 105–25.

Miller, R.E. (1969), 'Interregional Feedbacks in Input-Output Models: Some Experimental Results', *Western Economic Journal*, vol. 7, pp. 57–70.

Miller, R.E. (1986), 'Upper Bounds on the Sizes of Interregional Feedbacks in Multiregional Input-Output Models', *Journal of Regional Science*, vol. 26, pp. 285–306.

Miyazawa, K. (1960), 'Foreign Trade Multiplier, Input-Output Analysis and the Consumption Function', *Quarterly Journal of Economics*, vol. 74, pp. 53–64.

Miyazawa, K. (1966), 'Internal and External Matrix Multipliers in the Input-Output Model', *Hitotsubashi Journal of Economics*, vol. 7 (1), pp. 38–55.

Miyazawa, K. (1976), *Input-Output Analysis and the Structure of Income Distribution*, Springer-Verlag, Heidelberg.

Okazaki, F. (1989), *The 'Hollowing Out' Phenomenon in Economic Development*, paper presented at the Pacific Regional Science Conference, Singapore.

Schur, I. (1917), 'Uber Potenzreichen, die im Innern des Einheitskreises Beschrankt Sind', *J. Reine und Angew. Math*, vol. 147, pp. 205–32.

Sherman, J. and Morrison, W.J. (1950), 'Adjustment of an Inverse Matrix Corresponding to Changes in an Element of a Given Matrix', *Annals of Mathematical Statistics*, vol. 21, pp. 124–7.

Sonis, M., Guo, J., Hewings, G.J.D. and Hulu, E. (1997), 'Interpreting Spatial Economic Structure: Feedback Loops in the Indonesian Economy, 1980, 1985', *Regional Science and Urban Economics*, vol. 27, pp. 325–42.

Sonis, M. and Hewings, G.J.D. (1989), 'Error and Sensitivity Input-Output Analysis: A New Approach', in R.E. Miller, K.R. Polenske, and A.Z. Rose (eds), *Frontiers of Input-Output Analysis*, Oxford University Press, New York.

Sonis, M. and Hewings, G.J.D. (1991), 'Fields of Influence and Extended Input-Output Analysis: A Theoretical Account', in J.J. Ll. Dewhurst, G.J.D. Hewings and R.C. Jensen (eds), *Regional Input-Output Modeling: New Developments and Interpretations*, pp. 141–58, Avebury, Aldershot.

Sonis, M. and Hewings, G.J.D. (1992), 'Coefficient Change in Input-Output Models: Theory and Applications', *Economic Systems Research*, vol. 4, pp. 143–57.

Sonis, M. and Hewings, G.J.D. (1993), 'Hierarchies of Regional Sub-Structures and their Multipliers within Input-Output Systems: Miyazawa Revisited', *Hitotsubashi Journal of Economics*, vol. 34, pp. 33–44.

Sonis, M., and Hewings, G.J.D. (1998), *Feedbacks in Input-Output Systems: Impacts, Loops and Hierarchies*, Discussion Paper 98-T-2, Regional Economics Applications Laboratory, University of Illinois, Urbana.

Sonis, M., Hewings, G.J.D. and Gazel, R. (1995), 'An Examination of Multi-Regional Structure: Hierarchy, Feedbacks and Spatial Linkages', *Annals of Regional Science*, vol. 29, pp. 409–30.

Sonis, M., Hewings, G.J.D. and Guo, J. (1996), 'Sources of Structural Change in Input-Output System: A Field of Influence Approach', *Economic Systems Research*, vol. 8, pp. 15–32.

Sonis, M., Hewings G.J.D. and Guo, J. (2000), 'A New Image of Classical Key Sector Analysis: Minimum Information Decomposition of the Leontief Inverse', *Economic Systems Research*, vol. 12, pp. 401–23.

Sonis, M., Hewings G.J.D. and Lee, J-K. (1994), 'Interpreting Spatial Economic Structure and Spatial Multipliers: Three Perspectives', *Geographical Analysis*, vol. 26, pp. 124–51.

Thompson, W.R. (1965), *A Preface to Urban Economics*, Johns Hopkins Press, Baltimore.

Chapter 5

Estimating Sources of Regional Manufacturing Productivity using Shift-Share Extensions

Kingsley E. Haynes, Mustafa Dinc and Jean H.P. Paelinck

Introduction

Productivity, competitiveness and corporate downsizing, are hot issues, which have been occupying the American public policy agenda since the 1980s. These issues have preoccupied the agendas of scholars, researchers, public officials, politicians and individual citizens, partly because more and more international high value products dominate in the market. The last decade witnessed massive layoffs particularly from the large American corporations rationalized on the basis of restructuring for increased competitiveness. As a result, job insecurity has become a main concern of blue and white collar middle class Americans. This is exacerbated by the stabilization or decline in relative living standards of the average American family.

In spite of an increased focus on competitiveness and productivity issues, no consensus has emerged, due in part to the conflicting findings of a variety of studies. Some argued that these findings are by-products of the loss of international competitive dominance in an increasingly open and globalized market place (see for example Thurow, 1992; Tyson, 1992; Magaziner and Patinkin, 1990; Luttwak, 1993). A few admit the importance of productivity (see for example Thurow, 1992 p. 164; Porter, 1990, pp. 6, 37), but continue to focus on the competitiveness argument. On the contrary, other scholars argued that these changes have nothing to do with competitiveness. Paul Krugman, one of the most influential advocates of this view, for example, argued that the only way to increase living standards of Americans is to increase the productivity of workers (Krugman, 1991, 1994; see also Rivlin, 1992; Kendrick, 1973, 1984). According to Krugman (1991, 1994) and Rivlin (1992) productivity growth in the U.S. slowed after 1973, and so did wage increases and increases in living standards of Americans. On the other hand, Greiner et al. (1995) and van Ark (1995) argue that U.S. manufacturing has shown a strong recovery from the slowdown in output and productivity growth since the late 1970s. It is argued that productivity growth in the manufacturing sector of the US economy has been rapid over the past decade, and has been accompanied by a substantial reduction in employment.

Productivity growth is one of the most important sources of economic expansion and hence it is a key source of the rise in output and income per person employed. While the viability of firms in a long term competitive environment depends heavily on their efficiency, the overall efficiency or productivity of the economy of countries, states, or localities determines the general well-being of their people (Krugman, 1991; Rivlin, 1992).

In the regional development context, this issue becomes much more important because in the last couple of decades regional economies have become relatively more important for national economies, and in some cases dominate the national economy from a leading technology or entrepreneurial perspective. For examples see Camagni (1995), Hansen (1992), Ohmae (1993), Scott (1994), Scott and Storper (1992), Illeris (1993), Erickson (1994), Feldman and Florida (1994), and Sabel (1987). In addition, expansion of market boundaries and, to some degree elimination of trade barriers brings new opportunities to these regional economies/industries. However, at the same time this means more and more competition for regional industries in both domestic and foreign markets (Haynes and Dinc, 2000).

To restructure and improve their economies the states and local governments in the U.S. have developed different economic policies. These policies and programs impact to some extent the vitality and success of regions, firms and eventually the lives of people. Most of these policies involved some kinds of low interest loans, tax breaks, industrial recruiting and other traditional tools or a combination of them. Recent details of these policies have been presented elsewhere by Isserman (1994) and evaluated by Bartik (1994). However, as Gerking (1994) argued there is another more fundamental step in improving the regional economy over the long run: improved productivity. According to Gerking (1994) if regional productivity grows at a modest 1.5 per cent annually output doubles every 47 years with factor inputs held constant. Such a powerful effect on regional economic growth probably would be difficult to achieve by regional development policies.

There is another important aspect of productivity: its impact on employment change. While productivity growth plays a crucial role on economic growth in the long run, it has a negative impact on sector specific employment change in the short-run. In that sense, understanding, measuring and explaining productivity growth and its impact on the regional economy are very important and are a major concern to elected policy makers. This is also important in the promotion of sound economic development policies and programs. Therefore, robust regional analysis methods are needed to address these issues.

Such a method has been developed by Haynes and Dinc (1997). To assess the foundations of economic performance and employment change in manufacturing, Haynes and Dinc (1997) have taken account of industrial and regional differences in labor and capital (non-labor) productivity and the effects of productivity differences on regional manufacturing employment. To do so they have modified the Rigby-Anderson (1993) extension of the shift-share model by separating labor and non-labor factor contributions to productivity. They employed the total factor productivity approach of Kendrick (1961, 1973, 1983 and 1984). However, there are several alternative productivity measurement approaches, which need to be assessed and compared for stability and robustness.

This chapter reviews these alternative productivity measurement approaches and in the light of these methods develops a generalizable model in the Haynes-Dinc (1997) framework.

The organization of the chapter is as follows. The next section provides background information about shift-share models and productivity measurement methods. The new model and application are discussed in the following section. The fourth section analyzes and compares the findings. The final section presents conclusions.

Background

Shift-Share Basics

The classical shift-share model examines economic change in a region by decomposing it into three additive components: the reference area component, the industry mix, and the regional share (Dunn 1960). The variable so decomposed may be income, employment, value added, number of establishments or a variety of other measurements.

Some notation is needed. The subscript **i** indexes the industrial sector in region **r**. Hence $\mathbf{E_{ir}}$ is employment in sector **i** of region, **r**. The growth or decline rate in total employment in sector **i** of region **r** is $\mathbf{g_{ir}}$. The growth or decline rate in industry **i** in the reference area **n** is $\mathbf{g_{in}}$.

The reference area generally refers to the national economy and the influence of its growth (decline) rate is called the national share (for smaller regions such as counties it may refer to the state economy). It can be formulated as:

$$NS \equiv \sum_i g_n E_{ir} \tag{1}$$

The industry mix (composition shift, or structural effect) measures the industrial composition of the region and reflects the degree to which the local area specializes in industries that are fast or slow growing nationally. Thus, a region containing a relatively large share of industries that are slow (fast) growing nationally will have a negative (positive) proportionality shift:

$$IM \equiv \sum_i E_{ir} (g_{in} - g_n) \tag{2}$$

The regional share (competitive effect) measures the change in a particular industry in the region due to the difference between the industry's regional growth (decline) rate and the industry's reference area growth rate. This component indicates growth or decline in industries due to locational advantages or disadvantages. Although we do not always know what these advantages or disadvantages are, we can determine by looking at the differential shift component which industries are performing particularly well in the region. Again summing over sectors:

$$RS \equiv \sum_i E_{ir} (g_{ir} - g_{in}) \tag{3}$$

The total shift is the sum of three components; it is identically equal to the change in total employment:

$$\begin{aligned} TS &\equiv NS + IM + RS \\ &\equiv \sum E_{ir}\, g_n + \sum E_{ir} (g_{in} - g_n) + \sum E_{ir} (g_{ir} - g_{in}) \end{aligned} \tag{4}$$

This is known as the traditional shift-share model.

Following Rigby and Anderson (1993), Haynes and Dinc (1997) modified the shift-share model. They argued that Rigby and Anderson (1993) ignore the non-labor factors' contribution to productivity in their model. To improve the Rigby and Anderson extension they separate labor's and capital's (non-labor) contribution to productivity. By following Kendrick (1961, 1973, 1983, 1984), they employed the total factor productivity (TFP) approach to separate labor and capital (or non-labor) productivity. In this approach, productivity is defined as the relationship between output of goods and services and the inputs of resources and, usually expressed in ratio form, the ratio of aggregate output to the sum of inputs. Outputs are weighted by their unit costs at constant prices. The inputs are combined in terms of their share in total costs at constant prices. Hence, to maintain the simplicity of the shift-share model the later method is employed.

As a result the shift-share equations take the following forms:

1. To investigate employment change:

$$TSL \equiv NSL + IML + RSL \tag{5}$$
$$NSL \equiv NS(aL) + NS(bL) = \sum Eir\ (anL + bnL) \tag{6}$$
$$IML \equiv IM(aL) + IM(bL) = \sum Eir\ [(ainL\text{-}anL) + (binL\text{-}bnL)] \tag{7}$$
$$RSL \equiv RS(aL) + RS(bL) = \sum Eir\ [(airL\text{-}ainL) + (birL\text{-}binL)] \tag{8}$$

2. To investigate capital change:

$$TSK \equiv NSK + IMK + RSK \tag{9}$$
$$NSK \equiv NS(aK) + NS(bK) = \sum Kir\ (anK + bnK) \tag{10}$$
$$IMK \equiv IM(aK) + IM(bK) = \sum Kir\ [(ainK\text{-}anK) + (binK\text{-}bnK)] \tag{11}$$
$$RSK \equiv RS(aK) + RS(bK) = \sum Kir\ [(airK\text{-}ainK) + (birK\text{-}birK)] \tag{12}$$

Equations (5) and (9) can be written in a general form as:

$$\Delta E_{ir} \equiv TS \equiv [NS(a) + NS(b)] + [IM(a) + IM(b)] + [RS(a) + RS(b)] \tag{13}$$

where the a's represent the rate of employment change in the region (and reference area) resulting from variations in output over the given time period with constant productivity, and the b's represent the rate of employment change resulting from variations in productivity over the given time period with constant output.

In the case of the lack of reliable capital stock data at the state and sector level, only the employment portion of the model can be utilized. To determine the contribution of other factors – namely capital, technology, infrastructure raw material etc. – to total productivity, and hence their impact on employment change, let ΔE be the actual employment change over time in the region, and TSL the total shift (employment change) in the region or state resulting from the differential change in labor productivity and output. Then the difference between actual change and total shift will give the employment change resulting from the all production factors' contribution to total labor productivity, ΔEP. This can be formulated as:

$$\Delta EP = \Delta E - TS \tag{14}$$

Alternative Productivity Assessments

Total Factor Productivity Assessment

Productivity, in general, can be defined as the relationship between output and one or more of the associated inputs used in the production process. Interest in measures of productivity changes for the economy or its major sectors or regional economies arises in large part from the impact of productivity change on the standard of living. Historically, partial productivity measures, particularly ratios of output to labor inputs were the first type of productivity measures developed. The development of measures of multi-factor productivity (total factor productivity), which relate output to all inputs has lagged for several reasons. First, estimation of required data began on a systematic basis only after World War II. Second, the development of national economic accounting systems did not begin until about 1940 (Panel to Review Productivity Statistics, National Academy of Sciences (NAS), 1979).

Early estimates of total factor productivity (TFP) in the U.S. were prepared by Tinbergen in 1942, by Stigler in 1947 for manufacturing and by Barton and Cooper in 1948 for agriculture. There are several ways to calculate TFP, including econometric techniques that provide estimates of the trend-rate of productivity growth. The simplest method, yielding the most flexible measures, is to calculate the ratios of real product to real factor costs in successive periods. Calculation of TFP is simple and straightforward which is one of its advantages. With appropriate statistics on input quantities, input prices, output quantities and output prices one can directly estimate the TFP:

$$TFP = \frac{O}{aL + bK} \tag{15}$$

where O is the real product, L is the weighted averages of labor input and K is the weighted averages of capital (non-human) inputs; a and b are the per centage shares of labor and capital in the factor income originating in the sector or economy. Labor input is measured in terms of man-hours worked. Capital input is assumed to move proportionately with the real stocks of tangible capital assets. The inputs are estimated without allowance for changes in their quality or marginal physical productivity, so that changes in the ratios of output to input may be interpreted as reflecting all the diverse forces that affect the quality or productive efficiency of the factors (Kendrick, 1961, 1973, 1984; NAS, 1979; Kendrick and Grossman, 1980; Norsworthy and Malmquist, 1985; Wolff, 1985; Bronfenbrenner, 1985; Baumol, Blackman and Wolff, 1989). However, some have argued that this definition of total factor productivity may be misleading because intangible inputs resulting from research and development, education and training are not included with the tangible inputs, nor are the governmental services to business i.e. public infrastructure, included when the measures are confined to the private economy (NAS, 1979 pp. 44).

A solution, at least partially, came from Denison (1962). In this formulation, it is possible to expand inputs to include various qualitative elements that have improved the productive efficiency or intensity of use of the human and non-human factors of production. Denison (1962) made such an adjustment. He adjusted labor input (man-hours) so as to reflect the effects of increasing educational attainment of the work force and the assumed increase in man-hour output occasioned by declines in the average number of hours worked per week and per year. Denison then attempted to quantify the contributions of the other variables with his final residual representing advances in knowledge.

On the other hand Kendrick argued that he remains convinced that measures of tangible factor inputs, unadjusted for quality changes, and the associated total and partial productivity measures remain a useful point of departure for analysis of growth and change in economic aggregates and structure... it is not crucial whether we count certain variables as inputs or as part of the statistical explanation of the productivity residual – so long so we correctly sort out and identify the significant forces at work (Kendrick, 1973 p. 5).

As mentioned earlier, TFP is measured within an economic accounting framework as a ratio of real product to the associated real factor costs, the weights are changed periodically to reflect changes in the structure of production and in the relative prices of outputs and of inputs. The use of national accounts as the framework for output, input and productivity estimates contributes greatly to the consistency of the estimates. This also has the advantage that TFP for the business sector is a weighted average of TFP in the component industries. This means consistency with the measure for the entire industry. By changing factor input weights occasionally it is possible to avoid some restrictive assumptions, i.e. the underlying Cobb-Douglas production function assumption of linear homogeneity with unit elasticity of substitution between factors.

The weights for labor and capital are not obtained by fitting statistical production functions to data. Instead, they are obtained from national income estimates of the U.S. Department of Commerce. The exponents of statistical production functions are sometimes quite close to the shares revealed by national income estimates. However, the ability of the regression analysis to estimate parameters could be hampered by the high inter-correlation among the explanatory variables (Kendrick and Grossman, 1980).

If we are not concerned with the marginal and average productivity concepts used in static equilibrium theory and instead our concern is with the relationship between output and inputs in real terms, over time in a dynamic economy, then the basic objective of productivity estimates becomes to obtain at least rough measures of the impact of the investments and other variables on production. In that sense TFP approach provides a simplified solution.

Kendrick (1973), one of the pioneers of the multi-factor productivity or total factor productivity approach, defines productivity as the relationship between output of goods and services and the input of resources, human and non-human used in the production process. This relationship is usually expressed in ratio form and may be written as a modification of (15):

$$TFP = \frac{O}{bL + (1-b)K} \tag{16}$$

where O=output, L=labor, K=capital and b= weight of input (derived as the estimated share of factor income).

Kendrick (1973) argues that productivity estimates derived from output-input ratios are essentially interchangeable with those derived from statistical production functions, if the component variables and the underlying shape of the relationship are consistently specified.

He also argues later that total factor productivity can be viewed as the ratio of factor input prices to product prices. His argument is based on the following reasoning. When national product, Y, (output) is divided by average output prices (Po) real output, or final output (O) is obtained. Similarly when national income, Y, (factor costs) is divided by the average price of inputs (PI), real factor cost, or input (I) is obtained. Therefore, total factor productivity (O/I) can be viewed as the ratio of factor input prices to product prices:

$$\frac{O}{I} = \frac{Y}{P_O} \div \frac{Y}{P_I} = \frac{P_I}{P_O} = \frac{P_L + P_K}{P_O} \tag{17}$$

As a result changes in the ratio of input prices to output prices must be proportional to changes in total factor productivity, so the argument goes.

Baumol et al. (1989), Bronfenbrenner (1985), and Dollar and Wolff (1993) use a similar definition and measurement of productivity. In addition, Dollar and Wolff (1993) introduce the capacity utilization rate. In this definition TFP becomes:

$$TFP = \frac{O}{bL + (1-b)uK} \tag{18}$$

where u=capacity utilization rate.

Bronfenbrenner (1985) argues that it is possible to estimate separate productivities for inputs *K, L, . .* If the individual input productivities are Y/K, Y/L, and respective income shares are *r* and *w* the TFP becomes:

$$TFP = r\,(Y/K) + w\,(Y/L) + \ldots \tag{19}$$

From the identity:

$$Y \equiv wL + rK \tag{20}$$

one derives:

$$Y = \frac{Y}{L}(wL) + \frac{Y}{K}(rK) \tag{21}$$

which could be regressed to obtain *(Y/K)* and *(Y/L)*

Norsworthy and Jang (1992) indicated that the total factor productivity is the weighted average productivity of all purchased inputs, where the weights are the shares in total cost of production. Then TFP is simply the ratio of the total cost of producing all outputs to total costs of all inputs. They argued that this is the broadest measure of productivity, and the only measure whose increase is unambiguously beneficial, in the sense that it corresponds to a decline in the total unit cost of production:

$$Z = TFP = \frac{\sum w_j y_j}{\sum v_i x_i} \tag{22}$$

where *yj* = quantity of output *j*, *xi* = quantity of input *i*, *wj* = the share of output *j* in total revenue, *vi* = the share of input *i* in total cost.

After the familiar assumptions about competitive markets, the growth of TFP is equal to the aggregate rate of growth of output less the aggregate rate of growth of inputs:

$$\frac{dZ}{dt} = \sum w_j \frac{dy_i}{dt} - \sum v_i \frac{dx_i}{dt} \tag{23}$$

Equivalently, it can be shown that the growth of TFP is equal to the average rate of growth of input prices less the average rate of growth of output prices:

$$\frac{dZ}{dt} = \sum v_i \frac{dp_i}{dt} - \sum w_j \frac{dq_j}{dt} \tag{24}$$

Norsworthy and Jang assume that the capital inputs are quasi-fixed and in fact, in the short run it is assumed to be fixed; thus, TFP becomes:

$$TFP = \frac{\sum w_j y_j}{\sum v_i x_i + v_K k} \tag{25}$$

Since the growth rate of TFP is the average growth (share-weighted) rate of the productivities of all inputs:

$$\begin{aligned} \Delta TFP &= \ln Z_t - \ln Z_{t-1} \\ &= \sum \bar{v}_{it}\left(\ln\frac{y_t}{x_{it}} - \ln\frac{y_{t-1}}{x_{t-1}}\right) = \sum \bar{v}_{it}\left((\ln y_t - \ln y_{t-1}) - (\ln x_t - \ln x_{t-1})\right) \end{aligned} \tag{26}$$

From the above equation, one can derive the equation expressing output growth in terms of growth rates of inputs and of TFP:

$$\Delta Y = \ln y_t - \ln y_{t-1} = \sum v_i (\ln x_{it} - \ln x_{it-1}) + \Delta TFP \tag{27}$$

Output growth is then expressed in terms of the contributions of each input which is TFP. Finally, the growth rate of productivity of any particular input can be expressed in terms of the rates of growth of the ratios of all other inputs to that input, and the growth of TFP. For labor productivity:

$$\Delta LP = (\ln y_t - \ln y_{t-1}) - (\ln x_{Lt} - \ln x_{Lt-1}) = \sum_{i \neq L}^{m} v_i (\ln x_{it} - \ln x_{Lt-1}) + \Delta TFP \tag{28}$$

In the same way, non-labor factors' productivity can be estimated.

In addition to input factors, there are some other sources of growth, which affect productivity of a firm, sector or region. Norsworthy and Jang (1992) argue that these important sources of growth in TFP such as economies of scale, learning curve effect and changes in the quality of output (and input) cannot be derived by growth accounting techniques, but econometric models can be used for such estimates. These estimates can be incorporated in the growth accounting framework by portioning the TFP term:

$$TFP = TFP_{SE} + TFP_{LC} + TFP_R \tag{29}$$

The equation for output growth may be rewritten:

$$\Delta Y = \sum_i \Delta X + \Delta TFP_{SE} + \Delta TFP_{LC} + \Delta q_y + \Delta TFP_R \tag{30}$$

Here, output growth is explained in terms of the growth in inputs, scale effects (ΔTFP_{SE}), learning curve effects (ΔTFP_{LC}), changes in the quality of output (Δq_y) and residual or unexplained growth in TFP (ΔTFP_R).

Solow's Residual

Although Jan Tinbergen in 1942 performed the first empirical productivity measurements in the U.S., most of the later works on productivity are based on Solow's (1957) pioneering paper. At about the same time that multi-factor productivity was being measured using an economic accounting framework, Solow (1957) and other economists took a parametric approach to estimating productivity. Solow defined a production function as:

$$Q = F(K, L; t) \tag{31}$$

where Q=output, K=capital and L=labor inputs. Here t stands for time and represents technical change. This production function is, in fact, similar to the Cobb-Douglas function. Solow describes technical change as any kind of shift in the production function. According to this definition technical change covers all sorts of things such as demand slowdowns, assembly line speed-ups, improvements in the health and education of the labor force. Shifts in the production function are defined as neutral if they leave marginal rates of substitution untouched but simply increase or decrease the output attainable from given inputs. In the case that technical change is neutral, the production function takes the special form:

$$Q = A(t)\, f(K, L) \tag{32}$$

where A(t) measures the cumulated effect of shifts over time. By differentiating the above equation with respect to time and dividing by Q one gets:

$$\frac{\dot{Q}}{Q} = \frac{\dot{A}}{A} + A\frac{\partial f}{\partial K}\frac{\dot{K}}{Q} + A\frac{\partial f}{\partial L}\frac{\dot{L}}{Q} \tag{33}$$

Defining:

$$w_K = \frac{\partial Q}{\partial K}\frac{K}{Q} \quad \text{and} \quad w_L = \frac{\partial Q}{\partial L}\frac{L}{Q} \tag{34}$$

the relative shares of capital and labor can be substituted into the above equation (note that $\frac{\partial Q}{\partial K} = A\frac{\partial f}{\partial K}$) and one obtains:

$$\frac{\dot{Q}}{Q} = \frac{\dot{A}}{A} + w_K \frac{\dot{K}}{K} + w_L \frac{\dot{L}}{L} \tag{35}$$

From there one can calculate $\frac{\dot{A}}{A}$, by letting $Q / L = q$, $K / L = k$ and $w_L = 1 - w_K$

Note that $\frac{\dot{q}}{q} = \frac{\dot{Q}}{Q} - \frac{\dot{L}}{L}$ in the above equation; then equation (19) becomes:

$$\frac{\dot{q}}{q} = \frac{\dot{A}}{A} + w_K \frac{\dot{k}}{k} \tag{36}$$

Now if we disentangle the technical change index *A(t),* all we need are a data series for output per man-hour, capital per man-hour and the share of capital.

If $\frac{\dot{F}}{F}$ is independent of *K* and *L* (under constant return to scale only *K* / *L* matters) then shifts in the production function are neutral. If in addition $\frac{\dot{F}}{F}$ is constant over time, say equal to *a,* then $A(t) = e^{at}$ or in discrete approximation $A(t) = (1-a)^t$.

Following Tinbergen and also Solow (1957), Jorgenson and his associates (1972, 1987, 1995) developed a similar productivity index. Jorgenson and Griliches (1972) argued that if quantities of output and input are measured accurately, growth in total output is largely explained by growth in total input, and observed growth in total factor productivity is negligible. This statement has been the subject of the long lasting debate between Jorgenson and Griliches and Denison (see May 1972, Survey of Current Business).

Jorgenson and Griliches defined the growth rate of total factor productivity as the difference between the rate of growth of real product and real factor inputs. In this definition, they used the weighted averages of the rate of growth of individual products and factors. The weights are relative shares of each product in the value of total output and of each factor in the value of total input. According to Jorgenson the change in total factor productivity is the effect of 'costless' advances in applied technology, managerial efficiency, and industrial organization.

To derive the rate of growth of total factor productivity Jorgenson et al. employed the system of social accounts. In this system the value of output is equal to the value of input:

$$\Sigma q_i Y_i = \Sigma p_j X_j \qquad i = 1.\ldots m, \qquad j = 1.\ldots n \tag{37}$$

where Yi = quantity of output i, Xi = quantity of input, qi = price of output, pi =price of input. To define total factor productivity the above equation is differentiated with respect to time, and both sides divided by the corresponding total value:

$$\sum w_i \left(\frac{\dot{q}_i}{q_i} + \frac{\dot{Y}_i}{Y_i} \right) = \sum v_j \left(\frac{\dot{p}_j}{p_j} + \frac{\dot{X}_j}{X_j} \right) \tag{38}$$

where $w_i = \dfrac{q_i Y_i}{\sum q_i Y_i}$ and $v_j = \dfrac{q_j X_j}{\sum q_j X_j}$ are factor shares of output and input respectively with $w_i \geq 0$, $v_j \geq 0$ and $\sum w_i = \sum v_j = 1$

In terms of Divisia index numbers the definition of total factor productivity, P, is the ratio of the value of total output to the value of total input: $P = Y / X$ in the same way as the rate of total factor productivity growth may expressed as:

$$\frac{\dot{P}}{P} = \frac{\dot{Y}}{Y} - \frac{\dot{X}}{X} = \sum w_i \frac{\dot{Y}_i}{Y_i} - \sum v_j \frac{\dot{X}_j}{X_j} \tag{39}$$

or alternatively:

$$\frac{\dot{P}}{P} = \frac{\dot{p}}{p} - \frac{\dot{q}}{q} = \sum v_j \frac{\dot{p}_j}{p_j} - \sum w_i \frac{\dot{q}_i}{q_i} \tag{40}$$

By following the same reasoning, Jorgenson (1995) argued that the value of consumption and investment should be equal to the value of capital and labor services:

$$q_C C + q_I I = p_K K + p_L L \tag{41}$$

where C=quantity of consumption, I= quantity of investment, K= quantity of capital services, L= quantity of labor services, and q_C, q_I, p_K, p_L are corresponding prices. Following the above (39) and (40) the rate of total factor productivity growth may be written in the same way as:

$$\frac{\dot{P}}{P} = \frac{\dot{Y}}{Y} - \frac{\dot{X}}{X} = v_C \frac{\dot{C}}{C} + v_I \frac{\dot{I}}{I} - w_K \frac{\dot{K}}{K} - w_L \frac{\dot{L}}{L} \tag{42}$$

where the weights are relative value shares. These two approaches of Jorgenson et al. are similar to the above mentioned multi-factor productivity approaches.

Translog Assessment

Such a production function, called the transcendental logarithmic production function or simply the translog production function was developed by Christensen, Jorgenson and Lau (1973). In studies of productivity measurement, they have preferred to employ this specific form of the production function:

$$Z = \exp\left(\begin{array}{l}\alpha_0 + \alpha_X \ln X + \alpha_K \ln K + \alpha_L \ln L + \alpha_T T + \frac{1}{2}\beta_{XX}(\ln X)^2 + \beta_{XK} \ln X \ln K + \\ \beta_{XL} \ln X \ln L + \beta_{XT} T \ln X + \frac{1}{2}\beta_{KK}(\ln K)^2 + \beta_{KL} \ln K \ln L + \beta_{KT} T \ln K + \\ \frac{1}{2}\beta_{LL}(\ln L)^2 + \beta_{LT} T \ln L + \frac{1}{2}\beta_{TT} T^2\end{array}\right) \quad (43)$$

where Z= output, K = capital, L= labor and X= intermediate inputs. Necessary conditions for producer equilibrium imply that the value shares of intermediate, capital, labor inputs are equal to the elasticity of output with respect to these inputs:

$$v_X = \alpha_X + \beta_{XX} \ln X + \beta_{XK} \ln K + \beta_{XL} \ln L + \beta_{XT} T \quad (44)$$

$$v_K = \alpha_K + \beta_{XK} \ln X + \beta_{XK} \ln K + \beta_{KL} \ln L + \beta_{KT} T \quad (45)$$

$$v_L = \alpha_L + \beta_{XL} \ln X + \beta_{KL} \ln K + \beta_{LL} \ln L + \beta_{LT} T \quad (46)$$

The residual productivity growth rate is then equal to the rate of growth of output subtracting the contribution of all inputs explicitly taken into account:

$$v_T = \alpha_T + \beta_{XT} \ln X + \beta_{KT} \ln K + \beta_{LT} \ln L + \beta_{TT} T \quad (47)$$

The translog production function is characterized by constant returns to scale if and only if the parameters satisfy the conditions:

$$\begin{array}{l}\alpha_X + \alpha_K + \alpha_L = 1 \\ \beta_{XX} + \beta_{XL} + \beta_{XK} = 0 \\ \beta_{LL} + \beta_{LX} + \beta_{LK} = 0 \\ \beta_{KK} + \beta_{KX} + \beta_{KL} = 0 \\ \beta_{TX} + \beta_{TL} + \beta_{TK} = 0\end{array} \quad (48)$$

Now consider two discrete points in time (*t and t-1)*; the growth rate of output can be expressed as a weighted average of the growth rates of inputs, plus the average rate of productivity growth:

$$\ln Z_t - \ln Z_{t-1} = \bar{v}_X(\ln X_t - \ln X_{t-1}) + \bar{v}_K(\ln K_t - \ln K_{t-1}) + \bar{v}_L(\ln L_t - \ln L_{t-1}) + \bar{v}_t \quad (49)$$

and from this one gets residual factor productivity growth derived as:

$$\bar{v}_t = (\ln Z_t - \ln Z_{t-1}) - \bar{v}_X(\ln X_t - \ln X_{t-1}) - \bar{v}_K(\ln K_t - \ln K_{t-1}) - \bar{v}_L(\ln L_t - \ln L_{t-1}) \quad (50)$$

Cobb-Douglas Assessment

Following Solow's initial work, there has been further development of the production function approach using both the Cobb-Douglas function and other production functions involving different concepts of the production process. The well known assumptions of the Cobb-Douglas function are competitive markets, constant returns to scale, neutral technological change and constant shares of the factors in income. Other formulations, however, allow variable returns to scale, variable elasticities of substitution between the factors and biased technological change which means that changing technology may increase the demand for one factor relative to another.

Suppose a case of a single output Y (or aggregated output) and two inputs, labor L and capital K and consider a production function that has the Cobb-Douglas form:

$$Y = CL^{\alpha} K^{\beta} \tag{51}$$

where α and β are the factor elasticity of labor and capital, C is a constant representing productivity or technical change. Over a short period of time it is assumed that α remains constant. In such cases, changes in C measure changes in total productivity (Maddala, no ref.). Now assume two discrete points in time *t and t-1* and let the values of above variables be in time tY_t, L_t, and K_t, in time *t-1*, Y_{t-1}, L_{t-1} and K_{t-1}:

$$\begin{aligned} Y_t &= C_t L_t^{\alpha} K_t^{\beta} \\ Y_{t-1} &= C_{t-1} L_{t-1}^{\alpha} K_{t-1}^{\beta} \end{aligned} \tag{52}$$

from this expression productivity index $Ct / Ct\text{-}1$ is obtained.

To construct a productivity measure from (51) or (52) we need the value of the parameters α and β. To get these we use the share of labor and capital in total cost as α and β. In doing so we implicitly assume that in a given period the combination of inputs was chosen so as to maximize profits. Let the price of labor and capital be *PL* and *PK* respectively. The share of labor in total cost is:

$$\alpha = SL = LPL / (LPL + KPK) \tag{53a}$$

and similarly the share of capital in total cost is:

$$\beta = SK = KPK / (LPL + KPK) \tag{53b}$$

Factor Augmented Assessment

Sato (1970) developed a factor augmented production function to incorporate the bias of technical change into the production function:

$$Y(t)= F[A(t)K(t), B(t)L(t)] \tag{54}$$

where Y(t) = output at time t, L(t) = labor, K(t) = capital, and A(t) and B(t) are the efficiencies of capital and labor respectively. The growth rate of output over time can be written as:

$$\frac{\dot{Y}}{Y} = \alpha\left(\frac{\dot{K}}{K}\right) + \alpha\left(\frac{\dot{A}}{A}\right) + \beta\left(\frac{\dot{L}}{L}\right) + \beta\left(\frac{\dot{B}}{B}\right) \tag{55}$$

where α and β represent the share of capital and labor in output, and prime refers to time derivatives. Technical change as a residual is then:

$$T = \frac{\dot{Y}}{Y} - \alpha\left(\frac{\dot{K}}{K}\right) - \beta\left(\frac{\dot{L}}{L}\right) \tag{56}$$

The factor augmenting approach allows us to measure TFP growth. TFP growth is the weighted (by factor shares) growth rates of the efficiency parameters:

$$\Delta TFP = \alpha\left(\frac{\dot{A}}{A}\right) + \beta\left(\frac{\dot{B}}{B}\right) \tag{57}$$

By letting $y = Y/K$, $z = Y/L$, $x = L/K$, and w = the wage rate, r = the return on capital, Sato derives the following equations in order to isolate and calculate the individual efficiencies:

$$\frac{\dot{z}}{z} = \alpha\left(\frac{\dot{A}}{A}\right) + \beta\left(\frac{\dot{B}}{B}\right) - \alpha\left(\frac{\dot{x}}{x}\right)$$

$$\frac{\dot{w}}{w} = \left(\frac{\dot{B}}{B} - \frac{\alpha}{\sigma_{LK}}\right)\left(\frac{\dot{B}}{B} - \frac{\dot{A}}{A} + \frac{\dot{x}}{x}\right) \tag{58}$$

$$\frac{\dot{r}}{r} = \left(\frac{\dot{A}}{A} + \frac{\beta}{\sigma_{LK}}\right)\left(\frac{\dot{B}}{B} - \frac{\dot{A}}{A} + \frac{\dot{x}}{x}\right)$$

where $\sigma_{LK} \neq 1$

$$\frac{\dot{A}}{A} = \left(\frac{\sigma_{LK}\dfrac{\dot{r}}{r} - \dfrac{\dot{y}}{y}}{(\sigma_{LK} - 1)}\right)$$

$$\frac{\dot{B}}{B} = \left(\frac{\sigma_{LK}\dfrac{\dot{w}}{w} - \dfrac{\dot{z}}{z}}{(\sigma_{LK} - 1)}\right) \tag{59}$$

Sato estimates σ_{LK} as $\sigma_{LK} = \dfrac{w \cdot r}{-xy(\partial w / \partial x)}$

Frontier Assessment

Aigner, Lovell and Schmidt (1977) introduced the stochastic production frontier and suggested a new approach to the estimation of the frontier production function. Their approach involves the specification of the error term as being made up of two components, one normal and the other from a one-sided distribution.

In order to provide statistical properties to earlier estimation of parametric frontier production functions, Schmidt (1985) added a one-sided disturbance to the production function:

$$y_i = f(x_i; \beta) + \varepsilon_i \tag{60}$$

Aigner et al. (1977) decomposed the error term into two independent components:

$$\varepsilon_i = v_i + u_i \tag{61}$$

where v is a two-sided error term representing the usual statistical noise found in any relationship, u is a one-sided error term representing technical (in)efficiency. They argued that in doing so it is possible to estimate the variance of v and u, so to get evidence on their relative sizes. Another implication of this approach is that the productive efficiency should be measured by the ratio:

$$\frac{y_i}{f(x_i;\beta)+v_i} \tag{62}$$

rather than the ratio:

$$\frac{y_i}{f(x_i;\beta)} \tag{63}$$

This procedure simply distinguishes productive inefficiency from other sources of disturbance that are beyond the firm's control.

Later Jondrow, Lovell, Materow and Schmidt (1982) further developed the estimation of two components, v and u. They argued that the entire *(v-u)* is easily estimated for each observation but to separate it to its two components is problematic. They suggested a solution to this problem by considering the expected value of u conditional on *(v-u)*. They provided an explicit formula for the half-normal and exponential cases.

Greene (1980) argued that the half-normal distribution of the stochastic frontier model proposed by Aigner, Lovell and Schmidt (1977) is 'a bit inflexible' and modified it by allowing the one-sided part of the disturbance to have a two-parameter Gamma distribution. He found that the gamma model offers a promising alternative to the half-normal and exponential models for the stochastic frontier.

In summary, the present authors observe that all the previous approaches could be operationally synthesized as follows.

Take any production function:

$$y = f(x) \tag{64}$$

x being a vector of production factors, and by taking its logarithmic differential with respect to time:

$$\frac{d\ln y}{d\,\mathrm{t}} = \sum_i E_i \frac{d\ln x_i}{d\,\mathrm{t}} + \sum_i f_{it}{}'' \frac{x_i}{y} \tag{65}$$

where changes in the marginal productivity have been taken into account. This matches perfectly the isoquant approach in terms of input coefficients – mentioned above – as normalized and comparable quantities; their vector - $f_{it}{}''$ - corresponds to the vector of change of locations of sector or firm from one normalized isoquant to another, and the production coefficients appear explicitly in the second term of the right hand side of (65).

The production elasticity *Ei* are in principle not constant (which would reduce (64) to a Cobb-Douglas production function); to allow for variability one could specify that function in Box-Cox transformed variables as:

$$y^{\sigma} = \sum_i a_i x_i^{\mu i} + b \qquad (66)$$

leading to:

$$E_i = \frac{a_i \mu_i \sigma^{-1} x_i^{\mu i}}{y^{\sigma}} \qquad (67)$$

Shift-Share, Output and Productivity Change: A New Model

In the light of the above discussion of different approaches, productivity and output change can be integrated into shift-share models. From equations (4) and (13) for sector i in region r:

$$TS \equiv NS + IM + RS \qquad (68)$$

$$TS \equiv [NS(a) + NS(b)] + [IM(a) + IM(b)] + [RS(a) + RS(b)] \qquad (69)$$

We can rewrite the equation (68) in terms of employment growth rates as:

$$\Delta' \ln E_{ir} \equiv \Delta' \ln E + (\Delta' \ln E_i - \Delta' \ln E) + (\Delta' \ln E_{ir} - \Delta' \ln E_i) \qquad (70)$$

This equation corresponds to the traditional shift-share model and $\Delta \ln E$ represents **the national share**, $(\Delta \ln E_i - \Delta \ln E)$ represents **the industry mix**, and **the regional share** is represented by $(\Delta \ln E_{ir} - \Delta \ln E_i)$

Where:

$$\Delta \ln E \equiv \Delta \ln Q - (\Delta \ln \frac{Q}{E}) \equiv \Delta \ln Q - (\Delta \ln Q - \Delta \ln E) \qquad (71)$$

$$\Delta \ln E_i \equiv \Delta \ln Q_i - (\Delta \ln \frac{Q_i}{E_i}) \equiv \Delta \ln Q_i - (\Delta \ln Q_i - \Delta \ln E_i) \qquad (72)$$

$$\Delta \ln E_{ir} \equiv \Delta \ln Q_{ir} - (\Delta \ln \frac{Q_{ir}}{E_{ir}}) \equiv \Delta \ln Q_{ir} - (\Delta \ln Q_{ir} - \Delta \ln E_{ir}) \qquad (73)$$

Substituting (71), (72) and (73) into equation (70) we can rewrite the equation (69) as:

$$\begin{aligned} \Delta \ln E_{ir} &\equiv TS \equiv [\Delta \ln Q - (\Delta \ln \frac{Q}{E})] \\ &+ [\{\Delta \ln Q_i - (\Delta \ln \frac{Q_i}{E_i})\} - \{\Delta \ln Q - (\Delta \ln \frac{Q}{E})\}] \qquad (74) \\ &+ [\{\Delta \ln Q_{ir} - (\Delta \ln \frac{Q_{ir}}{E_{ir}})\} - \{\Delta \ln Q_i - (\Delta \ln \frac{Q_i}{E_i})\}] \end{aligned}$$

In equation (74), ($\Delta \ln Q$) represents NS(a) and ($\Delta \ln \frac{Q}{E}$) represents NS(b). Similar representations hold for the remaining components.

Now:

$$\Delta \ln Q \equiv \alpha \Delta \ln K + \beta \Delta \ln E + \tau \quad (75)$$

$$\Delta \ln \frac{Q}{E} \equiv (\Delta \ln Q - \Delta \ln E) \equiv \alpha \Delta \ln K + (\beta - 1)\Delta \ln E + \tau \quad (76)$$

$$\tau \equiv (\Delta \ln Q - \Delta \ln E) - \alpha \Delta \ln K - (\beta - 1)\Delta \ln E \quad (77)$$

$$\Delta \ln Q_i \equiv \alpha_i \Delta \ln K_i + \beta_i \Delta \ln E_i + \tau_i \quad (78)$$

$$\Delta \ln \frac{Q_i}{E_i} \equiv (\Delta \ln Q_i - \Delta \ln E_i) \equiv \alpha_i \Delta \ln K_i + (\beta_i - 1)\Delta \ln E_i + \tau_i \quad (79)$$

$$\tau_i \equiv (\Delta \ln Q_i - \Delta \ln E_i) - \alpha_i \Delta \ln K_i - (\beta_i - 1)\Delta \ln E_i \quad (80)$$

$$\Delta \ln Q_{ir} \equiv \alpha_{ir} \Delta \ln K_{ir} + \beta_{ir} \Delta \ln E_{ir} + \tau_{ir} \quad (81)$$

$$\Delta \ln \frac{Q_{ir}}{E_{ir}} \equiv (\Delta \ln Q_{ir} - \Delta \ln E_{ir}) \equiv \alpha_{ir} \Delta \ln K_{ir} + (\beta_{ir} - 1)\Delta \ln E_{ir} + \tau_{ir} \quad (82)$$

$$\tau_{ir} \equiv (\Delta \ln Q_{ir} - \Delta \ln E_{ir}) - \alpha_{ir} \Delta \ln K_{ir} - (\beta_{ir} - 1)\Delta \ln E_{ir} \quad (83)$$

In the above equations, one can estimate the value of the parameters α and β as the share of labor and capital in total cost. In doing so, it is implicitly assumed that in a given year the combination of inputs was chosen so to maximize profits, and was constant during the year. Let the price of labor and capital be P_L and P_K respectively. The share of capital in total cost is:

$$\alpha = SK = \frac{KP_K}{LP_L + KP_K} \quad (84)$$

and similarly the share of labor in total cost is:

$$\beta = SL = \frac{LP_L}{LP_L + KP_K} \quad (85)$$

Substituting corresponding productivity changes ($\Delta \ln \frac{Q}{E}$) into the components of the equation (74) and rearranging gives:

$$\begin{aligned}
\Delta \ln E_{ir} \equiv TS \equiv & [\Delta \ln Q - (\alpha \Delta \ln K + (\beta - 1)\Delta \ln E + \tau)] \\
& + [\{\Delta \ln Q_i - \Delta \ln Q\} - \{(\alpha_i \Delta \ln K_i + (\beta_i - 1)\Delta \ln E_i + \tau_i) \\
& - (\alpha \Delta \ln K + (\beta - 1)\Delta \ln E + \tau\}] \\
& + [\{\Delta \ln Q_{ir} - \Delta \ln Q_i\} - \{(\alpha_{ir} \Delta \ln K_{ir} + (\beta_{ir} - 1)\Delta \ln E_{ir} + \tau_{ir}) \\
& - (\alpha_i \Delta \ln K_i + (\beta_i - 1)\Delta \ln E_i + \tau_i)\}]
\end{aligned} \quad (86)$$

In equation (86):

$$NS(a) \equiv \Delta \ln Q \tag{87}$$

$$NS(b) \equiv (\alpha \Delta \ln K + (\beta - 1)\Delta \ln E + \tau) \tag{88}$$

$$IM(a) \equiv \Delta \ln Q_i - \Delta \ln Q \tag{89}$$

$$IM(b) \equiv \{(\alpha_i \Delta \ln K_i + (\beta_i - 1)\Delta \ln E_i + \tau_i) - (\alpha \Delta \ln K + (\beta - 1)\Delta \ln E + \tau)\} \tag{90}$$

$$RS(a) \equiv (\Delta \ln Q_{ir} - \Delta \ln Q_i) \tag{91}$$

$$RS(b) \equiv \{(\alpha_{ir} \Delta \ln K_{ir} + (\beta_{ir} - 1)\Delta \ln E_{ir} + \tau_{ir}) - (\alpha_i \Delta \ln K_i + (\beta_i - 1)\Delta \ln E_i + \tau_i)\} \tag{92}$$

Equation (86) takes into account output change and productivity change resulting from improvement of capital and labor including residual, τ, (faster than average regional technical progress, scale and external economies, infrastructure etc.) and at the same time it maintains the additivity property of the shift-share model. Total regional growth is obtained summing over i and r.

Another important development emerges from the above discussion. $\Delta \ln E$ can be written as:

$$\Delta \ln E \equiv \Delta \ln Q - \alpha \Delta \ln K - (\beta - 1)\Delta \ln E - \tau \tag{93}$$

by arranging equation (91) one can derive:

$$\Delta \ln E + (\beta - 1)\Delta \ln E \equiv \Delta \ln Q - \alpha \Delta \ln K - \tau \tag{94}$$

$$\beta \Delta \ln E \equiv \Delta \ln Q - \alpha \Delta \ln K - \tau \tag{95}$$

finally from equation (93):

$$\Delta \ln E \equiv \frac{1}{\beta} \Delta \ln Q - \frac{\alpha}{\beta} \Delta \ln K - \frac{\tau}{\beta} \tag{96}$$

where $\frac{1}{\beta}$ is output, $\frac{\alpha}{\beta}$ is capital and $\frac{\tau}{\beta}$ is average total productivity multiplier.

Regional Perspectives

In the regional economic context, researchers have employed the above mentioned approaches to investigate different aspects of regional productivity in terms of their impacts on productivity change and regional productivity differentials. Agglomeration economies have become an important issue in regional economic development. For a recent review discussion of regional dynamics see Haynes et al. (1997). Therefore at the regional level, in addition to labor, capital and material inputs, because of different factor endowments of regions (states, SMSA's, counties or census regions), infrastructure, urbanization, (dis)economies of scale, quality of labor force, unionization, industry mix of the region and business cycles play an important role on determining productivity. As a result at the regional level these factors have become a part of regional production (cost) functions in determining spatial productivity patterns. For examples see Moomaw (1983a),

Moomaw and Williams (1991), Hulten and Schwab (1984), Garofalo and Malhotra (1984), Beeson (1987), Mullen and Williams (1987, 1990), Fogarty and Garofalo (1988) and Williams and Moomaw (1989), Beeson and Husted (1989) Anderson (1990), Bjurek, Hjalmarson and Forsund (1990), Greene (1980) and Cornwell, Schmidt and Sickles (1990). For a detailed review of regional applications of these approaches see Gerking (1994) and Moomaw (1983b).

Data and Application

In the regional economic context, instead of partial productivity measures, i.e. labor productivity (output per worker), measures of TFP, output per unit of all inputs, when available, are in principle better guides to comparisons of efficiency than measures of output per unit of input alone (NAS, 1979). It is not always efficient, for example, for an employer, sector or region to invest in labor saving machinery to increase its output. If wages are high, the price of the new machinery is low, interest rates are low and the existing machinery is near the end of its useful life then investment in labor saving machinery could produce large gains in efficiency. If one or more of these conditions are reversed, however, it might be more efficient to continue to use existing machinery longer. The result is that an establishment with low output per hour of labor may be more efficient than one whose labor productivity is higher because the first establishment is economizing in the use of other inputs (for a similar discussion see Haynes and Dinc, 1997).

In the shift-share application, to capture the annual change in regional growth or decline in employment the dynamic shift-share approach of Barff and Knight in 1988 is incorporated with the new modification.

The period of investigation is from 1987 to 1994. During this period we have examined six sunbelt and six manufacturing belt states. The data employed are from the Annual Survey of Manufactures Geographic Area Series, and the Census of Manufactures Geographic Area Series. Labor inputs were measured by hours worked rather than the number of employees, to take account of temporal, sectoral and spatial variations in the length of the unit of work. The labor inputs include only production workers in manufacturing sectors which covers 70–75 per cent of total manufacturing employees in the United States. Output is measured by value added. To determine the share of labor in factors, the ratio of production wages to sector specific value added is used. Wages data of production workers are from the Annual Survey of Manufactures and Census of Manufactures. Value added data by industry were deflated using the GNP implicit price deflator (Economic Report of the President, 1997).

One of the major problems researchers face in regional productivity analysis is the lack of reliable capital stock data at the state level. Three alternatives have been proposed by various researchers to overcome this problem: 1. avoid the need to measure capital services (Sveikauskas, 1975), 2. constructing measures of capital, 3. use available proxies for capital (Aaberg, 1973; Moomaw, 1983a).

Each of these alternatives, however, has some limitations. Avoiding the need for capital stock data approach has given unstable estimates over time. Another important shortcoming of this approach is that estimating parameters of a production function without capital stock data requires restrictive assumptions (Gerking, 1994; Moomaw, 1983b). It is possible to construct one's own capital stock data by using the popular perpetual inventory method. In addition to the cost of developing capital stock estimates, there is a danger that unrecognized biases could arise, and depreciation rates of the capital may vary over time and space (Moomaw 1983b).

The third alternative, the use of proxies for capital data, may involve the danger of not knowing how closely the chosen variable substitutes for the capital data. Aaberg (1973) suggested the use of non-labor costs per unit labor as a proxy for capital intensity. Later Moomaw (1983a) compared productivity estimates using the non-labor income measure of capital intensity with those using the capital measure stock measure. He found that non-labor income estimates perform as well as, if not better than, the alternative...the manufacturing capital stock data developed for states do not provide a better proxy for capital services than non labor income data (pp. 85). Here non-labor income is equal to value added minus total labor costs per production worker. Therefore, in the analysis we use the non-labor income approach as a proxy for capital stock data.

Findings and Discussion

The new model proposed here captures all contributing factors to productivity change as oppose to earlier productivity related shift-share models. It is possible to investigate each of these factors separately, i.e., capital, labor and residual (infrastructure, technological advancement etc.). In this illustration, however, we present the results as aggregated. We also examine five manufacturing sectors (the fabricated metal products, the industrial machinery and equipment, electric and electronic equipment, transportation equipment and instrument and related product sectors) in detail. We assume that four of these sectors are core manufacturing sectors and the fifth one (instruments and related products sector) is the new growing high-tech sector. Further, four states (Kentucky, Texas, New York and Ohio) are investigated in detail.

The aggregated results of the analysis are presented in Table 5.1. Between 1987 and 1994 seven states posted a growth while five had a decline. From the sunbelt Arizona, Kentucky, Tennessee and Texas, and from the old manufacturing belt Illinois, Michigan and Ohio are the growing states in terms of manufacturing employment. On the other hand, California and Florida from sunbelt and Massachusetts, New York and Pennsylvania from the manufacturing belt are declining states.

A close investigation of Table 5.1 (p. 96) and Figure 5.1 (p. 100) reveals that the declining states have posted substantial productivity improvements and consequently had employment losses, although they had employment growth resulting from output change. Employment losses resulting from improvements in productivity outpaced employment gain from output growth in these states. Massachusetts and New York had the highest improvement in productivity and the largest decline in employment followed by California and Pennsylvania. On the other hand among growing states only Michigan improved its productivity during the study period. In the growing states, output growth and inferior productivity performances have helped employment gains. Kentucky had the largest growth due to its poor productivity performance and followed by Tennessee and Texas.

Table 5.1 Aggregated shift-share results, 1987–1994

	NS(a)	NS(b)	IM(a)	IM(b)	RS(a)	RS(b)	Total (a)	Total (b)	Total Shift	Actual Growth
Arizona	0.066	-0.057	-0.024	0.028	-0.009	0.117	0.033	0.089	0.122	0.122
California	0.066	-0.057	-0.003	-0.013	0.097	-0.232	0.161	-0.302	-0.141	-0.141
Florida	0.066	-0.057	0.031	-0.061	0.079	-0.136	0.176	-0.254	-0.078	-0.078
Illinois	0.066	-0.057	-0.003	-0.013	-0.066	0.094	-0.003	0.024	0.021	0.021
Kentucky	0.066	-0.057	0.029	-0.062	-0.221	0.373	-0.126	0.254	0.128	0.128
Massa-chusetts	0.066	-0.057	-0.003	-0.013	0.151	-0.367	0.215	-0.437	-0.222	-0.222
Michigan	0.066	-0.057	-0.003	-0.013	-0.026	0.052	0.038	-0.018	0.020	0.020
New York	0.066	-0.057	0.031	-0.061	0.056	-0.242	0.153	-0.360	-0.207	-0.207
Ohio	0.066	-0.057	-0.003	-0.013	-0.041	0.080	0.022	0.010	0.032	0.032
Penn-sylvania	0.066	-0.057	0.031	-0.061	0.090	-0.174	0.187	-0.292	-0.105	-0.105
Tennessee	0.066	-0.057	0.031	-0.061	-0.117	0.258	-0.019	0.141	0.121	0.121
Texas	0.066	-0.057	-0.003	-0.013	-0.057	0.190	0.007	0.120	0.127	0.127

Figure 5.2, in addition to sources of employment change illustrates regional advantages or disadvantages for the states under investigation. This figure reveals that the regional advantages (disadvantages) are the driving forces of employment growth (decline) in these states, although national trends had some impact on manufacturing employment growth.

In the fabricated metal products sector (Figure 5.3), six states (Arizona, Illinois, Kentucky, Michigan, Tennessee and Texas) had employment growth due to poor productivity performance, even though output declined in these states. On the other hand, in the remaining states output growth contributed to the employment growth but decline in employment resulting from productivity gains surpassed this growth contribution. In Ohio and New York, all regional and national factors had a negative impact on employment growth. Another important point in this sector is that the national effects were almost negligible, this sector is driven by regional factors.

Regional advantages and sources of employment change in the industrial machinery and equipment sector is presented in Figure 5.4. In this sector, seven states had employment growth between 1987 and 1994. In Florida, Kentucky, Tennessee and Texas despite the output decline employment grew in this sector due to their poor productivity performance during the study period. In Arizona, employment decline resulting from output decreases outpaced the employment gain from poor productivity performance of the state in this sector. On the other hand, California, Massachusetts, New York and Pennsylvania had rapid growth of productivity causing employment decline despite the increases in output. In this sector, five of the manufacturing belt states suffered employment losses due to productivity improvement. From the sunbelt only California improved its productivity so it lost employment. In this sector, regional factors were the driving forces in employment growth (decline).

Figure 5.5 shows that in the electric and electronic sector, only Tennessee and Texas had an employment growth. Eight of the remaining states had a decline in employment in this sector due mainly to productivity improvements. In two states, Illinois and Kentucky, employment losses resulted from the decline of output. In this sector, national trends had an important impact on employment growth. The good news is, however, there is substantial improvements in productivity in the electric and electronic sector. It is possible to speculate that increasing international competition may have forced this sector to improve its productivity.

In the transportation equipment sector, Illinois, Kentucky and Tennessee enjoyed employment growth while remaining states suffered a decline (Figure 5.6). In these three states, poor productivity saved employment despite the output decline. On the other hand, in Arizona, California, Florida, Massachusetts, Michigan and New York where employment decline occurred productivity gain was the main contributor to losses, even though output grew substantially in these states. In Pennsylvania and Texas regional output declined and had a negative impact on employment, but total output effect (including national effects) had a positive impact. In this sector, regional dynamics were more important than national trends.

Figure 5.7 illustrates sources of employment change in the instrument and related products sector. In this sector, during the study period Kentucky and Michigan were the only winners in terms of employment growth. The underlying driving force behind this growth was poor productivity performances of these states. Although output decreases caused a substantial employment decline, employment gains from poor performance saved them. The remaining states posted a decline in this period resulting mainly from productivity improvements driven either regional (in Arizona) or national (in California, Massachusetts, New York, Ohio, Pennsylvania, Tennessee, and Texas) trends.

Kentucky had employment growth in 15 manufacturing sectors between 1987 and 1994 (Figure 5.8). Although output decreases had a negative impact on employment growth, its inferior productivity prevented decline. In Kentucky, national effects had little impact on employment growth with the exception of the leather and leather products sector. Kentucky improved its productivity in four sectors (the textile mill products, apparel and textile products, the leather and leather products and the primary metal products sectors) and had employment decline in two of them. In the other two sectors, output growth prevented employment decline. The largest growth occurred in the transportation equipment sector in Kentucky due to slow productivity improvements.

Figure 5.9 shows that Texas had employment growth in 15 sectors resulting mainly from inferior productivity. The largest growth took place in the furniture and fixtures sector followed by the rubber and miscellaneous plastics, industrial machinery and equipment, fabricated metal products and the electric and electronic sectors. Texas improved its productivity in only three sectors, the food and kindred products, textile mill products and the stone clay and glass products. In seven sectors, the food and kindred products, textile mill products, paper and allied products, printing and publishing products, rubber and miscellaneous plastics, electric and electronic equipment, transportation equipment and the instruments and related products, national trends had a major impact on employment growth in Texas.

With the exception of the tobacco products sector, manufacturing employment in New York declined in all sectors between 1987 and 1994 (Figure 5.10). In most of these sectors, output grew but New York improved its productivity faster so ended up with employment decline. In the electric and electronic equipment, transportation equipment, and instruments and related products sectors, national factors had an impact on employment growth in New York during the study period. In the remaining sectors, regional factors were the driving force. Though New York suffered a decline in manufacturing employment between 1987–1994, it can be argued that it improved its competitive edge and could be better of in the long run.

Figure 5.11 shows that in Ohio, manufacturing employment grew in ten sectors and declined in nine between 1987 and 1994. Employment growth occurred where the productivity was poor even output declined with the exception of the food and kindred products and paper and allied products sectors. In these two sectors, regional productivity effect was not strong enough to surpass output growth effect so Ohio gained employment in these sectors. In the stone, clay and glass, electric and electronic equipment, and the instruments and related products sectors national factors had substantial impact on employment growth while remaining sector were mainly driven by regional forces.

As discussed earlier an important outcome of this study is the multipliers. Table 5.2 shows the average multipliers for selected sectors by state. In this table, output multiplier is represented by $\frac{1}{\beta}$, capital multiplier by $\frac{\alpha}{\beta}$ and residual productivity multiplier by $\frac{\tau}{\beta}$. The values of these multipliers are calculated as annual averages, and can be interpreted as similar to regression coefficients. For example, in Arizona, one unit growth in output in the fabricated metal products sector created on average 3.31 units growth in employment. Similarly, one unit capital expenditure created 2.31 units employment decline in this sector for a given year. Recall that this is an ex-post analysis and hence reflects the realized growth or decline based on multipliers. Therefore, a positive sign under the productivity multiplier heading is an indicator of poor productivity performance of a state in a given sector. In fact, the expected sign of this multiplier is negative. This table provides valuable information for the state industrial policy makers about understanding what happened in the state and determining of future policies.

Table 5.2 Average multipliers for selected sectors, 1987–1994

	Output Multiplier	Capital Multiplier	Productivity Multiplier
Fabricated Metal Products			
AZ	3.31	-2.31	0.19
CA	3.46	-2.46	-0.07
FL	3.38	-2.38	-0.02
IL	3.35	-2.35	0.03
KY	3.77	-2.77	0.09
MA	3.62	-2.62	-0.07
MI	2.68	-1.68	0.02
NY	3.14	-2.14	-0.02
OH	3.08	-2.08	0.00
PA	3.44	-2.44	-0.02
TN	3.31	-2.31	0.06
TX	3.55	-2.55	0.10
Industrial Machinery and Equipment			
AZ	4.66	-3.66	-0.05
CA	7.62	-6.62	-0.19
FL	4.63	-3.63	0.05
IL	3.86	-2.86	0.04
KY	5.10	-4.10	0.11
MA	5.83	-4.83	-0.32
MI	3.33	-2.33	0.04
NY	4.34	-3.34	-0.06
OH	3.61	-2.61	0.04
PA	3.81	-2.81	0.00
TN	4.17	-3.17	0.15
TX	5.25	-4.25	0.21
Instruments and Related products			
AZ	11.54	-10.54	-0.52
CA	6.65	-5.65	-0.25
FL	7.28	-6.28	0.03
IL	7.19	-6.19	-0.03
KY	3.78	-2.78	0.39
MA	6.26	-5.26	-0.24
MI	5.36	-4.36	0.14
NY	9.73	-8.73	-0.36
OH	6.13	-5.13	-0.06
PA	5.89	-4.89	-0.09
TN	6.94	-5.94	-0.07
TX	6.96	-5.96	-0.09
Electric and Electronic Equipment			
AZ	9.00	-8.00	0.06
CA	6.67	-5.67	-0.01
FL	8.27	-7.27	-0.07
IL	5.15	-4.15	0.01
KY	3.70	-2.70	0.02
MA	4.94	-3.94	-0.15
MI	3.64	-2.64	-0.04
NY	5.62	-4.62	-0.10
OH	5.19	-4.19	-0.04
PA	4.95	-3.95	-0.04
TN	3.70	-2.70	0.05
TX	8.91	-7.91	0.31
Transportation Equipment			
AZ	5.92	-4.92	-0.19
CA	5.57	-4.57	-0.36
FL	4.46	-3.46	-0.13
IL	4.78	-3.78	0.13
KY	7.19	-6.19	0.62
MA	5.33	-4.33	-0.33
MI	3.30	-2.30	-0.02
NY	3.86	-2.86	-0.16
OH	4.28	-3.28	-0.02
PA	4.25	-3.25	-0.02
TN	4.03	-3.03	0.21
TX	4.55	-3.55	-0.06

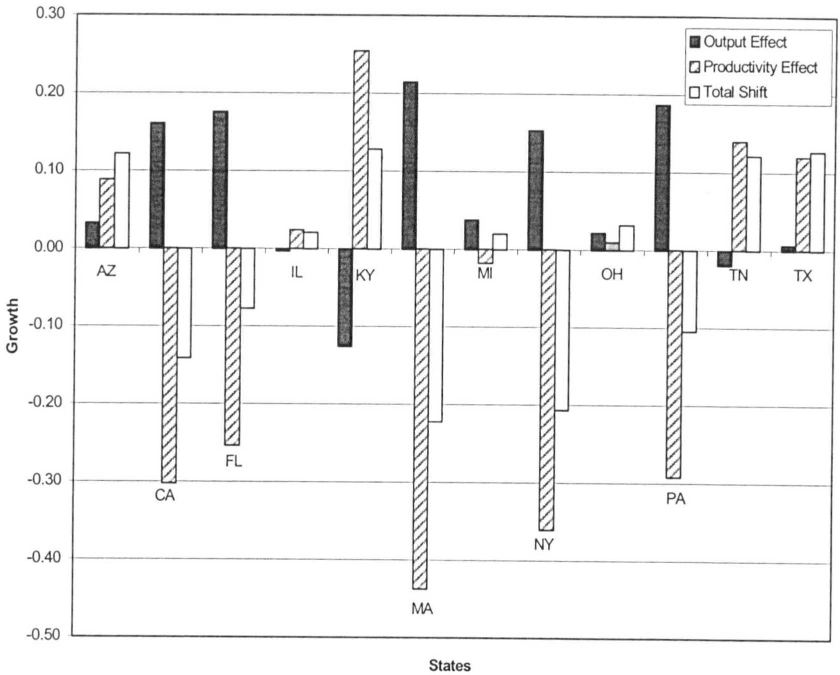

Figure 5.1 Sources of manufacturing employment change, 1987–1994

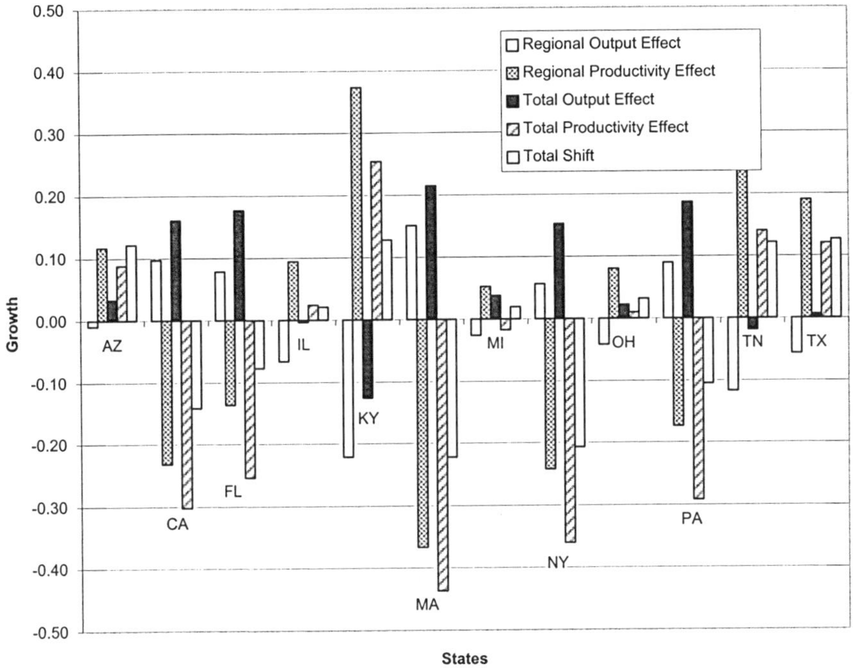

Figure 5.2 Regional advantages in manufacturing employment change, 1987–1994

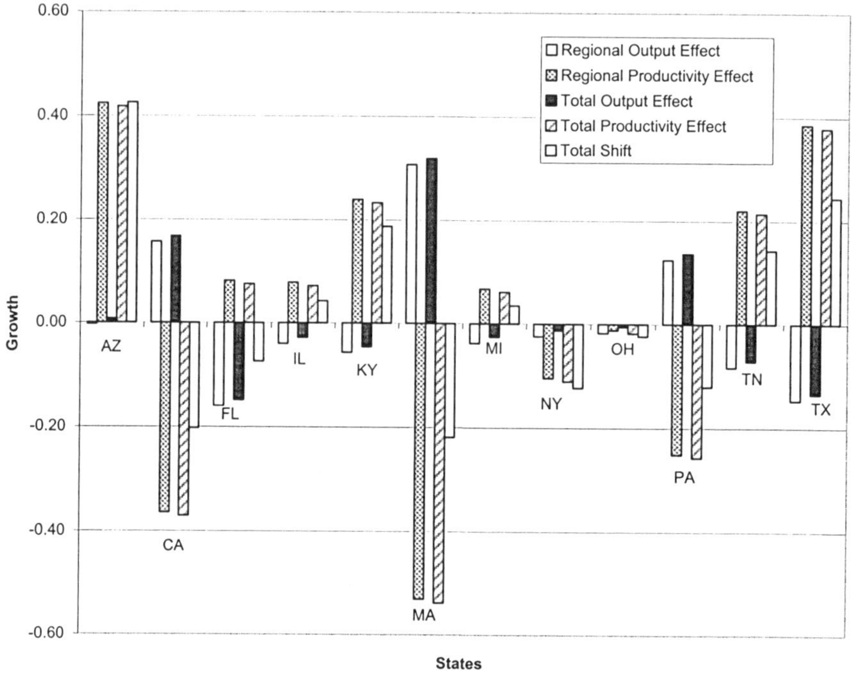

Figure 5.3 Regional advantages in the fabricated metal products sector, 1987–1994

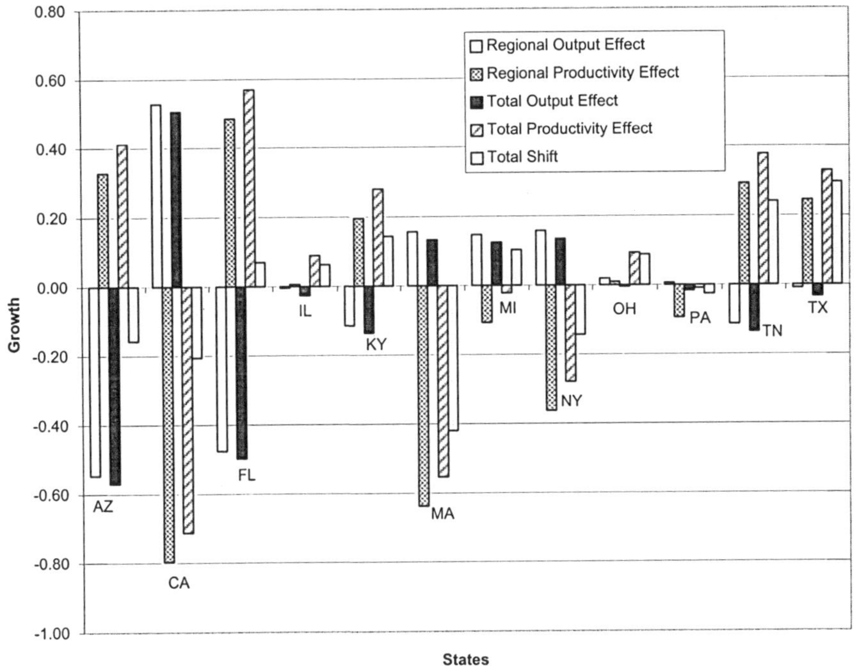

Figure 5.4 Regional advantages in the industrial machinery and equipment sector, 1987–1994

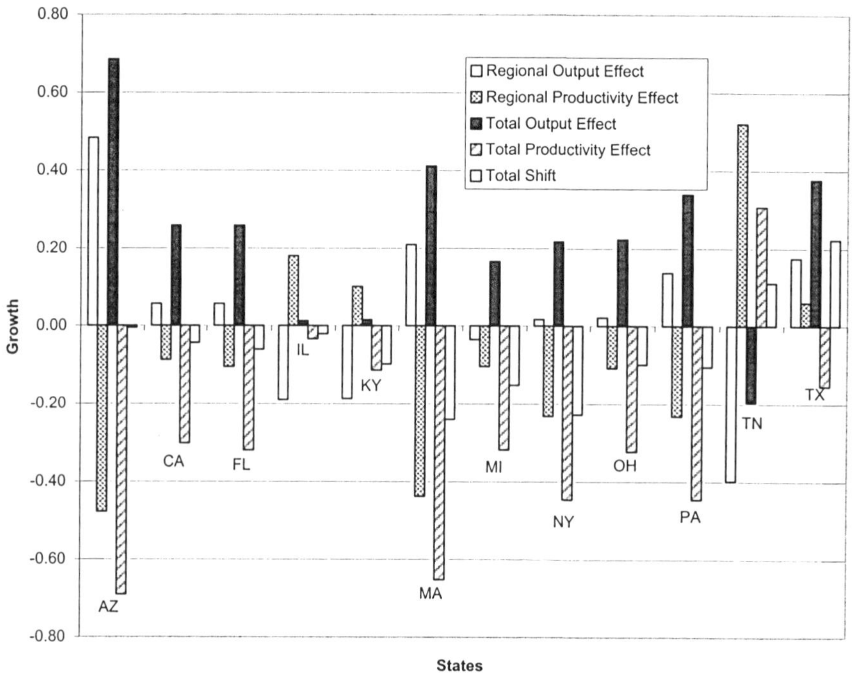

Figure 5.5 Regional advantages in the electric & electronic sector, 1987–1994

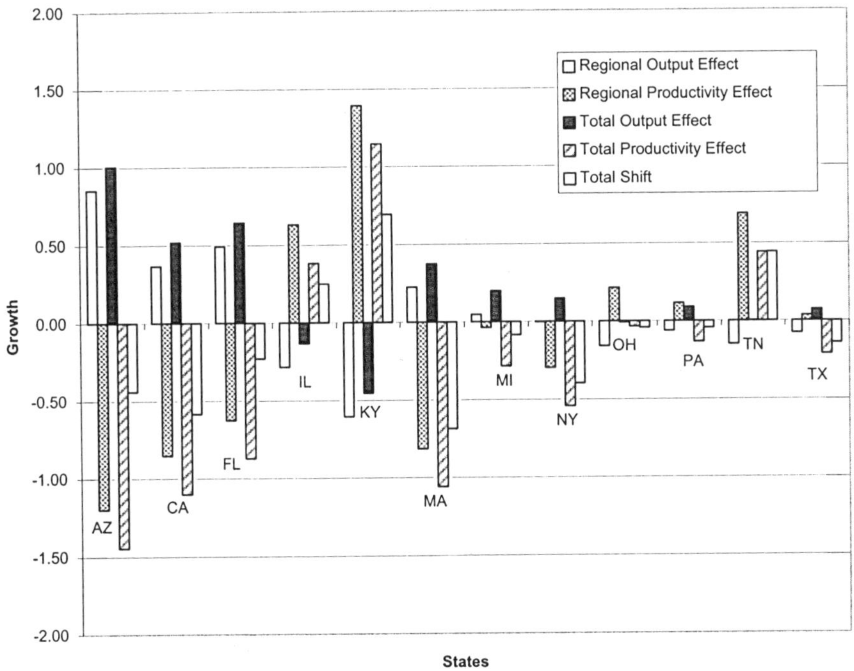

Figure 5.6 Regional advantages in the transportation equipment sector, 1987–1994

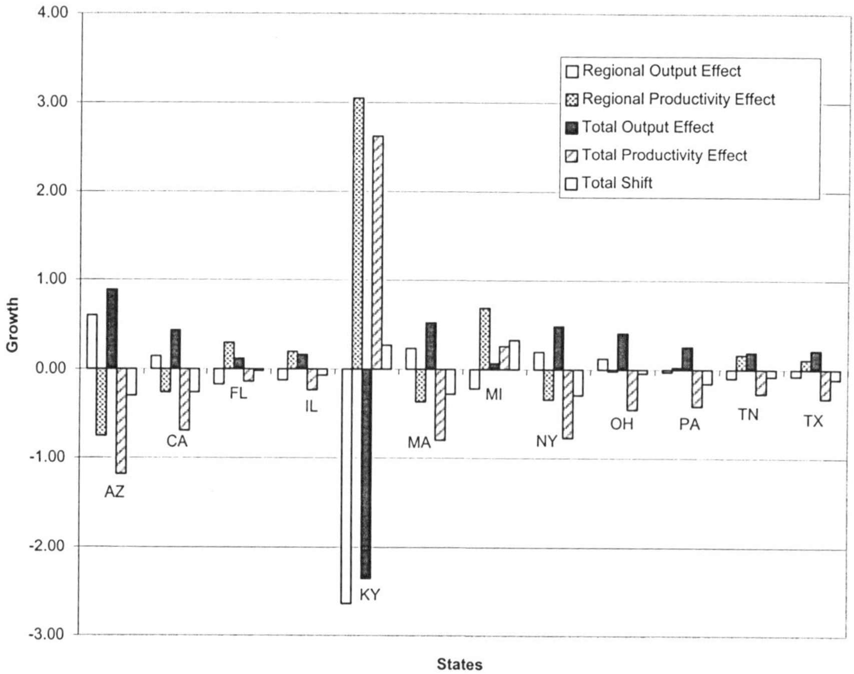

Figure 5.7 Regional advantages in the instrument and related products sector, 1987–1994

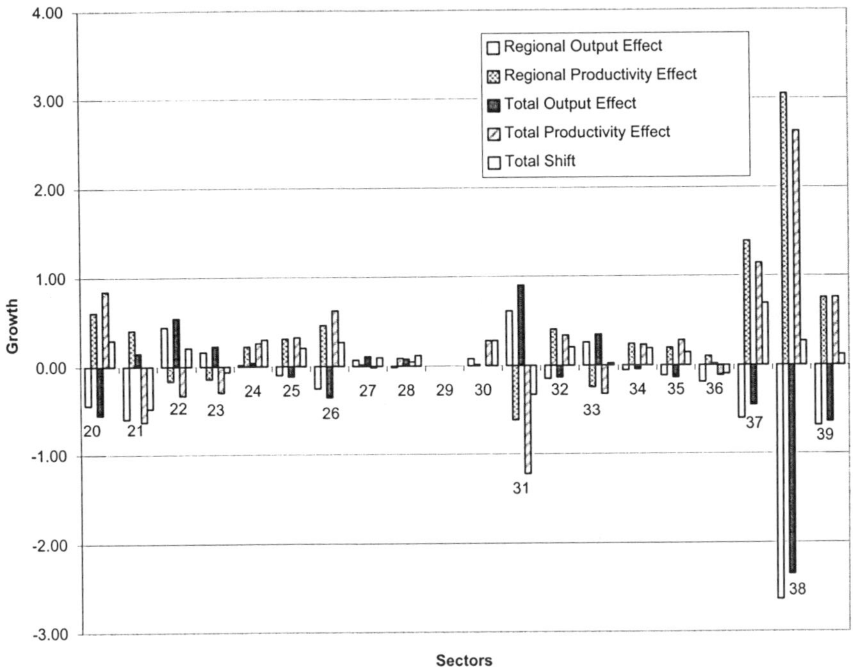

Figure 5.8 Regional advantages and sources of employment change in Kentucky, 1987–1994

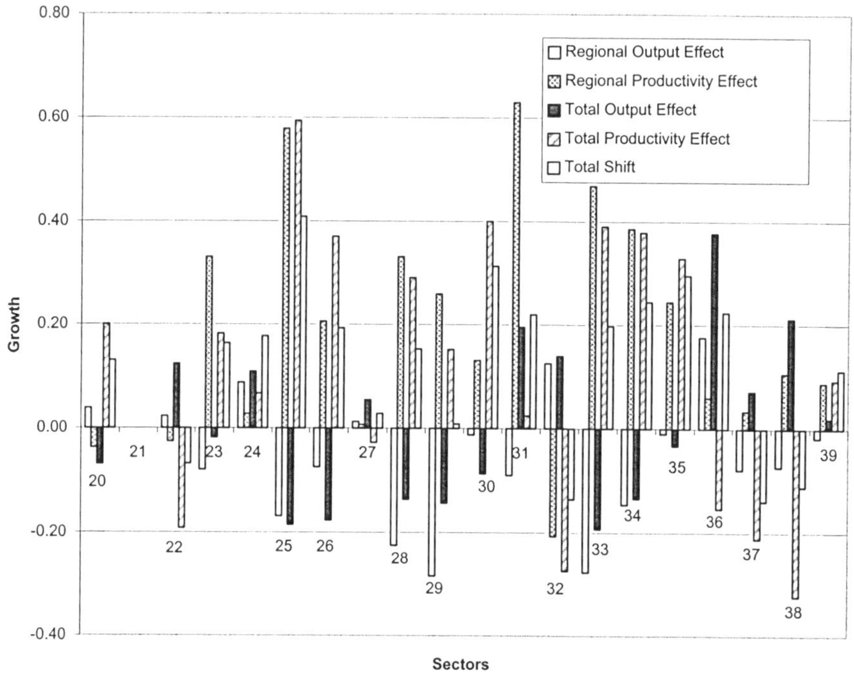

Figure 5.9 Regional advantages and sources of employment change in Texas, 1987–1994

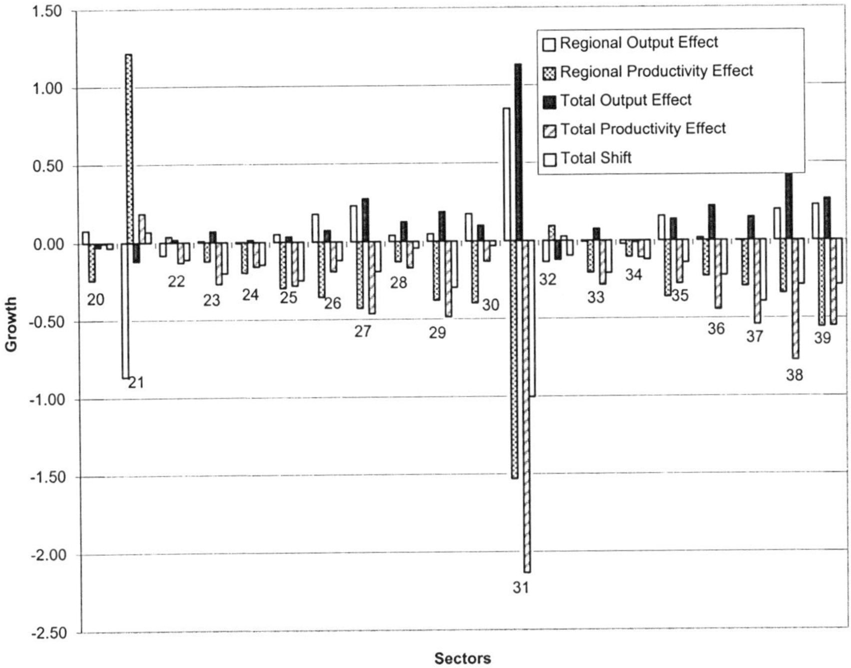

Figure 5.10 Regional advantages and sources of employment change in New York, 1987–1994

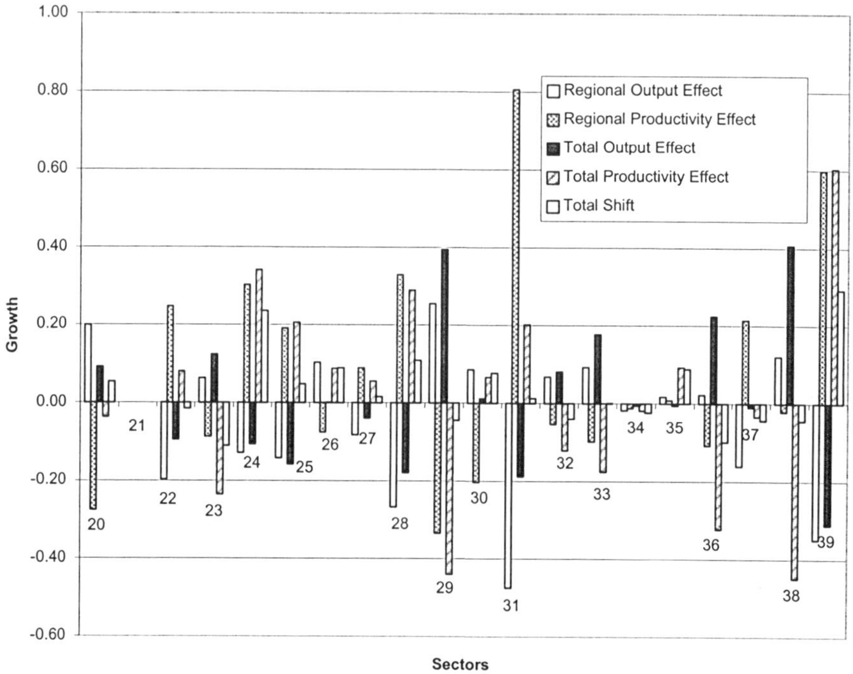

Figure 5.11 Regional advantages and sources of employment change in Ohio, 1987–1994

Conclusion

This chapter focused on the development of a new shift-share model in the light of earlier productivity and shift-share studies, and illustrated its application. The empirical analysis demonstrated that the new model is in fact useful and contributes to the general knowledge of regional modeling. Inclusion of all contributing factors to productivity and hence employment change provides a deeper understanding of the regional economy and employment change.

The findings from the empirical analysis suggest that manufacturing employment growth during the study period was basically driven by regional dynamics. National trends had little impact on employment change with the exception of a few sectors in a few states. Productivity played a significant role in manufacturing employment change. These findings give some support to the idea that the old manufacturing belt began recovering in this period (Federal Reserve Bank of Chicago, 1996).

The findings of this study may seem controversial in the way that productivity is presented as it is responsible for significant employment decline. Recall, however, that this analysis examined only production workers not total manufacturing employment. Non-manufacturing sectors were not investigated, either. Therefore, job expansion resulting from productivity improvements are not captured economy wide. Future research needs to focus on these wider issues.

References

Aaberg, Y. (1973), 'Regional Productivity Differences in Swedish Manufacturing', *Regional and Urban Economics*, vol. 3, pp. 131–56.

Aigner, D.J., Lovell, C.A.K. and Schmidt, P. (1977), 'Formulation and Estimation of Stochastic Frontier Production Function Models', *Journal of Econometrics*, vol.6, pp. 21–37.

Anderson, W. P. (1990), 'Labour Productivity Growth in Canadian Manufacturing: A Regional Analysis', *Environment and Planning A*, vol. 22, pp. 309–20.

van Ark, B. (1995), 'Manufacturing Prices, Productivity, and Labor Costs in Five Economies', *Monthly Labor Review*, July, pp. 56–72.

Bartik, T.J. (1994), 'Better Evaluation is Needed for Economic Development Programs to Thrive', *Economic Development Quarterly*, vol. 8. pp. 99–106.

Baumol, W.J., Blackman, S.A.B. and Wolff, E.N. (1989), *Productivity and American Leadership*, The MIT Press, Cambridge, MA.

Beeson, P. (1987), 'Total Factor Productivity Growth and Agglomeration Economies in Manufacturing 1959–73', *Journal of Regional Science*, vol. 27, pp. 183–99.

Beeson, P. and Husted, S. (1989), 'Patterns and Determinants of Productive Efficiency in State Manufacturing', *Journal of Regional Science*, vol. 29, pp. 15–28.

Bjurek, H., Hjalmarson, L. and Forsund, F.R. (1990), 'Deterministic Parametric and Nonparametric Estimation of Efficiency in Service Production: A Comparison', *Journal of Econometrics*, vol. 46, pp. 213–27.

Bronfenbrenner, M. (1985), 'Japanese Productivity Experience', in W.J. Baumol and K. McLennan (eds), *Productivity Growth and U.S. Competitiveness*, Oxford University Press, New York.

Camagni, R. (1995), 'The Concept of Innovative Milieu and Its Relevance for Public Policies in European Lagging Regions', *Papers in Regional Science*, vol. 74, pp. 317–40.

Christensen, L.R., Jorgenson, D.W. and Lau, L.J. (1973), 'Transcendental Logarithmic Production Frontiers', *Review of Economics and Statistics*, vol. 55, pp. 28–45.

Cornwell, C.P., Schmidt, P and Sickles, R.C. (1990), 'Production Frontiers with Cross-Sectional and Time Series Variation in Efficiency Levels', *Journal of Econometrics*, vol. 46, pp. 185–200.

Denison, E.F. (1962), *Soures of Economic Growth in the United States and the Alternative Before Us*, Committee for Economic Development, New York.

Dollar, D. and Wolff, E.N. (1993), *Competitiveness, Convergence, and International Specialization*, The MIT Press, Cambridge, MA.

Dunn, E.S. (1960), 'A Statistical and Analytical Technique for Regional Analysis', *Papers of the Regional Science Association*, vol. 6, pp. 97–112.

Erickson, R.A. (1994), 'Technology, Industrial Restructuring and Regional Development', *Growth and Change*, vol. 25, pp. 353–79.

Federal Reserve Bank of Chicago (1996), *Assessing the Midwest Economy*, No. 2, Chicago.

Feldman, M.D. and Florida, R. (1994), 'The Geographical Sources of Innovation: Technological infrastructure and Product Innovations in the US', *Annals of the A.A.G*, September.

Fogarty, M.S. and Garofalo, G.A. (1988), 'Urban Spatial Structure and Productivity Growth in the Manufactruing Sector of Cities', *Journal of Urban Economics*, vol. 23, pp. 60–70.

Garofalo, G.A. and Malhotra, D.M. (1984), 'Input Substitution in the Manufacturing Sector During 1970s: A Regional Analysis', *Journal of Regional Science*, vol. 24, pp. 51–63.

Gerking, S. (1994), 'Measuring Productivity Growth in U.S. Regions: A Survey', *International Regional Science Review*, vol. 16, pp. 155–85.

Greene, W.H. (1980), 'Maximum Likelihood Estimation of Econometric Frontier Functions', *Journal of Econometrics*, vol. 13, pp. 27–56.

Greiner, M., Kask, C. and Sparks, C. (1995), 'Comparative Manufacturing Productivity and Unit Labor Costs', *Monthly Labor Review*, February, pp. 26–38.

Hansen, N. (1992), 'Competition, Trust and Reciprocity in the Development of Innovative Regional Milieu', *Papers in Regional Science*, vol. 71, pp. 95–105.

Haynes, K.E., Button, K.J., Nijkamp, P. and Qiangsheng, L. (1997), *Regional Dynamics II*, Edward Elgar, Cheltenham, UK.

Haynes, K.E. and Dinc, M. (1997), 'Productivity Change in Manufacturing Regions: A Multifactor / Shift-Share Approach', *Growth and Change*, vol. 28, Spring, pp. 150–70.

Haynes, K.E. and Dinc, M. (2000), 'Globalization and the Borderless Economy: Perspectives for the Twenty-first Century Regional Science', in H. Kohno, P. Nijkamp and J. Poot (eds), *Regional Cohesion and Competition in the Age of Globalization*, Edward Elgar, Cheltenham, UK, pp. 26–45.

Hulten, C.R. and Schwab, R.M. (1984), 'Regional Productivity Growth in U.S. Manufacturing: 1951–78', *The American Economic Review*, vol. 74, pp. 152–62.

Illeris, S. (1993), 'An Inductive Theory of Regional Development', *Papers in Regional Science*, vol. 72, pp. 113–34.

Isserman, A.M. (1994), 'State Economic Development Policy and Practice in the United States: A Survey Article', *International Regional Science Review*, vol. 16, pp. 49–100.

Jondrow, J., Lovell, C.A.K., Materow, I.S. and Schimidt, P. (1982), 'On the Estimation of Technical Efficiency in Stochastic Frontier Production Function Model', *Journal of Econometrics*, vol. 19, pp. 233–8.

Jorgenson, D.W. (1995), *Productivity, Volume 1: Postwar U.S. Economic Growth*, The MIT Press, Cambridge, MA.

Jorgenson, D.W. and Griliches, Z. (1972), 'The Explanation of Productivity Change', *Survey of Current Business*, May, pp. 2–36.

Jorgenson, D.W., Gollop, F. M. and Fraumeni, B.M. (1987), *Productivity and U.S. Economic Growth*, Harvard University Press, Cambridge, MA.

Kendrick, J.W. (1961), *Productivity Trends in the United States*, Princeton University Press, Princeton, NJ.

Kendrick, J.W. (1973), *Postwar Productivity Trends in the United States, 1948–1969*, National Bureau of Economic Research, New York.

Kendrick, J.W. (1983), *Inter-industry Differences in Productivity Growth*, American Enterprise Institute, Washington, DC.

Kendrick, J.W. (1984), *Improving Company Productivity*, The Johns Hopkins University Press, Baltimore, MD.

Kendrick, J.W. and Grossman, E.S. (1980), *Productivity in the United States*, The Johns Hopkins University Press, Baltimore, MD.

Krugman, P. (1991), *The Age of Diminished Expectations*, The MIT Press, Cambridge, MA.

Krugman, P. (1994), 'Competitiveness: A Dangerous Obsession', *Foreign Affairs*, March/April, pp. 28–44.

Luttwak, E.N. (1993), *The Endangered American Dream*, Simon and Schuster, New York.

Magaziner, I.C. and Patinkin, M. (1990), *The Silent War: Inside the Global Business Battles Shaping America's Future*, Vintage Books, New York.

Moomaw, R.L. (1983a), 'Nonlabor Income Measures of Capital Intensity Versus Capital Stock Measures in Estimating the Determinants of Regional Labor Productivity Differentials: The Manufacturing Sector', *Annals of Regional Science*, vol. 17, pp. 79–93.

Moomaw, R.L. (1983b), 'Spatial Productivity Variations in Manufacturing: A Critical Survey of Cross-Sectional Analysis', *International Regional Science Review*, vol. 8, pp. 1–22.

Moomaw, R.L. and Williams, M. (1991), 'Total Factor Productivity Growth in Manufacturing: Further Evidence from the States', *Journal of Regional Science*, vol. 31, pp. 17–34.

Mullen, J. and Williams, M. (1987), 'Technical Progress in Urban Manufacturing: North-South Comparisons', *Journal of Urban Economics*, vol. 21, pp. 194–208.

Mullen, J. and Williams, M. (1990), 'Explaining Total Factor Productivity Differentials in Urban Manufacturing', *Journal of Urban Economics*, vol. 28, pp. 103–23.

National Academy of Science (1979), *Measurement and Interpretation of Productivity*, Washington, DC.

Norsworthy, J.R. and Jang, S.L. (1992), *Empirical Measurement and Analysis of Productivity and Technological Change*, North-Holland, Amsterdam.

Norsworthy, J.R. and Malmquist, D.H. (1985), 'Recent Productivity Growth in Japanese and U.S. Manufacturing', in W.J. Baumol and K. McLennan (eds), *Productivity Growth and U.S. Competitiveness*, Oxford University Press, New York.

Ohmae, K. (1993), 'The Rise of the Region State', *Foreign Affairs*, Spring, pp. 78–87.

Porter, M. (1990), *The Competitive Advantages of Nations*, Free Press, New York.

Rigby, D.L. and Anderson, W.P. (1993), 'Employment Change, Growth and Productivity in Canadian Manufacturing: an Extension and Application of Shift-Share Analysis', *Canadian Journal of Regional Science*, vol. XVI, pp. 69–88.

Rivlin, A.M. (1992), *Reviewing the American Dream*, The Brookings Institution, Washington, DC.

Sabel, C. (1987), 'The Reemergence of Regional Economies', Detroit (Mimeograph).

Sato, B. (1970), 'The Estimation of Biased Technical Progress and the Production Function', *International Economic Review*, vol. 11, pp. 179–208.

Schmidt, P. (1985), 'Production Frontier Functions', *Econometric Reviews*, vol. 4, pp. 289–328.

Scott, A.J. (1994), 'The Geographical Foundations of Industrial Performance', UCLA School of Public Policy, (Mimeograph).

Scott, A.J. and Storper, M. (1992), 'Industrialization and Regional Development', in A.J. Scott and M. Storper (eds), *Pathways to Industrialization and Regional Development*, Routledge, NY, pp. 3–17.

Solow, R.M. (1957), 'Technical Change and the Aggregate Production Function', *The Review of Economics and Statistics*, vol. 39, pp. 312–20.

Sveikauskas, L.A. (1975), 'The Productivity of Cities', *Quarterly Journal of Economics*, vol. 89, pp. 392–413.

Thurow, L. (1992), *Head to Head*, Morrow, New York.

Tyson, L.D. (1992), *Who's Bashing Whom*, Institute for International Economics, Washington, DC.

Williams, M. and Moomaw, R.L. (1989), 'Capital and Labor Efficiencies: A Regional Analysis', *Urban Studies*, vol. 26, pp. 573–85.

Wolff, E.N. (1985), 'The Magnitude and Causes of the Recent Productivity Slowdown in the United States: A Survey of Recent Studies', in W.J. Baumol and K. McLennan (eds), *Productivity Growth and U.S. Competitiveness*, Oxford University Press, New York.

Chapter 6

'Place' as 'Network': Applications of Network Theory to Local Communities

Roger E. Bolton

Introduction

This chapter[1] is a tentative exploration of the relevance of the theory of networks to local planning and other actions of local and regional governments. What stimulates me to think on these lines is a feeling that the theory might shed light on the phenomenon of a 'sense of place', which I have written about in earlier papers. I believe that we should be able to model a local community that has a sense of place as a network of certain kinds of social interactions. I also believe that one way to think about local and regional planning, very broadly conceived, is as government action to facilitate a social network so that it will create network benefits that accrue to many members of the community, and also to create incentives for residents to 'remain connected' and to contribute socially valuable interactions, rather than to exit and cease interactions.

Therefore, I shall use a bit of space at the beginning of this chapter to review the basic notion of a sense of place. The rest of the chapter has the following sections: general remarks on networks and their characteristics; comments on the value of three bodies of previous literature on networks and their effects; a summary of the theory of 'adoption externalities' from the economics literature on networks; remarks on the process of internalizing network externalities; comparison of adoption externalities to the 'tragedy of the commons' and introduction of a related concept, the 'tragedy of exit'; a suggestion that Albert Hirschman's analysis of 'exit, voice, and loyalty' can be related to social networks; and, in closing, some caveats on the sense of place that are suggested by consideration of networks.

Introduction to 'Sense of Place'

In various papers (Bolton 1989, 1992, 1995a; Bolton and Jensen 1995), I have offered an economic interpretation of a *sense of place*, a concept widely used by geographers, planners, and journalists, but relatively little by economists.

The sense of place 'refers to a complex of intangible characteristics of place that make it attractive to actual and potential residents and influence their behavior in observable ways' (Bolton, 1992, p. 193). An essential part of the sense of place is landscape and appreciation of it; an essential part of it is history and an appreciation of it; but another essential part of it is a sense of community, or shared reciprocal obligations, and trust. As part of this, there are restraints on self-interest and on free riding. The sense of community has been neglected by regional and urban analysts, relative to environmental and cultural amenities and to the fiscal packages of taxes and public expenditures that Charles Tiebout talked about.[2]

Social scientists who have had related ideas have written about 'social capital' or used similar terms, and in doing so have referred explicitly to social networks. The Harvard political scientist Robert D. Putnam (1993a, b, 1995a, b, c, 1996) is far and away the best known user of the term, but he stresses that he is following the eminent American sociologist James Coleman, who also explicitly used the phrase 'social capital' (1988a, 1990).[3] For Coleman, social capital 'inheres in the structure of relations between persons and among persons' and 'is lodged neither in individuals nor in physical implements of production' is not lodged in individuals or in physical objects (1990, p. 302). In generates trust, creates and enforces norms. It is a set of mutual obligations. It depends on the logistics of social contacts and depends on stability of contacts – individual mobility can be destructive of social capital. Finally, it is affected by ideology – a sometimes troubling aspect. I believe that a sense of place is a form of social capital in Coleman's sense, and I used the term 'social capital' explicitly in Bolton (1992, p. 192). Below I will return to some of the aspects of social capital just mentioned. Coleman referred to network analogies explicitly and so do some other writers who have used the concept of social capital.

In my own mind, the sense of place certainly is a form of social capital, but one formed and enjoyed in the context of a particular place, in a particular geographical, historical, and cultural setting. It is an intangible, location-specific asset: it does indeed have some of the characteristics of *capital.* 'Capital' immediately suggests two things, at least: *investment* and *returns.* In previous papers I have discussed the kinds of investment that help create and maintain a sense of place and the returns people enjoy when there is a strong sense of place. I will not repeat that discussion here, except occasionally to refer to it when necessary to amplify the present discussion of networks.

Many economists, on hearing mention of a sense or place or similar intangible concepts, say, 'Sure, there is something in that idea. But what is the theory? How can you measure it?'. It reminds me that the economist Stephen Goldfield once said an economist is someone who sees something working in practice and asks if it can work in principle. In fact, there are important pieces of economic theory that are relevant and that I have discussed in earlier papers: public goods; household production and consumer demand theory; option value; agglomeration. The other question, 'Can you measure it?' is harder, but I have suggested some research strategies I consider appropriate (Bolton, 1992, 1995a). I note that some other economists have begun to use the concept of social capital. A notable example is Gary Becker, who refers to social capital as a force in shaping individuals' preferences (Becker, 1996, ch. 1; see extended discussion in Bolton, 1997).

Networks

A network is a collection of objects or 'nodes' connected in some way or other by explicit links. The objects may be computers, or production/transportation facilities, or people, and the links may be physical connections – like electronic connections or transportation lines – or nonphysical connections such as face-to-face contacts in conversations. The network creates a situation in which the change in the state of an object can affect the state of other objects in the network, that is, the network creates interdependence. If the objects are people, the actions of one person have the potential to affect the welfare of other persons in the group.

A variety of terms are available for defining things further. For simplicity, I will follow closely the terminology of Liebowitz and Margolis (1994), who present some of the essential economic ideas about networks and who in addition have the great merit of warning against overselling the applicability of 'network benefits.' (Katz and Shapiro, 1985, 1994) are also valuable sources and go more deeply into business firms' strategies in the presence of network externalities, which strategies may be suggestive for analyzing local governments' actions resembling partial 'ownership' of the social network. Capello (1995) is useful although focused on telecommunications networks and on networks of firms as factors in regional economic development.

Liebowitz and Margolis have essentially a two by two classification scheme, which in turn is based partly on distinctions made in Katz and Shapiro (1985). A network may be either *literal* or *metaphorical*, and the effects of one user on another may be either *direct* or *indirect*. For simplicity, I will move immediately to a discussion in which the 'objects' are people and the 'flows' between people are conversation, argument, information, or similar intangibles.

A *direct* network is one in which reciprocal contacts – interaction – between two people are essential to produce the interdependence. A telephone network or a seminar are examples; a conference call is also an example, because 'interaction' includes interaction at a distance and is not limited to face-to-face contacts in spatial proximity. An *indirect* network is one in which there is interdependence, but not reciprocal contacts.

An example suggested by Katz and Shapiro and also by Liebowitz and Margolis is one where the existence of many buyers of some durable consumer good increases the viability of repair businesses. Thus, we might imagine that owners of some exotic sports car, the *Leopard*, will benefit if their numbers increase, expanding the repair market and allowing more repair shops of efficient scale to survive. The owners of *Leopards* need not interact with each other on a regular basis or even know who each other are. Their interdependence comes not from contact with each other, but from common dependence on one or a few central nodes in their network. The only interaction is between each car owner and the central node.

A *literal* network is one where the links are physical capital and the flows are limited to flows along those links; again a telephone or transportation or computer network comes to mind. A *metaphorical* network is one where there are not physical capital links connecting participants to each other, although of course some persons will use significant amounts of real capital in their own participation. There are, however, critical common interests and activities. A faculty seminar, a collection of people who speak the same language, a group of people who exchange stories of the past glories of a place – these may well be metaphorical. Obviously I have metaphorical networks in mind when talking about a sense of place. The geographer Melvin Webber undoubtedly also had metaphorical networks in mind in coining the phrase 'community without propinquity' (1963). Many remember Webber's famous phrase, although fewer remember or know that he actually discussed literal network connections as much or more than metaphorical ones. Many people are of course simultaneously in both literal and metaphorical networks, and they may switch rapidly back and forth between literal and metaphorical connections.

Metaphorical networks are critical mental constructs in thinking about the sense of place in a large region as an agglomeration of senses of place in smaller localities (Bolton, 1992, p. 194). Each locality is in some sense a metaphorical network, but there is also a larger metaphorical network of those smaller networks, or an agglomeration of agglomerations. Even though there are not *frequent* interactions across the boundaries of the smaller networks, nevertheless there are the critical commonalities that metaphorical networks depend upon, including of course some *minimal* amount of interaction.

The distinction between literal and metaphorical admittedly is imprecise. A faculty seminar usually meets in a room in a building, or on a suitably developed patch of grass, perhaps, thus requiring some real capital, yet it seems useful to call it metaphorical or at least to think of it as different from the most obvious literal networks.

There are probably not very interesting or useful examples of networks that are both indirect and literal. They would have physical capital links connecting persons but not require interaction among the persons to produce network benefits. It is true that in an indirect network there must be a physical connection between each participant and the central node – one thinks again of the sports car owners, who need to drive or be pulled by towtrucks on streets to the garage. However, there need not be any physical links that have the primary purpose of connecting participants *with each other*.

One caution on metaphorical indirect networks: an expansion of the network may create benefits for some members, but do so wholly or partly at the expense of others so that the whole group collectively does not benefit (Liebowitz and Margolis, 1994, p. 137). For example, assume that initially only a few people own *Leopards*, and there is monopoly in repairing them. If then more people buy *Leopards*, the market will expand and entry of new firms will drive down the price of repairs.

Assume this happens not by reducing repairers' production costs but rather by eroding the original monopoly's profit margin. The result is an efficient expansion of the market but also a transfer of rents from repairers to car owners. The transfer clearly benefited the car owners, but it was not an increase in efficiency. One needs to be careful not to see an efficiency gain when in fact there is none. It is worth noting that in this example even the increase in efficiency did not result from cost reductions, but rather by reducing a preexisting market imperfection, and thus is not quite the same thing as we usually think of when considering network effects.

Three Literatures

A priori, one expects three strands of literature on networks to be helpful in modeling places as networks. First, the literature from engineering and transportation analysis, and graph theory, on flows through literal networks of physical capital. Second, the literature from economics on 'adoption externality', which occurs when adding a participant to a network not only creates value for the marginal participant but also adds value to other participants (that is, is not merely an internal transfer). The marginal benefit to all participants collectively exceeds the marginal benefit to the new participant alone, thus marginal *social* benefit exceeds marginal *private* benefit. Third, the literature from sociology on 'social relations' among people connected in various ways.

At first glance, the first type of literature, on physical link networks, may seem relevant to transportation and communications planning but not to the more metaphorical networks I have in mind when talking about a sense of place (a standard elementary reference in this literature is Bradley, 1977, ch. 8 and Appendix C; another text reference is Hillier and Lieberman, 1986, ch. 10; and two recent examples are Casti, 1995 and Johnson, 1995). However, in fact this literature is very useful in forcing us to think about heterogeneity of nodes and links, about bottlenecks, missing links, roundabout connections, etc. Indeed, I am struck by how much the second literature, on adoption externality, tends to gloss over such complications.

Too often it is limited to analysis of networks of participants assumed to be homogeneous in certain ways, so that what is important is the sheer number of participants but not any other characteristics of them or of the links. One explanation is that models with only one variable – N, the number of participants, is easily manipulated mathematically. (In some models participants do have different willingness to pay for connection to a network of size N, but the willingness to pay is not modeled explicitly as a function of the *other participants they interact with or characteristics of the links with them*; see Katz and Shapiro, 1985; Economides and Himmelberg, 1995.)

As I argue below, any application of adoption externality to social networks must recognize the highly heterogeneous nature of participants and the links between them. Not every participant is a 'node' exactly like all other 'nodes.' The literature on physical path networks recognizes heterogeneity from the very start and thus is a useful corrective. Nodes with large or small capacities for interaction, links with narrow bridges and one-way restrictions – these physical features have analogues in social networks.

The third body of literature, from sociology, seems very promising indeed. Two especially valuable ideas are the role of common language in facilitating network interactions and the identification of 'leaders' as important 'nodes'. Unfortunately, incorporation of insights from this literature must await another paper. In the present chapter, then, I will concentrate primarily on the application of the theory of adoption externalities, taking account of some insights from models of literal networks.

Adoption Externality

There are many ways to introduce and elaborate adoption externality: numerical examples, graphical analysis, or algebra and calculus. I will use all of these, and shall start with a simple numerical example. Table 6.1 is a simple example of the benefits participants get from a network. The network is a direct one, either literal or metaphorical:

Table 6.1 Benefits of a direct network

Person added	Added benefit to person	Added benefit to others	Total added to all	Total cumulative benefit
A	0	0	0	0
B	100	100	200	200
C	200	200	400	600
D	300	300	600	1200
E	100	60	160	1360
F	25	0	25	1385

The benefits are monetary equivalent values, per some time period – month or year, perhaps.

One person – A – does not make a network, so there is no benefit. When B is added, B and A interact with each other: B values her two-way contacts with A at 100 per period and A values the contacts at the same amount. The result is the second line of the table; note that the total added benefit from B's joining exceeds the benefit to her alone. Now assume that when C joins, there is again a 100 value per potential contact. C can contact two persons, A and B, so his benefit is 200. A gets added value of 100 from the new ability to interact with C, and the same for B, so we have a marginal external benefit of 200. Again, total benefit to all persons rises by more than the value to the marginal joiner alone, specifically by 400 compared to 200. It is obvious that there is an *agglomeration* effect here.

If D is added, and again the valuation is 100 per potential contact, then we have the fourth line: D can contact three persons, A and B and C, so the benefit to D is 300. Each of the others gets 100, so we have increase in total benefit = 600.

Under these oversimplified assumptions, we have the following pattern for variation of N between 1 and 4:

Marginal Private Benefit of Nth member =
a(N-1) = aN - a for N = 1, 2, 3, ...

where N = number of participants, and the value of each potential contact is constant at a. We also have:

Average Benefit $= a(N\text{-}1) = aN - a$
Total Benefit $= TB_N = N$ **times average** $= Na(N\text{-}1) = aN^2 - aN$
Marginal Social Benefit of Nth member $= TB_N - TB_{N-1} = 2a(N\text{-}1)$

The key feature of this example is that marginal social benefit exceeds marginal private benefit (it is being twice as large is purely a function of the 'linear' example, with identical members and constant marginal private benefit).

If we simplify by making the participation a continuous variable, and let the benefit function be more general, but keep the assumption that all participants have the same benefit function, then we have:

Marginal Private Benefit of Nth unit $= F(N)$
Average Benefit $= F(N)$
Total Benefit $= TB_N = NF(N)$
Marginal Social Benefit $= dTB_N/dN = F(N) + N(\partial F/\partial N)$
$>$ **Marginal Private Benefit**

Again, the key feature is that marginal social benefit exceeds marginal private benefit.

Figure 6.1 shows marginal private benefit and marginal social benefit for the case of identical participants and a constant marginal benefit function (a similar diagram is in Liebowitz and Margolis, 1994, p. 142 and of course in many other standard references on networks).

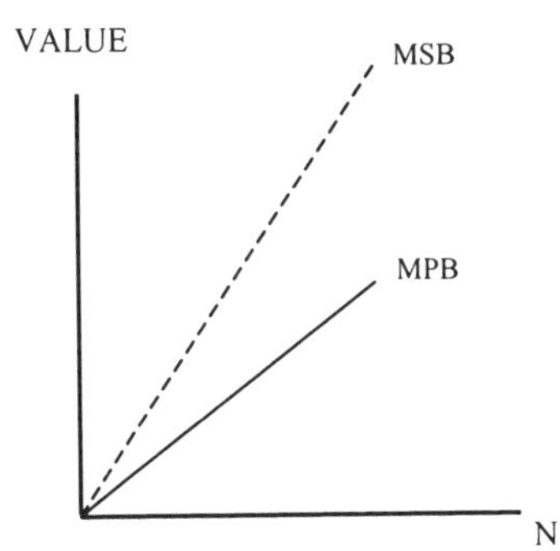

Figure 6.1 Marginal private and social benefit

But wait. Such a good thing cannot go on forever. Return to the numerical example (Table 6.1). When E joins up, assume he does not value the network much; his benefit is only 25 per connection, and each other person values communication with him at only 15. And when F is added, his private benefit is only 5 per contact, *and no other person values the contact with him at all.* Total benefit no longer rises dramatically.

If inframarginal participants collectively get any positive added benefit, as happens up through the joining of E, then marginal social benefit exceeds marginal private benefit. That is the 'adoption externality'. But the externality is not necessarily large. Furthermore, if not all previous participants get a positive addition, then the adoption externality might not even be positive. In our example, there is no adoption externality of F's decision to join: after E the externality is no longer 'marginal'. The network is already large enough that additions benefit only the new joiner. More generally, it is only natural that once a network gets large, there are a lot of zeroes, and even some negatives, for the benefits to people already in. Any one who belongs to an electronic discussion list recognizes that. The heterogeneity of the members is a crucial complication.

Thus the specification of the private benefits function is crucial in any realistic model, and we expect it to depend on characteristics of all the users and on the precise patterns of contacts and interactions among them. And we expect it to depend on the spatial context – on people's attitudes about the place where the interactions occur. These attitudes are part and parcel of what we might call the 'sense of place'. We can incorporate the sense of place as part of the specification of a network model, and the heterogeneity of the nodes and links is an important aspect of the specification. To repeat, this is an insight from the literature on physical link networks that is often missed by economists specifying network externality models.

A graphical representation is in Figure 6.2. For simplicity, it assumes that 'participation' is a continuous variable and that all persons are alike. Marginal private benefit rises steadily up to N = D, as in the upper part of Table 6.1, but after N = D the marginal private benefit and the adoption externality decline in a way similar to the pattern in the lower lines of the table. Beyond N = E, the inframarginal participants receive no marginal benefits and the externality is no longer 'marginal'.

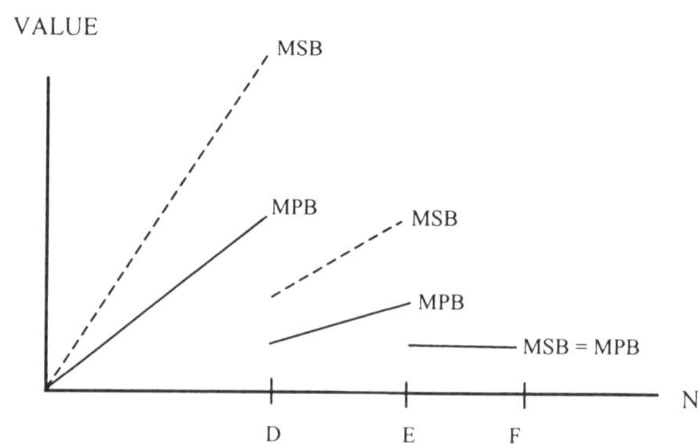

Figure 6.2 Network externality model

One might describe the pattern of interactions by various matrices, with each row and column representing a person and with each element capturing some dimension of their interactions. An *adjacency matrix*, for example, has as each element a_{ij} either a one, if persons *i* and *j* have interaction or are connected in some way, or a zero, if not (Casti, 1995, p. 6; Coleman, 1964, pp. 444–55). A more complicated matrix would have a continuously varying index of interaction or connection as each element. Other matrices may describe the distance – social distance as well as physical distance – between persons. These sorts of matrices may be useful ways to capture the structure of social relations, but it remains to be seen whether one can establish empirical regularities between particular matrix patterns and certain kinds of economic behavior, which is what would be necessary to relate matrix patterns to a sense of community or a sense of place. This is an important area of future research.

However, one can get some insights immediately from economics, based on *substitutability*. Assume a network already has a substantial number of participants who are broadly similar in various ways. Persons *i* and *j* are in the network. The value of adding new participant *k* is limited, because for both *i* and *j* their interaction with each other is substitutable for contact with *k*. Each already has access to a satisfactory range of personalities. If *j* leaves and *k* replaces him, then *i* would not lose much, except in the case where duration of interaction or other special feature has created a special attachment between *i* and *j*.

But surely this case – of special attachment – is a common one, and an important aspect of research is to discover geographical and historical settings that foster such special attachments. *Special attachments are obvious analogues to high capacity links in a physical link network.* Special attachments are especially prevalent in families, but they are present even in communities defined politically or geographically. An adjacency or connectivity matrix or similar matrix must reflect both high and low substitutability, wherever each is present. Not only are such matrices difficult to construct, they are inherently dynamic and not static.

What if there are not special attachments between *i* and *j*, and the community enlarges? The value of *i* and *j* to each other may well change as the size of the whole matrix enlarges, if the new members are substitutable for old ones. In other words, when the whole matrix is expanded by adding new rows and columns, the 'old' regions of the matrix also change.

Surely comments such as these have been made before, but I believe they have not received sufficient attention, either in the literature on applications of networks, especially metaphorical ones, or in the literature on places in economics and geographical and planning. The concept of adoption externality, enriched by an appreciation of the heterogeneity of members in a community, offers promise of helping us understand the differences between places, and also understand the desire of government officials and planners to maintain population when there is job loss. Job loss raises the threat of moving in reverse from that described in the example – moving up in Table 6.1 rather than down. These network effects augment other motivations to maintain population, such as the desire to avoid losing tax base and the labor pool that produces economies of agglomeration in producing market goods and services.

Internalizing Externalities

Let me now turn to the optimal scale of the network. It is the scale at which social marginal benefit equals social marginal cost of providing the network. The notion of the cost of providing a network is itself a complicated subject, especially for nonliteral networks, which I cannot go into here. But assuming we can specify it, the optimal scale is N^* in Figure 6.3, which is drawn for a situation where there are still marginal externalities at the optimal scale. If a single entity owns the network and prices it in a nondiscriminatory way, this owner can attain the optimal scale by charging a price, P^*, and accepting N^* members (Liebowitz and Margolis, 1994, pp. 141–2, discuss this rule but only for the simpler 'linear' case described in Figure 6.1). Figure 6.3 shows a case where MPB is still rising at N^*, so that the owner must ration membership to be no more than N^*. The key result here is that the optimal price is *below social marginal cost.* In Figure 6.3 average cost is increasing at the optimal scale, to highlight that pricing below social marginal cost is not required by economies of scale but by a fundamentally different condition, namely adoption externalities.

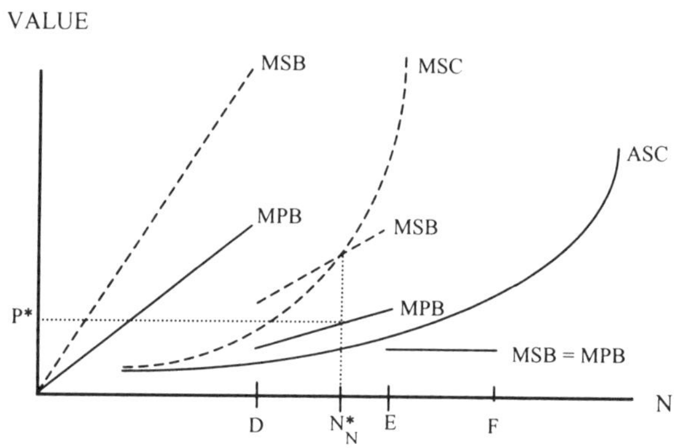

Figure 6.3 Internalizing externalities

While the single network owner can achieve the optimal scale, it is another, separate question whether the implied price will raise enough revenue to cover total cost. One must know the average cost curve to determine that. In Figure 6.3, revenues are sufficient to cover cost, but optimum pricing may of course be greatly complicated if a nondiscriminatory price were to imply a loss. Subsidies, multipart pricing schemes, and price discrimination become relevant.

The theory of the single network owner is a prominent part of the economics literature on literal networks, such as in telecommunications, computer networks, and transportation. Indeed a major concern of that literature is the comparison of monopoly and competitive provision of literal networks (for some examples, see Katz and Shapiro, 1985, 1994; Economides and Himmelberg, 1995). In applications to urban and regional planning of metaphorical networks, the notion of a single owner is less relevant. I suggest it is useful, however, to model local governments as *partially* 'owning' social networks, in the sense that they seek to internalize some of the adoption externalities. In doing this they act as investors, as bankers and subsidizers, and as entrepreneurs.

Governments make investments in 'network-augmenting capital', for example. Such capital includes all sorts of things ranging from community meeting facilities to ceremonial celebrations to historic preservation to institutions that improve the political process. Governments develop service pricing and subsidy schemes aimed at maintaining population size when it is threatened by external events. And of course they try to be selective and target desirable additions to the community. What is essential to understand is that this motive is over and above more traditional motives of expanding tax base and increasing employment opportunities, although certainly it may complement those traditional motives.

Furthermore, it is at least conceivable that one community is still below the optimal scale while another is past it, because the latter's network no longer has marginal externalities. In that case, even an action that increases one community's size at the expense of another's is efficiency-enhancing in the nation as a whole. It is a task of empirical research, albeit informed by value judgments on what network effects are genuine social benefits, to disentangle efficiency-enhancing effects from pure rent transfer effects.

An understanding of the details of the network will suggest policies to attract particular kinds of people. Prices and subsidies will be selective and targeted. Governments inevitably must act as entrepreneurs, making forecasts and taking risks. Even if a neutral observer finds the competitive process distasteful, and suspects it is nothing more than rent-seeking, at least he or she will understand better what is going on if he or she has the mental model of a network.

In addition to government efforts to internalize externalities there will be actions by private individuals or groups. Groups can establish their own organizations, informal or formal, to commit themselves to place-prosperity policies: staying connected, as it were, interacting frequently, and shouldering some of the costs of creating, augmenting, and maintaining the social network to encourage and facilitate other people staying connected. They establish their own norms and sanctions in order to encourage these activities. Some groups may be large enough to achieve economic benefits that cover their costs, the benefits external to each member of the group becoming benefits to other members and thus internal to the group; some shoulder costs out of altruistic motives. Even single individuals may engage in such action altruistically. All of these are alternatives to full or partial 'ownership'. Indeed, one might think of government action as simply a special case of this phenomenon of individuals and groups acting to internalize externalities of interaction or to provide network-augmenting capital.

We can get insights into such actions by noting certain behavior in private markets, where buyers of some goods cooperate with each other to augment network capital. The 'user group' is a prime example, and it is not only in computer software that one can find it. There is a literature in network economics about such buyer cooperation. We should expect to find something similar in the case of less tangible goods that are important in communities. Indeed, one indicator of a strong sense of place will be the frequency and strength of such behavior. Nonprofit organizations such as churches and charitable groups are critical actors in this regard. So are groups of school parents: in many places it is in schools where we observe much of the private and public action to augment the community's network. (Coleman's discussion of 'zeal' and the creation of sanctions in enforcement of norms is useful in thinking about the voluntary actions of individuals and groups suggestive; see Coleman, 1988b; 1990, pp. 273–8.)

Before leaving adoption externalities, it is useful to repeat that the network effect discussed here is different from the phenomenon of economies of scale in production. Under certain conditions, economies of scale provide another, separate rationale for preferring more to less population, at least up to a point, but it is a different rationale, and it is important not to confuse adoption externalities with economies of scale.

Economies of scale cause average cost of production to fall as output rises, and if average cost is falling then marginal cost is necessarily lower than average cost. If there is average cost pricing, as so often in the public sphere, then additional production will expand output, reduce average cost, and reduce price. But this could happen even if there were no interaction among members of the community – could happen, in other words, if the only network is an indirect one like the one of car owners referred to earlier. Furthermore, while the efficient exploitation of economies of scale requires reducing price to as near marginal cost as possible, it does not require or even permit pricing *below* marginal cost, as happens with adoption externalities. Nor are the specific details of contacts among users relevant, as they are in the network case – rather, only total output is relevant. If any subsidies are needed, they are rather different in kind from the ones that might be used in the network case, where governments are conscious of the value of adding particular kinds of people to the network and encouraging particular kinds of interactions.

Of course, in the real world the two phenomena – adoption externalities and economies of scale – may coexist, in the sense that there are economies of scale in certain goods and services that have adoption externalities or that augment the social network. Pricing then of course is much more complicated, and as noted earlier may require multipart pricing, discriminatory pricing, or subsidies.

The Tragedy of Exit

Return to the basics of network externalities for a moment. Liebowitz and Margolis refer to network externality as the 'tragedy of the commons turned on its head' (1994, p. 141). Remember that in the tragedy of the commons, people *over*use some common resource – pasture, fishery, a waste sink of limited assimilative capacity. Each user takes into account only his or her own costs and benefits, but in using the resource causes congestion of some sort that results in loss of value for all the other users – a negative externality.

In the case of the network, users *under*use it. Each participant increases benefit or reduces cost of other participants – at least up to a point – and that is a positive externality, but the added participant does not take the benefit into account.

An interesting angle is to move through Table 6.1 in the opposite direction – upward, with a loss of population. Then we are talking about marginal private losses and marginal social losses, and starting with the exit of D marginal social loss exceeds marginal private loss. A person leaving the network creates an externality. Coleman referred to that explicitly, with the example of a family moving away from a community (1990, p. 316). While my numerical example is terribly oversimplified, I think it conveys a basic truth. It helps us understand why local governments are so concerned when population size per se falls. As we have seen above, this concern for the social network is not simply a concern to achieve economies of scale in production of goods and services, and it is not simply an effort to protect rents.

If indeed the network externality is the 'tragedy of the commons turned on its head', one can say the deterioration of the social network is a tragedy – the *tragedy of exit* (Bolton, 1995b). Exit from the community, in self-interest shaped perhaps by desperation – exit compared to voice and loyalty, to use Hirschman's (1970) phrase – helps destroy the capital in the social network. The choice by community members between exit and voice, or continued participation, is fundamentally important in coping with stress, for exit destroys valuable social capital. In network terms, it is disconnect. Regional and urban economics needs more research on voice to balance its concerns with exit, i.e., migration out of the community.

Hirschman's Exit, Voice, and Loyalty[4]

Albert Hirschman's provocative distinctions between exit and voice (1970) are relevant to an understanding of networks and a sense of place. Hirschman did not refer to networks, but a reasonable interpretation of his analysis is that people's perceptions of the quality of the social network shape their choice between exit and voice – a choice people may feel compelled to make as a response to a decline in the quality of life in their community. 'Exit is outmigration; voice is persistence and participation in public discussion' (Bolton, 1999, p. 13).

Of course, the possibility of exit gives force to voice. Potential exit complements voice, actual exit competes with voice. 'The relative balance of these two responses in a declining community, or in any community undergoing major change, might be taken as an *a priori* indicator of the sense of place, and a suitable quantifiable proxy for the sense of place …' (*ibid.*). Local government will work to facilitate voice, at least for some citizens – again, we must recognize that governments know the importance of selective, targeted policies. This is a challenge: voice is essentially an '*art* constantly evolving in new directions' (Hirschman, 1970, p. 43, italics in original), and society must invent new institutions that increase the effectiveness of voice.

People have consumer surplus from membership in an organization. Hirschman noted that persons who have the most surplus are most likely to exercise voice, because they have the most to lose by either acquiescence or quick exit; they will continue to speak up and delay exit as long as much of their surplus is still intact (1970, pp. 49–50). The analogue to Hirschman's surplus is what I call 'place surplus' (Bolton, 1997, 1999). I suggest that a goal of local planning is to operate a network that generates large place surpluses for many citizens, thus creating incentive for voice and delaying exit. It is an empirical question whether local planners actually have that goal. Related empirical questions are whether individuals that have large place surpluses fill prominent roles – as nodes or links – in the social network, and whether planners design policies to create incentives for such individuals to serve those functions.

Hirschman also discusses loyalty, a 'special attachment' (Hirschman, 1970, p. 79). To translate Hirschman's theory of organizations into one of places, we must recognize that loyalty can reinforce place surplus as a force promoting voice rather than exit, and it can actually be a partial substitute for place surplus. If the surplus is large, the desire to avoid losing it is sufficient in itself, so loyalty is superfluous. But if surplus is small, then the cost of exit is low and the motivation for voice depends on loyalty (Hirschman, 1970, pp. 79–81; Bolton, 1999, p. 16). From my point of view the critical research question is how social networks build loyalty in their members.

Some Caveats in Closing

I mentioned many pages ago that a strong sense of place has its good points and its bad points. It may go along with insularity, discrimination against outsiders – who are too often minorities. While it may promote cooperation with one's fellow oldtimers, it inhibits cooperation with newcomers. This I think is in fact the main problem with sense of place, and an economist who finds value in a sense of place must maintain a balance between hard-headed analysis and soft-hearted concern, as Nancy Birdsall (1995) put it recently in a quite different context. We are reminded that Coleman recognized explicitly that social capital has an ideological component. 'A local population that has a strong sense of place may also have other preferences that are undesirable from the point of view of the larger society' (Bolton, 1992, pp. 197–8). These objectionable preferences may be ones that create negative elements in the interaction matrices referred to earlier.

One interesting angle here is the question whether a sense of place helps explain metropolitan fragmentation, and resistance of suburbs to racial and economic integration of housing and schools. These are problems discussed at length recently by Anthony Downs, just to name one example (1994). While we usually don't think of American suburbs as having a strong sense of place, this may be a too-hasty generalization, and thinking about social networks and sense of place in suburbs may help us understand the phenomena Downs is writing about and also help us to appreciate some of the bad things about a strong sense of place.

The task of both economic theory and economic policy analysis is to recognize the values of a sense of place but also to recognize the cost of achieving and maintaining them. Sense of place is not an unalloyed good. If I have overemphasized the values, it is only because I feel they have been neglected, especially by economists in their customary zeal to alert society to the cost of everything.

To repeat, we need both hard-headed analysis and soft-hearted concern.

Notes

1 I originally developed some parts of this chapter for one or more of the following unpublished papers and have borrowed from them here: Thirtieth Anniversary Lecture, Regional Research Institute, West Virginia University, Morgantown, October 1995; Charles M. Tiebout Memorial Lecture, Pacific Northwest Economic Conference, Portland, Oregon, May 1996; paper read at meeting of American Collegiate Schools of Planning, Toronto, July 1996; paper read at North American meeting of Regional Science Association International, Arlington, Virginia, November 1996; paper read at meeting of Pacific Regional Science Association, Royal Waikoloan Resort, Hawaii, February 1997; and paper read at meeting of Association of American Geographers, Fort Worth, Texas, March 1997. I thank the many colleagues who gave helpful comments on those occasions. I also thank participants in seminars at: Department of Economics, Williams College; Department of Applied Economics and Statistics, University of Nevada-Reno; Department of Geography, University of Washington. I am grateful to Andrew Isserman, John Mitchell, William Beyers, Douglass Shaw, and Alison O'Grady for special assistance.

2 There are exceptions of course. See for example Bartik (1991, pp. 65–66), and Bartik, Butler, and Liu (1992).

3 Coleman (1988a; 1990, ch. 12) credited Glenn Loury (1977, 1987) with earlier use of the term 'social capital'. Loury had in mind a relatively narrow range of applications, namely the effects of social relationships on the development of labor skills, thus the effects of social capital on investment in human capital. This narrow range of applications is, however, vitally important in many communities, and the effects of social capital on human capital are very important for economic development. Putnam, though indicating his greatest debt is to Coleman, has also cited Loury and has also noted that Jane Jacobs used the term 'social capital' as early as 1961 (Putnam 1995a, p. 78, citing Jacobs 1961, p. 138). In a classic paper (1985) Mark Granovetter referred to 'embeddedness', and both Coleman and Putnam rightly acknowledge Granovetter's influence as well. Until Putnam began to make the general concept and the specific term 'social capital' so well known, urban economists were probably more likely to cite Rothenberg (1967, pp. 147–8), who used the terms 'neighborhood adjustment capital' and 'neighborhood interaction capital', and who cited not only Jacobs but Schorr (1963, Chs. 1–2), or perhaps they would cite Dynarski (1981), who used the term 'value of community'.

4 This section is based on Bolton (1999).

References

Bartik, T.J. (1991), *Who Benefits From State and Local Economic Development Policies?*, W.E. Upjohn Institute for Employment Research, Kalamazoo, MI.

Bartik, T.J., Butler, J.S. and Liu, J-T. (1992), 'Maximum Score Estimates of the Determinants of Residential Mobility: Implications for the Value of Residential Attachment and Neighborhood Amenities', *Journal of Urban Economics*, vol. 32, September, pp. 233–56.

Becker, G. (1996), *Accounting for Tastes*, Harvard University Press, Cambridge, MA.

Birdsall, N. (1995), 'Hard-Headed Analysis and Soft-Hearted Concern', *Convocation Address on Development Economics*, September, Williams College, Williamstown, MA.

Bolton, R. (1989), 'An Economic Interpretation of a 'Sense of Place'', *Research Paper No. 130*, Department of Economics, Williams College, Williamstown, MA.

Bolton, R. (1992), ''Place Prosperity' vs. 'People Prosperity' Revisited', *Urban Studies*, vol. 29:2 (1992), pp. 185–203; shortened version reprinted in R.D. Norton (ed.), *Structuring Direct Aid: People versus Places*, vol. 9 of *Research in Urban Economics* series, JAI Press, Greenwich, CT, pp. 79–98.

Bolton, R. (1995a), 'New Regional Science and New Economics', *Australasian Journal of Regional Studies*, vol. 1, pp. 31–8.

Bolton, R. (1995b), 'An Economist's Interpretation of a 'Sense of Place'', Thirtieth Anniversary Lecture, October, *Regional Research Institute*, West Virginia University, Morgantown, WV.

Bolton, R. (1997), 'A Critical Examination of the Concept of Social Capital', paper read at *North American Meeting of Regional Association International*, November, Buffalo, NY.

Bolton, R. (1999), 'Place Surplus, Exit, Voice, and Loyalty', paper read at *Uddevalla Symposium on Evaluation of Regional Policies*, June, Fiskebäckskil, Sweden.

Bolton, R. and Jensen, R.C. (1995), 'Regional Science and Regional Practice', *International Regional Science Review*, vol. 18, pp. 133–45.

Bradley, S.P., Hax, A.C. and Magnanti, T.L. (1977), *Applied Mathematical Programming*, Addison-Wesley, Reading, MA.

Capello, R. (1995), 'Network Externalities: Towards a Taxonomy of the Concept and a Theory of their Effects on the Performance of Firms and Regions', in C.S. Bertuglia, M.M. Fischer and G. Preto (eds), *Technological Change, Economic Development and Space*, Springer-Verlag, Berlin, pp. 208–37.

Casti, J.L. (1995), 'The Theory of Networks', in David Batten, John L. Casti, and Roland Thord, (eds), *Networks in Action: Communication, Economics and Human Knowledge*, Springer-Verlag, Berlin, pp. 3–24.

Coleman, J.S. (1964), *Introduction to Mathematical Sociology*, The Free Press of Glencoe, New York.

Coleman, J.S. (1988a), 'Social Capital in the Creation of Human Capital', *American Journal of Sociology*, vol. 94, pp. S95–S120.

Coleman, J.S. (1988b), 'Free Riders and Zealots: The Role of Social Networks', *Sociological Theory*, vol. 6, pp. 52–57.

Coleman, J.S. (1990), *Foundations of Social Theory*, Belknap Press of Harvard University Press, Cambridge, MA.

Downs, A. (1994), *New Visions for Metropolitan America*, Brookings, Washington, DC.

Dynarski, M. (1981), *The Economics of Community: Theory and Measurement*, Ph.D. dissertation, Johns Hopkins University, Baltimore, MD.

Economides, N. and Himmelberg, C. (1995), 'Critical Mass and Network Size with Application to the US Fax Market', *Salmon Center Working Paper S-95–26*, Stern School of Business, New York University, NY.

Granovetter, M. (1995), 'Economic Action and Social Structure: The Problem of Embeddedness', *American Journal of Sociology*, vol. 91 (November 1985), pp. 481–510, reprinted as Appendix D in M. Granovetter, *Getting A Job: A Study of Contacts and Careers*, second edition, University of Chicago Press, Chicago, IL, pp. 211–40.

Hillier, F.S. and Lieberman, G.J. (1986), *Introduction to Operations Research*, fourth edition, Holden-Day, Oakland, CA.

Hirschman, A. (1970), *Exit, Voice, and Loyalty: Responses to Decline in Firms, Organizations, and States*, Harvard University Press, Cambridge, MA.

Jacobs, J. (1961), *The Death and Life of Great American Cities*, Random House, NewYork.

Johnson, J. (1995), 'Links, Arrows, and Networks: Fundamental Metaphors in Human Thought', in D. Batten, J.L. Casti and R. Thord (eds), *Networks in Action: Communication, Economics and Human Knowledge*, Springer-Verlag, Berlin, pp. 25–48.

Katz, M.L. and Shapiro, C. (1985), 'Network Externalities, Competition, and Compatibility', *American Economic Review*, vol. 75, June, pp. 424–40.

Katz, M.L. and Shapiro, C. (1994), 'Systems Competition and Network Effects', *Journal of Economic Perspectives*, vol. 8, Spring, pp. 93–115.

Liebowitz, S.J. and Margolis, S.E. (1994), 'Network Externality: An Uncommon Tragedy', *Journal of Economic Perspectives*, vol. 8, Spring, pp. 133–50.

Loury, G.C. (1977), 'A Dynamic Theory of Racial Income Differences', in P.A. Wallace and A.M. LaMond (eds), *Women, Minorities, and Employment Discrimination*, Lexington Books, Lexington, MA, pp. 153–86.

Loury, G.C. (1987), 'Why Should We Care About Group Inequality?', in *Social Philosophy and Policy*, vol. 5, pp. 249–71.

Putnam, R.D. (1993a), *Making Democracy Work: Civic Traditions in Modern Italy*, Princeton University Press, Princeton, NJ.

Putnam, R.D. (1993b), 'The Prosperous Community: Social Capital and Public Life', *The American Prospect*, vol. 13, Spring , pp. 35–42.

Putnam, R.D. (1995a), 'Bowling Alone: America's Declining Social Capital', *Journal of Democracy*, vol. 6, January, pp. 65–78.

Putnam, R.D. (1995b), 'Bowling Alone, Revisited', *The Responsive Community*, vol. 5, Spring, pp. 18–33.

Putnam, R.D. (1995c), 'Turning In, Tuning Out: The Strange Disappearance of Social Capital in America', *PS: Political Science and Politics*, vol. 28, December, pp. 664–83.

Putnam, R.D. (1996), 'The Strange Disappearance of Civic America', *The American Prospect*, vol. 24, Winter, pp. 34–48.

Rothenberg, J. (1967), *Economic Evaluation of Urban Renewal*, Brookings Institution, Washington, DC.

Schorr, A.L. (1963), *Slums and Social Insecurity*, U.S. Department of Health, Education, and Welfare, Washington, DC.

Webber, M.M. (1963) 'Order in Diversity: Community without Propinquity', in Lowdon Wingo, Jr. (ed.), *Cities and Space: The Future Use of Urban Land*, Essays from the Fourth Annual Resources for the Future Forum, Johns Hopkins Press for Resources for the Future, Baltimore, MD, pp. 23–54.

Chapter 7

The Spatial Structure of the City: A North American Perspective on Trends, Prospects and Research Directions

William P. Anderson

Introduction

No topic should be of more interest to geographers and regional scientists than the spatial structure of cities. No 'inherently geographic' topic affects the day-to-day existence of people more. Yet one gets the feeling that the effort to analyses cities in a rigorous and explicitly spatial way has been running out of steam.

Starting around mid-century, there was a succession of analytical approaches with different conceptual and methodological bases. These include concentric and sectoral generalizations; density gradients; mathematical land use theory; urban ecological studies; integrated urban models; and probably a few more. Some of these have an abstract bent, while others are more empirically motivated, but they all employ some sort of formal analysis and they all treat distance or space explicitly.

Browsing recent issues of journals, it seems that this succession of new ideas is petering out. There is continuing work in the mathematical land use tradition and some rekindling of interest in integrated urban models. But, with the exception of work along the lines of fractals and cellular automata, there are not a lot of new ideas – especially when contrasted with other fields of spatial analysis such as migration analysis, epidemiology, and the cluster of topics under the umbrella of 'new economic geography'.

A possible explanation is that trends in urban spatial structure confound the spatial mechanisms we traditionally have built our theoretical and empirical models around. Analytical geographers view the world as held together by the friction of distance. As the attenuation of distance becomes less powerful, what is left to hold things together? What structure is left to model?

At the same time, there is a growing interest in the policy aspects of urban spatial structure. Environmental problems, fiscal pressure on local governments, and growing social inequalities have all been blamed on spatial trends that are too highly segregated and too dispersed. In my view, these policy questions are sufficient motivation for geographers and regional scientists – as the social scientists best equipped to deal with spatial questions – to refocus their attention on the shape of the city.

My purpose in this chapter is to play up some of the most important issues to consider in conducting research on urban spatial structure. I will not make specific methodological prescriptions, nor will I attempt a comprehensive review of the literature. Rather, what follows is a series of observations based on my experience working in the fields of urban transportation modeling, integrated land use and transportation modeling, urban environmental analysis, and urban and regional economic modeling. (The biases that arise from this experience will be evident to many readers.)

My discussion is set in the context of North American (meaning American and Canadian) cities. This is because I am most familiar with them, having lived and worked in both countries. I do not mean to suggest, however, that the processes driving the evolution of North American cities are necessarily typical, or that observations about them can be applied directly to, say, European or Asian cities. I also do not devote much attention in this chapter to the very important social, economic, and political differences between cities in the U.S. and Canada.

The chapter begins with a set of conceptual definitions related to urban spatial structure and a brief review of trends and debates about those trends. This is followed by a review of policy issues with direct connections to urban spatial structure that have emerged recently. In the next section I review a couple of examples of how well-received ideas about spatial structure may turn out to be wrong, or only partly right. (The intention is to remind us of the limits of our understanding.) This is followed by a discussion of some major trends in society that are likely to affect the future shape of cities. The final section presents some general research directions, with an emphasis on topics that are neglected in the current literature.

Urban Spatial Structure

The spatial aspects of a city may be viewed in terms of three interrelated concepts: urban form, urban spatial interaction, and urban spatial structure (Bourne, 1982). *Urban form* refers to the spatial distribution of fixed elements in the city, including the spatial distribution and densities of land uses and associated structures, and the spatial patterns of transportation, water, and other infrastructure. *Urban spatial interaction* refers to movements of people, goods, and information occurring on a regular basis within the city. It includes commuting patterns, patterns of non-work trips, patterns of deliveries of goods, and even such movements of information as funds transfers and phone calls.

Urban spatial structure is a more comprehensive concept, comprising urban form, urban spatial interaction, and organizing principles that define the relationships between the two. The key point here is that urban form influences and constrains urban spatial interaction, but it does not determine it. It is easy to imagine two very different commuting patterns that might overlay the same urban form: the first in which people commute short distances to jobs located near their homes, and the second in which people commute much longer distances, bypassing nearby employment opportunities. In the first instance, people have chosen their residential locations in order to be close by their jobs because minimizing the cost of commuting is an important organizing principle. In the second, other organizing principles such as the desire to attain social status or to live nearby amenities have determined the relationship between urban form and urban spatial interaction. For reasons that I will explain later, the distinction between urban form and urban spatial structure is important for understanding trends in urban land use and transportation.

In North America, it is well known that the prevailing trend in urban form has been toward a low density pattern generally known by the pejorative term *urban sprawl.* While there is no universally accepted definition of sprawl, it usually refers to a development pattern with four elements: 1. a rapid outward expansion of the metropolitan boundary, 2. a general decline over time in the density of both population and employment, 3. a high density of roads providing good accessibility to all points, even in the periphery, and 4. a segregation of residential and other land uses, with most residential growth occurring in peripheral suburbs. I say the term sprawl is pejorative because urban analysts tend to decry it as a degenerate trend, but until fairly recently there has been little negative reaction to it from the economic and political mainstream. Most North Americans are suburbanites and despite some gentrification trends they seem happy that way.

Urban sprawl generally implies a highly dispersed or disorganized spatial pattern – a kind of high-entropy city. As is the case with spatial interaction models, high entropy leads to high transport costs. Thus, sprawl is associated with the wasteful use of resources. But there is considerable argument about just how disorganized urban form has become. The vision of a dense but declining central city surrounded by a field of uniformly low density development does not necessarily fit the facts. Low overall densities may reflect the existence of a few peripheral subcenters of fairly dense commercial development within a field of very low density residential development (Greene, 1980). Such a pattern is perhaps not as efficient as a highly compact city, but much more efficient than a single CBD surrounded by low density, because the average distance from any residence to the nearest commercial center is much shorter (Haynes, 1986). The terms *multinucleated city* and *polycentric city* appear in the literature with reference to such patterns.

This notion was expanded upon and popularized by Garreau (1991) who coined the term *edge city* to refer to major peripheral commercial developments around North American cities. He identified edge cities around older cities such as New York and Boston as well as around newer cities such as Houston and Atlanta. In stark contrast to other urbanists, who tend to express nostalgia for traditional urban forms, Garreau sees edge city development as a new frontier in urbanization, which is more conducive to life styles of the late twentieth century. He even claims that this type of development should reduce commuting effort since people can work close to their homes. The argument that peripheral development saps the life out of central cities is rejected on the grounds that of the metropolitan areas in which he has identified major edge city development, only one (Detroit) has lost downtown employment. Others, such as Boston, New York, and Toronto, have experienced downtown real estate booms.

While the polycentric vision of urban development is perhaps more realistic than the more negative notion of urban sprawl, the argument that this type of development leads to more efficient transportation patterns is questionable. Here it is easy to fall into the trap of assuming a direct causal relationship from urban form to urban spatial interaction. The fact that someone lives close to an edge city does not necessarily mean that he will work there, or even shop there. (This general problem is related to the jobs-housing balance issue, which is discussed at some length below.)

There is also some dispute as to whether polycentric development is a universal trend. While Garreau employs specific definitions for edge cities, his approach is somewhat anecdotal. Statistical analysis incorporating data for entire metropolitan areas do not necessarily yield the same sort of conclusions. Bourne (1989) observed only limited evidence of polycentric development in Canadian metropolitan areas. Looking at data for Los Angeles in 1970, 1980, and 1990, Gordon and Richardson (1996) concluded that the trend is toward increasing dispersion rather than polycentricity.

From the forgoing discussion, the link between urban form and urban transportation is evident. Recognizing that the connection is mediated by organizing principles, urban form provides the spatial context within which transportation patterns (urban spatial interaction) evolve. The causality is not in only one direction, however. Elements of the transportation system – notably transportation technology and transportation infrastructure – have important influences on the long-term evolution of urban form. The spatial extent of cities has expanded with each major innovation in personal transportation. Both the shift from wagons to rail and from rail to private automobiles permitted greater separation of homes and workplaces, and therefore served as enabling technologies for suburbanization.[1]

All transportation technologies require infrastructure, and the spatial patterns of infrastructure networks affect the spatial pattern of land development. For example, a strictly radial pattern of roads or railways promotes a radial patterns of development along transport corridors, as is the case in Paris or Stockholm (Orrskog and Snickars, 1992). Circumferential elements, such as beltway roads, promote a more dispersed pattern of development, although peripheral centers may develop at the intersections of radial and circumferential elements. Thus it is not just the car that promotes (or permits) dispersion, but also the infrastructure that defines the car's mobility. In this way, addition of new infrastructure can have a profound and irreversible effect on the shape of the city (Wegener, 1986).

From a theoretical perspective, the explanation is clear. A new road increases the accessibility of the land around it, and therefore improves the economic feasibility of upgrading that land to higher valued land uses. In practice, however, the direction of causality is not that clear. New land development may occur as part of a contagious pattern at the urban edge, despite the fact that adequate transportation infrastructure has not yet been developed. This creates a demand on the public sector. Anyone who is familiar with the politics of North American metropolitan areas can cite examples of suburban communities agitating for roads or rail lines that will improve their accessibility. Despite this, it is almost an article of faith in the planning literature that construction of new roads promotes dispersed development. It is only recently that this assumption has been subjected to empirical tests (Darovny, 1998; Hansen, Gillen, and Puvathingal, 2001).

Policy Objectives

The literature on urban spatial structure has both positive and normative components. The normative literature addresses questions regarding the type of urban forms that are most desirable and the policies that may be used to foster them. Or to put it differently, this literature addresses problems that are closely associated with prevailing trends in urban form. Three such problems are considered here: environmental pollution in cities, the high costs of municipal service provision, and poor economic opportunities for low income populations.

Environmental Pollution

There is a large and varied literature on how urban spatial structure affects environmental quality. Most of it is focused on emissions of air pollutants from transportation, although the affect of land development patterns on water pollution is also an important issue. The majority of the people writing in this field take the position that low-density development has led to over reliance on automobile transportation and therefore increased air pollution. It follows that more compact, European-style development will lead to a healthier environment.

Since I have already reviewed this literature elsewhere (Anderson, Kanaroglou, and Miller, 1996; Bureau of Transportation Statistics, 1996), I prefer here to illustrate the difficulties of drawing a direct link between urban spatial structure and urban environmental quality by means of a hypothetical comparison. Consider two hypothetical cities of a million population with similar economies. The first is a compact city where the majority of people live at high densities in attached or multilevel housing and most employment and services are concentrated near the city center. The second is a dispersed city, covering about three times as much area as the compact city, where most people live in detached homes in low-density suburbs and employment and services are scattered throughout the urban area. Which of these cities is likely to have the healthier environment?

To answer this question we have to consider two factors: the rates at which pollutants are generated and the pollutant concentrations to which urban residents are exposed. Starting with the former, it is likely that the compact city will generate less of a number of important pollutants. Since the two cities' economies are similar, there is no reason to expect a difference in the total emissions into air and water from manufacturing industries, although the spatial distributions of those emissions may be different. Households, however, can be expected to produce more emissions in the dispersed city. One reason is that suburban residents generally consume more interior living space, requiring more energy for heating and cooling, and consequently more air pollution. Trips for work, shopping, and recreation are generally longer in the dispersed city, and since low-density areas are not served efficiently by public transportation they are mostly made by private automobile. Consequently, each household consumes more energy and produces more air pollution in the course of its daily activities. Other factors associated with the suburban lifestyle may also contribute to higher rates of air pollution, including the use of gasoline powered lawn mowers and the heating and cooling of huge commercial spaces such as shopping malls.

Water pollution may also be higher in the dispersed city. A high proportion of the space in this city will be paved over for roads and parking areas onto which are discharged pollutants related to fuel combustion, coolants and lubricants, and brake and tire wear from the large number of automobiles. Run-off from these surfaces is one of the main sources of water-borne pollutants. Run-off from suburban lawns contains pesticides and fertilizers which degrade the quality of drinking water and contribute to eutrophication in water bodies. Furthermore, the covering over of more land with hard surfaces and the rapid diversion of rainwater from surfaces such as roofs and lawns into storm drains reduces natural water storage capacity. This can lead to flooding problems downstream. It can also reduce the ability of land to naturally filter pollutants from rainwater before it reaches rivers, lakes, and harbors. Solid waste disposal may also be higher in the dispersed city, primarily due to clippings and leaves from lawns, which are currently a major input to many landfills.

Based on these observations, it would be easy to arrive at the conclusion that dispersion of urban population and activities necessarily leads to accelerated environmental degradation. But such a conclusion may be premature because it is based on observation of the *typical* dispersed city, which does not represent the only option for dispersed development. For example, if the locations of jobs in the periphery were well coordinated with the locations of workers residences, commuting trips could actually be shorter in a dispersed city than in a compact city with a single, central employment zone. Run-off and pollution problems associated with suburban lawns could be mitigated if suburbs were designed with smaller private spaces and larger common spaces that could be maintained in a more natural state. Mixed residential and commercial land use with adequate facilities for non-motorized transport could reduce the amount of space needed for roads and parking lots. In this light, it is important to consider the differences not only between compact and dispersed urban forms, but also between different types of dispersed forms.

Furthermore, the notion that dispersion is bad for the environment will strike a discordant note with many people, especially in North America where most people live in the suburbs. Was not the desire to escape pollution in central cities one of the main reasons they moved to the suburbs in the first place? This seeming paradox points out the need to consider the second factor mentioned above: the pollutant concentrations to which urban residents are exposed. Take air pollution. In the compact city, total emissions are lower but they are concentrated into a smaller area, so emissions per hectare, as opposed to per capita, may be higher.

Following the adage that 'dilution is the solution to pollution' one might conclude that more dispersed emissions are less of a threat to human health. For some pollutants that are known to have direct health effects this is indeed true. For example concentrations of carbon monoxide and air borne particulates drop off quickly with distance away from a busy road. Since the typical suburban resident spends relatively little time in close proximity to such roads, her exposure to these pollutants is lower than a central city resident who may live with a block or so of an arterial road. Of course there is a question of equity here. Some of the most dispersed cities still have heavily congested urban cores. In these places it is often the urban poor who are most exposed to emissions from cars belonging to suburbanites.

There are other air pollutants, most notably smog, that are more regional than local. Their spatial distribution may owe as much to landforms as to the distribution of emissions. Suburban developments located in valley bottoms may have higher concentration than downtown areas. The mechanisms of smog formation are too complex to consider here but it is fair to say that it is one air quality problem which cannot be overcome by separating populations from the sources of emissions. Since the emissions that cause smog come, in large part, from cars, it is a problem that is only exacerbated by higher rates of driving in dispersed cities.

The purpose of this hypothetical comparison is not to draw any conclusions about the kind of spatial structure that is desirable from an environmental perspective. Rather, it seeks to drive home two points: first that spatial structure has important impacts on urban environmental quality, and second that the nature of these impacts are not simple – they often involve trade-offs between the reduction of emissions and the reduction of exposures. Only when these complex relationships are well understood can spatial planning be used as an effective tool to improve urban environments.

Municipal Service Provision

In North America, local municipal governments are responsible for the provision of a large number of public services, including primary and secondary education; water and sewage; construction and maintenance of local roads; solid waste disposal; police and fire protection; and a variety of health and social services. It has been argued that trends in the evolution of urban form have increased the costs of providing these services for two reasons. The first is that political fragmentation that emerges from a process of dispersed urban growth retards the ability to achieve scale economies in service provision. The second is that many services are more expensive to provide to low density populations.

Political fragmentation occurs by two mechanisms. In the first, as the metropolitan boundary expands, it incorporates pre-existing communities that were formally rural, but which have their own local charters and government institutions. A classic example is Boston, whose metropolitan area encompasses around 50 cities and towns, many of which were formally established well before the American Revolution. In the second mechanism, new communities are formed on the urban periphery with the expressed purpose of avoiding control by the urban government. For example, industrial firms may establish new communities to avoid urban taxes and regulations or affluent social groups may establish independent towns where they can enforce exclusionary policies.

The positive side of political fragmentation is that it provides urban residents a choice among different bundles of public services (the Tiebout hypothesis) and it provides some level of competition which promotes efficient service provision. The negative side is that it facilitates segregation of social groups (discussed further below) and it tends to create administrative units that are two small to achieve scale economies in service provision. This can be overcome by the establishment of service districts or metropolitan governments comprising several municipalities. This solution is more widely used in Canada than in the U.S., where adherence to local autonomy is stronger. Also, in some U.S. cities in the South and West there is less political fragmentation because governments of central cities have been able to annex peripheral land as they expand.

The argument that per capita costs of providing municipal services increases with decreasing density applies to those services involving linear infrastructure (roads, water, and sewage) and those with a substantial transportation component (solid waste disposal or even schools). The argument can be illustrated by the simple observation that if houses are more widely spaced, it takes more pipe to connect each house to the water network, so provision of water is more expensive. Also, garbage trucks and school buses have to cover more ground between houses. This argument has been around since the 1970s (Real Estate Research Corp., 1974), but it has gained prominence in the 1990s (Blaise, 1995; DiNino and Baetz, 1996; Office of Technology Assessment, 1995). This probably reflects the fact that in both The United States and Canada, the flow of funds from higher levels to municipal governments has slowed or stopped, thus creating greater pressure to economize. Furthermore, municipalities cannot escape their financial problems by promoting growth, since new residents living in dispersed developments may imply service costs that are not covered by incremental property taxes (Office of Technology Assessment, 1995).

Access to Economic Opportunity

One of the most distressing side effects of the trend to dispersed urban forms is the way it has reinforced social segregation in the United States. With the exception of a few fashionable urban enclaves, the highly educated, highly skilled, and highly paid live in suburban communities while disadvantaged groups live in central cities and older 'near' suburbs. Racial segregation by place of residence is even more profound. This problem is perhaps less stark in Canada, where central cities are more heterogeneous, but it still exists.

Socio-economic segregation is strongly reinforced by political fragmentation, because local governments have primary responsibility for both the funding and delivery of public education. Suburban school districts provide more and better teachers and equipment, and suburban students significantly outperform their urban contemporaries on standardized tests and in admissions to university. The best evidence of this is the dominant influence that the quality of school systems have on residential real estate values in some U.S. metropolitan areas.[2]

Another way that trends in urban spatial structure reinforce social segregation is through the declining accessibility of central city residents to employment opportunities. During the 1950s and 60s, residential locations moved from the core to the periphery more rapidly than workplace locations. More recently, the suburbanisation of jobs has progressed as rapidly or more rapidly than the suburbanisation of people in most cities. With most of the job growth occurring on the periphery, central city residents lose their greatest traditional advantage: access to employment. (See, for example, Hughes, 1991; Simpson, 1992.)

It is especially difficult for central city residents to take jobs in the suburbs because of the limited ability of public transportation systems to serve highly dispersed suburban workplaces. Thus, lack of car ownership is a major impediment to employment. This problem places limits on the potential of 'welfare to work' programs in both the U.S. and Canada.

Given an increasing awareness of the link between dispersed urban expansion and the environmental, economic, and social problems described above – not to mention the nagging problem of congestion arising from excessive automobile dependence – it is not surprising that a number of policy proposals to reverse established trends have emerged in recent years. These proposals fall into two general categories: those concerned with governance and those concerned with design.

Policies regarding governance address the inefficiencies and inequities arising from excessive political fragmentation. As such, they are not directed explicitly at urban spatial structure, since in principle a compact city can be fragmented and a dispersed city can be under a single jurisdiction. For the reasons described above, however, fragmentation tends to emerge as a by-product of spatial growth.

The most direct way to eradicate the problems created by political fragmentation is to stretch the boundaries of the central city to include all or most of its suburbs (Rusk, 1993). This solution has been adopted in some form in Ontario, where elimination of the smallest level of municipal governments has been achieved in Metropolitan Toronto[3] and proposed for Ottawa and Hamilton. In the U.S., amalgamation of well-established municipalities would face major political hurdles. Downs (1994) sees fragmentation as one of a set of problems resulting from low-density growth. He proposes imposition of an urban growth boundary as part of a mixed strategy.

Design policies deal explicitly with the spatial layout of the city. They generally go beyond the idea of an urban growth boundary to create coordinated development patterns for different activities, and place particular emphasis on the promotion of public transportation and non-motorized transportation. Peter Calthorp (1993) is the most prominent proponent of this type of planning. His *transit oriented development* strategy envisions small to medium clusters of mixed land use at high density around nodes that serve as transit stations. This vision of suburban development is quite different from current practice, but it is being adopted in a number of metropolitan areas including Portland, Oregon and San Diego, California. The 'neotraditional' approach to residential development

(Christofordis, 1994) is complementary to this approach, although it is concerned primarily with local rather than regional patterns.

The new vision of suburban development is not without its detractors. The most potent argument is that low-density development represents the true preferences of North American families. Any attempt to artificially restrict land consumption by households will only drive up housing prices and may have the perverse effect of forcing development to exurban areas where densities are not restricted (Audirac, Shermyen, and Smith, 1990). Also, some transportation analysts dispute the argument that lower density leads to more pollution, arguing that dispersed homes and workplaces lead to less congestion, and therefore much lower emissions on a per mile basis (Gordon and Richardson, 1994).

There are also a number of institutional factors that work against the new suburban vision. For example, for transit oriented development to work, both commercial and residential land uses need to be clustered around transit stations. For reasons that will be explained later, municipal governments get a greater fiscal benefit from commercial development. They may therefore choose to zone land around stations exclusively for commercial use (Boarnet and Crane, 1997). There may also be resistance to any form of high-density residential development because of fears that it will attract low-income residents.

Two Misapprehensions

The preceding section suggests that environmental, economic, and social objectives may be achieved by policy measures that intervene in the evolution of urban spatial structure. This presupposes, however, a good understanding of the forces that drive that evolution. Without such an understanding there is little hope of formulating effective policy. Recent evidence indicates, however, that our understanding may not be as good as we sometimes think it is. I offer two examples to illustrate how easy it is to formulate and accept explanations of processes that do not stand up to empirical verification.

Jobs-Housing Balance

The general dynamics of metropolitan dispersion in the post-war period can be roughly described as a period of residential dispersion with jobs remaining centralized, followed by a period of continued decentralization of population and rapid decentralization of employment. One might therefore have expected to see growth in the length and duration of work trips in the first period, followed by a gradual reduction as the spatial distributions of residences and workplaces became more similar. However, with some notable exceptions, work trip lengths and durations have continued to grow. (See for example U.S. Department of Transportation, 1993.)

So what is going on here? A possible explanation is that despite the similarity in general spatial patterns, the specific patterns of housing and employment were not conducive to efficient commuting. Cervero (1989) and others coined the term *jobs-housing balance* (or rather the lack thereof) to describe this spatial mismatch. This idea had a natural intuitive appeal and leant itself to a number of policy prescriptions. To achieve the desired balance, all new development should accommodate roughly equal numbers of jobs and workers. In this way, a level of self-containment within development nodes could be achieved, reducing the need for long commutes.

A number of empirical analyses have been conducted to concerning this hypothesis. Several of them used optimization methods to decompose observed commuting miles into a component that is necessary, given the spatial distribution of jobs and workplaces, and a residual component called *excess commuting*. Studies conducted on data for Baltimore (Cropper and Gordon, 1991), Los Angeles (Giuliano and Small, 1993), and Hamilton, Ontario (Scott, Kanaroglou, and Anderson, 1997) all conclude that more than half of commuting is excess commuting.

Since commuters are already driving much further than the existing spatial pattern of jobs and housing would require, it is unlikely that much could be gained by creating a better jobs-housing balance. Cervero (1996) took a somewhat different approach. He compared measures of jobs-population balance in communities around San Francisco with measures of self-containment based on actual commuting patterns and found that the two were not strongly correlated.[4]

Perhaps these results should not be too surprising, given that attempts to promote self-contained communities have generally failed and that there is no *necessary* relationship between spatial patterns and commuting behavior (Giuliano, 1991). But how are we to interpret this very high degree of excess commuting? The most probable answer is that commuting efficiency is only one of a variety of factors that contribute to the household location decision. Most people would be willing to drive a bit further to reduce their mortgage payments, and housing prices tend to be lowest in highly segregated residential areas. Also, since more than half of automobile travel is for purposes other than journey-to-work, the locations of shopping and recreational facilities may have as much influence as workplace location. Some people may actually prefer inaccessible spots where they are away from traffic and close to natural areas.

The misapprehension that growing average commute length is primarily a function of a jobs-housing mismatch illustrates two things. First, cities are sufficiently complex entities that perfectly plausible explanations of things observed in them may turn out to be wrong, or only partly right. Policies based on 'common sense' explanations may therefore be wasteful or even counter-productive.

Second, the importance of Bourne's organizing principles in urban spatial structure is evident here. Assuming that jobs-housing balance necessarily leads to efficient commuting amounts to assuming a direct causal link between urban form and urban spatial interaction. As it turns out, the expected outcome does not occur because minimizing commute distance is not the only organizing principle at work.

Flight from Blight

A vision of central city residents moving to the suburbs is at least implicit in most models of the evolution of urban spatial structure. Debates center not so much on whether this happens as on why. The two opposing arguments are the 'flight from blight' hypothesis and the 'natural evolution' hypothesis. In the flight from blight, conditions in the center city become so bad that residents flee to the suburbs. According to the natural evolution vision the move from the city to the suburb is a natural outcome of changing production and transportation technologies and changes in preferences induced by rising incomes. In either case, the suburbs are substituted for the central city.

A recent paper by Adams *et al* (1996) cast doubt on the basic assumptions underlying these two arguments. Looking at migrants to the suburban components of 51 U.S. metropolitan areas over the periods 1975–80 and 1985–90 they found that most new suburbanites come not from the adjacent central city but rather from outside the metropolitan area. (This is consistent over the two time periods.) New migrants to central cities also come primarily from outside the metropolitan area. Furthermore, the proportion of growth due to migration in central cities and suburbs is highly correlated in the cross-section. In other words, those suburbs that attract a lot of outside migrants are associated with central cities that also attract a lot of outside migrants.

This contradicts the fundamental notion that suburban growth occurs *at the expense of* the central city. It implies a kind of complementarity whereby urban and suburban growth are mutually reinforcing. It also indicates the high level of long-distance mobility among Americans, where city-to-city moves are more common than city-to-suburb moves. It is the type of information that makes one rethink a lot of the conventional wisdom.

Inexorable Forces

It is not my purpose here to try to make predictions about urban form. The discussion earlier under the heading Policy Objectives suggests, however, that there is a growing dissatisfaction with established low density trends, and that we may see an increasing use of policy instruments that attempt to contain the spatial extend of urban growth. Of equal or greater importance to policy measures, however, are inexorable forces of change in society that are bound to have profound effects on the evolution of urban spatial structure. What follows are some speculations about the form those effects may take.

Family Structure and Demographics

One of the most important changes in the economies of the affluent countries over the past thirty years is the rapid integration of women in the labor force. While this transformation may appear to be complete, it actually has some way to go. Many working women are still employed only part time or in occupations known as 'pink collar ghettoes'. Over the next twenty years or so, we should see the dissimilarities in employment patterns between the sexes diminish, as barriers fall and more highly educated women enter a broader variety of occupations.

The gender differences in employment patterns are evident in commuting patterns. On average, women commute shorter distances and are more likely to use public transportation. This in part reflects the employment of women in household oriented service industries (retail, banking, health care, etc) whose spatial patterns are geared to the residential distribution. Over the longer term, these differences should also diminish, although they may be preserved somewhat due to a culture that still places primary responsibility for childcare on women.

From the perspective of urban spatial structure, the ability of the two-worker household to choose residential locations geared to efficient commuting is very much restricted. It is unlikely that a husband and wife will work in the same vicinity, so it is also unlikely that they can choose a house that gives them both a short commute – even if minimizing commuting difference is a high priority to them. Typically, one will have a short commute and the other a long one, or they may split the difference and live half way between jobs.[5]

To illustrate the effect of this on urban spatial structure, consider a city in which each household has one worker, and assume that within constraints on housing type, price, etc., each household chooses a location that minimizes that worker's commute. Now consider a city with the same urban form but where each household has two workers, and the locations of the workers' jobs are independently distributed. Assume further that each household chooses a location to minimize the sum of the two commutes. The average length of commute will be higher in the second case than in the first, despite the fact that the disutility of commuting remains the same. Thus, the relationship between urban form and urban spatial interaction changes because the underlying organizing principles have changed. It is not clear how much (if any) of the increase in average commute length can be attributed to the increase in the proportion of two worker households. This effect should only be magnified as the difference between male and female employment patterns decline.

An equally profound change will occur early in the next century when the baby-boom generation reaches its sixties and the proportion of retired people increases. One could speculate at length on what effect that will have on urban spatial structure. The mix of commuting and discretionary trips; preferences for housing types and locations; the proportion of people without access to private transportation; and the fiscal structure of municipalities will all change. One could probably make an argument that this will cause either an acceleration in dispersion or a reconcentration of population.

Information Technology

One of the main outcomes of ongoing advances in information and communication technologies is to create a particular kind of mobility. The essence of this mobility is that the fixed connection between the things that you do and the places where you do them breaks down. For example, telecommuting uses technology to loosen the bond between the act of working and the location of the workplace. You now have the choice to work in two places: at work or at home. Miniaturization of computers will take this trend even further. Dertouzos (1997) predicts the introduction of powerful computing devices that can be worn as clothing, rather than fixed in place or carried like a brief case. With these technologies you will be able to work anywhere.

What will be the impact of this new mobility on the shape of the city? The facile answer is that it will result in an acceleration of the long-term dispersion trend. People who are not tied down to their jobs can live where they like, and people appear to prefer low-density living.

Those who have examined this issue carefully, however, advise caution (Nijkamp and Salomon, 1989; Gillespie, 1992). For one thing, all technological changes require some institutional changes to be broadly adopted. This is especially true of changes involving the workplace. This is probably why the adoption of telecommuting has been slower that many would have predicted in the 1980s. Another important point is that access to the workplace already plays a diminished role in residential locations, so people's location choices may not change all that much after they are freed from the need to commute.

Affluence

It is important to remember that the radical changes in urban spatial structure that have occurred over the past fifty years are the outcome not only of changes in transportation technology, but also of the unprecedented growth in personal income. It was this growth in income which made widespread car ownership possible. A quite separate argument is that land is an income elastic good. As incomes rise, an increasing proportion of households spend an increasing proportion of their incomes on land, so expansion in the spatial extent of the city is a necessary outcome. This effect is independent of either increasing car ownership or population growth.

Despite the dismal economic predictions of the 1970s, the North American economies (U.S. and Canada) have shown remarkable resilience over the past twenty years. Wage growth has slowed, but total income growth has been quite healthy. Increasing affluence is a well-entrenched trend, at least for the foreseeable future. A critical question is therefore whether rising incomes will continue to translate into more dispersed development.

It seems likely that the rate of growth in per household car ownership will slow, first because it is already so high and second because households are getting smaller. Whether the consumption of land per household will continue to grow with income per household is a more interesting question. It cannot be viewed in isolation from other trends in household preferences. For example, with increasing income to spend on time-consuming leisure pursuits, the availability of time may be critical to maximizing household utility. An interesting question is therefore what is the income elasticity of time? And are time and land substitutes or complements? If time is highly income elastic, long commutes and the investment of time in maintaining large properties may become less attractive. Unfortunately, most empirical analyses of household consumption patterns do not treat time explicitly (more about this later).

Research Directions

The forgoing discussion raises quite a few issues that have implications for the type of research that is needed to get a better understanding of urban spatial structure. I do not want to consider specific models or methods here, but rather to identify a few major areas where the current body of research is seriously lacking. They fall into three categories: the need to consider a broader range of actors whose decisions affect spatial structure; the need to treat space and time explicitly; and the need to set spatial structure in the context of broader social and economic trends.

Who are the Actors?

Urban economic theory is based on the interplay of spatial decisions by two categories of actors: households and firms. This makes sense because it is they who ultimately derive utility and profit from location choices. But two other categories of actors – land developers[6] and municipal governments – are at least as important in the evolution of urban form. Their roles involve the creation of spatial choice sets.

Developers are primarily responsible for expanding the urban edge. Only rarely does an individual firm or household purchase rural land and build a home or factory for its own use. More frequently choices are made from among sites on offer in a large-scale housing survey or industrial park. This is not to say that developers dictate the evolution of urban form. In order to maximize profit they respond to a variety of market signals, including the spatial pattern of prices in existing properties. However developers' supply side factors, such as the most efficient scale of survey and the density of development that maximizes profits given prices of land and other inputs, will have an effect on the type of housing that is provided.

This is an important issue since the spatial distribution of housing surveys contributes more than any other single factor to changes in the shape of the city over time. Yet it is surprising how little empirical work there is on where and at what density developers choose to build new housing.[7] Part of the problem is that, compared to the location choices of households, the choices of developers are lumpy, idiosyncratic, and there are relatively few players in the market. Thus convenient economic assumptions may not apply. It may therefore be fundamentally wrong-headed to try to *predict* the behavior of developers. That should not, however, prevent us from trying to understand it.

If developers are unpredictable, municipal governments are even more so. But because they control zoning and the placement of linear infrastructure, they effectively constrain the choices of developers. (In particular, the placement of trunk sewer lines may be the most neglected issue in research into urban form.)

Municipal governments are under two different types of pressures from their constituents. The first is pressure to maintain the homogeneous character, especially of affluent communities. This usually results in some policy of *growth management*, such as moratoria on new development and large lot size and setback[8] regulations. These policies generally have a pecuniary benefit for existing residents in the form of higher property values and a corresponding cost to potential new residents (Downs, 1994). They may have environmental benefits, such as preservation of wetlands and open spaces. But they generally result in more dispersion as development is pushed to communities at the urban edge whose governments welcome new housing as a means of developing a tax base.

The second kind of pressure is from the fiscal squeeze due to reductions in intergovernmental transfers and the tax payers' revolt of the 1970s and 80s, which resulted in restrictions on residential property taxation. An interesting outcome of this is an increased preference for commercial over residential development. Municipal governments have learned that the ratio of service provision cost to property tax revenue is lower for a new shopping mall or office building than it is for new housing survey. Given that many suburban communities have a limited amount of land left to develop, and that they are already predominantly residential, governments actively seek commercial development to improve their balance sheets. As Cervero (1996) observed in California, this has lead to an increasing balance of jobs and housing (but as I observed above, balance does not necessarily imply containment). It may also have lead to an accelerated dispersion of metropolitan employment.

Space and Time

For the most part, empirical research on urban spatial structure is not what I would call explicitly spatial. Much of the empirical work involves comparisons of crude spatial categories such the central city vs. the suburbs.[9] After fifty years of suburbanization, suburbs have become so varied that it makes little sense to think of them as an aggregate. Some central cities are even more heterogeneous. (I would not be surprised if the 'central city' of Boston contains both the most expensive and cheapest real estate in the entire metropolitan areas.) Data are available at smaller spatial units, both through the American and Canadian censuses and from special purpose employment, housing, and transportation surveys.

New methods and technologies are now available to analyze spatial data sets. Spatial statistics, which was for some time a rather esoteric topic, is now coming into the main stream of geographical research. Geographical information systems (GIS) make it much easier to manipulate and display spatial data and to convey the results of analyses in graphical forms that are more compelling than numerical tables. With these tools there is an opportunity to address explicitly spatial questions such as the spatial relationship between infrastructure and land development; the spatial extent of positive and negative externalities; spatial accessibility measures based on the interplay of networks and activity patterns; and the spatial pattern of the advancing urban edge.

Integrating time into spatial analyses of cities is important for a variety of reasons. One is that there is great ambiguity about directions of causality in processes such as the links between construction of infrastructure and land development. Time series of observations on, say, the spatial pattern of the road network and residential patterns and densities are needed to untangle these relationships. Unfortunately, such information is available only sporadically from secondary sources. Developing spatial time series may therefore require some extraordinary measures, such as compilation of municipal records from municipalities. The use of remote sensed land use data is another option worth exploring.

At a more behavioral level, it is time and not distance that people and firms try to conserve when they make location and transportation decisions. (This point has been well established in empirical research on urban transportation.) Methods of analysis that incorporate time should therefore be developed further. An excellent example of this is the theoretical model of Lakshmanan and Hua (1983) which integrates a time budget into a conventional utility maximizing approach. Another promising trend is the more behavioralistic models that come under the heading of 'activity analysis' in transportation demand literature. While these models generally take urban form as given, their is great scope to extend this idea to take advantage of the fact that different locations provide different activity schedule choice sets.

The Larger Context

My final point is that the evolution of urban spatial structure cannot be analyzed in isolation from everything else that is happening in the world. As I have already noted, trends that are national or international in scope affect the way that evolution occurs. These include growth in income; changes in the relationships between federal, state/provincial, and local governments; technological trends in transportation, communications, and information; changing gender roles; demographic changes; and even trends in race relations.

It is equally important to recognize that trends in urban spatial structure have important influence on things we normally think of as belonging to the regional or national level. An obvious example is the relationship between cities and the automobile industry. The availability of affordable cars and complementary infrastructure has made suburbanization possible. But it is the inexorable trend toward dispersed development that has continuously expanded the demand for cars. Given the enormous role of the automobile industry, it is clear that aggregate economic figures for both Canada and the U.S. would look very different today had it not been for suburbanization.

To put it in more general terms, most of the economic activity in North America occurs in cities. The spatial structure of cities has profound effects on the composition and efficiency of that activity. It therefore stands to reason that urban spatial structure has a profound effect on the composition and rate of national economic growth. The nature and magnitude of this effect is a virgin field for analysis.

Conclusions

My purpose in this chapter has been to play up some of the most important issues to consider in conducting research on urban spatial structure. This is not an exhaustive review. There are a number of issues (such as crime and personal safety) that strike me as important, but which are beyond my expertise. I am sure there are also important issues that have not even occurred to me.

One generalization that can be drawn from all this is that the role of distance has changed. Measuring distance from the central business district at each point in the urban field will provide little basis for an explanation of spatial patterns. The traditional focus on the distance that must be overcome in the journey-to-work trip is misplaced, given the wide variety of factors that affect location decisions and location choice sets.

The role of distance has diminished, but I do not think it has disappeared. The traditional distance measures are not as potent as they once were (or as we once imagined them to be) but there are more distance variables to consider. In particular, the distances defining the extent of spatial externalities deserve more attention. Also, distance is not the only important spatial concept. Boundaries – especially those defining municipal jurisdictions – may be just as important in determining location choices.

As a final note, one might easily conclude from the discussion in this chapter that the spatial structure of cities is so complicated that any attempt at formal modeling is doomed to failure, and therefore not worth the effort. I could not disagree more with that conclusion. It is because the system under study is so complex that some exercise in modeling – i.e., stripping away detail or isolating components – is so necessary. The results of many different types of models, including traditional urban economic theory, can yield valuable insights. The key point is that they must be interpreted as insights and not as conclusions. Useful policy direction can only come from a synthesis of information from various modes of analysis.

Notes

1 See Muller (1995) for a historical review.
2 A recent edition of *Boston Magazine* ran an article called 'The Best Places to Live'. The article was almost exclusively about the relative merits of local public schools.
3 This amalgamation does not, however, include the fastest growing suburbs on the fringe of the metropolitan area, whose local governments have resisted any form of amalgamation or even co-ordination in service provisions.
4 Similar results for towns in the United Kingdom were presented by Michael Breheny at the 1998 meetings of the Association of American Geographers.
5 If the disutility of commute distance is marginally decreasing, the latter option is less attractive.
6 Of course developers are a class of firms, but urban economic theory is primarily concerned with firms that produce goods and services at a given location on an ongoing basis.
7 With one of my graduate students I recently did a statistical analysis of the location of new housing surveys in Hamilton, Ontario over a period of 15 years (Darovny and

Anderson, 1998). We were surprised at how few similar studies we could find in the literature.

8 The setback is the minimum allowable distance from the road or lot line to a house or other structure.

9 A notable exception is the class of *integrated urban models* which generally define variables over small zones or the links of detailed road networks. (See Southworth, 1995, for a recent review.) The *cellular automata* models constitute a new approach to modeling cities that incorporate significant spatial detail. (See Batty, 1997.)

References

Adams, C.F., Fleeter, H.B., Kim, Y., Freeman, M. and Cho, I. (1996), 'Flight From Blight and Metropolitan Suburbanization Revisited', *Urban Affairs Review*, vol. 31, pp. 529–43.

Anderson, W.P., Kanaroglou, P.S. and Miller, E. (1996), 'Urban Form, Energy, and the Environment: A Review of Issues, Evidence, and Policy', *Urban Studies*, vol. 33, pp. 7–35.

Audirac, I., Shermyen, A.H. and Smith, M.T. (1990), 'Ideal Urban Form and Visions of the Good Life: Florida's Growth Management Dilemma', *Journal of the American Planning Association*, vol. 56, pp. 470–82.

Batty, M. (1997), 'Cellular Automata and Urban Form: A Primer', *Journal of the American Planning Association*, vol. 63, pp. 266–74.

Blaise, P. (1995), *The Economics of Urban Form*, prepared for the GTA task force by Berridge, Lewingberg, Greenberg, Dark, Gabot. Ltd. , Toronto.

Boarnet, M. and Crane, R (1997), 'L.A. Story: A Reality-Check for Transit Based Housing', *Journal of the American Planning Association*, vol. 63, pp. 189–204.

Bourne, L.S. (1982), 'Urban Spatial Structure: An Introductory Essay on Concepts and Criteria', in L.S. Bourne (ed.), *Internal Structure of the City*, 2nd Edition, Oxford University Press, New York.

Bourne, L.S. (1989), 'Are New Urban Forms Emerging? Empirical Tests for Canadian Urban Areas', *The Canadian Geographer*, vol. 33, pp. 312–28.

Bureau of Transportation Statistics (1996), *Transportation Statistics Annual Report 1996: Transportation and the Environment*, U.S. Department of Transportation, Washington, (W.P. Anderson one of 14 major contributors, principal author of Chapter 8, 'Transportation and Air Quality: A Metropolitan Perspective').

Calthorpe, P. (1993), *The Next American Metropolis: Ecology, Community, and the American Dream*, Princeton Architectural Press, New York.

Cervero, R. (1989), 'Jobs-housing Balance and Regional Mobility', *Journal of the American Planning Association*, vol. 55, pp. 136–50.

Cervero, R. (1996), 'Jobs-Housing Balance Revisited: Trends and Impacts in the San Francisco Bay Area', *Journal of the American Planning Association*, vol. 62, pp. 492–511.

Christofordis, A. (1994), 'New Alternatives to the Suburb: Neotraditional Development', *Journal of Planning Literature*, vol. 8, pp. 429–40.

Cropper, M.L. and Gordon, P.L. (1991), 'Wasteful Commuting: A Re-examination', *Journal of Urban Economics*, vol. 29, p. 2013.

Darovny, M. (1998), *Residential Development in Hamilton-Wentworth 1980–1994*, Master of Arts Thesis, McMaster University, Hamilton, Ontario, Canada.

Dertouzos, M. (1997), *What Will Be*, Harper, San Francisco, CA.

DiNino, T. and Baetz, B.W. (1996), 'Environmental Linkage Between Urban Form and Municipal Solid Waste Management Infrastructure', *Journal of Urban Planning and Development*, vol. 122, pp. 83–100.

Downs, A. (1994), *New Visions for Metropolitan America*, Brookings Institution, Washington, DC.

Garreau, J. (1991), *Edge City: Life on the New Frontier*, Anchor, New York.

Gillespie, A. (1992), 'Communications Technologies and the Future of the City', in M. Breheny (ed.), *Sustainable Development and Urban Form*, Pion, London.

Giuliano, G. (1991), 'Is Jobs-housing Balance a Transportation Issue', *Transportation Research Record*, vol. 1305, pp. 305–12.

Giuliano, G. and Small, K.A. (1993), 'Is the Journey to work Explained by Urban Structure?', *Urban Studies*, vol. 30, pp. 1485–500.

Gordon, P. and Richardson, H.W. (1994), 'Congestion Trends in Metropolitan America', in *Curbing Gridlock*, vol. 2, Transportation Research Board Special Report 242, National Academy Press, Washington, DC.

Gordon, P. and Richardson, H.W. (1996), 'Beyond Polycentricity: The Dispersed Metropolis, Los Angeles, 1970–1990', *Journal of the American Planning Association*, vol. 62, pp. 289–95.

Greene, D.L. (1980), 'Urban Subcentres: Recent Trends in Urban Structure', *Growth and Change*, vol. 11, pp. 29–40.

Hansen, M., Gillen, D. and Puvathingal, M. (2001), *Freeway Expansion and Land Development: An Empirical Analysis of Transportation Corridors*, University of California Transportation Center, Research, Paper 511.

Haynes, V.A. (1986), 'Energy and Urban Form: A Human Ecological Critique', *Urban Affairs Quarterly*, vol. 21, pp. 337–53.

Hughes, M.A. (1991), 'Employment Decentralization and Accessibility: A Strategy for Stimulating Urban Mobility', *Journal of the American Planning Association*, vol. 57, pp. 288–98.

Lakshmanan, T.R. and Hua, C-i. (1983), 'A Temporal-Spatial Theory of Consumer Behavior', *Regional Science and Urban Economics*, vol. 13, pp. 341-61.

Muller, P.O. (1995), 'Transportation and Urban Form: Stages in the Spatial Evolution of the American Metropolis', in S. Hansen (ed.), *The Geography of Urban Transportation*, Guilford, New York.

Nijkamp, P. and Salomon, I. (1989), 'Future Spatial Impacts of Telecommunications', *Transportation Planning and Technology*, vol. 13, pp. 275–87.

Office of Technology Assessment (1995), *The Technological Reshaping of Metropolitan America*, U.S. Government Printing Office. (OTA-ETI-638), Washington, DC.

Orrskog, L. and Snickars, F. (1992), 'On the Sustainability of Urban and Regional Structures', in M. Breheny (ed.), *Sustainable Development and Urban Form*, Pion, London.

Real Estate Research Corporation (1974), *The costs of Sprawl: Environmental and Economic Costs of Alternative Residential Development Patterns on the Urban Fringe*, U.S. Government Printing Office, Washington, DC.

Rusk, D. (1993), *Cities Without Suburbs*, Woodrow Wilson Center Press, Washington, DC.

Scott, D.M., Kanaroglou, P.S. and Anderson, W.P. (1997), 'Impacts of Commuting Efficiency on Congestion and Emissions: Case of the Hamilton CMA, Canada', *Transportation Research*, D 2(4), pp. 245–57.

Simpson, W. (1992), *Urban Structure and the Labour Market*, Clarendon Press, Oxford.

Southworth, F. (1995), *A Technical Review of Urban Land Use–Transportation Models as Tools for Evaluating Vehicle Travel Reduction Strategies*, ORNL-6881, prepared for the Office of Environmental Analysis and Sustainable Development, U.S. Department of Energy by Oak Ridge National Laboratory.

U.S. Department of Transportation (1993), *Journey-to-work Trends in the United States and Major Metropolitan Areas 1960–1990*, Federal Highway Administration, U.S. Government Printing Office, Washington, DC.

Wegener, M. (1986); 'Transport Network Equilibrium and Regional Deconcentration', *Environment and Planning A*, vol. 18, pp. 437–56.

Chapter 8

Behavioral Adaptations to Traffic Congestion

Robert E. Skinner, Jr.

Introduction

Without a doubt, among the great transportation challenges facing the United States, and many other countries throughout the world is congestion – the decline in transportation service levels that results from travel demand growth that is not matched by commensurate increases in supply. Between 1985 and 1994, for example, vehicle-miles of travel on the U.S. highway system increased by nearly 40 per cent while expressway mileage grew by just five per cent (FHWA, 1985–1995). Not surprisingly, available data and indices, such as the one developed by the Texas Transportation Institute (Schrank and Lomax, 1997) show a fairly consistent rise in highway congestion.

The growth in congestion is not expected to abate, raising the prospects of serious mobility declines and slowed economic growth. Policy prescriptions for dealing with this dilemma very widely and include building new highways, using intelligent technology to increase the capacity of existing highways, introducing road pricing to suppress travel demand, improving transit, and changing land use and development patterns. Hard choices are called for.

It is possible, however, that the expected scale, nature, and timing of future transportation crises occasioned by congestion may be overstated. They might be overstated not because the root causes are not real, but rather because our forecasts of congestion and its impacts overlook society's capacity to adapt or modify its behavior to mitigate the impacts of congestion or delay its onset. To the extent that forecasts of future congestion are overstated, the desirability and timing of remedial policy actions might be affected.

The theme of this chapter is that such 'adaptations' have taken place in the place, are likely do so again in the future, and collectively may result in significant changes in travel characteristics.

Some Examples

Behavioral adaptations involve tradeoffs that individual travelers, households, and employers make in the face of growing travel congestion. These tradeoffs may involve sacrificing the preferred travel schedule, mode, route, trip destination, or even the degree of safety or residential location to reduce the impact of congestion on the time spent traveling. It can be viewed as 'choosing the lesser evil' or more elegantly as utility maximization. Either way, it does involve an added cost to the traveler; and in some cases, one can argue that the tradeoffs are not in society's best interest. Nevertheless, from the standpoint of the individual, they are clearly understandable and rational.

The sections below illustrate several adaptations that have already been made to growing travel demand and congestion.

Higher Highway Speeds **and** *Higher Capacity*

As traffic engineers well know, when traffic density increases (vehicles per hour per lane) and approaches the maximum flow rate, average speeds drop sharply. But this empirically derived relationship has changed over time, as documented by successive editions of TRB's *Highway Capacity Manual* (Figure 8.1). On a freeway lane operating at 1800 passenger cars per hour, for example, the 1965 edition reports an average speed of about 37 mph while the 1994 edition reports an average speed of 59 mph, an increase of 59 per cent.

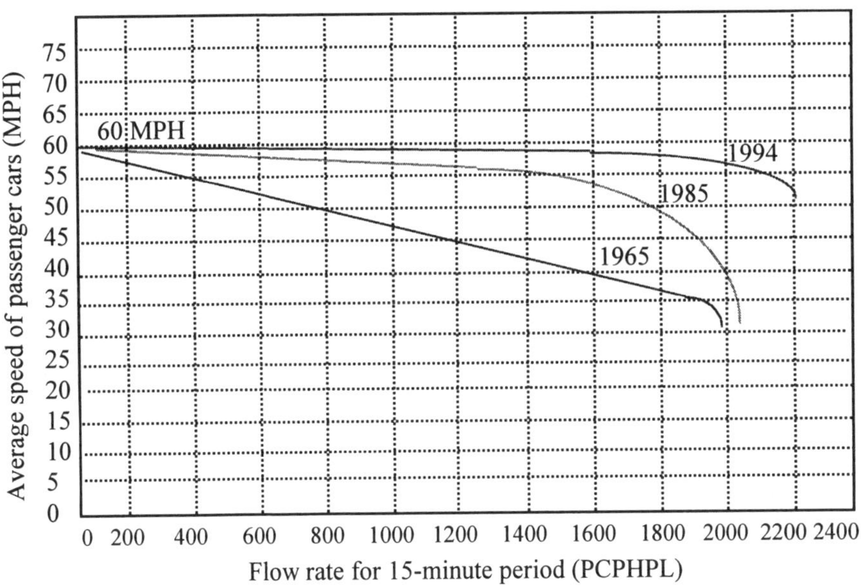

Figure 8.1 Freeway speed vs flow rate (HRB 1965; TRB 1985; TRB 1994)

Acting individually, drivers have squeezed more capacity out of the highway system than traffic engineers ever imagined or desirable possible three decades ago. They have done this by accepting shorter and shorter gaps between vehicles traveling at high speed. This phenomenon may reflect a more experienced, more confident generation of drivers, but it also represents a tradeoff between speed and safety and probably stress levels. It is not a tradeoff that society as a whole or highway agencies explicitly encouraged, but it has had the effect of mitigating the consequences of traffic growth. And it has done this without travelers changing their mode, their schedule, or their route.

Finding Better Routes in the Aftermath of an Earthquake

In January of 1994, the Northridge earthquake shook the Los Angeles region damaging eight freeways, especially the I-5 near Sylmar, the SR-14 near Santa Clarita, and the I-10 in central Los Angeles. This massive loss of freeway capacity forced motorists and commuters to make immediate changes to their trip making habits, and fortunately these changes have been well documented (Giuliano et al., 1996). The experience is a testament to the adaptability of travelers, and rich source of information about the preferences of travelers.

In brief, in the most heavily impacted corridors, automobile commuters most frequently changed their route and their departure times; changing mode was much less frequent. Some trips were simply not made, and as one would expect, nonwork trips were the most likely to be discontinued. Also, as expected, commuters reported, on average, increases in their travel times. According to Giuliano et al. (1996), these results are generally consistent with those of other emergency or special events such as the 1989 Loma Prieta earthquake in the San Francisco Bay Area and the 1984 Los Angeles Summer Olympics.

The Northridge aftermath results of special interest to this chapter concern travel times and route changes. Apparently, some commuters rediscovered arterial streets that, in their view, provide equal or better service than the freeway routes they replaced. Although average travel times consistently increased after the earthquake, the Commuter Transportation Services survey (CTS, 1994) reported 25 per cent of commuters who changed routes said they would stay with the new routes after the freeways reopened. For commuters with trips of less than 10 miles, the fraction was even higher – 37 per cent.

This result is a reminder that travelers, even commuters repeatedly traveling between the same origin and same destination, do not always know the full range of options available, and that their choices may be biased, for example in favor of freeway routes. In this case an immediate disruption forced travelers to reassess their options. It is certainly plausible that a similar reassessment process will occur, albeit gradually, as congestion and delays increase on the overall freeway network. If arterial routing options are available, the impacts of mounting freeway congestion will be mitigated as travelers utilize arterial networks more fully. Indeed, this is one of the rationales for providing drivers with real-time traffic information.

Commuters Inventing New Options

In the previous examples, motorists acting individually found ways to continue to drive and mitigate the impacts of congestion or disruptions to the highway network. Although we might overlook the impact of these sorts of adaptations, they should not be surprising. The growing willingness to travel at high speeds with narrow gaps between vehicles has been apparent to traffic engineers (as well as motorists themselves) for many years, and travel forecasters have devoted considerable energy to understanding and modeling route choice decisions.

This example, although applicable in only very specific circumstances, illustrates that travelers can be quite inventive and devise on their own a new travel option that transportation planners would be unlikely to propose, and some might actively discourage. It involves the formation of ad hoc carpools near access points to high-occupancy-vehicle (HOV) express lanes.

Reno et al. (1989) evaluated ad hoc carpools formed in Springfield area of Northern Virginia to use express HOV lanes on the Shirley Highway to reach downtown Washington, D.C or the Pentagon. They found that 2500 strangers formed carpools each workday morning which resulted in considerable travel time savings to drivers and passengers. Moreover, because most of the passengers would use public transit if they did not join the ad hoc carpools, the passengers saved transit fares (compensation to the driver was infrequent), and the public transit agency reduced the number of peak period buses and therefore reduced its operating costs.

Ad hoc carpools of this type depend upon the presence of HOV lanes that offer a considerable time advantage over regular lanes, parallel transit services (as backup and for return trips), and convenient park-and-ride lots. While these conditions may not be met in many travel corridors, there may other creative responses to congestion that travelers will develop in the future. Parenthetically, it is worth noting that there are some advantages to letting approaches like ad hoc carpooling develop naturally rather than under the guidance of government. Reno et al. (1989) suggest that issues like compensation, carpool etiquette, and perhaps security are more easily handled by the indigenous carpools than by government sponsored programs designed to achieve the same end.

Keeping Work Trip Times Steady

While a number of definitional and data problems exist related to the measurement of highway congestion, the available information shows that congestion has generally increased on major highways in U.S. urban areas. For example, the Texas Transportation Institute (TTI) index mentioned earlier indicates a steady rise in congestion between 1982 and 1994 for but a handful of major U.S. urban areas (Schrank and Lomax, 1997), see Table 8.1. The U.S. Department of Transportation (DOT, 1995) reports that daily vehicle miles of travel per lane mile has increased steadily, especially on major facilities, between 1983 and 1993.

The previous examples in this section are suggestive of the adaptations individual travelers have made to deal with this rise in traffic congestion. Is there any evidence at a larger, more aggregated scale to demonstrate that these behavioral adaptations make a difference? Based on work trip travel time data, the answer is yes.

Table 8.1 TTI Roadway congestion index for U.S. urban areas

Urban area	1982	1986	1988	Year 1990	1992	1993	1994
Northeastern average	0.92	0.99	1.03	1.04	1.05	1.07	1.08
Midwestern average	0.80	0.87	0.91	0.94	0.97	0.99	1.01
Southern average	0.86	0.92	0.97	0.98	1.00	1.01	1.02
Southwestern average	0.83	0.93	0.91	0.93	0.95	0.96	0.97
Western average	0.95	1.09	1.16	1.20	1.20	1.21	1.21
Total average	0.86	0.95	0.99	1.01	1.03	1.04	1.05

Gordon and Richardson (1994) reviewed data from national self-reported travel surveys which show, despite the evidence of increased congestion, remarkable stability in work trip travel times; in some cases actual declines are reported. One of the data sources used by Gordon and Richardson, for instance, is the American Housing Survey (AHS). It shows that average one-way work trip travel time for homeowners, for instance, was nearly a constant 21 minutes between 1975 and 1989 after a jump of one minute from the 1974 average; for renters, the average varied began this period at 18 minutes and ended at 19 minutes (Figure 8.2).

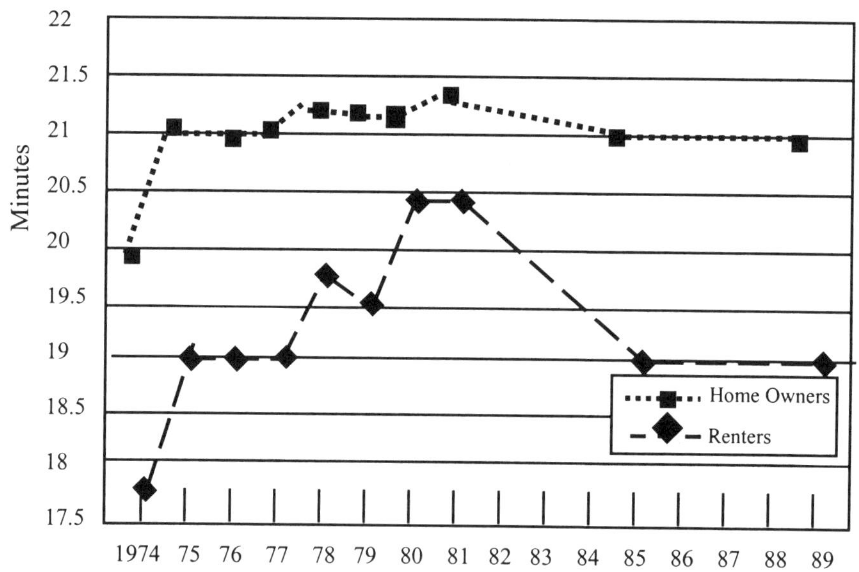

Figure 8.2 Travel time to work AHS survey trends (Pisarski 1992)

Gordon and Richardson attribute the stability in work trip travel times to suburbanization of employment and residential locations – individual employers and workers changing location in ways that counteract the influence of congestion on work trip travel times. No doubt this is true, but other adaptations such as new routes, altered schedules, changes in mode, and so on have surely contributed as well.

Finding Added Capacity in the Skies

Although this chapter is focused on surface transportation and adaptations to highway congestion, it at least worth mentioning that there are examples elsewhere in transportation where sharp growth in demand has been accommodated without the reductions in service levels that might have been expected.

Since 1979 commercial air flights within the United State have increased by approximately 50 per cent and domestic air passenger volumes have increased by over 80 per cent (FAA, 1996). Yet only one major airport has been constructed since 1974, the failure to upgrade air traffic control technology is well known, and a TRB expert committee (TRB, 1991), which assessed the changes in air service during the first decade of economic deregulation (1978–1988), concluded that air service had improved during that period in terms of cost and availability.

Although the author knows of no comprehensive analysis that explains precisely how this accommodation was reached, several possibilities are likely. Few new airports have been built, but the utilization of many has increased significantly including airports that previously had little or no scheduled air service; peaking can be smoothed by pricing flexibility that did not exist before deregulation; and despite the lack of equipment upgrades, air traffic controllers have found ways to manage a significant increase air traffic flow with a work force comparable in size to the one that existed before the 1981 strike.

While these adaptations were not the result of decisions made by individual travelers, they were not the result of a master plan nor were they clearly foreseen in advance. Airlines, airport authorities, and the air traffic controllers all played roles, and while these roles were clearly impacted by the actions of others, the decision making is largely independent.

Further Adaptations to Congestion

The previous section attempted, selectively and certainly not exhaustively, to illustrate behavioral adaptations to congestion that are already taking place, in some cases for decades. There is no reason to believe that such changes in behavior will not continue, although some may have reached the point of dimensioning returns (higher capacity via shorter gaps between vehicles) and others may have limited potential (ad hoc carpools). This section will cite two adaptations which may become far more significant in the future than they have been in the past.

Using Telecommunications and Information Technology to Reduce Travel

Telecommuting is more of a real possibility today than ever in the United States, and it will be even more so in the future. However, so far it has not became sufficiently common to show significant increases in the percentage of at-home workers. Indeed, Pisarski (1992) reports AHS derived data which show a decline in at-home workers between 1985 and 1989.

But there are more variants of Telecommuting than just working at-home exclusively, and these variants seem more apparent all the time. They include workers spending a portion of each day or a portion of each week working at home and shared work sites closer to home but not at the main employer location. The availability of computers, faxes, and email plays a role but other factors certainly contribute – more relaxed views about the extent and nature workplace supervision, and the transition from a manufacturing economy to a service-oriented economy.

As the technology improves, highway congestion increases, and the economy increasingly becomes a service-oriented economy, Telecommuting in its various forms will become increasingly attractive. Although there are skeptics about the potential for Telecommuting to replace work trips to any significant degree, it would be shortsighted to prematurely dismiss the technological possibilities and the inventiveness of commuters.

Rejuvenation of Smaller and Medium Sized Cities and Rural America

One way Americans have reduced the impact congestion is through suburbanization of jobs. Now there are signs that this process of escaping congestion, high housing costs, and other urban problems will move to a higher level – businesses and employment moving to smaller and medium sized cities and even rural America. Anecdotal evidence abounds – for example, Southern California businesses relocating or expanding in places like Tucson, Reno, and Boise. Solid statistical evidence of this migration is still thin, but certain a number of medium-sized cities, particularly in the West are growing rapidly. And the gap between non-metropolitan growth and metropolitan area growth has narrowed, and done so because of migration (Johnson and Beale, 1996). Impacts on the larger metropolitan areas of this phenomenon may be less apparent because of their size, continued growth of their outer suburbs, and for some the impact of immigration from abroad.

The rejuvenation of smaller and medium-sized cities and rural American, if indeed it happens, will be facilitated by the on-going revolution in information and communications technology. As the movement of backroom financial operations from major cities attests, Des Moines is just as convenient as New York City when business is conducted over the telephone and large data bases are no longer bound to huge computer facilities.

This shift may or may not be good social policy, but it would have the effect of redistributing travel demand to areas that have less congested highways and sometimes a greater ability to add new highway capacity.

Conclusion

It is virtually certain that metropolitan areas in the United States, and much of the developed world, face traffic growth that will exceed the growth in highway capacity. The policy debate about the increase in congestion that will result is often framed as follows: the traveling public will inevitably suffer delay and travel disruption unless government responds with new investments or new policies that reduce congestion. How government should respond – new highways, transit, new traffic management technology, land use controls, etc. – is the subject of considerable debate.

The lack of consensus about the appropriate policy response, coupled with the many barriers governments face in financing and/or implementing such far reaching public policies, may lead one to believe that travelers are doomed to suffer mounting traffic congestion. While this is probably so, a variety of behavioral adaptations illustrated in this chapter may mitigate or delay the onset of congestion. The adaptations may not lead to desirable public policy outcomes, and surely they come at price to individual travelers, households, and employers. Nevertheless, experience indicates that they are just as inevitable as traffic growth and cumulatively can have significant impacts, which planners and public officials should take into account.

References

Abbreviations:

CTS	Commuter Transportation Services, Inc.
DOT	U.S. Department of Transportation
FHWA	Federal Highway Administration (DOT)
HRB	Highway Research Board (now TRB)
TRB	Transportation Research Board

CTS (1994), *State of the Commute*, Los Angeles, CA.

DOT (1995), 1995 *Status of the Nation's Surface Transportation System: Conditions and Performance*, Report to Congress.

FAA (1996), *FAA Aviation Forecasts – Fiscal Years 1996–2007*, U.S. Department of Transportation.

FHWA (1985–1995), *Highway Statistics* (annual), U.S. Department of Transportation.

Giuliano, G., Golob, J., Bahl, D., Lee, W. and Y.C. Liao, Y.C. (1996), *Impacts of the Northridge Earthquake on Transit and Highway Use*, Summary Report, School of Urban Planning and Development, University of Southern California, Los Angeles, CA.

Gordon, P. and Richardson, H. (1994), *Curbing Gridlock, Peak-Period Fees to Relieve Traffic Congestion Volume II*, in TRB Special Report 242, TRB, National Research Council, Washington, DC, pp. 1–31.

HRB (1965), *Highway Capacity Manual Second Edition*, Special Report 87, National Research Council, Washington, DC.

Johnson, K.M. and Beale, C.L. (1996), *The Reemergence of Population Growth in Nonmetropolitan Areas of the U.S. in the 1990s: The Rural Rebound*, Working Paper No. 10, Demographic Change and Fiscal Stress Project, Loyola University, Chicago, IL.

Pisarski, A. (1992), *Travel Behavior Issues in the 90s*, Office of Highway Information Management, FHWA, Washington, DC.

Reno, A.T., Gellert, W.A. and Verzosa, A. (1989), 'Evaluation of Springfield Instant Carpooling', in *Transportation Research Record 1212*, TRB, National Research Council, Washington, DC, pp. 53–62.

Schrank, D.L. and Lomax, T.J. (1997), *Urban Roadway Congestion – 1982 to 1994*, Volume I, Annual Report, Texas Transportation Institute, The Texas A&M University System, College Station, TX.

TRB (1985), *Highway Capacity Manual Third Edition*, Special Report 209, National Research Council, Washington, DC.

TRB (1991), *Winds of Change, Domestic Air Transport Since Deregulation*, Special Report 230, National Research Council, Washington, DC.

TRB (1994), *Highway Capacity Manual*, Third Edition Updated, Special Report 209, National Research Council, Washington, DC.

Chapter 9

A Simultaneous Model of Long-Term Regional Job and Population Changes

Ingvar Holmberg, Börje Johansson and Ulf Strömquist

Introduction

Contemporary economic development has been associated with an increasing knowledge intensity of labor supply and an increasing input share of R&D resources. At the same time the importance of scale economies has been emphasized. This chapter examines a model structure that can project multiregional job and populations dynamics. Such dynamics include the attraction (and lack of attraction) of firms and households to each functional region. Firms are attracted by a region's economic milieu, whereas people are attracted by the corresponding household milieu. The former can be related to every region's market potentials for firms, whereas the latter makes reference to the household market potentials. In addition, we show how a region's infrastructure affects its market potentials. One background in this endeavor is the contributions in Elhance and Lakshmanan (1986) and Lakshmanan and Hansen (1965). The approach with market potentials makes it possible to shed new light on population and job dynamics in a system of functional regions.

Market Potentials, Infrastructure and the Size of a Functional Region

In Lakshmanan and Hansen (1965) market potential is used as a means to describe economic concentration and the opportunities of making contacts in and between such concentrations on the basis of a spatial discount function. In the subsequent analysis we stress the importance of making a precise distinction between a region's internal and external market potential. The method to identify a region's internal market potential is in a fundamental way related to the delineation of the geographic extension of a functional region.

A functional region is distinguished by its concentration of activities and of its infrastructure which facilitates particularly high factor mobility within its interaction borders. In particular, a functional region has an integrated labor market, in which commuting as well as job search is intensive (Johansson, 1998). To a certain extent this idea has a place in more or less all urban models. New urban economics, as formalized in Fujita (1989), identifies an urban region by deriving increasing commuting cost from increasing distance to the city center, which is the host of all work paces.

Going back to von Thünen (1826), Lösch (1943), Hirsch (1967) and many others, we find an assumption that products vary with regard to the contact or interaction intensity associated with their input and output transactions. These contributions make an additional assumption that interaction costs are much lower when a transaction is made inside a region than when it is carried out between regions. Contact-intensive products can be considered to have distance-sensitive transactions. Hence, for such products one would expect that their geographic transaction costs would rise sharply as the interaction crosses a regional border. As a consequence, the interaction frequency associated with distance-sensitive products can be assumed to decrease, as contacts have to be made at increasing distance from the central parts of the region.

In view of the above observations, the market-potential theory presented here recognizes that the contact intensity associated with selling and delivering different products (goods and services) varies considerably. For distance-sensitive products (with a high contact intensity), the geographic transaction costs are assumed to be much lower for interactions with customers inside the regional border than for interactions carried out across the border (Johansson, 1998). This also implies that products can be distance sensitive as regards input transactions. The same argument applies in a natural way to the labor market, in the sense that individuals search for a job, supply their capabilities and carry out their work primarily inside the region where they live.

With this background, the model outlined in the sequel distinguishes between the internal and external market potential of firms located in a given region. Firms supplying distance-sensitive products must find a sufficiently large demand for their sales inside their own region. When strong internal scale economies prevail, a firm cannot obtain positive profits when locating in a region with an internal market potential which is too small. This latter conclusion relates to recent empirical studies of regional economies saying that 'economic density' matters (Ciccone and Hall, 1996; Johansson, 1996; Johansson, Strömqvist and Åberg, 1998).

The size of the internal market potential of a functional region depends on the infrastructure provision in the region. Infrastructure for interaction has the role of offering high density combined with low transaction costs, such that a supplier has a large accessibility to customers and such that a producer has a large accessibility to suppliers of specialized inputs as well as to households supplying specialized labor inputs.

Modern research concerning the importance of infrastructure for economic performance and development started around fifty years ago with contributions such as Rosenstein-Rodan (1943) and Nurkse (1953). In a survey of this field of research Lakshmanan summarizes the post-war research in the following way:

> This literature attributes a two-fold return to the nation or the region from the provision of social overhead capital. First, the delivery of improved education, health care and recreation directly augments the welfare of human resources or individuals in the form

of better skills, reduced absenteeism, etc. Second, the provision of roads, airports, utilities, etc., improves the productivity of producer capital (machinery, equipment, livestock, etc.) and of consumer capital (housing and residential structures). In the long run the impact of infrastructure creation will be such as to lead to extensive modification in the relative prices both of factors of production and final products. The expectation is that there will emerge a new equilibrium of costs and prices at a higher level of income and employment.

Infrastructure, according to Lakshmanan has two fundamental roles. First, it influences both the consumption and production possibilities of the society. Second, it is intrinsically a collective good. It is not only common to all households – it is common to both households and industry. As a consequence, infrastructure will influence, in a basic way, the size of the internal and external market potential of a region, 1. by extending its links for interaction through space and 2. by creating accessibility of regions. At the same time infrastructure extends over time through its durability. In this way it creates sustainable conditions of production, consumption and welfare.

Resource Based and Scale Based Theories

The traditional analysis of comparative advantages is in particular associated with the names Ricardo, Heckscher and Ohlin. Models in this tradition emphasize the abundance of resources located in each individual region. As a whole this way of thinking is a resource-based theory.

The resource-based theory has been challenged in recent decades by scale-based models, which explain location and trade patterns in a context of internal and external economies of scale. In our analysis we attempt to combine resource-based and scale-based assumptions into the same theoretical framework. This is primarily done by associating 1. resource-based advantages to input market potentials of each sector and 2. scale-based advantages to customer market potentials of each sector.

In the doctrines of economic theory we find that scale economies are emphasized already in Adam Smith's notion of division of labor, which has the form of a successive decomposition of production into a system of sub activities as output grows (Arrow, 1979; Stigler, 1951). The pre-requisite for Smith's scale phenomena is that demand is large enough to encompass a larger output. The associated decomposition may take place inside a firm but also by outsourcing the original production to a set of new (interacting) firms.

In the model formulations used in this chapter, the first option is represented by internal economies of scale, whereas the second option sometimes may have the form of external economies of scale. Koopmans (1957) relates internal scale economies to the existence of one or several productivity-enhancing indivisibilities such as indivisible equipment, set-up costs including learning how to do it. Following Krugman (1990) this type of phenomena could be represented by a fixed cost factor, referring to a catalyst which must be present in the production process without being used up. This includes knowledge resources, patents as well as material and non-material networks. Other contributions where specialization is based on internal scale economies can be found in regional economics (e.g. Beckmann, 1958; Tinbergen, 1967; Kaldor, 1970).

The impact of external economies of scale (localization economies) was emphasized by Marshall (1920). Chipman (1970) formalized external economies of scale by describing how a firm with constant scale economies can benefit from positive external influences from the output from other firms (in the same region). Associated approaches are found in urban and regional economics as well as in models of spatial product cycles in works of Hirsch (1967), Mills (1967) and Henderson (1986). We could also observe that Ethier (1979) shows how the Marshallian notion of external economies of scale can play a major role in explaining trade between countries and how Marshallian economies can be combined with traditional trade modeling that is based on comparative advantage theory.

External economies of scale include externalities which are transmitted through the market and extra-market influences in the form of various forms of information spillovers. This chapter argues that internal and external scale economies generate specialization dynamics with similar properties. In large urban regions economic density and agglomeration are based on combinations of internal and external economies of scale.

Moreover, both input and customer market potentials tend to vary with the size of an urban region. This makes it possible to combine resource-based and scale-based regional specialization and growth processes. Modern resource-based models also emphasize the supply of knowledge-intensive labor as a primary specialization factor. We include the pertinent labor location-dynamics by considering the household market potentials referring to housing and job opportunities as well as the supply of services and amenities. Equipped with this two-sided view of firms' and households' market potentials, we investigate a process where jobs follow households at the same time as households follow jobs.

Infrastructure and Cumulative Interaction between Jobs and Population

Given the outline in the two previous subsections, we are now in a state where we can combine the phenomena of scale economies and market potential into a model of regional cumulative growth. The self-reinforcing process is assumed to have the form an interdependent dynamics between economic activity and population size in regions. In this theoretical framework infrastructure for interaction functions like an arena which brings resource-based and scale-based models of regional development together.

The market potential of a firm refers to its accessibility to customers, input suppliers and its potential labor supply. Infrastructure facilitates the development of the market potential. As for the household, its location factors include accessibility to jobs, household services and amenities. Again the same infrastructure helps to create accessibility. Observe that density of jobs and supply of household services is part of economic density and firms' market potentials.

This is the basis for the empirical model to be estimated and studied. In view of this, the chapter examines the simultaneous interaction between the change of population and jobs in a system of regions.

Empirical models that emphasize the described form of dynamic interdependence can be found in Mills and Carlino (1989) and Holmberg and Johansson (1992) and Johansson (1996). A basic idea in this approach is that not only physical infrastructure but also the market potentials are slowly adjusting variables.

Other studies investigating the impact of regional infrastructure on the growth process are Mera (1973), Elhance and Lakshmanan (1986), Johansson (1993) and Sasaki, Kunihisa and Sugiyama (1995). These are related to cross-section studies of the relation between infrastructure and regional productivity. This group includes Wigren (1984), Munell (1990), Andersson, Anderstig and Hårsman (1990) and Seitz (1995).

Outline of the Study

The next section broadens the views introduced previously and makes the assumptions about endogenous growth of functional regions more precise. The focus is on the interaction between population changes and the development of economic activity. This framework also considers the knowledge intensity of the labor force. A major concern is to combine the two conflicting assumptions that 1. people follow jobs and 2. jobs follow people. The section thereafter provides an overview of the population and job distribution across Swedish regions. In this section the model is formalized and described by two interdependent temporal equations.

A subsection presents the approach applied in the statistical investigation. The approach is based on the assumption that the household and job dynamics are interdependent. It presents the econometric model to be estimated and provides an assessment of the econometric results. In the last section the results are further discussed and conclusions are drawn.

Endogenous Growth and Density of Functional Regions

This section defines functional regions and their overall internal market potentials. Moreover, it outlines how resource-based and scale-based models can be combined into the same framework. With this as a basis the dynamic interdependence between job and population development is formulated.

Market Potential and the Density of a Functional Region

In Sweden a functional region normally consists of several interacting municipalities. Such a group of municipalities is considered to be integrated into a region when the interaction between the municipalities is intensive. According to spatial interaction theory, the interaction intensity is a falling function of the time distance between origin and destination (Sen and Smith, 1995). Hence, a functional region is characterized by short time distances between its municipalities. Empirical observations of labor market commuting and similar forms of trip making inform us that short distance often means less than 30–40 minutes.

Figure 9.1 describes the propensity of the labor force to commute to the location of a workplace as a function of time distance. Point A refers to the origin of such trips. Very close to this point movements may not be classified as trips, but once trip making starts the frequency gradually declines as predicted by, e.g. a gravity model. The depicted curve has the following message: to the right of point B the frequency of work trips is likely to be low. Now, we may consider point A to be located in given municipality. If a major part of the jobs in a second municipality is located to the right of point B, the labor market interaction will be low. Next, suppose that infrastructure for labor market travelling is improved. Then this means that the second municipality moves to the left of point B on the time-distance axis. Such a change implies that the labor markets of the two municipalities become integrated and we may also think of the result as an enlargement of the functional region associated with the first municipality.

Labor market trips can be viewed upon as a representative form of frequent interaction, which means that similar conditions apply to other forms of frequent interaction, e.g. transactions and deliveries between a supplier and his customers. Thus, our conclusions about labor commuting should be valid also for business contacts and transactions that require direct contact. Recalling that a functional region can be defined as an area that allows for frequent market interactions, we may conclude that the borders of a labor market region will approximate the borders of a functional region. The internal market potential is a measure of the market opportunities that exist inside the borders of the region.

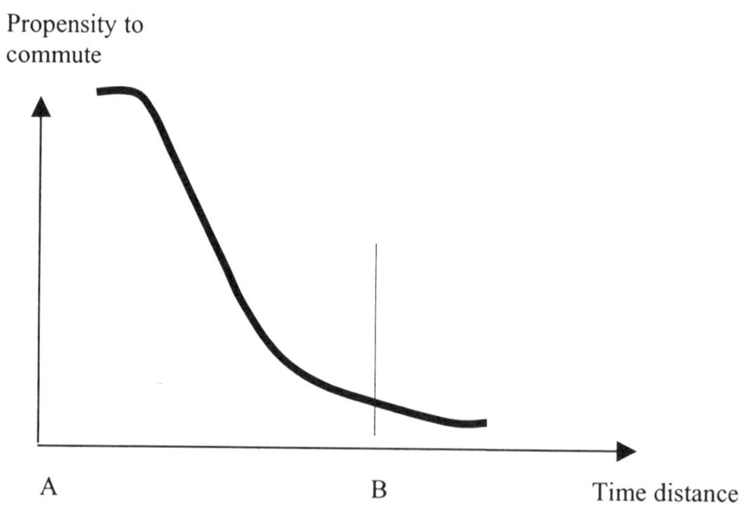

Figure 9.1 Propensity to commute as a declining function of time distance

In a precise analysis one has to define the market potential with regard to each specific group of products (or each specific group of economic activities). However, in this chapter we want to emphasize the impact of a generalized market potential concept, represented by the size and density of the region. Having said this, observe that the accessibility criterion applied in Figure 9.1 implies that all parts of a region must satisfy a minimum level of contact intensity. Thus, with such a delineation of a functional region, the size of the region in terms of population, purchasing power or GDP will reflect the size of a market, which satisfies a strict criterion of interaction density. In particular, for regions with roughly the same GDP per capita, one may conclude that the size of the population also reflects the relative size of a region's purchasing power. In the sequel we shall use the term 'overall market potential', denoted by M, to signify this measure.

Combining Resource Based and Scale Based Models

How can one use the variable M in a model where the number of jobs and the number of inhabitants interact in a slow dynamic process? In this subsection we present a sketch of how a set of self-reinforcing processes all imply that a region's market potential may grow (or decline) in a process of endogenous change. We shall do this by referring to 1. a firm's customer market potential, 2. a firm's input market potential, 3. a firm's labor-input market potential. For the individual household one may also identify its 1. job market potential, 2. housing market potential, and 3. consumption market potential. Finally, in the following subsection the role of interaction infrastructure is introduced as a support factor in the development process.

Before we start, observe that the input market potential and the labor input market potential together are core variables in a resource-based model of regional specialization and development. The customer market potential refers to the opportunities of firms to benefit from both internal and external scale economies. The job market potential is merely a measure of how low the friction is when households, with given location, search for jobs with acceptable commuting conditions. A combination of large job and housing market potentials increases a household's opportunity of finding an efficient match of job and housing location.

Consider now the customer market potential and let M denote the overall market potential. To each economic activity, i, one can associate a coefficient, k_i, showing this activity's demand intensity. Then the activity-specific internal market potential is given by k_iM. For activities with distance-sensitive products, the size of k_iM is vital for the possibility of firms associated with these activities to locate in the region. Internal scale economies will imply that for any activity one can identify a minimum level of output, $\bar{x}_i$, below which the firm cannot cover fixed and variable costs. Hence, location is possible only if $k_iM \geq \bar{x}_i$, and with $k_iM >> \bar{x}_i$, the region may host several firms.

Suppose now that at a given point in time, when $M = M(0)$, this criterion is satisfied and stimulates the activity to locate in the region, possibly substituting previous imports to the region. What is the consequence of such an introduction of a new activity? We should expect the number of jobs and the income in the region to increase. This will in turn bring the market potential to increase to a new level $M(1) > M(0)$. If this augmentation is significant, one may also predict an expansion of already existing activities. In addition, the increase by $\Delta M = M(1) - M(0)$ may trigger the introduction of still more new activities (new firms) into the regional market. As a consequence one can expect a cumulative change process of the kind illustrated in Figure 9.2. Observe also that a shrinking market potential will make the direction of the arrows to switch into the opposite direction, implying cumulative decline.

The size of export flows to other regions is often small for distance-sensitive products. However, as the production grows the cost per unit output falls, due to scale economies. And this allows prices of interregional exports to decline, which may bring about growing exports flows. In such a development, the external market potential grows as a share of the total market potential.

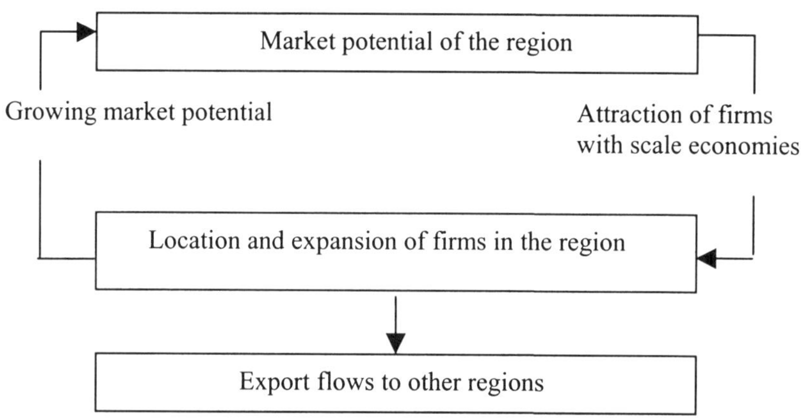

Figure 9.2 Cumulative growth of the market potential due to scale economies

In relation to Figure 9.2 one should observe that internal and external scale economies may be present simultaneously. The effect of external economies is that firms with similar activities are attracted to each other. In the latter case they also stimulate input suppliers to locate in the region, to the extent that their deliveries are distance sensitive, in combination with scale economies in their production.

To be more precise, let for a given activity, i, the demand for distance-sensitive inputs be $h_i x_i$ and let the corresponding supply be y_i. Let in a similar way the demand for specialized labor inputs be $n_i x_i$ and the corresponding supply in the region be z_i. With a sufficiently large input-market potential for activity i we have that $y_i \geq h_i x_i$ and $z_i \geq n_i x_i$. Observe also that the same output as y_i and the same type of labor as z_i may have other customers than firms engaged in activities of type i. In such cases $y_i >> h_i x_i$ and $z_i >> n_i x_i$. From this we understand that a large overall market potential can ascertain and stimulate the development of input-market potentials in general. This will further improve the production conditions of activity i as well as other activities with similar input requirements. In summary, the described phenomena will give rise to the cumulative process illustrated in Figure 9.3.

In the described process the internal market-potential expands and this can generate falling output prices, which in turn will stimulate exports to other regions. In this way the external market potential gets a growing importance for the cumulative growth trajectory.

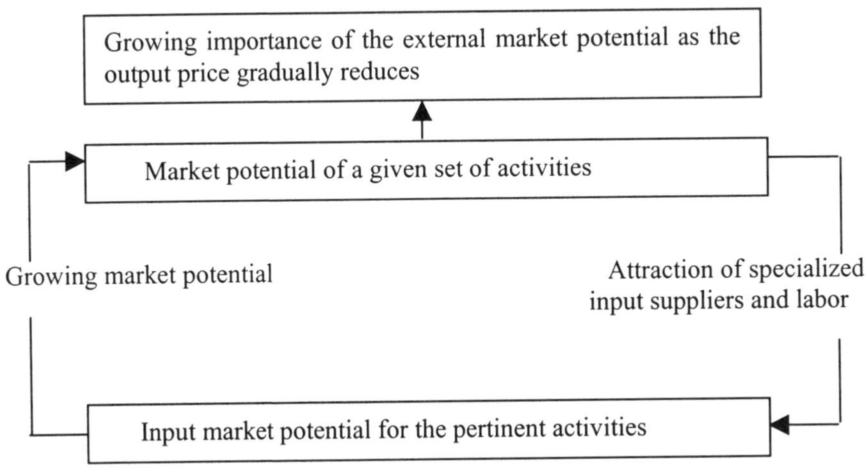

Figure 9.3 Dynamic interdependence between market potential and input market potential

Special attention should be given to knowledge-intensive sectors, which have a large share of knowledge-handling labor, often registered as a high share of employees with university education. One may also recognize another form of knowledge dependence, which reveals itself as large input shares from knowledge-intensive firms. This gives us a distinction between knowledge-oriented and less knowledge-dependant sectors. Suppose that sector i in our previous example belongs to the former category. Then an increase of x_i will stimulate an increase of y_i, and together this will imply an overall increase of the region's knowledge intensity. The cumulative consequence is that we can observe a simultaneous or interacting expansion of the job market potential of knowledge-intensive households.

Formulating the Dynamic Processes

The market potential variables discussed in the previous subsection represent resources that adjust on a slow time scale. This means that a region's overall market potential, as well as its specific components, has the same role as infrastructure. A region's market potentials provide an arena for processes that adjust on a fast and medium-speed time scale. Moreover, the input market potentials comprise the regional supply of capital, labor (with different skills and education) and built environment, which are all factors emphasized in resource-based models with historical adherence back to Ricardo.

What about the knowledge intensity of the labor force? Many studies provide empirical support to the assumption that households with university education and other skill attributes are attracted to migrate to and stay in regions that offer an attractive household milieu. The latter includes natural and artificial amenities as well as climatic attributes. In addition, the milieu is strongly affected by the household infrastructure which comprises the region's housing market potential and the accessibility from housing areas 1. to the supply of household services, 2. to the supply of amenities of various kind, and 3. to job opportunities in workplace areas. This may be thought of as the household milieu or the household market potentials.

The above ideas imply that a region's household milieu is a partly independent attractor of household location and regional labor supply. To the extent that this is true one may conclude that regional labor markets must adjust by means of a process where firms follow the location of labor supply, rather than the opposite. Before we address this question we shall investigate the role of infrastructure for interaction.

Infrastructure for interaction in an urban region is, first of all, the entire built environment with its various networks for transport and communication. It also includes the links connecting the region with other regions and the associated external market potentials. The internal infrastructure has the role of making it possible to combine high economic density with low interaction costs – with regard to all the different types of markets specified in the preceding subsection.

High density and low geographic transaction costs imply 'thick' markets with large demand, many customers and suppliers and frequent transactions. Moreover, interaction infrastructure may also enlarge a market in a complementary way by including previously separated geographic domains. In this case extension of transport facilities integrates new areas by reducing the time distances to these new areas. This form of enlargement also implies that the internal market potential of the regions grows.

The overall market potential (size and density of a region) is an infrastructure phenomenon in itself. It changes in a process of very slow adjustments and provides collective market opportunities that benefit both households and firms.

Figure 9.4 depicts how the location of households and jobs form a self-reinforcing dynamic process, i.e., a process with positive feedback. In addition the figure emphasizes how the formation of regional infrastructure affects the process by gradually building up a milieu for households and for firms. Naturally, the economic milieu is partly determined by the job-location process. However, we assume that the economic milieu as a whole changes at a much slower pace than the location of jobs does. Hence, in limited time perspective we treat the milieu characteristics as approximately invariant. The same argument applies to the relation between the household milieu and the dynamics of household location.

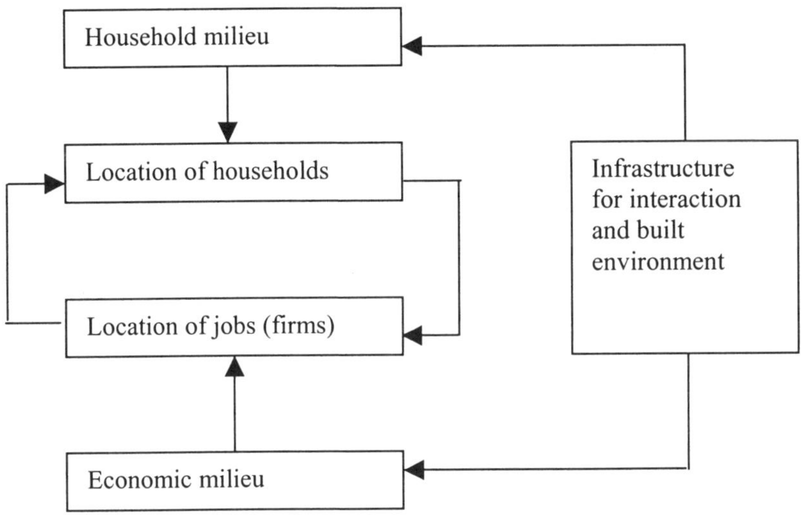

Figure 9.4 Household and economic milieu in the regional development process

The regional change process in Figure 9.4 has the form of interdependent dynamics such that jobs and households mutually adjust to each other. A formulation like this is in sharp contrast to the so called export base model, according to which economic activities locate independently, whereas the labor supply of households is assumed to adjust to the demand for labor, partly through in-migration. In this case households follow jobs. Regional change processes of this kind are usually associated with the 'industrial society' characterized by homogenous labor employed in factories.

An opposite relation is suggested in Quigley (1990) and Maclellan (1990). They observe in the late 20th century Europe and US a change process according to which jobs follow household. This form of causation is associated with the 'knowledge society' in which the growing economic sectors have a high demand for knowledge-intensive labor, primarily with university education. Under these conditions knowledge-intensive households select residential locations in areas and regions with an attractive household milieu and firms with a large demand for the associated labor inputs have to adjust their location accordingly.

The next section will present our model for long term projection of employment and population growth in Swedish municipalities. The strategy employed refers to Figure 9.4. Two structural equations are estimated simultaneously, one for projection of job development and one for household development in individual municipalities. The relation between these two projections is illustrated by Figure 9.5. From our previous discussion it is obvious that the household milieu, economic milieu and infrastructure attributes are slowly changing factors. As a consequence the interdependencies have to be estimated over a long time period.

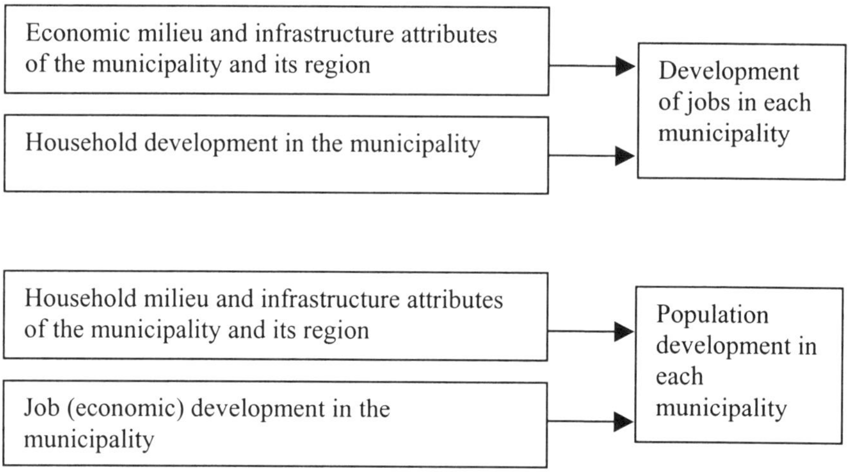

Figure 9.5 Structure of two interdependent change processes

Specifying the Model Structure

In preceding subsections we have stresses that most Swedish municipalities do not have a labor market of their own. This means that the number of persons dwelling in a municipality (and having a job) depends on the number of jobs in the functional region. The size of the economically active population in Swedish municipalities is only to a lesser degree determined by the size of the population in each individual municipality. And in the long run the sustainable size of the entire population in a municipality can be assumed to depend on the size of the economically active population.

An analysis of Swedish municipalities during the beginning of the 1990s shows that the variation in population size of municipalities can explain only 40 per cent of the corresponding variation in the size of the economically active population. The reason for this is simply that a large share of the working population has a job in other parts of the functional region. In other words, the local labor market is much larger than the municipality and a balance is achieved by commuting between different municipalities in a region.

To illustrate this phenomenon one can study the relation between a municipality's daytime and nighttime population. The former variable refers to the number of jobs in the municipality, whereas the latter refers to the number of persons living in the municipality. In order to make these two populations comparable they should be defined for the same age classes. If this is done, the ratio between the daytime and the nighttime populations will show how dependent a given municipality is of the local labor market. Table 9.1 illustrates this relation and shows that 2/3 of all municipalities are dependent on job opportunities in other municipalities, basically within the same region.

Table 9.1 Municipalities with excess demand for and supply of labor, Sweden, 1990–1994

Local labor market dependency	Ratio of daytime population to nighttime population. Per cent	Number of municipalities
Strongly dependent on labor inflow	110–	24
Dependent on some labor inflow	101–109	38
Relatively independent	99–101	24
Dependent on external job opportunities	91–98	69
Strongly dependent on external job opportunities	–90	133
All municipalities		288

Close to one half of the Swedish municipalities are strongly dependent on other municipalities for employment opportunities. Municipalities of this type are either suburbs of the large metropolitan municipalities or lying in the vicinity of regional centers. For about 10 per cent of the municipalities the internal labor market is relatively balanced. Another ten per cent of the Swedish municipalities have a marked excess demand for labor and are hence strongly dependent on commuting inflows from other municipalities. In this group we find the large metropolitan municipalities and some of the large regional centers.

To be able to describe in model terms such a situation would require the construction of a set of labor market regions (functional regions) with self-sufficient labor markets and thus very small flows of job commuters into or out of the region. Another possible solution is to use the municipalities as observation units and to explicitly take into account the commuting between municipalities as a balancing factor. In the present study the latter approach has been adopted.

Our next task is to bring our discussion in the preceding sections down to a set of structural equations, which can describe the dynamic interaction between jobs and population in each municipality. At the same time we should take into account properties of the household and economic milieu.

The household milieu also depends on the job market potential, which is partly reflected by the number of jobs in the municipality and partly by the commuting characteristics of the municipality. Since this does not provide the whole picture of the pertinent market potential, we have to include also other infrastructure and milieu variables.

In a reciprocal way the size of the population reflects part of the labor input market potential. In addition, the total population also reflects the size of the customer market inside the municipality. However, also in this case additional variables are needed, as will be made clear subsequently.

So far two basic variables have been emphasized, i.e., the number of jobs which will be denoted by S and the number of inhabitants, denoted by B. In formulating our two-equation model we follow the work by Carlino and Mills (1987). For each municipality, the equation describing the number of jobs (or economic activity level) includes three categories of variables, namely *S*, *B* and $I = (I_1,...I_n)$, where the latter is a vector of municipality characteristics describing infrastructure, market potentials and other aspects of the economic milieu. The corresponding variables referring to the size of the population are *S*, *B* and $H = (H_1,...,H_k)$, where the latter is a vector of municipality characteristics describing infrastructure, market potentials and other aspects of the household milieu. Obviously, some components of the *I* and *H* vectors are likely to be the same. The two equations incorporate the dynamic interdependence among variables in the following way:

$$S_{t+\tau} = F(S_t, B_{t+\tau}, I_1,..., I_n) \tag{1}$$

$$B_{t+\tau} = G(B_t, S_{t+\tau}, H_1,..., H_k) \tag{2}$$

where

$S_t =$ number of jobs (daytime population) at time t = 1980, whereas $S_{t+\tau}$ refers to the number of jobs at time $t+\tau$ = 1994.

$B_t =$ total population at time t = 1980, whereas $B_{t+\tau}$ refers to the population size at time $t+\tau$ = 1994.

$I =$ municipality characteristics describing the economic milieu during the period 1980–1994.

$H =$ municipality characteristics describing the household milieu during the period 1980–1994.

In order to avoid size problems in the estimation process we shall, as will be explained further on, express both employment and population as densities by dividing the corresponding numbers by the total area of each one of the municipalities.

The model (1)-(2) describes a long-term interdependent change process that eventually will lead to an equilibrium, where the population and job adjustments have come to rest, given the composition of slowly changing milieu characteristics of each municipality.

One may then ask how fast population and job densities approach the equilibrium point. One important factor in this process is the mobility of jobs and households between municipalities and regions, which obviously influences the rate of change in population and job densities. Mills and Carlino (1989) show that in the American economy densities change at an extremely slow rate. According to model estimates, it takes more than 50 years before the long-term equilibrium point (in the model) is reached. Similar conclusions can be drawn from Holmberg and Johansson (1992).

These observations imply that an implicit final equilibrium of the system (1)-(2) may have only indirect meaning, since such an equilibrium will most likely be displaced due to changes in infrastructure and in other factors not included in the model specification. This does not exclude that the estimated change model describes and explains the development in a shorter time perspective of 15–30 years. Our conclusion is that it is exactly in this time perspective that the model is useful both for projections of multiregional change and for qualitative analysis.

Population and Job Distribution across Swedish Regions

This section starts by identifying large market potential areas and macro regions with a dense household milieu. Thereafter population and job density patterns are described. These exercises form the basis for specifying the econometric model and interpreting the estimation results.

Distribution of the Swedish Population across Regions

Sweden is characterized by an uneven distribution of its population with an average of 21 inhabitants per square kilometer in the 1990s. However, one can identify two major macro regions with high population densities. Within each of these regions every municipality center is surrounded by at least 50 000 person inside a circle of 30 kilometers radius. The first of these two macro regions is located in the eastern part of Sweden with Stockholm as a center point. It unfolds along three corridors as described below:

1. Stockholm-Uppsala-Gävle, 2. Stockholm-Örebro-Karlstad, and 3. Stockholm-Norrköping-Linköping. When a municipality belongs to this macro region, this is recognized in the regression equations by the dummy variable:

$$A_1 \tag{3}$$

The second of these macro regions is located in western and southern Sweden and can be described by two corridors as follows:

1. Trollhättan-Göteborg-Malmö-Kristianstad-Kalrskrona, 2. Trollhättan-Skövde-Jönköping-Värnamo-Ljungby. When a municipality belongs to this macro region, this is recognized in the regression equations by the dummy variable:

$$A_2 \tag{4}$$

Practically every municipality in these two macro regions belongs to a large or medium-sized functional region. In addition to this regional characterization we have also arranged two groups of municipalities with very large internal and nearby market potentials. This gives us two market potential areas, where both are associated with metropolitan regions. The first area is associated with the Stockholm region and the second with a west-coast area comprising the Göteborg and Malmö regions:

The first market-potential area is the *Mälardal area*, with about 2.4 million inhabitants. For this area we use the dummy variable:

$$B_1 \tag{5}$$

The second market-potential area can be called the *West coast area* comprising the Göteborg and Malmö regions. This area hosts 1.6 million inhabitants and is recognized in the estimation equations by the dummy variable:

$$B_2 \tag{6}$$

In summary one can conclude that the municipalities in the two macro regions (A_1 and A_2) have a dense household milieu. On the other hand, in the two large market-potential areas (B_1 and B_2) each municipality belongs to a large functional region. Finally, one should observe that the intersection between the sets A_1 and B_1 is considerable. Likewise, the two sets A_2 and B_2 contain to a large extent the same municipalities.

Population Density Patterns

Our regressions will be focussed on two slowly changing variables, population and job densities. Although the population density adjusts at a slow pace, the population size in municipalities can change considerably during a decade. In the period 1980–1994 one can observe that 25 municipalities had a population increase by more than 20 per cent, almost exclusively municipalities belonging to a metropolitan region (suburbs).

Table 9.2 The ten municipalities with the highest population increase, 1980–1994

Municipality	Market potential area	Population increase, per cent
Vaxholm	B1 (Stockholm region)	64.9
Värmdö	B1 (Stockholm region)	45.4
Kungsbacka	B2 (Göteborg region)	38.6
Vallentuna	B1 (Stockholm region)	32.4
Ekerö	B1 (Stockholm region)	29.6
Håbo	B1 (Stockholm region)	26.5
Vellinge	B2 (Malmö region)	26.2
Tjörn	B2 (Göteborg region)	25.2
Höör	B2 (Malmö region)	25.0
Österåker	B1 (Stockholm region)	24.9

Source: Statistics Sweden.

During the same period around 20 municipalities lost more than 10 per cent of their population. These are municipalities belonging to small and peripheral functional regions, often in northern Sweden but also municipalities dominated by a single export industry.

Table 9.3 The ten municipalities with the largest population loss, 1980–1994

Municipality	Population loss 1980–1994, per cent
Filipstad	-10.9
Hagfors	-11.2
Kiruna	-11.9
Hofors	-12.3
Sorsele	-12.7
Oxelösund	-14.8
Åsele	-15.6
Bjurholm	-15.6
Hällefors	-15.8
Laxå	-16.2

Source: Statistics Sweden.

How slow is then the change of the population density? Between 1980 and 1994 the average density increased from 20.2 to 21.5, i.e., by 6 per cent. For some areas the change is clearly larger. For the majority of municipalities the change was less than 10 per cent in absolute value. In general the density rises more rapidly in already dense municipalities.

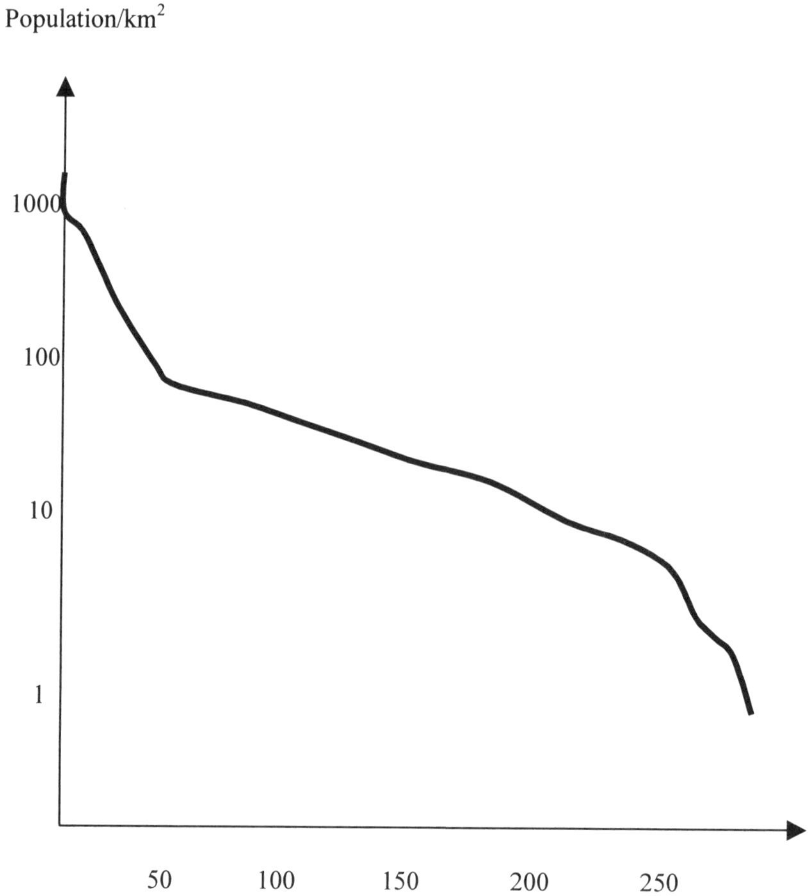

Figure 9.6 Population density across Swedish municipalities

The diagram in Figure 9.6 illustrates the density of municipalities when they are ranked according to population density. To the left side of the curve one finds the municipalities that belong to metropolitan regions. For a large majority of municipalities the density fall within the interval 10 to 100 persons per square kilometer.

Job Density Patterns

The density of jobs (or work places) can be measured and described in the same way as was done for population in the preceding subsection. The corresponding statistical observable is called daytime population and records all persons having a job in a given municipality (irrespective of the residential location of those persons). The range of variation in job densities is even greater than that of population densities. In the Stockholm region one can find several municipalities with more than 1000 work places per square kilometer. At the same time there were more than 60 municipalities with less than 5 jobs per square kilometer. During the period 1980–1994 the average density reached its maximum in 1990. Due to the sluggish economic development in the four following years, the density decreased somewhat in this period.

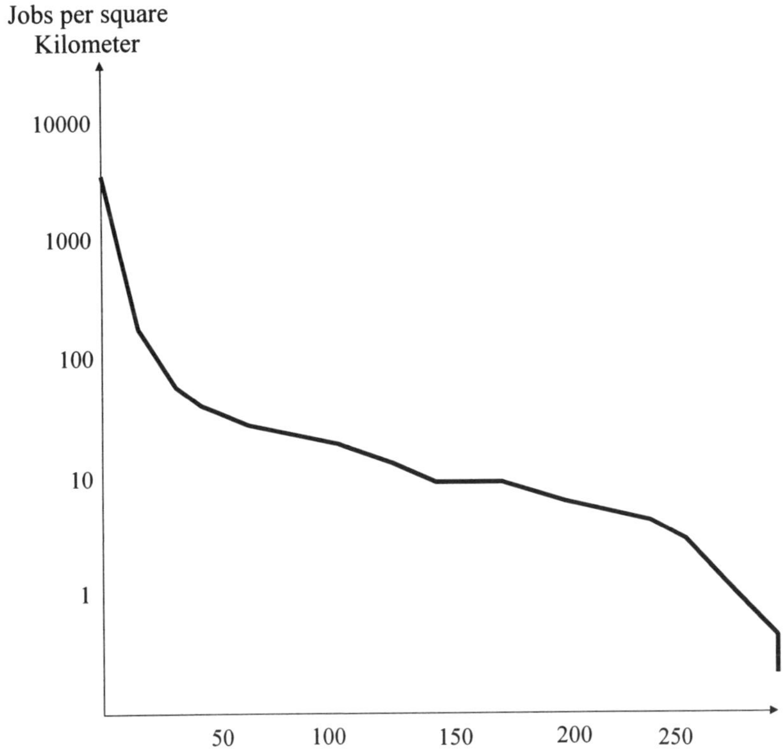

Figure 9.7 Density of jobs across Swedish municipalities, 1994

The economic recession in Sweden that followed after 1990 made the average job density fall from 11 to 10 persons per square meter. Table 9.4 shows that the job density still had increased considerably between 1980 and 1994 in some municipalities. Table 9.5 on the other hand is focussed on the ten municipalities with strongest reduction in job density.

Around 70 of the Swedish municipalities experienced a growth in their job density in the period after 1980. In another 200 municipalities the job density decreased. In this latter category we also find the three largest municipalities Stockholm, Göteborg and Malmö. This is illustrated in Table 9.5 where one can see that the largest reductions of jobs per square meter took place primarily in municipalities that had a very high job density from the start.

Table 9.4 The ten municipalities with the largest increase of job density, 1980–1994: number of jobs

Municipality	Market potential area	Increase in job density
Sundbyberg	(B1) Stockholm region	217.0
Solna	(B1) Stockholm region	119.0
Sollentuna	(B1) Stockholm region	102.3
Täby	(B1) Stockholm region	81.2
Danderyd	(B1) Stockholm region	68.3
Huddinge	(B1) Stockholm region	56.2
Partille	(B2) Göteborg region	32.2
Järfälla	(B1) Stockholm region	28.9
Mölndal	(B2) Göteborg region	27.7
Tyresö	(B1) Stockholm region	25.3

Source: Statistics Sweden.

Table 9.5 The ten municipalities with the largest decrease in job density, 1980–1994: number of jobs

Municipality (Market potential area)	Decrease in job density
Helsingborg (B2)	-7.2
Karlskoga (B1)	-9.1
Bjuv (B2)	-10.8
Hallstahammar	-16.5
Burlöv (B2)	-19.1
Landskrona (B2)	-28.2
Göteborg (B2)	-43.0
Oxelösund	-46.2
Malmö (B2)	-115.1
Stockholm (B1)	-159.3

Source: Statistics Sweden.

Two Structural Equations

In this section we introduce our two structural equations referring to the job density in 1994, $S(94)$, and the population density the same year, $B(94)$. The objective of these two regression equations is to 1. show the dynamic influence from the economic and household milieu and 2. show how job and population densities mutually influence each other over time. We start by specifying the counterpart of equation (7), which describes the change process of job densities. Two major explanatory variables are the job density in 1980, $S(80)$, and the population density in 1994, $B(94)$. The whole regression equation is specified in formula (7). The remaining explanatory variables are presented in Table 9.6.

$$S(94) = \alpha_0 + \alpha_1 S(80) + \alpha_2 B(94) + \alpha_3 B_1 + \alpha_4 B_2 + \alpha_5 C_1 + \alpha_6 C_2 + \alpha_7 T + \alpha_8 K + \alpha_9 M + \alpha_{10} U \tag{7}$$

Table 9.6 Explanatory variables in equation (7)

Variable	Definition
B_1 and B_2	Dummy variables representing the two large market-potential areas 1. the *Mälardal* and 2. the *West coast.*
C_1	Average rate of commuting into the municipality, 1987–90
C_2	Average rate of commuting out of the municipality, 1987–90
T	General accessibility to other municipalities
K	Dummy variable representing university municipalities
M	Dummy representing the central Stockholm region (Stockholm, Solna and Sundbyberg municipalities)
U	Average rate of unemployment in the municipality 1994

The two dummy variables, B_1 and B_2, refer to the two large market potential areas, as defined in (5) and (6). The two commuting variables, C_1 and C_2, characterize each region's relation to the entire labor market of the corresponding functional region during the estimation period. This relation is also reflected by the variable *T*, which describes each municipality's accessibility to other municipalities in the form of the following population potential:

$$T_r = \sum_s B_s \exp\{-\lambda d_{rs}\} \tag{8}$$

where T_r denotes municipality *r*'s accessibility to the populations, B_s, in the municipality itself and in other municipalities *s*, where d_{rs} is the distance between *r* and *s* in travel time by car, and where λ represents the generalized travel cost per unit distance.

Knowledge or university municipalities are recognized by the dummy variable *K*, whereas the special character of the central Stockholm region is captured by the variable *M*. Finally, the influence of the unemployment during 1994 is identified by the variable *U*.

Turning to the population density equation, we observe that the population density in 1980, $B(80)$, and the job density in 1994, $S(94)$, are explanatory variables in the regression equation (9). The remaining independent variables are presented in Table 9.7.

$$B(94) = \beta_0 + \beta_1 B(80) + \beta_2 S(94) + \beta_3 A_1 + \beta_4 A_2 + \beta_5 C_1 + \beta_6 C_2 + \beta_7 D + \beta_8 K + \beta_9 M + \beta_{10} U \tag{9}$$

Table 9.7 Explanatory variables in equation (9)

Variable	Definition
A_1 and A_2	Dummy variables representing the two macro regions defined in (3) and (4)
C_1	Average rate of commuting into the municipality, 1987–90
C_2	Average rate of commuting out of the municipality, 1987–90
D	Proportion of detached houses for a single family and for two families
K	Dummy variable representing university municipalities
M	Dummy representing the central Stockholm region (Stockholm, Solna and Sundbyberg municipalities)
U	Average rate of unemployment in the municipality 1994

We may observe that the two equations (7) and (9) have five explanatory variables in common, namely C_1, C_2, *M*, *K* and *U*. As we shall see subsequently, all these except *K* have opposite signs in the two equations. It is also natural to find that the housing variable *D* only occurs in the population density equation. Moreover, the market-potential variable *T* that describes a municipality's general accessibility is not included in the population density equation.

The data for the estimation are collected for the time period 1980–1994. As indicated in the preceding subsection, some variables are assumed to reflect characteristics that are assumed to be more or less invariant during the period, whereas the unemployment variable *U* is introduced for the terminal year to correct for the downturn of economic activities in the end of the period.

The equations in (7) and (9) are structural equations, which are estimated by a two-stage least-square method from the SPSS package. The result from the estimation is presented in Tables 9.8 and 9.9. The first table presents the estimated parameters of the job density equation.

Table 9.8 Parameter estimates of the job density equation (7)

Variables	Parameter values	t-values
Intercept	-1.2508	-12.2
$S(80)$ = job density 1980	0.1579	3.8
$B(94)$ = population density 1994	0.8264	19.9
B_1 = Mälardal market potential	-0.0211	-2.0
B_2 = West coast market potential	0.0019	0.1
C_1 = rate of in-going commuter flows	0.0016	16.9
C_2 = rate of out-going commuter flows	-0.0012	-12.6
T = general accessibility (market potential)	0.0526	5.9
K = university municipality	0.0139	0.9
M = central Stockholm region	-0.1812	-3.6
U = unemployment rate	-0.0174	-6.5
R-square (adj.)		**0.998**

From Table 9.8 we can see that two parameters are not statistically significant, namely B_2 and *K*. Hence, having a university in a municipality does not in itself stimulate job densities. However, we shall soon see that it influences the population density. Clearly, the unemployment rate has a negative effect on the job density. Moreover, the Mälardal-region dummy, B_1, as well as the central-Stockholm dummy, *M*, has each a dampening effect on the increase of job density of municipalities.

Among variables with a positive effect on the growth of job densities we find the already established job density, *S*(80), and the growth of population – as represented by *B*(94). The high parameter value for the latter variable is a first indication of a pattern where jobs follow population. Then we have a set of slowly changing, structural characteristics, with a positive effect on the growth of job densities. These are 1. in-going commuter flows, and 2. general accessibility, i.e., the direct market potential of a municipality. Finally, a large out-going commuter flow pattern has a dampening effect on the growth of job densities. In general, the estimated parameters have a sign, which is compatible with the assumptions of the theory outlined in previous sections, and the R-square is indeed high. The latter is, of course, partly a result of using lagged variables for slow processes.

Our second equation, (9), reflects the change of population densities. It has four structural variables in common with equation (7): C_1, C_2, *K* and *M*. As we shall see, the associated parameters for C_1, C_2 and *M* come out with opposite signs in the population and job density equations. All parameter values are presented in Table 9.9.

Table 9.9 Parameter estimates of the population density equation (9)

Variables	Parameter values	t-values
Intercept	0.2821	8.1
B(80) = population density 1980	0.4908	3.8
S(94) = job density 1994	0.5189	19.8
A_1 = macro region 1, defined in (3)	-0.0156	-1.7
A_2 = macro region 2, defined in (4)	-0.0009	-0.1
C_1 = rate of in-going commuter flows	-0.0010	-15.5
C_2 = rate of out-going commuter flows	0.0009	23.3
D = attractiveness of housing market	0.0013	4.3
K = university municipality	0.3400	3.2
M = central Stockholm region	0.1143	3.4
U = unemployment rate	0.0097	5.1
R-square (adj.)		**0.999**

The macro region dummies are not statistically significant, especially not for A_2. We may also observe that many of the municipalities associated with A_1 are also associated with B_1. Everything else equal, in these municipalities both job and population densities tend to have a reduced growth rate.

Let us next turn to the structural characteristics which appear in both equations and observe the following pattern:

1. The share of in-going commuter flows stimulate growth in job densities and dampen the growth in population densities.
2. The share of out-going commuter flows dampen the growth in job densities and stimulate the growth in population densities.
3. A location in the central Stockholm region reduces the growth of job densities and increases the growth of population densities.
4. The effect of having a university is insignificant as regards growth in job densities but has a significant positive effect on the growth in population densities.

Next we observe that a high unemployment rate has not the negative growth effect as it had in the job density equation. Moreover, the attractiveness of a municipality's housing market has a positive growth effect on population densities.

Having reached these conclusions, what can we say about the coupled variables *S* and *B*? First we note that the already established population density has a strong influence on the growth in population density and this effect is much stronger than the corresponding effect for job densities. This result points in a clear direction: the path dependence of population density is much stronger than the path dependence of job density.

Second, the influence from growth in job density on population density seems to be stronger than the influence in the opposite direction. Our two last remarks both indicate that the location dynamics of households (population) has an impact on the location dynamics of economic activities (jobs) which is stronger than the impact of the reversed feedback. In the next subsection we shall try to substantiate this conclusion further.

Interpretation of Results

The results in the preceding subsection are very much in accordance with the theoretical framework outlined in the previous section. We do find that the integration of municipalities into functional regions has a clear impact on change of both job and population densities of municipalities. This is reflected by the highly significant parameter values for established patterns of commuting between municipalities. We also find that the general market potential variable (general accessibility) has a clear impact on the job density dynamics.

One way of taking our discussion a little bit further is to transform the estimated structural equations in the previous subsection into reduced-form equations. The parameters in the latter equations are calculated from the initial parameters when we insert the relevant variables from one structural equation into the other. The result of this operation is displayed in Table 9.10.

Before we proceed, one may observe that in the reduced form the job dynamics are influenced indirectly by all variables in the two equations. This influence works itself through an 'initial' impact on the population dynamics and this effect is then 'transmitted' to the job dynamics. In this indirect way the job-density growth is stimulated by 1. the attractiveness of the housing market and 2. the existence of a university. In a similar way the general accessibility affects the growth of population density.

In order to further illuminate the relative strength of different influences, we can calculate elasticities of various regression variables. For several variables these elasticities are equal to the coefficients in Table 9.10. This happens when logarithmic values of the variables have been used in the estimation. For all other variables, the elasticity has been evaluated around the mean value.

Table 9.10 Parameter estimates of the reduced-form equations

Variables	Job density	Population density
Intercept	-1.7101	-0.5572
S(80) = job density 1980	0.2652	0.1301
B(80) = population density 1980	0.7184	0.8715
A_1 = macro region 1	-0.0216	-0.0262
A_2 = macro region 2	-0.0013	-0.0016
B_1 = Mälardal market potential area	-0.0354	-0.0174
B_2 = West coast market potential area	0.0031	0.0015
C_1 = rate of in-going commuting	0.0013	-0.0003
C_2 = rate of out-going commuting	-0.0007	0.0006
T = general accessibility (market potential)	0.0884	0.0434
D = attractiveness of housing market	0.0018	0.0022
K = university municipality	0.0703	0.0685
M = central Stockholm region	-0.1460	0.0427
U = unemployment rate	-0.0158	0.0020

The result in the first two rows of Table 9.11 has a distinct message: the impact of population density on the two simultaneous change processes is markedly higher than the same type of impact from job density. A second observation is the high elasticity for the variable 'general accessibility', which suggests a strong influence from a municipality's market potential (via its accessibility to neighboring municipalities plus its internal accessibility). This influence is high for both the job and the population density.

Table 9.11 Estimates of impact elasticities

Variables	Job density	Population density
$S(80)$ = Job density	0.27	0.13
$B(80)$ = Population density	0.72	0.87
C_1 = In-going commuting	0.14	-0.03
C_2 = Out-going commuting	-0.13	0.10
T = General accessibility	1.06	0.52
D = Attractiveness of housing	0.12	0.14
U = Rate of unemployment	-0.11	0.01

Conclusions

In the first part of this chapter we provide arguments suggesting that a study of multiregional development should use functional regions as spatial observation units. However, we have shown that it is possible to model multiregional change processes at a lower level of spatial resolution (with municipalities as observation units), given that each municipality's association with its functional region is reflected by variables such as accessibility and inter-municipality commuting etc.

The empirical exercise has one overall message as regards spatial resolution. Aggregate geographical areas have much less importance than fine level areas. This is reflected by the following result:

The two aggregate areas A_2 and B_2 are not statistically significant as dummy variables. The other two areas, A_1 and A_2, may have parameters different from zero, but these two dummy variables have a weak influence on the change process.

The three most important factors, as given by the impact elasticities in Table 9.11, are reflecting local characteristics. In order of importance these factors are 1. general accessibility that basically reflects the market potential of a municipality together with its closest neighbors, 2. population density and 3. job density. The latter two definitely reflect a local phenomenon. One can also note that the attractiveness of the local housing market has a dynamic impact on both job and population densities.

The rest of this story is that 1. in-going commuting links have an impact on job density, whereas out-going commuting links affect population density. Table 9.12 summarizes this discussion by ranking how different factors contribute to the two, coupled change-processes.

Table 9.12 Ranking of the combined direct and indirect effects on the development of job and population densities

Factors influencing job-density development	Factors influencing population-density development
General accessibility (+)	Population density (+)
Population density (+)	General accessibility (+)
Job density (+)	Attractiveness of housing (+)
In-going commuting (+)	Job density (+)
Out-going commuting (-)	Out-going commuting (+)
Attractiveness of housing (+)	
Rate of unemployment (-)	

How could the findings in the empirical be further examined and tested? A first obvious option is to recapitulate the econometric exercise, but now with functional regions as spatial units. With such an approach one could define both density of a region and the density variation within the region, or one could define intraregional and interregional accessibility as two separate variables. Another extension of the study would be to explicitly test for the two-way causality and the relative strength in jobs follow households and households follow jobs.

Finally, it should be stressed that the theoretical framework, which is outlined in this chapter, is but a sketch. The empirical results provide an incentive to continue the work to formulate a consistent theory of multiregional interdependent dynamics.

References

Andersson, Å.E., Anderstig, C. and Hårsman, B. (1990), 'Knowledge and Communication Infrastructure and Regional Economic Change', *Regional Science and Urban Economics*, vol. 20, pp. 359–76.

Arrow, K.J. (1979), 'The Division of Labor in the Economy', in G.P. O'Discroll Jr. (ed.), *Adam Smith and Modern Political Economy*, Iowa State University Press, Ames.

Beckmann, M. (1958), 'City Hierarchies and the Distribution of City Sizes', *Economic Development and Cultural Change*, IV, vol. 3, pp. 343–8.

Carlino, G. and Mills, E.S. (1987), 'The Determinants of County Growth', *Journal of Regional Science*, vol. 27, pp. 39–54.

Chipman, J.S. (1970), 'External Economies of Scale and Competitive Equilibrium', *Quarterly Journal of Economics*, pp. 347–85.

Ciccone, A. and Hall, R.E. (1996), 'Productivity and the Density of Economic Activity', *American Economic Review*, vol. 86, pp. 54–70.

Elhance, A. and Lakshmanan, T.R. (1986), 'Infrastructure-Production System Dynamics in National and Regional Systems; an Econometric Study of the Indian Economy', *Regional Science and Urban Economics*, vol. 18, pp. 511–31.

Ethier, W. (1979), 'National and International Returns to Scale in the Modern Theory of International Trade', *American Economic Review*, vol. 72, pp. 389–405.

Fujita, M. (1989), *Urban Economic Theory*, Cambridge University Press, Cambridge, MA.

Henderson, J.V. (1986), 'Efficiency of Resource Usage and City Size', *Journal of Urban Economics*, vol. 19, pp. 47–70.

Hirsch, S. (1967), *Location of Industry and International Competitiveness*, Oxford University Press, Oxford.

Holmberg, I. and Johansson, B. (1992), *Growth of Production, Migration of Jobs and Spatial Infrastructure*, Report ISRN KTH/RP/AR-92/6-SE, Regional Planning, The Royal Institute of Technology, Stockholm.

Johansson, B. (1993), 'Infrastructure, Accessibility and Economic Growth', *International Journal of Transport Economics*, vol. 2, pp. 131–56.

Johansson, B. (1996), 'Location Attributes and Dynamics of Job Location', *Journal of Infrastructure, Planning and Management*, vol. 530/IV-30, pp. 1–15.

Johanssson, B. (1998), *Infrastructure, Market Potential and Endogenous Growth*, paper presented at the Kyoto workshop 1997, Department of Civil Engineering, Kyoto University, Japan.

Johansson, B., Strömqvist, U. and Åberg, P. (1998), *Regioner, handel och tillväxt (Regions, Trade and Growth)*, RTK, Stockholms läns landsting, Stockholm.

Kaldor, N. (1970), 'The Case for Regional Policies', *Scottish Journal of Political Economy*, vol. 17, pp. 337–48.

Koopmans, T.C. (1957), *Three Essays on the State of Economic Science*, McGraw-Hill, New York.

Krugman, P. (1990), *Rethinking International Trade*, MIT Press, Cambridge, MA.

Lakshmanan, T.R. (1989), 'Infrastructure and Economic Transformation', in Å.E. Andersson, D.F. Batten and B. Johansson (eds), *Advances in Spatial Theory and Dynamics*, North-Holland, Amsterdam.

Lakshmanan, T.R. and Hansen, W.G. (1965), 'A Retail Market Potential Model', *Journal of the American Institute of Planners*, vol. 31, pp. 134–43.

Lösch, A. (1943), *Die Raumliche Ordnung der Wirtschaft*, Gustav Fischer, Stuttgart.

Maclellan, D. (1990), 'Urban Change through Environmental Investments', in *Urban Challenges*, SOU 1190:33, Stockholm, pp. 51–76.

Marshall, A. (1920), *Principles of Economics*, Macmillan, London.

Mera, K. (1973), 'Regional Production Functions and Social Overhead Capital: An Analysis of the Japanese Case', *Regional and Urban Economics*, vol. 3, pp. 157–86.

Mills, E.S. (1967), 'An Aggregative Model of Resource Allocation in a Metropolitan Area', *American Economic Review*, vol. 57, pp.197–210.

Mills, E.S. and Carlino, G. (1989), 'Dynamics of County Growth', in Å.E. Andersson, D.F. Batten and B. Johansson (eds), *Advances in Spatial Theory and Dynamics*, North-Holland, Amsterdam, pp. 195–206.

Munell, A. (1990), 'How does Public Infrastructure Affect Regional Economic Performance?', in A. Munell (ed.), *Is there a Shortfall in Public Capital Investment?*, Boston, Federal Reserve Bank.

Nurkse, R. (1953), *Problems of Capital Formation in Underdeveloped Countries*, Basil Blackwell, Oxford, UK.

Quigley, J. (1990), 'The Quality of Housing', in *Urban Challenges*, SOU 1990:33, Allmänna Förlaget, Stockholm, pp. 39–50.

Rosenstein-Rodan, P.N. (1943), 'Problems of Industrialization of Eastern and South-Eastern Europe', *Economic Journal*, p. 53.

Sasaki, K., Kunihisa, S. and Sugiyama, M. (1995), 'Evaluation of Road Capacity and its Spatial Allocation', *Annals of Regional Science*, vol. 29, pp. 143–54.

Seitz, H. (1995), 'The Productivity and Supply of Urban Infrastructures', *Annals of Regional Science*, vol. 29, pp. 143–154.

Sen, A. and Smith, T. (1995), *Gravity Models of Spatial Interaction Behavior*, Springer-Verlag, Berlin.

SOU (1990), *Challenges*, Allmänna Förlaget, Stockholm, 1990:33, pp. 51–76.

Stigler, G. (1951), 'The Division of Labour is Limited by the Extent of the Market', *Journal of Political Economy*, vol. 59, pp. 185–93.

von Thünen, J.H. (1826), *Der Isolierte Staat in Beziehung auf Nationale Ökonomie und Landwirtschaft*, Gustav Fischer, Stuttgart.

Tinbergen, J. (1967), 'The Hierarchy Model of the Size Distribution of Centres', *Papers of the Regional Science Association*, vol. 20, pp. 65–80.

Wigren, R. (1984), 'Measuring regional Efficiency – A Method Tested on Fabricated Metal products in Sweden 1973–75', *Regional Science and Urban Economics*, vol. 14, pp. 363–79.

Chapter 10

Economic Development and Health Patterns

David E. Andersson

Introduction

A discussion of the current health patterns of specific societies and of likely future changes to those health patterns can benefit from a historical economic perspective. Each stage of economic development has been associated with a typical mortality and morbidity profile. The empirical regularities are in fact so strong that if we know the stage of economic development of a society, we can mostly predict the general outlines of the actual mortality statistics.

While culturally determined behavioral differences do persist (no matter what stage of economic development we are studying), these differences are relatively small compared with inter-stage differences. Since economic development is such a good predictor of the health structure, it may therefore be worthwhile to take a closer look at what determines economic development, since the forces of economic development are arguably the most important underlying causes for the health patterns of any region, as reflected in mortality and morbidity statistics. Moreover, the pace of economic development seems to be associated with the pace of illness alleviation. And the greatest (and generally swiftest) economic restructuring a region can experience – industrialization – is accompanied by the most dramatic reduction of the incidence of infectious and parasitic diseases.

This chapter will take a look at these underlying causes, by first discussing the broad determinants of economic development, and then look at the health structure associated with various stages. We shall also discuss the implications of economic development for individual behavior.

The starting point of the analysis is that the most fundamental determinant of economic development is the division of labor. This realization is however not enough. Rather, we start from Adam Smith's insight that the division of labor is limited by the extent of the market (Smith, 1776).

The reason for focusing on the extent of market is that this is the link between several important factors. One such factor is space-bridging infrastructure. Improvements to such infrastructure expand the extent of the market, and thus increase opportunities for the division of labor. More generally, space-bridging infrastructure is likely to promote economic development. The second section below shall look at economic development from this infrastructural, market-extending perspective, following Andersson and Strömquist's theory that the transformation from one stage of development to the next stage (e.g. early capitalist to industrial society) coincides with a phase transition. Such a phase transition takes place when a critical link is added to an existing, space-bridging, network, or alternatively, that a new space-bridging invention superimposes a new, more efficient, network (Andersson and Strömquist, 1988).

However, the extent of the market is crucial from another perspective as well. This is because larger economies rely more on impersonal economic relationships, which encourages the development of formal institutions. This is the so-called 'soft infrastructure' of the rule of law and property rights. Following Kasper's approach to institutional evolution, we shall in the third section describe how institutional innovations are related to the network-induced economic transformations (Kasper, 1998a).

Extending the market also increases the efficiencies associated with competition. A greater number of actors implies that there is a greater potential for competing suppliers of the same good or service. A less widely known phenomenon that also increases efficiency is the potential for efficiency-inducing inter-jurisdictional competition. The fourth section will look at how constrained governments – which is often explained by inter-jurisdictional competition – has indeed accelerated economic development in various advantaged regions of the world, while a lack of such competition ultimately leads to stagnation.

Ultimately, it is people (either as individuals or in organizations) who shape the soft and hard infrastructures and who compete against each other. Whether we are discussing institutions, technology, or economic behavior, it is important to understand that it is individuals who introduce such disparate things as, for example, property rights, roads, vaccines, and voluntary exchange (trade). Thus we should not forget the role of the entrepreneur, a term which should be understood in a more general sense than the conventional one of a resourceful risk-taking businessman. Instead, an entrepreneur is anyone who, through personal risk-taking, introduces system-wide or localized, inherently unpredictable, 'positive shocks' to a system.

Space-bridging Infrastructures and the Growing Division of Labor

Andersson and Strömquist (1988) argue that the physical infrastructure – especially transportation and communication networks – are of crucial importance in explaining long-term economic growth and restructuring. They especially emphasize critical links and the creation of new networks.

When a new link connects two regions with different resource bases, it is inevitable that gains from integration will arise. This is because the effect of joint resource exploitation always exceeds the sum of the effects from two isolated resource bases. The evolution of ever larger trade and production areas reflects the marginal creation of links between pairs of regions. A critical link is a link that bridges two already established networks, and which results in a dramatic expansion to the extent of the market.

When non-critical links are added to existing networks, we will experience a slowly changing evolution of the economic system. When a critical link is added, however, a revolutionary restructuring of the entire economy will result. Andersson and Strömquist call such a revolutionary restructuring of the economy a 'logistical revolution'.

However, a logistical revolution does not imply that the preceding economic system will disappear in its entirety. Rather, the new system will be superimposed on the preceding system. The newer system will however be of greater importance in terms of its overall contribution to the economy, even if most people continue to work within the older system in the initial phase of the new developmental stage.

An example of how a critical link caused a logistical revolution is the arrival of trade capitalism in the 13th century. This was caused by the establishment of a new shipping route from the Mediterranean to the Baltic sea – which new shipbuilding technology facilitated – and a new bridge linking northern and southern Europe (Pirenne, 1936). These two links together caused a total transformation of the economy. Thousands of new cities appeared in the following one hundred years. An urban network economy was thus superimposed on a predominantly rural, feudal system. The new urban economies became centers of trade and culture with workshops and manufactories for the production of goods to exchange with the agricultural surplus. Transactions were facilitated by means of specie money and middlemen. A new urban capitalism thereby emerged.

Sometimes, however, the revolutionary trigger is not a critical space-bridging link, but a critical space-bridging technology. For example, the new post-industrial, globalized economy, which has been superimposed on industrialized, national economies since the 1970s, has been made possible only through the emergence of a new integrated computing and communication technology. It is through this technology that the transaction costs associated with international financial flows have been brought down. It has also led to a globalization of the availability of knowledge and information.

Institutional Evolution

A parallel development to the gradual extension of the market through reductions in transport and communication costs, has been the gradual evolution of institutions, the most important being the establishment of private property rights and the rule of law.

The earth was initially inhabited by small communities of hunters and gatherers without any concept of private property. These tribal communities were small enough for everyone to know and trust each other. Moreover, in small communities with shared beliefs and a shared quest for survival, altruistic and collectivistic forms of social organization tend to arise naturally (Hayek, 1988). Anthropologists have shown that this form of organization does not lead to opportunistic behavior among individuals in communities of up to 60 or 70 people. Personalized relationships and informal sanctions inhibit abuse of jointly owned assets. However, in larger groups, the 'tragedy of the commons' is a prevalent phenomenon (Hardin, 1993). This phenomenon may also explain why small groups are relatively adept at non-opportunistic, altruistic behavior in modern societies, whereas larger groups are generically afflicted with opportunistic behavior by some members of the group.

What then caused tribal society to break down? It seems that it was the population growth of certain communities in unusually well-endowed regions of the world. The most favored regions are regions that have a combination of unusually fertile soil and a below-average rate of infectious diseases and dangerous animals.

The Neolithic revolution of some 10,000 years ago marks the beginning of both agricultural society and the introduction of private property rights (Kasper, 1998b). It should come as no surprise that this occurred independently in certain mild and dry areas of the world (the Mediterranean, parts of Asia and the Americas). Conversely, tribal societies have persisted the longest in infertile, inaccessible or disease-prone regions (i.e. in sub-arctic, mountainous, or equatorial regions). In other words, an inhospitable natural environment delays the emergence of large communities with attendant propensities for both opportunistic individualism and impersonal large-group interaction. It is this lack of opportunistic individualism and impersonal relationships which prevents small-scale tribal societies to develop the ultimate causes of sustained economic development: the division of labor and private property rights.

However, property rights are chronologically prior to a (successful) formalized rule of law (Hayek, 1988). Agriculture and the domestication of animals generally trigger the adoption of private property (although the distribution of property may differ as a reflection of different tribal power structures. There are instances of both hierarchical and egalitarian tribes, in the same way as there are patrilineal, matrilineal, and ambilineal tribes). However, in all post-tribal societies there is a mixture of formal and informal institutions. Formal institutions denote the rule of law and formal punishments. Informal institutions denote rules of conduct with informal sanctions (reputation effects or shaming). However, as societies grow larger or more heterogeneous, reliance on formal institutions (e.g. the court system) tends to grow. Perhaps the best illustration of this is Anglo-Saxon common law. This is the process where informal, generally accepted, rules of conduct are gradually adopted by the formalized rule of law.

Sometimes the institutional setting is referred to as the non-material infrastructure, to reflect its similarity with the material infrastructure in shaping the economic structure of society. Another similarity is that extended periods of slow institutional evolution is punctuated by institutional revolutions. This is when critical institutional innovations are introduced which reshape the fundamentals of economic life. We have already noted the Neolithic revolution as the foundation for agricultural society. It is perhaps less well known that certain institutional innovations in England (which were later imitated elsewhere) was a prerequisite for the industrial revolution of the late 18th century. On the formal side were the introduction of modern financial institutions and the enclosure of agricultural land. But perhaps more important was a new informal (i.e. internal) institution that first arose among English entrepreneurs (Andersson and Strömquist, 1988). In the preceding period of trade capitalism, the economic actors treated the production technology as given by the resource endowments of a given region. The new, internalized, rule of economic behavior was to treat the production of goods as an optimization problem. The new industrial capitalist attempted to find the production method and resource use which maximized profits. In industrial society, the search for more efficient production technologies and a more specialized division of labor became key features of entrepreneurial behavior. It was this new non-material infrastructure of common rules of behavior that Adam Smith so cogently observed in the 'Wealth of Nations' (Smith, 1776).

The Role of the State and Inter-Jurisdictional Competition

So far we have discussed economic development without reference to the dynamics of political power. Political constraints have, however, had an enormous impact on the functioning of the economy at all stages of development. There are also certain commonalities that democratic and authoritarian societies share regarding the accumulation of state power.

Stable territorial governments have a marked tendency to grow over time, as has been observed by historians and economists, no matter what the geographical or historical context of their investigation. In discussing the growth of the public sector in democracies, Mancur Olson outlined a compelling theory of the impact as well as the formation and proliferation of interest groups (Olson, 1965, 1982). Olson showed how small, well-organized interest groups can obtain substantial resources for the members of the group by securing politically administered transfers from society at large. At the same time, the members of the larger polity have insufficient incentives to check this resource flow, since the burden imposed on each of them is relatively insignificant by comparison. However, the combined impact of all transfers to interest groups from unorganized segments of the population may be substantial. Olson also showed that one can expect the quantity of redistributive activities to grow over time in stable societies. Moreover, this growth of government not only leads to a redistribution of resources, but also to a diversion of activity away from productive pursuits toward lobbying for political favors. Hence, economies tend to grow faster after external shocks (such as a war or a revolutionary transformation of the economic structure) have shattered the power alliances between established interest groups and political parties.

The tendency for governments to grow is reinforced by the self-interested behavior of politicians and bureaucrats (Niskanen, 1971; Mueller, 1989). This conclusion is based on the assumption that individuals pursue their self-interest in public organizations just as they pursue their self-interest in market relationships. Mueller (1989) further argues that this economic impact of self-interested behavior can be expected to increase as the size of the public sector grows, since it is easier to misrepresent the true prices and quantities of government-provided goods and services when budgets are large and complex. The impact should be especially pronounced when there are no private alternatives against which to gauge the performance of a specific government activity, as in the case of public sector monopolies (Borcherding, 1977).

While public choice theory was developed to analyze the rent-seeking behavior of interest groups in democracies, this does not imply that rent-seeking is confined to democratic societies, only that the relative transparency of democracies makes it easier to observe and conceptualize (Tullock, 1987). Indeed, we would expect the secretive nature of dictatorships to increase the scope for rent-seeking by small groups of politically well-connected people. Likewise, the lack of media scrutiny and democratic checks on the abuse of power would seem to magnify the problem of rent-seeking by politicians and bureaucrats in autocracies.

Several historical studies of economic development have shown how periods of rapid economic growth and technological progress have been associated with weak or decentralized governments. The sinologist Joseph Needham (1954) described how Chinese technological inventions mostly occurred in the more anarchic and turbulent periods of Chinese history. In his study of Egyptian civilization, Pirenne described how an initial period of limited autocratic government with individual property rights allowed that civilization to flourish, but that the subsequent accumulation of state power eventually led to a protracted economic stagnation (Pirenne, 1934). In the European context, the rise of urban capitalism from the 13th century onwards occurred in decentralized or lightly governed settings such as the towns of northern Italy (Baechler, 1975; Hayek, 1988). In the 20th century, the East Asian experience shows how small, peripheral countries with a greater exposure to international markets outperformed centralistic, self-contained states such as China or India. The limits placed on rent-seeking behavior imposed by the autocrats of the (initially) undemocratic New Industrialized Countries were a response to the lack of domestic natural resources and capital, as well as the need to build strong economies capable of staving off external threats.

The tendency for societies to evolve from a productive state to a redistributive state has prompted economists to propose possible countermeasures against rent-seeking. Olson (1982) argued for recurrent reorganizations of the governmental structure, since this would upset established relationships between interest groups and politicians. Noting the relative success of Switzerland's institutional structure at limiting the growth of rent-seeking activities, Tullock proposed the increased use of referenda (Tullock, 1993). Kasper has noted how political decentralization inhibits rent-seeking behavior through interjurisdictional competition and the importance of 'exit votes' (Kasper, 1998b). Some public choice economists, such as Rowley (1993), even go so far as to suggest that political fragmentation is the only efficiency-inducing political objective.

Stages of Development and Health Patterns

As was argued at the beginning of this chapter, general principles of economic development is of some interest for our understanding of general health patterns, because each stage of economic development tends to produce a specific mortality and morbidity profile. In this section we shall briefly discuss different stages of economic development and describe the characteristic health profile, drawing on statistical data for societies that roughly correspond with a specific level of development. Although it would be preferable to trace the changes to the profile for various regions over time, the lack of reliable historical observations makes this a cumbersome task.

In the preceding sections we have described the general characteristics of socio-economic development. We have seen how both the physical and non-material infrastructures undergo slow evolutionary changes, which are infrequently interrupted by revolutionary phase transitions. Further, the political power structures have an analogous tendency for a slow accumulation of power, which is only shattered by system-wide shocks to the structure, although the power accumulation process can be checked by institutional or external constraints.

The phase transitions have in fact been extremely infrequent in from a genuinely long-term perspective, although they have become less infrequent over time. In general, four phase transitions (and five archetypal stages of economic development) have been observed over the past 10,000 years. These transitions do, however, happen in various localities and regions in a rather uncoordinated fashion, rather than simultaneously on a global scale. Therefore, there are still local instances of all five stages, although the balance is continuously changing in favor of later stages of development.

Two phase transitions have proved to have an especially profound impact: the transition from tribal to agricultural society and the industrial revolution. This is because these transitions involved a fundamental reshaping of the value structure, rather than a sudden reduction to spatial transaction costs.

The first of these fundamental transitions marked the introduction of private property rights and the second transition involved the acceptance of optimizing, technology-driven production. The reason that these transitions are more fundamental is that it is not merely a superimposition of a new layer of development that slowly crowds out an underlying layer of development. Rather, the effects of the new internal institutions quickly spread to all parts of a region's economy. For example, the industrial revolution not only involved new mass production technologies, but also a new optimizing way of organizing agricultural production.

By contrast, the early capitalist revolution that began in 13th century Europe involved the creation of a new urban network economy on top of what was still essentially a feudal rural society. Although the importance of the urban relative to the rural economy steadily grew over the next five centuries, the organization of agriculture remained more or less the same.

It is still too early to tell whether the current transition from an industrial to a post-industrial society involves a fundamental shift of the social value structure akin to the industrial revolution, or whether it heralds a double-layered society akin to the pre-industrial regions of Europe with capitalist cities and feudal hinterlands.

What is clear however, is that it is not easy to find a purely agricultural/feudal region in today's world, and it is equally difficult to find a pure post-industrial region.

In the discussion of the general economic structure and health patterns, we therefore use the following trichotomy:

1. Tribal society.
2. Agricultural or early capitalist/agricultural society.
3. Industrial or industrial/post-industrial society.

Tribal Society

The defining feature of a tribal society is a collectivistic conception of the individual and an attendant inability to establish generally accepted private property rights. The typical tribal community is small in size and the economy is dominated by hunting and gathering which is sometimes augmented by some subsistence agriculture. While tribal communities have engaged in trade with other tribes or non-tribal communities, this trade has arisen from a group consensus as to the desirability of exchange, rather than on the actions of enterprising individuals. Although some agricultural production may exist in tribal groups, it is different from agricultural society in that there are limited incentives for productivity improvements owing to the collective ownership of the land, and a lack of division of labor into specialized hunter/gatherers and growers of specific crops. The identification of the individual with the group to which she belongs is also sometimes reflected in not attaching any rights or duties to any individual external to the tribal community.

While all human cultures are ultimately derived from tribal societies, it is only in Sub-Saharan Africa that the internal institutions of tribal society still permeate human relationships. Even though Sub-Saharan Africa has nation states, large cities, and often a formal rule of law derived from French or British sources, these decidedly non-tribal features were the result of European colonialism, rather than an expression of a native institutional evolution. The reason for calling Sub-Saharan Africa a tribal society is the lexicographical priority of internal institutions (customs, rules of behavior). The African world view is sometimes summed up by the word 'ubuntu', which, among other things, refers to the conception of the individual as having no independent status apart from that of his membership of a (tribal) group, and that all material possessions are shared within the group.

Because of this pervasive world view, the imposition of a judicial system derived from a general acceptance of private property rights has been a failure. Formal institutions are only successful if they derive from the informal, internal institutions of a society.

Since the collectivistic internal institutions of much of Sub-Saharan Africa only are compatible with small, tribal communities, the creation of cities and Western-style nations states also has had a disruptive impact. As has been noted by Fukuyama (1995), the urbanization of Africa has been accompanied by a breakdown of social trust. Moreover, if the internal institutions imply that all material wealth belongs to everyone in the group jointly, Western notions of the rule of law will result in there being a lot of theft, a concept which in itself is incompatible with tribal societies. The essence of the African dilemma is a mismatch between informal and formal institutions, and over-sized agglomerations of people (as opposed to a natural process of urbanization).

It is however important to distinguish between social and individual adaptability. Individual Africans, for example emigrants to Europe, can internalize the institutions of industrial society by adapting to the host community relatively quickly. On the social level changes generally occur much more slowly. Thus, it is unlikely that an agglomeration of individuals with internalized tribal rules of behavior will quickly adopt incompatible rules entirely derived from external sources.

Sub-Saharan Africa thus serves as our empirical example of the health profile of tribal societies. While Sub-Saharan Africa is the best approximation to a tribal society, it is not a pure tribal society. While infectious diseases have always been a predominant cause of death in tribal societies, these diseases are somewhat less deadly in Africa because of vaccination programs. Even though the life expectancies in the region are the world's lowest, pure tribal societies (in similar climatic environments) had even shorter life expectancies. On the other hand, certain communicable diseases, such as AIDS, may be more prevalent in Africa than they would have been in pure tribal societies, owing to higher population densities.

In comparing the health structure of different societies, we have chosen to focus on cause-specific mortality rather than morbidity. The reason for this is that the definition of death is unambiguous and equal across societies. Morbidity and disability, by contrast, vary regarding their definitions and measurements. This is true even among countries at a similar level of economic development (for example, official disability figures may be influenced by insurance and retirement policies).

When describing mortality patterns across societies, there are two common measures. The simplest measure is simply to divide all deaths into different causes. However, even for this simple measure, some problems arise. This is because deaths are often accompanied by several potentially fatal conditions. The convention in unclear cases is to record a death as being caused by the condition which has the highest probability of causing a fatal outcome. For example, if an individual suffers from a potentially fatal neuro-psychiatric condition and AIDS, it is AIDS which is recorded as the cause of death. Similarly, if an AIDS sufferer commits suicide, the cause of death is recorded as intentional self-inflicted injury. This means that in societies with a high incidence of infectious diseases or fatal injuries, a cursory reading of the mortality statistics may lead one to spuriously infer that less assuredly fatal conditions, such as respiratory ailments or cardiovascular diseases, may seem less common than they in fact are. Additionally, societies with relatively low life expectancies, such as Sub-Saharan Africa, will have a lower proportion of deaths caused by conditions that typically occur at high ages.

In the case of Sub-Saharan Africa, we can see that more than half of all deaths are caused by various communicable diseases such as infections (Table 10.1). Non-communicable diseases such as malignant neoplasms (i.e. cancer) and cardiovascular diseases, are relatively rare as the direct cause of death.

Table 10.1 Deaths by cause, Sub-Saharan Africa, 1990

Cause	Per centage
Infectious and parasitic diseases	**42.1**
Tuberculosis	4.7
Sexually transmitted diseases	4.0
Diarrheal diseases	11.6
Childhood-cluster diseases	10.5
Other infections and parasitic	11.3
Respiratory infections	**12.5**
Maternal conditions	**2.3**
Perinatal conditions	**6.1**
Nutritional deficiencies	**1.8**
Non-communicable diseases	**22.7**
Malignant neoplasms	5.2
Neuro-psychiatric conditions	0.5
Cardiovascular diseases	9.9
Respiratory diseases	2.6
Digestive diseases	1.9
Other non-communicable	2.6
Unintentional injuries	**6.5**
Intentional injuries	**5.9**

Source: Murray and Lopez (1996).

A drawback associated with a simple enumeration of deaths by causes is that it gives equal weight to all causes of death, no matter at what age they occur. Arguably, conditions occurring early in life should be regarded as more serious health problems. This has been the motivation for introducing the 'Years of Life Lost' measure (YLL) (Murray and Lopez, 1996), which is an exponential function with several prespecified constants. However, a problem with this measure is that it incorporates several arbitrary assumptions, in addition to the multiple-cause problem also associated with the simple death-by-cause measure.

First, an 'ideal' life expectancy is introduced. In Murray and Lopez (1996), this life expectancy is 80 years for men and 82.5 years for women. Second, a discount rate is introduced to account for time preference. The annual discount rate used implied by our YLL tables is three per cent, which is, of course, a highly arbitrary rate. Third, and perhaps not always preferable, Murray and Lopez use an age-correction factor to control for demographic differences. In the case of Sub-Saharan Africa, this means that 'childhood cluster diseases' are given a lower weight than one might have expected, because of the characteristic pyramid-shaped age structure of less developed societies.

Table 10.2 YLLs by cause, Sub-Saharan Africa, 1990

Cause	Per centage
Infectious and parasitic diseases	**48.5**
Tuberculosis	4.2
Sexually transmitted diseases	4.2
Diarrheal diseases	13.8
Childhood-cluster diseases	13.0
Other infections and parasitic	13.3
Respiratory infections	**13.3**
Maternal conditions	**2.4**
Perinatal conditions	**7.6**
Nutritional deficiencies	**2.1**
Non-communicable diseases	**12.4**
Malignant neoplasms	2.6
Neuro-psychiatric conditions	0.4
Cardiovascular diseases	4.6
Respiratory diseases	1.4
Digestive diseases	1.3
Other non-communicable	2.1
Unintentional injuries	**7.3**
Intentional injuries	**6.4**

Source: Murray and Lopez (1996).

Overall, if YLLs rather than deaths by cause is used as the mortality measure, the importance of communicable diseases increases (Table 10.2). Conversely, the contribution of malignant neoplasms and cardiovascular diseases to aggregate mortality is more than halved.

Agricultural/Early Capitalist Society

Agricultural and pre-industrial capitalist societies are characterized by an expansion of population agglomerations that necessitate an acceptance of impersonal relationships and the adoption of private property rights. In both agricultural and pre-industrial capitalist societies, rural areas typically take on feudal characteristics. This means that the majority of the rural population engages in subsistence agriculture. However, in feudal o quasi-feudal societies, there is also a group of privileged landowners. These land-owners differ from subsistence farmers in that they attempt to maximize the land rent by imposing fees and taxes to appropriate the surplus production of the subsistence farmers, who mostly do not own but lease the land they cultivate. These rural conditions were not only typical of medieval and early capitalist Europe, but also of India and China for most of their long histories.

Although some capital accumulation occurs in feudal societies, the accumulation process is impeded by the lack of incentives for capital accumulation among the subsistence farmers. Agricultural productivity gains thus tend to be sluggish in feudal and pre-industrial capitalistic societies.

Of the major world regions, the Indian subcontinent is probably the region that best approximates a society with a network of cities with features akin to pre-industrial capitalist society in Europe, interspersed with a rural agricultural society. The majority of India's rural population practice subsistence agriculture with a limited division of labor. At the same time, there are also (higher-caste) landowners engaging in rent-maximizing agriculture. In the cities, meanwhile, personalized trade and small-scale, relatively primitive, manufacturing predominate. (Admittedly, there are localized instances of activities with an industrial or even post-industrial character, for example, the computer industry in Bangalore and the Mumbai stock exchange.)

Table 10.3 Deaths by cause, India, 1990

Cause	Per centage
Infectious and parasitic diseases	**28.2**
Tuberculosis	8.0
Sexually transmitted diseases	0.7
Diarrheal diseases	9.8
Childhood-cluster diseases	5.5
Other infections and parasitic	4.2
Respiratory infections	**13.1**
Maternal conditions	**1.2**
Perinatal conditions	**7.0**
Nutritional deficiencies	**1.3**
Non-communicable diseases	**40.4**
Malignant neoplasms	5.4
Neuro-psychiatric conditions	1.1
Cardiovascular diseases	24.2
Respiratory diseases	2.8
Digestive diseases	2.7
Other non-communicable	4.2
Unintentional injuries	**6.9**
Intentional injuries	**1.7**

Source: Murray and Lopez (1996).

Tables 10.3 and 10.4 present deaths by cause and YLLs by cause for India, respectively. The main difference compared with Sub-Saharan Africa is that the contribution of infectious and parasitic diseases to overall mortality has been substantially reduced. By contrast, the share of all deaths caused by cardiovascular diseases is higher. Malignant neoplasms, on the other hand, remain at low levels as we move from tribal to agricultural/pre-industrial societies.

Table 10.4 YLLs by cause, India, 1990

Cause	Per centage
Infectious and parasitic diseases	**35.3**
Tuberculosis	6.3
Sexually transmitted diseases	1.0
Diarrheal diseases	14.3
Childhood-cluster diseases	8.5
Other infections and parasitic	5.2
Respiratory infections	**16.5**
Maternal conditions	**1.7**
Perinatal conditions	**11.1**
Nutritional deficiencies	**1.8**
Non-communicable diseases	**22.6**
Malignant neoplasms	3.3
Neuro-psychiatric conditions	0.9
Cardiovascular diseases	10.1
Respiratory diseases	1.6
Digestive diseases	2.1
Other non-communicable	4.6
Unintentional injuries	**9.0**
Intentional injuries	**2.0**

Source: Murray and Lopez (1996).

Industrial and Post-Industrial Societies

The industrial and post-industrial types of capitalism differ from the pre-industrial type in several ways, of which two are crucial. First, there is an optimizing approach to production. Second, impersonal markets and financial institutions replace personal exchange and credit. As regards the difference between the emerging post-industrial society vis-à-vis industrial society, two features are especially noteworthy as post-industrial traits: The production of knowledge-intensive services and the globalization of markets and financial institutions. We have chosen to describe the health patterns of industrial and post-industrial societies by dichotomizing between early industrial society and late industrial/early post-industrial societies.

Lundgren (2001) has argued that the economic reforms since 1979 in China marks a decisive structural break with the past by amounting to the implementation of the institutional infrastructure of early industrial society. This is not only because the reforms led to the emergence of widely dispersed *de facto* ownership of land, but also because of the wholesale adoption of the optimizing approach to production. The massive inflows of foreign direct investment in modern production facilities by multi-national corporations illustrate the psychological acceptance of industrial institutions. Pre-1949 China, by contrast, was much more akin to contemporary India, whereas the intervening period (1949 to 1979) marked the suspension of economic rationality by an all-powerful, centralized, state.

Tables 10.5 and 10.6 give deaths by cause and YLLs by cause for China in 1990. The tables illustrate how the industrial revolution coincides with a concurrent revolution in mortality patterns. All communicable, maternal, perinatal and nutritional conditions are much less important as causes of death in China than in India. This is especially true of infectious and parasitic diseases. Industrialization also coincides with the greatest increase in the number of deaths and YLLs accounted for by malignant neoplasms, which is in part a reflection of increased life expectancies.

Table 10.5 Deaths by cause, China, 1990

Cause	Per centage
Infectious and parasitic diseases	**6.1**
Tuberculosis	3.1
Sexually transmitted diseases	0.0
Diarrheal diseases	1.0
Childhood-cluster diseases	0.6
Other infections and parasitic	1.4
Respiratory infections	**5.3**
Maternal conditions	**0.3**
Perinatal conditions	**3.1**
Nutritional deficiencies	**0.9**
Non-communicable diseases	**72.7**
Malignant neoplasms	16.5
Neuro-psychiatric conditions	1.1
Cardiovascular diseases	28.9
Respiratory diseases	17.2
Digestive diseases	4.6
Other non-communicable	4.4
Unintentional injuries	**7.1**
Intentional injuries	**4.4**

Source: Murray and Lopez (1996).

In one category, China stands out compared with societies at other developmental stages: the unusually high proportion of deaths and YLLs caused by respiratory diseases. This is probably because air pollution levels are highest at the earliest stages of industrialization (Hua, 2001), at the same time as the highest proportion of the workforce is employed in heavily polluted industrial environments. It is no coincidence that several of the world's most polluted cities are Chinese.

Table 10.6 YLLs by cause, China, 1990

Cause	Per centage
Infectious and parasitic diseases	**8.3**
Tuberculosis	3.0
Sexually transmitted diseases	0.0
Diarrheal diseases	1.8
Childhood-cluster diseases	1.5
Other infections and parasitic	2.0
Respiratory infections	**9.5**
Maternal conditions	**0.8**
Perinatal conditions	**7.9**
Nutritional deficiencies	**1.8**
Non-communicable diseases	**51.5**
Malignant neoplasms	14.4
Neuro-psychiatric conditions	1.4
Cardiovascular diseases	16.7
Respiratory diseases	8.1
Digestive diseases	4.8
Other non-communicable	6.1
Unintentional injuries	**13.0**
Intentional injuries	**7.3**

Source: Murray and Lopez (1996).

In advanced industrial or post-industrial societies – here consisting of the 'established market economies' of Western Europe, North America, Japan, and Oceania – we can detect a further strengthening of the tendencies already exhibited by China. For example, deaths caused by infections and parasitic diseases decline from 6.1 per cent in China to 1.6 per cent in the established market economies (Table 10.7). In terms of YLLs, the per centage is reduced from 8.3 per cent to 3.0 per cent (Table 10. 8).

But perhaps the most pertinent feature of the morbidity patterns of the advanced societies is that purely involuntary causes of death to a large extent are replaced by, on the one hand, health conditions resulting from behavior-induced causes and, on the other hand, by causes generally occurring in old age. The behavioral tendency is even visible when we consider communicable diseases in isolation. Sexually transmitted diseases causes over 60 per cent of all YLLs attributed to infectious and parasitic diseases in the established market economies. The corresponding figure for Sub-Saharan Africa is less than 10 per cent, even though that region has the world's highest incidence of HIV infection.

Table 10.7 Deaths by cause, established market economies, 1990

Cause	Per centage
Infectious and parasitic diseases	**1.6**
Tuberculosis	0.2
Sexually transmitted diseases	0.6
Diarrheal diseases	0.0
Childhood-cluster diseases	0.0
Other infections and parasitic	0.8
Respiratory infections	**3.9**
Maternal conditions	**0.0**
Perinatal conditions	**0.6**
Nutritional deficiencies	**0.3**
Non-communicable diseases	**87.4**
Malignant neoplasms	24.7
Neuro-psychiatric conditions	2.9
Cardiovascular diseases	44.6
Respiratory diseases	4.8
Digestive diseases	4.3
Other non-communicable	7.1
Unintentional injuries	**4.3**
Intentional injuries	**2.0**

Source: Murray and Lopez (1996).

In fact, all diseases that are linked with dangerous – but voluntary – activities increase in relative importance as societies develop. Apart from sexually transmitted diseases, such conditions include road traffic accidents, cirrhosis of the liver, cardiovascular diseases, and lung cancer. This observation is especially pertinent when looking at mortality patterns from a 'public health' perspective. Although regular attendance at the orgies of ancient Rome may have caused a higher risk of dying from sexually transmitted diseases or cirrhosis of the liver, behavioral causes nevertheless have a minimal impact on life expectancies in underdeveloped societies.

This implies that the maximization of life expectancies may almost be a legitimate (i.e., Pareto-sanctioned) aim in primitive societies. In such societies, the aim has most efficiently been pursued through vaccination and water purification programs. However, in advanced societies, the maximization of life expectancies would among other things imply the prohibition of road transportation, dangerous sports, pre-marital sex, and tobacco, as well as the rationing of alcohol and junk food. From the standpoint of an individual who is prepared to incur an increased risk of early death in exchange for some activity valued by that individual, the public policy objective of maximizing his life expectancy becomes an undesirable obstacle to pursuing his personal objectives. And yet the objectives of many advanced countries' health policies assume that the maximization of life expectancies is a universally accepted objective.

Table 10.8 YLLs by cause, established market economies, 1990

Cause	Per centage
Infectious and parasitic diseases	**3.0**
Tuberculosis	0.2
Sexually transmitted diseases	1.9
Diarrheal diseases	0.0
Childhood-cluster diseases	0.0
Other infections and parasitic	0.9
Respiratory infections	**2.4**
Maternal conditions	**0.0**
Perinatal conditions	**3.1**
Nutritional deficiencies	**0.2**
Non-communicable diseases	**75.3**
Malignant neoplasms	26.1
Neuro-psychiatric conditions	3.1
Cardiovascular diseases	30.8
Respiratory diseases	3.6
Digestive diseases	4.6
Other non-communicable	7.1
Unintentional injuries	**10.3**
Intentional injuries	**5.6**

Source: Murray and Lopez (1996).

Perhaps the emphasis on maximizing life expectancies is just one instance of how social aims outlive their serviceability. As noted above, the internalized values of each individual tends to equate individual values and collective values in tribal societies. However, in impersonal and heterogeneous societies each individual pursues individual objectives. Still, much of contemporary political life is geared toward allegedly shared objectives, rather than toward facilitating each individual's pursuit of her unique set of objectives.

References

Andersson, Å.E. and Strömquist, U. (1988), *K-samhällets framtid*, Prisma, Stockholm.

Baechler, J. (1975), *The Origin of Capitalism*, Blackwell, Oxford.

Borcherding, T.E. (1977), *Budgets and Bureaucrats: The Sources of Government Growth*, Duke University Press, Durham NC.

Fukuyama, F. (1995), *Trust: The Social Virtues and the Creation of Prosperity*, The Free Press, New York.

Hardin, G. (1993), 'The Tragedy of the Commons', in D.R. Henderson (ed.), *The Fortune Encyclopedia of Economics*, Warner Books, New York.

Hayek, F.A. (1988), *The Fatal Conceit: The Errors of Socialism*, Routledge, London.

Hua, C.I. (2001), 'Pollution Transitions and Economic Growth in Asia', in D.E. Andersson and J. Poon (eds), Asia-Pacific Transitions, Palgrave, New York.

Kasper, W. (1998a), 'Transitions and Institutional Innovation – Reflections on the Current Economic Crisis', *Malaysian Journal of Economic Studies*, July, pp. 54–65.

Kasper, W. (1998b), *Property Rights and Competition: An Essay on the Constitution of Capitalism*, The Centre for Independent Studies, Smithfield NSW.

Lundgren, K. (2001), 'The Chinese Kaleidoscope: Chinese Economic Development in the Light of the New Institutional Theories', in D.E. Andersson and J. Poon (eds), Asia-Pacific Transitions, Palgrave, New York.

Mueller, D.C. (1989), *Public Choice II*, Cambridge University Press, Cambridge.

Murray, C.J.L. and Lopez, A.D. (eds) (1996), *The Global Burden of Disease*, Harvard University Press, Cambridge.

Needham, J. (1954), *Science and Civilization in China*, Cambridge University Press, Cambridge.

Niskanen Jr, W.A. (1971), *Bureaucracy and Representative Government*, Aldine-Atherton, Chicago.

Olson Jr, M. (1965), *The Logic of Collective Action*, Harvard University Press, Cambridge.

Olson Jr, M. (1982), *The Rise and Decline of Nations: Economic Growth, Stagflation, and Social Rigidities*, Yale University Press, New Haven.

Pirenne, J. (1934), *Histoire des institutions et du droit prive de l'ancienne Egypte*, Edition de la Fondation Egyptologique Reine Elisabeth, Bruxelles.

Pirenne, H. (1936), *Economic and Social History of Medieval Europe*, London.

Rowley, C.K. (1993), *Liberty and the State*, Edward Elgar, Cheltenham.

Smith, A. (1776), *An Inquiry into the Nature and Causes of the Wealth of Nations*, Oxford University Press (1976), Oxford.

Tullock, G. (1987), *Autocracy*, Kluwer Academic Publishers, Boston.

Tullock, G. (1993), *Rent Seeking*, Edward Elgar, Cheltenham.

Chapter 11

Growth and Development Policy under Economic Globalization

Åke E. Andersson

A Globalizing World Economy

National and regional economies are increasingly becoming globalized. Dependency upon foreign markets for goods and services, exports and imports, increasing in most parts of the world, has been growing rapidly during the last two decades. Some of this growth in dependency of foreign markets is a reflex of the growth of world production. Normally, a growth of world production of around three per cent per year should be expected to be associated with a growth of world exports of between 3.5 to 4 per cent, annually. But in the late 1980s this regularity changed in an unexpected way. Between 1987 and 1994 world production increased by 3.3 per cent per year, while world exports was growing at a rate of 6.2 per cent, annually. This was not only a reflection of the remarkable growth of export volumes from East Asia. However, a closer scrutiny of the statistical data shows that the increase in the export growth rates was equally large in the developed western market economies. The recent past of real economic globalization is shown in the following table.

Table 11.1 Development of production and trade, 1979–2002; annual per centage rate of growth

	1979–86	1987–94	1995–97	Forecast (IMF) 1998–2002
World disposable gross product	3.1	3.3	4.0	4.5
Global trade	3.5	6.2	7.4	6.7
Volume of exports from the western market economies	4.4	7.4	10.0	8.0
Volume of exports from Asia	6.4	12.8	10.0	10.7

Source: IMF-WEO, 1997–98.

The table clearly indicates that there is a remarkable phase transition occurring between the period 1979–1986 and the period 1987–1994. Evidently the scale of production increased at a more rapid pace than before but the rate of expansion of trade is much more than proportional to growth of production and higher than what would have been expected if data on trade elasticities had been used from earlier periods. Moreover, the expansion of world trade is expected to proceed also into the future, even if Japan and the developing East Asian economies would be growing at a sluggish rate.

Also in other respects there has been rapid increase in the degree and extent of global interdependencies in real terms over the latest decades. Global research collaboration as measured by international co-authorship data are increasing at two-digit expansion rates, annually, and this is one of the explanatory variables behind the rapid growth of international air travel (Andersson and Persson, 1993).

Global financial integration is another aspect of economic globalization. The financial integration of the world happened during the time period of globalization of trade and other real interaction between different parts of the world. The most remarkable financial globalization was in terms of cross-border transactions of equities and bonds. In the USA such transactions amounted to less than 10 per cent in most developed countries in 1980. By 1985 it had already grown to 35 per cent of GDP in USA and to 63 per cent in Japan. In 1990 it had grown to 90 per cent of GDP in the USA and to a high of 120 per cent in Japan. As a consequence of the depressed state of the Japanese economy after 1990 it declined to 83 per cent of GDP by 1996. However, in the same time period the share of GDP had risen to more than 150 per cent of GDP in the USA, Germany, France and Canada. In Italy, cross-border transactions of equities and bonds had risen from only 4 per cent of GDP in 1985 to 435 per cent in 1996.

The financial integration of the world economy is also reflected in the relative share of GDP allocated to foreign direct investments. In the period 1975 to 1979 Japan allocated 0.6 per cent of its GDP to such foreign direct investments. By 1980 to 1984 it had risen to 2.6 per cent and in the period 1985 to 1989 it jumped to 5.9 per cent. A fifteen-country average for OECD countries indicates a similar transformation. In 1975 to 1979 this average amounted to 2.2 per cent of GDP. It increased to 2.9 per cent in the period 1980 to 1984. In the period 1985 to 1989 it reached an average of 6.8 per cent and in the period 1990 to 1995 it had risen above 9 per cent of GDP.

All statistical indicators show that real and financial globalization progressed at a very rapid pace from the mid 1980s. The rate of globalization is by now fast enough to warrant a description of the process as a *phase transition*.

The Reasons for the Phase Transition into a Globalized Economy

I have at other instances claimed that dramatic expansion of trade is a phenomenon to be expected on trade and transaction networks subject to expansion above the number of links and nodes (Andersson, 1986).

My arguments in that context have later on been strengthened by the simulation experiments conducted by the biologist Stuart Kauffman (1996). In these simulations Stuart Kauffman assumes that new links between a predetermined set of nodes are generated randomly. Any pair of nodes can be connected with each other in each period of time and earlier connections do not play any role at each period of the interactive process. Figure 11.1 describes the consequence of the process during the simulation.

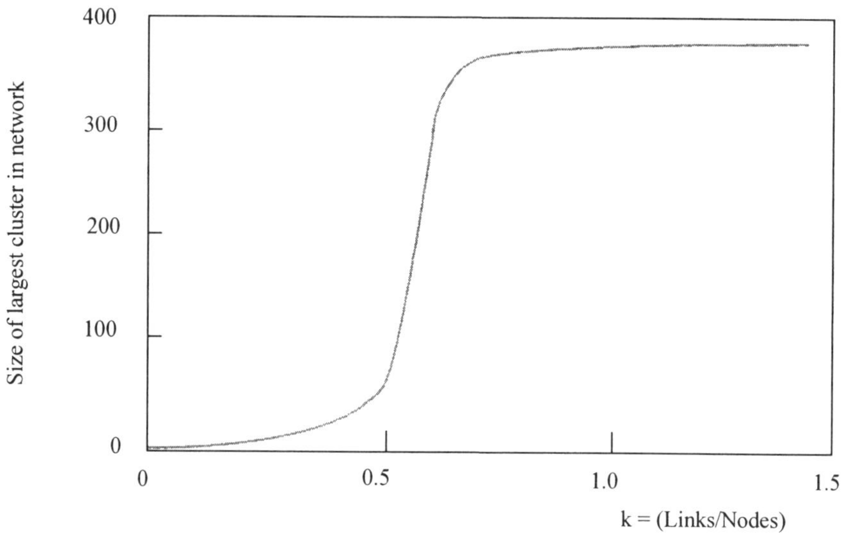

Source: Kauffman (1996).

Figure 11.1 Network integration as a function of the ratio between the number of links and of nodes in a random network formation computer simulation

What this simulation shows is a remarkable phase transition occurring when the number of links has passed 50 per cent of the number of nodes. Then, suddenly, the size of the largest integrated cluster jumps from around 10 per cent to more than 90 per cent of the total number of nodes. There is no need for any grand vision or plan to generate such a 'globalized' system of interacting nodes. Random network interaction possibilities will sooner or later generate a phase transition from a weakly integrated into a globalized system of interaction possibilities.

National Economic Policies in a Globalized Economy

The empirical data used in the introduction indicate a parallel real and financial phase transition into a globalized economy. The classical separation of growth and development analysis into one real and one financial part can no longer be used as a simplifying device. This also excludes the assumption and theory construct so often used in the literature, according to which national monetary policies can be an important determinant of national and regional real economic development.

National monetary policies are now subordinated to global financial market mechanisms, operating in the equities, bonds and currency markets. However, the monetary subordination does not mean that national and regional public development policies will be ruled out. In this chapter it is claimed that regional public policies can still be a powerful determinant of the possibilities of economic development, provided the regional (and national) monetary and fiscal policy making is valued favorably in the long time perspective of global investors and their expectations of long-term performance of the regional and national economy as a whole. To be continuously scrutinized by global investors is a new experience for national and regional policy makers. In the long run, the benefits of this globalized evaluation of politicians will by far outweigh the considerable disadvantages experienced by politicians in the short run.

Rates of Growth and Interest

In the modern economy with few possibilities of rapid demographic change and a majority of employees already working in modern sectors of the economy, growth of employment has ceased to be an important explanation on the rate of growth of the developed economy. This is reinforced by the fact that in most modern economies increasing labor productivity tends to be followed by shorter working hours. In the OECD-countries a 10 per cent increase in labor productivity tends to be accompanied by a reduction of the number of working hours per year of 2 to 3 per cent.

In this context we will make the assumption that the rate of growth of capital (including education and other human capital) will determine the rate of growth of production. It is thus assumed that increasing the rate of growth of capital in the form of infrastructure, machinery, other capital equipment and human capital will increase the rate of growth of the regional or national economy. At this stage of the argument we further assume that the price structure is not changing during the growth process. This means that there is no qualitative appreciation of the commodities produced in the economy, but that the GNP is composed of goods and services of an unchanging quality and valuation by the consumers. It should here be stressed that this is just a simplification used at this stage of the analysis, which is to be relaxed in a later section of the chapter.

Decisions on the rate of expansion of capital are assumed to be determined by the ruling rate of interest in the market for financial capital. This is not any drastic assumption from an empirical point of view. Nowadays, most of the investors investing in real capital tend to have the opportunity of alternative investments into equities and bonds. Thus, the link between savings and investments have been considerably weakened over the years. In the individual regions there is no obvious link between the regional rate of savings and the rate of capital accumulation occurring in the region. What counts is the expected profitability of investments into new capital and the cost of new capital in the global financial market. At given profitability expectations associated with the accumulation of real capital, an increase in the rate of interest is assumed to lead to a reduction in the rate of capital accumulation of the economy (be it regional or national).

The assumption about the rate of accumulation of real capital being a monotonically falling function of the rate of interest and the assumption that the rate of growth is a monotonically increasing function of the rate of capital accumulation implies that *the rate of growth of the economy is a monotonically decreasing function of the rate of interest charged in the financial markets.*

But this is not the whole story. In order to complete the picture we have to consider the workings of the globalized financial markets and the formation of expectations of the future in the individual region. Most financial investors, buying securities and bonds and similar instruments of credit, tend to keep a close watch of what is happening to the region or nation into which the financial investment funds are channeled. If the individual region or nation is growing at a very high rate of growth of its regional or national product, most financial investors tend to be expecting problems in the goods, services and factor markets of that region or nation mounting into the future. Both at the regional and national level, increasing the rate of growth beyond certain levels will surely lead to bottleneck problems in the labor markets and in the markets for producer and consumer services. Such expectations can furthermore reinforce the increasing demand for land for speculative reasons, leading to shortages of opportunities of location, reducing the profits from investments in property.

Beyond a certain point, there is thus a rather clear positive functional relation between the rate of growth of the economy and the expectation of risks, associated with financial investments in that region or nation. The strength of this positive functional relation between the rate of growth and the risk associated with financial investments is also clearly influenced by the expected capacity of the policy makers to control emerging problems of land speculation and other aspects of lacking control of bottleneck problems, emerging at the regional level. In some European countries financial investors have been reluctant to supply financial resources at stages of rapid economic growth, because of the tendency of politicians to increase public investment during such periods of private sector growth. The development in Malaysia has given ample illustrations of how an excessive willingness to invest in public projects, accompanying a rapid growth of private capital and GNP, has increased the perceived risk to the financial investors, active in the globalized financial markets.

The growing body of corporate finance literature has established a firm relation between the level of expected risk and the rate of interest on equities and bonds, purchased in the financial markets. A real capital investor, financing a large investment project in a region, expected to develop a large political risk, will have to pay a very high rate of interest in order to attract the necessary global funds to that region. In large parts of Asia such risks have increased over recent years and the high expected risks have been reinforced by expected inefficiency of the political system of many Asian countries and regions. Thus, at any given expected rate of real growth of the regional or national economy, financial investors have demanded a higher rate of risk compensation for their financial investments. The most important way of increasing the rate of interest is by decreasing the level of prices of equities and bonds.

If we thus assume that the relation between the rate of growth and the perceived risk to the financial investors is monotonically increasing and if an increased perceived risk must be accompanied by an increase in the rate of interest paid to the financial investors into equities and bonds, we can deduce *a monotonically increasing functional relation between the rate of growth and the rate of interest* faced by the real investors of the region.

The Equilibrium of Interest and Growth Rates

We have found that the rate of capital accumulation and the rate of growth of the economy are negatively related to the rate of interest charged in the financial markets, while on the other hand there is a positive relationship between the rate of growth and the rate of interest, charged by the globalized financial investors. The complete picture of the interdependency between the rate of interest and the rate of growth is thus such, that the equilibrium rate growth and interest is determined by the intersection of these two functional relations, as illustrated in Figure 11.2.

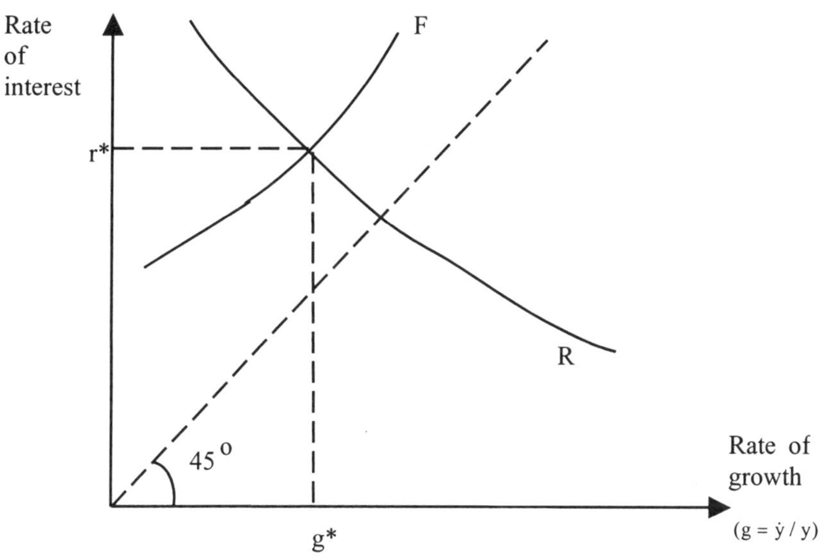

F: financial function
R: real economic function

r*= equilibrium rate of interest
g*= equilibrium rate of growth

Figure 11.2 Financial and real economic growth equilibrium

The stability of this equilibrium is highly dependent on the slope of the financial function. A region that would have a larger or more efficient supply of productive infrastructure in the form of publicly available knowledge or communication and transportation networks would have a higher efficiency of capital accumulation and would thus achieve a higher rate of growth at any level of the rate of interest. With given expectations of risks, associated with financial investments in the region the equilibrium combination of rate of interest and rate of growth of the economy would be higher than in a region with a lower supply of productive infrastructure.

Similarly, a region in which financial investors would expect a high rate of growth of improductive public capital (as in Kuala Lumpur) would have an equilibrium combination of a lower rate of growth and a higher rate of interest than in regions with similar real conditions of growth but more responsible public policy makers.

In von Neumann's theory of economic growth there is a strong duality relation between the rate of interest and the rate of growth of the economy (von Neumann, 1937). In fact, in von Neumann's paper on equilibrium growth there is an exact duality, requiring the rate of interest in equilibrium to be *equal* to the rate of growth of the economy, generating a 45° line through origo. This is grossly at variance with our theory, according to which the rate of interest must necessarily be larger than the rate of growth. In this theory the von Neumann duality is a limiting case, that can only occur if there would be no uncertainty in the financial market. In the von Neumann world of economic growth the equality of real interest and the rate of growth is a direct consequence of the deterministic nature of his theory of growth equilibrium. This is also the case in the more sophisticated analysis by Morishima (1964).

Globalization of financial markets has led to important changes of the preconditions for successful policy making both at the national and the regional levels. At the national level it is now impossible to formulate fiscal and monetary policies, based on the Keynesian and neo-classical assumptions of internationally weak dependence of national states and their central banks. Operating in a globalized world means in this context the formulation of policies, viable in a world of complex interdependencies and strong perception of risks among the decision makers, active in the globalized financial markets. The integration of these global financial markets is slowly but steadily leading towards equalized risk-compensated real rates of interest. In the developed economies this has led to equalization of marginal efficiencies of investment and to bankruptcies of corporations, who were formerly protected by national subsidy systems or in other ways being shielded against international competition. In the developing and newly industrialized countries the new global openness of financial markets has, on the whole, implied a better and a more inexpensive access to loanable funds to support their real capital accumulation.

Public spending on investments, public consumption and transfers to firms and households have normally been increasing along with private investments in the developed market economies, especially in Western Europe. This process has led to a rapid increase in the relative role of the public sector. To a large extent this expansion of public expenditure even in periods of booming private investments, has led to inflation and other bottleneck problems in many of these economies. Sudden devaluations of currencies have until recently been used by national governments to protect the balance of payments and the level of employment. These actions were possible as long as national, institutionally protected financial systems were the rule rather than the exception. But nowadays in the globalized financial markets such national policies are regularly and rapidly transformed into financial risks, which must be compensated by higher interest rates. Today any increase of public spending that will not support growth and development will lead to a crowding out of private investments as a consequence of repercussions in the global financial markets. Only such public investments that will support growth and development will not disturb the regional or national position in the financial markets. Policy makers in all regions and national policy making bodies are now forced to take actions and develop public investment strategies that will lead to reduction of the risks, perceived by financial investors, often located in distant nations and regions.

All OECD nations have been involved in a process of reformation of their financial institutions – banks, insurance companies, stock exchanges etc. – in order to ensure transparency, openness, fairness between national and international investors and lowered transaction costs in the financial markets. The speed of this transformation has been very uneven, it has been almost completed in the United States, is well under way in Western Europe (with the exception of France) and has recently been initiated in Japan, South Korea and Taiwan.

Growth versus Development

The real economy of the world is currently in a process of two structural transformations, caused by the improvement of communication systems and increasing global competition. Competitive industrialization is one of these two major transformations influencing all newly industrializing countries as well as the formerly Soviet-dominated economies. The OECD-countries, and especially their advanced regions, are in a process of transformation away from the industrial system into a post-industrial system of C-regions. In these C-regions the production system is increasingly being based upon the exploitation of the modern Communication systems, Cognitive skills of the population, Creativity in research, development and design activities and the advantages of increasing the Complexity of the goods and services produced and marketed at a global level.

Increasing complexity of the products is a powerful means of reducing the use of energy and other natural resources. In any research and development project there is a tendency to increase the input of information and knowledge, thereby saving on the use of labor, energy and raw materials. Modern pharmaceuticals, airplanes, cars and other transportation equipment, communication equipment, computers and other information technology equipment, give ample examples of this substitution of natural resources and labor for knowledge and information complexity (Andersson, 1995).

This transformation is leading the advanced economies away from the simple growth paradigm within which the quantities of goods and services are increasing, while the valuation of these products, as measured by their world market prices, are kept fairly constant. The market consequence of the increasing complexity of the products in the direction of growth of the *value of the products* rather than in growth of the quantity of goods and services. A consequence of a high research intensity in the industry of a region is increasing complexity of its products and improvements in the willingness to pay for these products, when they are sold in the globalized product markets. In the same way as investments into material capital will require a marginal efficiency at least corresponding to the risk compensating rate of interest, ruling in the globalized financial market, there is a similar requirement of efficiency of investments into research, development and new designs. This means that the rate of growth of complexity is determined by the ruling rate of interest in the financial market.

The fundament of efficient complexity policies by research, development and design is formed by the education and research strategies at the regional, infrastructural level. In this sense, regional education and university policies are becoming a central focus of a viable long-term development strategy for the C-region of the future. In the industrializing region, investments into infrastructure is essential, but in that case infrastructure means railroads, roads, ports and other terminals for transportation. Infrastructure for the C-region is instead education and research institutions, international airports and access to global information and communication systems. Also the housing and cultural and natural environmental infrastructure is of great importance, primarily because it constitutes the attractiveness to well educated and creative labor supply.

The Complete Picture of Growth and Development Equilibrium within a Globalized C-Region

We have already sketched out the conditions of growth equilibrium as determined by the equalization of a financial and real economic response function. At this intersection, shown in the following figure, the equilibrium rate of interest and rate of growth is determined. This determination of an equilibrium interest rate is conditional upon the attractiveness of regional and national policy making in the globalized financial market. If the political risk of the region or nation is deemed to be large, then the price will be paid in terms of a higher rate of interest and a lowered rate of growth. But the rate of interest will also determine the rate of transformation from an industrialized region into a C-region. The ruling rate of interest will determine the rate of growth of complexity, which is dependent upon the rate of growth of knowledge by creative activities in research, development and design in the region (in collaboration with other C-regions). A high rate of interest will stifle the rate of such knowledge accumulation and thus the potentials for long term economic development of the region.

In Figure 11.3, this is illustrated by the second quadrant, in which the rate of growth of complexity is assumed to be proportional to the rate of growth of knowledge. The ultimate consequence of increasing complexity is increasing willingness to pay for the product in the world market. In Figure 11.3 it is assumed that a higher rate of growth of complexity by a higher rate of growth of knowledge will determine a higher rate of growth of the willingness to pay for the product (as indicated by $\dot{p}/p$). Finally, the stage of development of the economy is determined by the intersection of the growth rate of the willingness to pay and the growth rate of the quantity of production. In D-space of the figure we would find the C-regions of the world. At early stages of industrialization a region would be located close to the $\dot{y}/y$ – axis of the figure in the G-space.

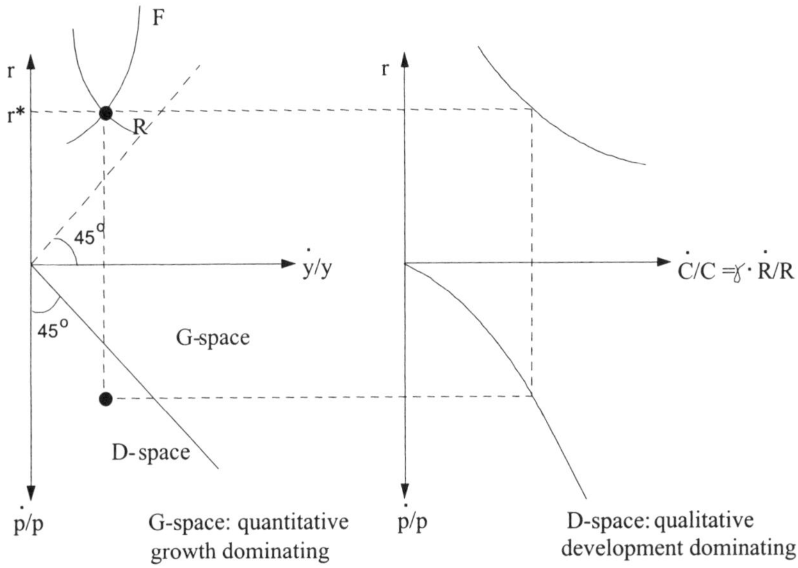

Figure 11.3 The complete picture of growth and development equilibrium

Conclusions

The information and communication technology revolution has played a key role in the transformation into a globalized economic system. The globalization process is a consequence of a major phase transition of the networks for transmission of the information and knowledge. In this chapter it is shown that such a phase transition is bound to appear, even if all the individual links and nodes are created by random forces.

The creation of a globalized financial system was already completed in the early 1990s. But after 1987 there has also been a very rapid increase in world trade in goods and services, as well as an extremely rapid expansion of the transfer of knowledge by cooperative research and development activities.

The world economy is now in a process of economic transformation, triggered by globalization of the financial as well as goods and service markets. Advanced nations are forced to harmonize their economic policies under the pressure of globalized financial markets. Regions of the advanced countries are redefining their policies so as to increase their long-term attractiveness for globalized multi-domestic corporations and their increasingly qualified labor in terms of educational and creative capacity.

In the chapter I have also shown that it is possible to formulate a dynamic equilibrium model in which the relative degree of growth versus development can be determined. In this model development is defined to be a process of increasing willingness to pay for the products in the world market, while growth is defined to be the expansion of the scale of production at constant values (i.e. prices) in the world market.

References

Andersson, Å.E. (1986), 'Presidential Address: The Four Logistical Revolutions', *Papers of the Regional Science Association*, vol. 59, pp. 1–12.

Andersson, Å.E. (1995), *Product Complexity and Sustainable Development*, paper delivered at the Honda Prize Ceremony, Tokyo.

Andersson, Å.E. and Persson, O. (1993), 'Networking scientists', *The Annals of Regional Science*, Springer Verlag, Heidelberg.

Kauffman, S. (1996), *At Home in the Universe*, Penguin Books, London.

Morishima, M. (1964), *Theory of Economic Growth*, Clarendon Press, Oxford.

von Neumann, J. (1937), 'A Model of General Economic Equilibrium', translated from the German original 1945–6, *Review of Economic Studies*, vol. 33, pp. 1–9.

Chapter 12

On the Processes Generating Impacts from Transportation Improvements: The Impacts of Air Transportation on Recreation Tourism

William L. Garrison, David Gillen and Christopher R. Williges

Introduction

Our interest is in the effects, impacts, or benefits of transportation improvements and we use those words interchangeably. The topic is hardly new. The effects of technology improvements, as well as those following facility or equipment investments, the honing of management techniques, or the relaxation of the constraints of economic regulation, have been the subject of countless studies. Debates about improvements have been fueled by claims and counter claims about benefits (and costs). We focus on the processes creating benefits in order to clarify the situation.

We were challenged to reexamine ideas about the processes generating benefits during a recently completed study of the relations between the development of air transportation and its impacts on the tourism-recreation industry (Garrison, Gillen and Williges, 1997). In the course of that study, much effort was given to the specification of the processes through which impacts are generated and positioning these processes in the context of the air transportation and recreation industries. This chapter tells the results of that process specification effort. It turns imprecise conversations into a full story. Comments on our empirical work are limited to the illustration of our approach and findings.

Do we find that transportation service enhancements result in the disappearance of distance? Disappearance is a seductive metaphor, but we think it slights both processes and outcomes. We view the friction of distance as moderated by the dynamics of the evolution of the supply of transportation services and the interacting dynamics of the evolution of demand: improved access begets mobility enhancements as innovative actors do new things and reshape old activities. Progress is achieved as reductions in the friction of distance enable innovations and more variegated production and consumption.

What we will Discuss and Why

There are lots of topics and interrelations on our plate, so to speak. To deal with these we need a general equilibrium-like framework that accommodates the major process at work. We will now begin to outline such a framework.

Imagining and debating the impacts of transportation improvements is a game many can play and many do. Investment in facilities, promotion of services, subsidy and regulation are pulled by claims of development impacts. Commenting on the situation in a 1996 paper, Peter Mackie, a British critic, remarked that the transportation analyst's concentration on attributes such as cheaper, faster and better does not meet the development interest of promoters, politicians and policy makers. The same situation holds in the US and elsewhere, where enthusiasms about the development effects of transportation improvements permeate political debates about investing in one program or another: transit investment is needed to give us livable cities and highway investment is needed to improve the competitiveness of regions and the nation. Debates about high speed rail service or improved access to air or marine ports also have broad development content.

This is not news. The student of US transportation policy might remind us that mercantilism with its optimism about development effects drove rail, inland waterway, highway, airport and other programs. It still does and the more than 200-year conflict between mercantilism and feudalism continues as promoters promote and those with interest in the status quo resist.

Turning from the policy context to analysis, the effects examined by analysts are of a cheaper, faster, better sort and they are scoped to what may be termed 'on-system' considerations. An investment in improved train control, for example, is seen as reducing the interference of one train with another, improving schedule adherence, saving fuel and reducing possibilities of collisions (cheaper, faster, better, safer). Highway pavement management systems aim for cost reductions and longer lasting pavements (cheaper for the pavement provider). A new runway at an airport is to reduce congestion delays (better service). This thinking focuses entirely on the production of services.

We have striven to look beyond these 'on-system' concerns to 'off-system' effects – the ways in which transportation improvements impact production *and* consumption activities throughout the economy. While many might say that conventional approaches extend to such impacts, we disagree because those approaches do not consider the ways in which transportation improvements create choices and the economic welfare gains from increased choices.

Transportation is conventionally viewed as an intermediate activity in production chains. So the individual, household, or manager of a production activity is viewed as using more transportation as services are improved or using the same amount of transportation at less cost. Also, transportation may be substituted for some other input in the production process. In the case of households, there may be travel to more distant recreational or shopping activities.

An extensive literature has stemmed from these views. It is partially reviewed in our 1997 Report (already cited) and recent work on cost function analysis is available in a 1996 review by Gillen. A pioneering paper on the impacts of infrastructure investment is that by Elhance and Lakshmanan (1988).

Having touched on the conventional view, how does our approach differ from that view? Two shorthand expressions begin to answer that question. Going beyond on-system enhancements and use-more or cost-less effects on established activities, we think of transportation improvements as enabling:

- Doing old things in new ways.
- Doing new things.

Reference is to the production and consumption of goods and services and new ways and new things flow from innovations; they are the results of innovations. So, put simply, transportation improvements are thought of as enabling innovations in the ways people produce and consume. In turn, and because innovations are a major force for social and economic development, the innovation emphasis informs the question of how transportation may act as an agent in development.

Doing old things in new ways involves technology shift-based productivity improvements. That is, technology development makes for the more effective uses of capital, labor and other factors of production by changing production recipes. Considering consumption, the innovation of new things increases the variety of products and services available. Such products and services offer consumers increased choices. Consumers may shift their consumption recipes/activities and thus enhance their quality of life.

An All-Inclusive Recipe for Impacts

Referring to doing old things in new ways and doing new things reminds us of Schumpeter's 1934 recipe for economic progress. He used the 'in new ways' words and stressed how innovation creates new things. He went on to emphasize how innovation and technology development accelerates economic development. His tie to transportation improvements was through increases in market and supply areas and the organization of more efficient production. Earlier, those ideas were explored in 1776 by Adam Smith in his chapter on specialization. Smith considered the contribution of specialization to comparative advantage.

Ingredients

Our recipe for impacts begins with Schumpeter-like and Smith-like ingredients. To these we add the ways transportation improvements may energize innovations and increase production and consumption choices.

Smith, Schumpeter and lots of industry location analysts observe that improving transportation enlarges market and supply areas and may bring new resources into the economy. Specialization follows from opportunities to increase market segmentation, as well as from increases in quantities produced. Using new-to-the-market low sulphur iron ore to produce metal and then scissors configured for left handed customers may be cited as an example outcome. But such an example slights processes – the imagining, experimenting and learning undertaken by suppliers and consumers.

Specialization is one mechanism and combining, a word used by Schumpeter, is another. Schumpeter spoke of 'carrying out new combinations' as the essence of innovation. The new combinations emphasis is certainly proper, but the word essence may be too strong. Adopting the widely held view that usefulness enters the innovation equation, we would ask for new combinations that serve markets. A new combination serving an existing market provides old things in new ways; new things require new markets.

Extending the Recipe

The new combinations ingredient in the processes generating impacts threads modal histories. On-system, transportation has seen new combinations followed by new combinations; sometimes broadly scoped and sometimes narrow. The modes were birthed by combining facility, equipment and management and operations protocols. For example, the railroads combined the steam engine with tramway-like fixed facilities and the funding, pricing and operations procedures used by canals and toll roads.

Within-existing-mode combining has transformed and retransformed systems as new propulsion capabilities, facilities, or management and control procedures have been adopted, for example, diesel locomotives, interstate highways and deregulation. The air transportation system was reshaped or transformed as jet aircraft services replaced piston engine aircraft.

The 'combining-specialization' on-system processes that yield new transportation services is also at work off-system as new services are combined with other things. Much discussed today are reductions in the number of warehouses in distribution systems and an increased frequency of smaller, longer distance shipments. Along with changes in inventory, this is carrying out transportation-logistics in new ways. On-system, innovations bring together new pricing and service elements, intermodal capabilities, improved communication and control and other things to provide new services. Off-system, transportation is combined with other elements in production and consumption processes to yield more flexible manufacturing, increased varieties of consumer choices and other new things.

Reflection will remind us of the many off-system innovations enabled by on-system service improvements. Sometimes advances have been massive. The railroads, for example, made winter obsolete in many areas as patterns of production and consumption that had been limited by seasonal constraints on canal and road services disappeared and new patterns appeared. Railroad services along with the telegraph allowed for the development of large-scale continuous production processes, such as those that emerged in steel mills. Yesterday's streetcars triggered innovations in urban living marked by the suburbs and outlying recreation and shopping centers.

Market Clearing

Subject to tieing-in to networks, risk and other constraints, entrepreneurs extend new services wherever there are profits on the horizon and those who are not served clamor for services. The result is a rush to deploy. When much facility construction is required, as was the case for highways and railroads, deployment may require decades. But even before networks are fleshed-out, there will be some action in the market. We recall this as the case when the truck substituted for the horse and wagon in turn of the century cities prior to improvements in roads linking cities.

Access is a key word. Although differing from network to network, access in some form becomes widely available early on in diffusion processes.

The availability of access enables innovations and over a period of time users combine transportation with other things. Streetcar and automobile suburbs are a reminder of innovations by housing, shopping center and other suppliers and by consumers. There is learning how to use new transportation services and related learning by transportation service suppliers – they learn how to provide services suited to emerging markets.

We think of mobility as the result of the interrelated evolution of the user and supply sides. A partial analogy is to individuals who are said to have mobility if they can adapt to and take advantage of transportation services. The analogy is broader when we remember that services evolve in response to what individuals demand and that mobility involves making use of the activities enabled by using transportation services.

Thinking About Air Transportation

Having sketched the way we think about the processes generating impacts and the ingredients in impact generating recipes, we now turn to the transformations that occur as the evolution of transportation services enable development of transportation-using industries. Air transportation was the service examined. We will comment on the structure of service provision and the provision of services on the US network.

Production of Services

Air transportation is produced by airline firms using navigation, airframe, funding, reservation, management and other technologies or protocols and firms work in lockstep with suppliers of airports and air traffic control. To conceptualize this production system, imagine vector A_t with elements a_i, where an element represents the ith technical attribute of the system at reference time t. Such an element might represent, say, engine thrust or horsepower in year 1960. Working with airport and other actors, the airline firm converts these building-block technologies to services, which we represent as B_t with elements b_j. We think of a service as, say, a flight between and origin and destination using a particular aircraft type, offering in-flight services of a certain sort, etc. The task of converting building blocks to services may be represented this way:

$$A_t\text{<---------->}B_t$$

An input-output like structure is suggested, but will not follow-up on that suggestion because combining is the operative concept in the innovation process. Our emphasis is not so much on the interdependencies in already established production processes that are captured in input-output analyses.

Combining does not take place independent of markets, so we have represented the conversion as two way and that is because a service attribute may affect the technological building blocks, as well as the reverse being true.

The production task for the airline, then, is to convert building-block technologies to services and, recognizing feedbacks, create or cause to be created appropriate building block technologies.

So far, a mouthful, but quite simple.

Continuing to leave service consumer considerations pretty much aside, let us think about the temporal pattern for changes in services. In a rough, approximate way technology development went somewhat like this.

Early-on, there was biplane mail and passenger services competing with rail services between large mainland cities. Over-water services competing with ferries and liners were also in early market niches.

A family of propeller driven aircraft emerged in the 1930s (B-207, DC-2 and DC-3) that could provide commercially viable services between large city pairs, as well as along links on networks with intermediate steps. As technologies, these aircraft combined structures, engines, landing gear, navigation and other then state-of-the-art technologies. At a system scale, developing airports, air traffic control, organization of firms and their financing, navigation aids, regulatory protocols and other building blocks combined with the availability of aircraft in providing services.

The 1930s template held through the 1950s as the quantity of service grew and aircraft and other building blocks increased in size to accommodate growth. It was broken in the 1960s as jet powered aircraft entered service. There was a certain recombining of the system as firms, airports, financing and other building blocks adjusted to change.

The rough and much simplified sketch represents the period from the 1920s to today in which air services proliferated. Today's situation is represented by today's vector of services. Extending beyond the equipment-oriented summary of the growth and development dynamic:

- The variety of services increased.
- Specialized services evolved in market niches.
- Market penetration of an s-curve sort occurred.
- Progress was achieved through functional refinement and discovery.

The words refinement and discovery refer to how old things in new ways and new things are achieved. Recall that innovations occur as building blocks are combined to provide services in market niches. Once a successful product or service emerges, there is a period of process-of-production refinement, as well as product refinement. Refined production and product technologies yield productivity gains. Products and production recipes may be tailored this way or that and specialized to markets. Tailoring involves discovery and its result is increased product variety. Gifford and Garrison applied these concepts to air transportation in a 1993 paper and they extended the concepts to infrastructure development of many types.

Networked Services

So far, the discussion of services has been aspatial, yet services are provided on networks connecting consumers with the places where the recreational services we examined are offered. How did network considerations enter our thinking?

Networks are means of commercial and social and cultural interactions. They connect places and regions and, as time goes by, connections may be improved or deteriorate. For instance, the 500-year expansion of the Roman road system aided exertion of Roman power over much of Europe. The breaking of the road network by marauding Goths and Moors was part of the story of the decline of Roman power, the decline and fall of Rome.

There is the presence of a network and the question of how well it serves, and, as already stressed, our thinking captures these considerations using the concepts of access and mobility. Considering access first, we think of access in an opportunity fashion. It has to do with the choice set available and the freedom of the population to do this or that.

By the 1930s enthusiasms for services had initiated government programs promoting access. Federal initiatives included promotion of flivver (Ford Model T-like) aircraft, steering air mail subsidies in the interest of creating nationwide services, provision of aids to navigation, the use of antitrust laws to break corporate ties between the airline companies and airframe builders, the licensing of pilots and the certification of the safety of aircraft. In addition to safety regulation, federal economic regulation was initiated. As time went by, these activities were extended. Cities and counties created airports and the federal government and some states began to aid design and construction. What had been support for the design of flivver aircraft shifted to science and technology development programs.

Enthusiasms resulted in the provision of access. Air service was made available nationwide and at a fine enough scale that medium size and many small cities had airports – places to access the system.

As we said, we think of mobility as the result of the taking up of access opportunities. The kernel is that of market response, and the market for air transportation responded strongly. The result on the supply side included the introduction of jets in the late 1950s with increases in speed and ride quality. As the jet fleet expanded, size and performance characteristics of aircraft were specialized to routes and market niches. Airways and airports were modified to accommodate jet aircraft. Deregulation in 1978 interacted with market and management forces to yield a broad range of fares and services. Hub and spoke service strategies by airlines emerged and most customers could take advantage of an array of services to a larger number of destinations.

Traffic growth doubled from 1955 to 1965 and doubled again by 1985. Cheaper, faster and better played roles here, but surely most growth resulted from more choice – the growth of access opportunities. Business travel could be undertaken in ways not practicable before and a similar comment held for travel of many types.

Just looking at measures of cheaper, faster, better, there were social savings as lower fares stemmed from greater airline competition, economies of scale, specialization of equipment and services and honing of the technology. Gains were magnified as reduced fares and improved services resulted in increased market growth. Morrison and Winston (1995) estimate that gains amount to $4 billion annually. Although the extent to which deregulation has increased competition is discussed, there is no debate about the existence of gains.

There have been additional gains. Tailoring services to markets and offering completely new services, such as helicopter lifts to remote fishing streams, provided variety gains. To be considered also are substitutability gains that arise from increased varieties of existing services. The notion here is that the greater the degree of substitutability between goods (as measured by the elasticity of substitution) the more welfare increases (Dixit and Stiglitz, 1977). This is observing that as products or services become more substitutable consumers have to sacrifice less to substitute.

Thinking About Tourism-Recreation

To extend analysis beyond on-system effects, we concentrated on the tourism-recreation industry, and our thinking about tourism-recreation followed the pattern described for air transportation services. There is the combining building blocks aspect, and there are specialization and market niche aspects as well. A 1996 paper by Garrison and Souleyrette provides an extensive discussion of such transportation-enabled combining processes. As is pointed out, sometimes transportation improvements enable the transfer and/or diffusion of something already known. In other situations, there is the creation of something entirely new. The idea of combining transportation with other technologies is also explored in a 1994 paper by Braun and Joerges. They say recombining and show how transportation technologies merge with biological-medical, computer and information technologies. The result is the European organ transplantation system, a system that matches donors and receivers, transports organs and takes advantage of tissue matching. It is a new way of doing old things.

Turning to dynamics, the tourism-recreation innovation processes can be sketched in a serial fashion somewhat similar to the rough sketch provided for air transportation. The story begins in the 1600s when wealthy young men traveled from court to court as barriers of the feudal system were reduced. To aid such recreational travel, Flemish geographer Gerhardus Mercator produced an Atlas of Europe in 1570, and that Atlas was a building block for the recreation innovation. As the royal and new-rich merchant classes increasingly sought recreation, the gambling, bathing and social visiting Mediterranean coast emerged in the 1700s. As English railroads spread, Thomas Cook innovated tours for the artisan classes of the 1850s. Cook's services spread and spread and appealed to a wider audience. Transportation services were combined with bread and board, scenery and other things.

At about Cook's time, Prince Albert is reported to have remarked at the opening of the London Exhibition in 1851, '... communications and transport have erased the vast distances that once separated mankind'. He could just as well have remarked on how the Exhibition was enabled by then transportation services. The growth and development of amusement parks, for another example, were enabled by streetcar services. Coney Island was a site for several parks, each somewhat specialized. Already, variety was available to those seeking recreation.

Today's list of tourism-recreation options or varieties ranges from outdoor recreation for one or many (e.g. Rocky Mountains) to world scale gambling and resort entertainment (e.g. Las Vegas) and recreation park clusters of activities (e.g. Orlando, Florida). Other lists emerge at regional and local scales.

Extending the diagram used to characterize the way building blocks were combined to produce air services, the combining of air transportation services with other building blocks is realized as demand and vector D_t represents that demand. But just as vector B_t was built-up of the elements of A_t, there are building blocks for D_t. Think of a vector E_t as containing elements that translate into D_t. The situation looks like this:

$$A_t \text{<--------->} B_t \text{<--------->} D_t \text{<--------->} E_t$$

So although we imagine a world partitioned into building blocks for this and for that, it is a permeable world, 'pass through' catches the situation. To illustrate from the recreation side, combining ski slopes with transportation (on site and for traveling to the site) says that demand asks for a way to ship skis. In turn, that asks for appropriate services and, say, a transportation service building block such as disposable boxes for skis. Such development illustrates how transportation improvements energize off-system innovations and those innovations, working through markets, steer innovations in transportation services.

A Rorschach Chart?

The relationships connecting the building blocks for transportation innovation (A_t) to the building blocks for tourism-recreation innovation (E_t) might be said to be Rorschach chart-like – what one sees says something about the mind of the beholder. We have sketched what we think. First, we see relations running at least in two ways as innovation in transportation services energize innovations in tourism-recreation and as developments in tourism-recreation influence transportation. The puzzle is leverage – to what extent is transportation (or tourism-recreation) pushed and pulled?

As our sketch of the dynamics of technological development indicated, we see the A_t to E_t connections as steered by that dynamic. To what extent is that dynamic controlling? Has historic path dependence steered development? May the tapering of returns from mature systems be seen?

Saviotti says that increased productivity implies reduced labor inputs but that greater product variety (new products) require labor inputs (Saviotti, 1996). He asks if progress comes more from productivity gains than variety gains or the reverse. We have that question in mind, and admit to a variety bias. But the puzzle is that of how to address the question. It turns on the definition of what is new and what is old. That question does not answer crisply because the new grows out of the old, there is 'nothing new under the sun'.

There is also the question of gains in welfare from innovations by producers and those by consumers. It may well be the welfare improvements flow in a large and overlooked way from the choices innovated and taken by consumers.

Another matter – what is progress? Not everyone finds the diffusion of choices and varieties of opportunities socially desirably. One hears laments that transportation improvements have lead to mass culture, the texture of society has changed. That comment has been addressed especially to the effects of automobilization and the primary and interstate highway programs and it is increasingly addressed to air services. At the same time, critics lament how today's mobility along with modern advertising, communications, publishing and educational curricula are divisive. Folk are turning away from commonly held views and values and critics say this does not bode well for social welfare.

Thinking About the Transportation-Recreation Interrelation

Our brief remarks on air transportation and on tourism-recreation touched on interrelations here and there. Now, we will look more closely at how we thought about interrelations.

Our thinking about tourism-recreation activities takes advantage of the literature that has evolved dealing with the uses of time (e.g. Robinson, 1977). Leisure activities can be roughly defined as what one does when not obligated to do something else, i.e. obligatory activities such as sleeping, childcare and working. Recreation is a leisure activity and we say tourism-recreation to indicate away-from-home activities. Although not very precise, that is a usable definition. It lets us imagine individuals seeking recreational activities at local, regional and national and international scales. That is geographic scale and there is also temporal scale – do we have a few minutes, hours, or days available for recreation activities? And, of course, what is done depends on how consumers value things, skills and experiences, resources available for expenditures and other things.

When recreation is considered, transportation is mostly thought of as a modifier of time and spatial scales – faster affects the use of time and cheaper may mean further. So a cheaper, faster, better improvement in transportation affects consumers' expenditures of time and money at places and, say, a resident of New York City may ski in Colorado rather than New England or Switzerland. Considering budgets, consumers may elect to spend more on recreation and less on, say, housing.

Variety Comes in Layers

Consuming this or that and more or less is one outcome of transportation improvements. The consume here or there outcome is a bit more complex. One might say that skiing is skiing, but at the same time skiing in Switzerland is not the same as in Colorado. The experiences differ.

So in addition to the consumer having a variety of improved air services to choose from, the consumer also has a variety of look-alike recreation choices and can do old things in new ways.

Another layer of variety emerges as we consider changes in production recipes. There is the variety of choices created when transportation is combined with other building blocks to produce new ways of doing not-so-look-alike old things or new things. How do we think about these?

Recreation is a big business and sources ranging from travel surveys, public and private state, national and regional agencies, to OECD and United Nations reports provide estimates of numbers of travelers and expenditures (Cook, 1990). Newspaper recreation sections, industry yearbooks, firm-specific data (such as K-101 reports) and other sources told us about changes in the provision of services and their markets (e.g. Waters, 1995). From these data, it is clear that there has been lots of innovation of a packaging-combining sort. A much referred to example is the evolution of amusement park complexes. Location-wise, these have evolved from urban street car-served zoos with entertainment rides through auto accessed suburban waterworlds and other amusement centers, to complexes of parks with different offerings served by air and long distance auto travel. The complex of recreational offerings in the Orlando, Florida area is a much cited example.

We have also identified evolutionary paths for gambling and gambling combined with amusement park-like services, outdoor recreation and other activities.

A role for transportation appears in every evolutionary path, what is systematic about roles? 1. By increasing the potential for larger markets, transportation enables market segmentation and increases producers' opportunities to vary products. 2. Working through the same market area mechanism, consumer oriented agglomeration advantages emerge. It works this way. Individual recreation suppliers may produce a particular package. The consumer may choose that particular offering (variety) and is advantaged if other offerings are in the area. Florida, California and the Pacific Northwest are advantaged by having many building blocks for combining things. We think that national parks, such as Yosemite, anchor agglomerations of associated activities and ought to be thought about in that fashion.

Continuing, 3. transportation availability may allow using spatially fixed natural resources – surf, sea, mountains, etc. – as recreational building blocks. Cultural resources may be thought about in the same way. The result may involve doing old things in new ways, but there are also opportunities for things that have not been done before (e.g. touring Antarctica). 4. Finally, transportation may allow taking advantage of special institutional arrangements (opportunity for gaming on Indian reservations; promotional willingness of governments).

The list of the ways recreation offerings may be provided goes on and on. Eventually we get to cruise ships, African safaris and just about anything one can imagine. Again, a role for transportation is ever present and it may be seen how transportation improvements enabled changes in production and consumption recipes.

Converting Our Thinking to Analysis

We traced the evolution of air services and changes in tourism-recreation activities in control and sample cities from 1955 to 1995. Thirteen cities were examined representing different levels and types of innovation in the recreation-tourism industries (Table 12.1).

For instance, Honolulu represented a tropical resort center, Las Vegas a gambling center, Orlando and amusement park center and Bozeman a gateway city to Yellowstone National Park. Columbus, Tulsa and Knoxville were among the cities included in the set to broaden the range of recreation-tourism observations beyond cities where much development was expected.

Table 12.1 Cities studied

Bozeman, Montana	Columbus, Ohio	Honolulu, Hawaii
Jackson, Mississippi	Knoxville, Tennessee	Las Vegas, Nevada
Orlando, Florida	San Antonio, Texas	Seattle, Washington
Tulsa, Oklahoma	Twin Cities, Minnesota	Tucson, Arizona
Denver, Colorado		

County data were used for the most part when examining activities associated with the cities. We collected data from several sources for five year intervals 1955–1995 on employment in eating and drinking establishments, hotels and other lodging, motion picture theaters and amusement and recreation establishments. Cluster analyses identified cities with similar employment trends over the study period.

To deal with the mobility aspect of the evolution and provision of air transportation services 1955–1995, we developed indices of the ways the cities were served by transportation network. We referred the cities to the 10 largest generators of air traffic in the US in 1960 and an index was formed by a composite of travel time and fare. A second index examined each city's ease of accessing those cities with greatest traffic involvement.

We used a modified shift-share technique to interpret urban area data on employment in tourism-recreation industries and tied the results of that interpretation to the mobility indices. The mobility and tourism-recreation changes interrelated strongly when we examined cities such as Bozeman, Orlando and Las Vegas where tourism-recreational developments have been great and where services loom large in the urban economies. Although present, the results were not as crisp across the other cities we analyzed. Cluster analysis and comparisons of trend lines aided our analysis.

Our study was data intensive, yet the data left a lot to be desired. There were incomplete data sets on air travel and fares. The employment data were at the two digit SIC code level so there was activity aggregation, as well as the spatial aggregation forced by the use of county data. (Disclosure issues required the two-digit aggregation; our study used data collected prior to the creation of the SMSA reporting units.) Also, the evolution of mobility provided by air services interrelated with many activities, so only a partial explanation for tourist-recreation driven mobility changes on the US network was to be expected.

Critique

We sought to clarify the relations between innovation in transportation and in tourism-recreation activities. The identification of relations in the analysis model made use of employment and mobility measures to approximate the elements of the vectors B_t and D_t discussed earlier and the use of approximations limited the richness of the analysis.

Interpretation? The analysis did point to increased specialization in recreation activities. It also said that the diffusion of air transportation improvements had improved mobility across markets varying in character. Much interpretation, however, was based on information external to the analysis model, information from industry sources on developments at places and on changes in the varieties of air services available. In this way, the analysis confirmed what was already known or suspected. But as we said earlier when referring to Rorschach charts, there is room for varied interpretations.

Technological change appears in myriad ways, so there remains the challenge of the full scoping of the ways transportation enhancements enable innovative activities taking place from time to time and here and there. And the valuation issue also remains. We speak of variety – doing old things in new ways and doing new things – but have yet to implement evaluation measures bearing on increased variety.

Disappearance of Distance

Paraphrasing remarks in the introduction when referring to the disappearance of distance, the dynamics of the evolution of the supply of services and the evolution of demand are driven by innovative actors doing old things in new ways or doing new things. As services are improved, the constraint of the friction of distance is relaxed.

A metaphoric game may aid in answering questions about relaxed constraints. Think of a movie fast-forwarding over the decades. It is showing a game where there is a table representing the US and there are air service and recreation service players (service providers). The air transportation players place their access and mobility cards and by the end of the movie the table is covered. The recreation players set down cards where things can be combined to provide recreation services. By the end of the game the air service and recreation cards form hills here and valleys there.

This is a complicated game because the plays are not independent, there is historic path dependence. What an air service player does depends on what other air service players have done and might do. A similar statement may be made about recreation service providers. In addition, recreation service providers depend on air services for the recreation opportunities they create and air service providers respond to the recreation market. The situation may appear to be of mind-boggling complexity, but it is tamed somewhat because competition and profits motivate plays of the game.

Not to be overlooked are the consumers of air transportation and recreational services. Their choices are working through markets and steering the actions of service providers. For analysis, what do we look for, what do we expect to see? The way the game is played forms one question. The recreation player lays a card; how does the air service player respond. The reverse is also at question: as air service is improved, how does recreation follow?

The disappearance of distance? One metaphor asks for another. So we say ... Results in an ever richer, more vibrant, changing and chancy tapestry for designs of production and consumption, for the designs of the lives and fortunes of individuals, activities and places.

References

Braun, I. and Bernward, J. (1994), 'How to Recombine Large Technical Systems: The Case of European Organ Transplantation', in J. Summerton (ed.), *Changing Large Technical Systems*, Westview Press, Boulder, CO, pp. 25–52.

Cook, S.D. (1990), 'Recreational Travel and Tourism Data: Needs, Resources, and Issues', in *Data Resources for National Transportation Decision Making*, Transportation Research Record 1253, pp. 56–70.

Dixit, A. and Stiglitz, J. (1977), 'Monopolistic Competition and Optimal Product Diversity', *American Economic Review*, vol. 67, pp. 297–308.

Elhance, A.P. and Lakshmanan, T.R. (1988), 'Infrastructure Production System Dynamics in National and Regional Systems: An Econometric Study of the Indian Economy', *Regional Science and Urban Economics*, vol. 18, pp. 511–31.

Garrison, W.L. and Souleyrette, R.R (1996), 'Transportation Innovation and Development: The Companion Innovation Hypothesis', *The Logistics and Transportation Review*, vol. 32, pp. 5–37.

Garrison, W.L., Gillen, D. and Williges, C.R. (1997), *Impact of Changes to Transportation Infrastructure and Services: How Changes in Air Transportation Infrastructure and Services Enabled Innovations in Recreational Activities, 1955–1995*, Institute of Transportation Studies, July 1997, (UCB-ITS-RR-97-4).

Gifford, J.L. and Garrison, W.L. (1993), 'Airports and the Air Transportation System: Functional Refinements and Functional Discovery', *Technological Forecasting and Social Change*, vol. 43, pp. 103–23.

Gillen, D. (1996), 'Transportation Infrastructure and Economic Development', *Logistics and Transportation Review*, vol. 32, pp. 38–62.

Mackie, P.J. (1996), 'Induced Traffic and Economic Appraisal', *Transportation*, vol. 23, pp. 103–19.

Morrison, S. and Winston, C (1995), *The Evolution of the Airline Industry*, Brookings Institution, Washington, DC.

Robinson, J.P. (1977), *How Americans Use Time: A Social-Psychological Analysis of Everyday Behavior*, Praeger, New York.

Saviotti, P.P. (1996), *Technological Evolution, Variety and the Economy*, Edward Elgar, Cheltenham.

Schumpeter, J.A. (1934), *The Theory of Economic Development*, Harvard University Press, Cambridge, pp. 65–6.

Smith, A. (1776), *The Wealth of Nations*, University of Chicago Press, Chicago, IL (1976 republication of the original).

Waters, S.R. (1995), *Travel Industry World Yearbook*, Child and Waters, Rye, NY.

Chapter 13

Transportation and Energy Policy: Retrospect and Prospect

David L. Greene

Introduction

After twenty-five years, transportation remains a major, growing user of fossil fuels, the key factor in the US oil dependence problem and a significant source of environmental pollution. Twenty-five years ago, the US transportation system used 17.7 quads of energy, about 96 per cent of which was petroleum (Davis, 1997, tables 2.7 and 2.8). This year, transportation will use about 24.7 quads of energy, 97 per cent of which is petroleum fuels (U.S. DOE/EIA, 1997a, table 2.5).[1] In 1972, transportation accounted for half of the petroleum consumed by the US economy, today it comprises two thirds (Davis, 1997, table 2.5). All US highway vehicles traveled 1.26 trillion miles in 1972 at an average fuel economy of 12 miles per gallon.

By 1995, vehicle miles of travel had nearly doubled to 2.42 trillion and average fuel economy had improved to 17 mpg.[2] In 1973 the US imported 6.0 million barrels per day (mmbd) of oil, 35 per cent of its total consumption (U.S. DOE/EIA, 1997a, table 1.8). Last year, the US imported 8.5 mmbd, 46 per cent of total consumption and this year, almost a quarter century after the first oil price shock in 1973, the US economy will break all previous records for oil imports and import dependency.

But what does all of this mean? Have things gotten better, or worse? And what lessons have been learned from 25 years of struggling with transportation energy issues that can help us address the energy problems of the future?

How have Transportation's Energy Problems Changed?

The transportation energy problems of 1970s centered around depletion of energy resources, dependence on imported petroleum and environmental pollution as a of energy use (notably urban air pollution, acid rain and petroleum spills).

The problems facing us today are in many ways similar, but there have been some significant changes and, perhaps more importantly, we now perceive transportation energy issues in significantly different ways.

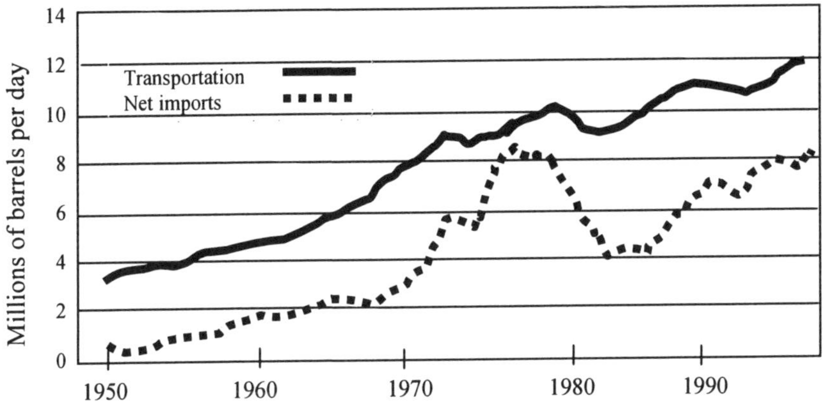

Source: U.S. DOE/EIA, Annual Energy Review 1996, DOE/EIA-0384(96), tables 5.1, 5.12b.

Figure 13.1 US transportation petroleum consumption and US net petroleum imports, 1950–1996

The oil price shocks of the 1970s and 1980s taught us that the costs of oil dependence were real and large.[3] But the oil price crash of 1986 showed that they were not necessarily permanent. Worry about 'running out' of oil has changed into concerns about the economic, strategic and military costs of oil dependence, as well as the global environmental impacts and sustainability of its continued use.

Oil Dependence

Despite the fact that oil today is plentiful and relatively inexpensive, oil dependence remains an immediate problem for the US transportation system. At $20 per barrel, oil is certainly cheaper today than it was in the 1980s, when prices topped $55 per barrel (1996 $). Yet it is still almost twice as expensive as it was in 1972 and twice as expensive as the best estimates of what oil would cost if the world oil market were competitive (e.g. Berg et al., 1997, p. 50). Thus, even today, oil producers are extracting monopoly rents from oil consumers. Over the period 1972 to 1996, the resulting transfer of wealth from the US economy to foreign oil producers amounted to $1.4 trillion (1996 $). In 1997, US oil imports will exceed all previous records for both quantity and share of domestic demand. Not only is there a continuing loss of wealth to monopoly pricing, but also a continuing vulnerability of our economy to possible future price shocks. The impacts of an oil price shock on US GDP depend on a variety of factors, but most critically on the oil cost share of GDP, which today is about the same as it was in 1972.

The question of whether there will be another world oil price shock in the near future remains an open one. The answer will depend on a number of factors. First, it will depend on the objective economic factors that determine OPEC's market power. Most important of these are the price elasticity of world oil demand, the price elasticity of non-OPEC oil supply and OPEC's share of the world oil market. The sizes of short- and long-run elasticities both matter. Second, it will depend on global politics, the internal stability of OPEC states and their relations to each other and on the cohesiveness of the cartel, as such.

As usual, there is good news and bad news. The good news is that OPEC's market share has not yet regained its high of 50 per cent in the 1970s and has been stalled at just over 40 per cent for several years. The fact that the world's oil demand is not growing at anything like the 7–8 per cent per year rates of the early 1970s is also good news. Increased supply from non-OPEC producers is more good news. The bad news is that OPEC still holds the majority of the world's proven reserves and, according to our best estimates (Masters, Attanasi and Root, 1994), the majority of the world's ultimate oil resources. Furthermore, OPEC is drawing down its reserves at half the rate of the rest of the world. The bad news includes the fact that US oil imports have reached a new high and the fact that transportation's share of petroleum consumption has increased. Transportation petroleum demand is notoriously price inelastic (Gately and Rappaport, 1988).

While it is likely that oil demand has become less price elastic, oil supply has almost certainly become more price elastic. Technological improvements such as 3-D seismic imaging, horizontal drilling and improved offshore drilling technology have significantly reduced the costs of finding and developing oil in many areas (e.g. Fagan, 1997). But the question of whether even these changes have made a sufficient impact on the ROW oil supply to forestall the possibility of future oil price shocks remains open (Salameh, 1995). The analysis of the total aggregate impacts on ROW supply elasticities has yet to be done.

Transportation, Energy and the Environment

Transportation's use of energy remains a major source of environmental pollution, yet transportation vehicles today generate less total pollution than they did 25 years ago despite more than a doubling of transportation activity. Transportation vehicles produce 78 per cent of all carbon monoxide emissions, 45 per cent of nitrogen oxide emissions, 37 per cent of hydrocarbon emissions and 27 per cent of anthropogenic emissions of fine particulates (U.S. DOT/BTS, 1996, Chapter 7).[4] Yet despite a more than doubling of vehicle miles traveled between 1970 and 1994, total transportation emissions of lead have been virtually eliminated, hydrocarbon emissions have been cut by half, carbon monoxide emissions are 30 per cent lower, particulate emissions are down 10 per cent and nitrogen oxide emissions increased by only 10 per cent. As a result of the achievements in transportation and other sectors, fewer urban areas fail the National Ambient Air Quality Standards and air quality has generally improved (U.S. DOT/BTS, 1997).

Essentially all of the improvement in emissions from transportation has come as a result of technological change implemented in response to federal emissions control regulations. By setting grams-per-mile emissions limits for new vehicles, fleet emissions rates have been dramatically improved. Were it not for reductions in per-mile emissions, transportation vehicles would produce 4.5 times as much hydrocarbon emissions, 3.2 times as much CO emissions and twice as much nitrogen oxides. Imagine the economic cost of trying to achieve these kinds of emissions reductions by reducing the demand for vehicle travel. Only technological solutions could clean up cars so cost-effectively.

There are other environmental problems associated with transportation and its energy use (e.g. oil spills, noise, acid rain and habitat disruption) and other externalities associated with transportation, such as traffic congestion. Many of these problems are also most effectively addressed by technical fixes, but others are not. The direct and indirect impacts of transportation on land use and habitats, for example, has yet to submit to a sweeping technological solution.

An environmental problem that was barely visible a quarter century ago, global climate change now occupies center stage in energy policy debates. Transportation is a major source of the anthropogenic greenhouse gas emissions driving climate change, accounting for about one third of US CO_2 emissions (U.S. DOE/EIA, 1996). Emissions of CO_2, the principal greenhouse gas, are directly related to the combustion of fossil fuels to power transportation equipment and the carbon content of the fuel. Three aspects of the greenhouse gas problem make it extremely difficult to solve: 1. there is enormous uncertainty about what the impacts of global climate change will actually be; 2. any effective solution will require a high degree of international cooperation; 3. at present, the available technological solutions are simply not good enough.

It has been estimated that stabilizing atmospheric CO_2 concentrations at current levels will require reducing global CO_2 emissions by 50 per cent to 80 per cent from their present levels (NRC, 1990, p. 21; IPCC, 1990). With today's technology, we simply do not know how to do that at anything less than a horrendous economic cost. A recent report by five National Laboratories on the potential for technology to reduce greenhouse gas emissions by 2010, concluded that an all-out effort to develop and implement energy efficient, low-CO_2 technology might, with luck, be able to reduce CO_2 emissions to 1990 levels by 2010 (Interlaboratory Working Group, 1997). However, the study concluded that the transportation sector would not even be able to hold CO_2 emissions to 1997 levels in 2010. It appears that with today's technology we cannot solve the problem of global climate change at a price we are willing to pay. Therefore, if we are to solve the problem, we must change the rules of the game by creating new technological options.

Sustainable Transportation

The doctrine of sustainability is superceding environmentalism as the guiding paradigm for humanity's relationship to the global environment. Lack of sustainability may well be the ultimate 'market failure'.

It is common to begin a discussion of sustainability by acknowledging that it lacks a precise, accepted, scientific definition (e.g. Toman et al., 1994; Pearce et al., 1994), as if this might prevent the concept from taking hold and having an impact on social policy. To this day, there is no precise, generally accepted, scientific definition of the term externality and yet its impact on the way we think about our economy and formulate environmental policy has been profound (e.g.

Greene and Jones, 1997). This is because the concept of externality is intuitively understood and there are adequate working definitions, as well (e.g. Baumol and Oates, 1988, p. 17).

The same applies to sustainability. Intuitively we know that the problem of sustainability is the paradox posed by economies growing without limit in a finite world. The most widely cited definition of sustainable development is still that of the Brundtland Commission, which states that '... sustainable development meets the needs of the present without compromising the needs of future generations to meet their own needs' (World Commission on Environment and Development, 1987).[5]

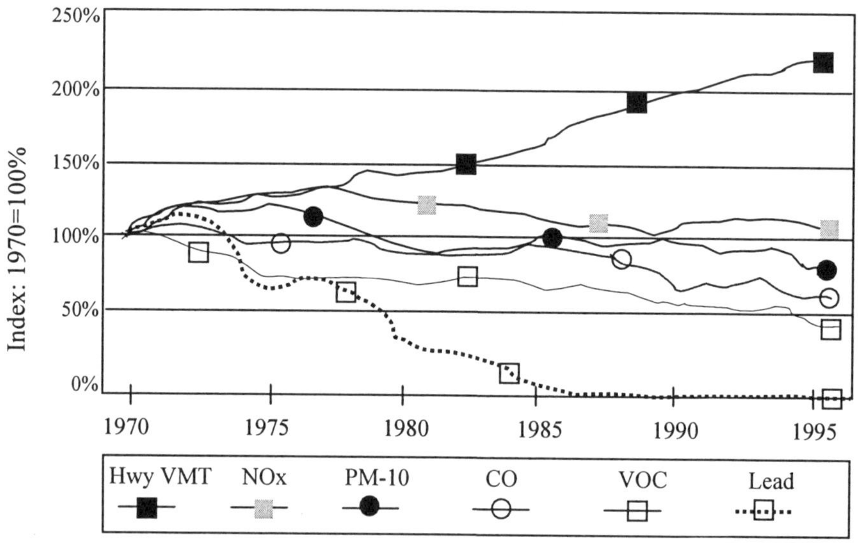

Source: U.S. EPA, National Air Pollutant Emissions Trends, 1900–1996.

Figure 13.2 Transportation emissions trends, 1970–1996

Sustainability could be the ultimate market failure. On the one hand, the prospect of an ever accelerating world economy racing towards a precipice of environmental and natural resource catastrophe is certainly compelling. The ability of markets to solve the problem of sustainability is hampered by the existence of environmental externalities. Worse, there is no guarantee that even if all environmental externalities were internalized, markets would produce a sustainable development path (Pearce and Warford, 1996; Toman et al., 1994). At best, perfect markets can be shown to maximize social welfare for the living. Put another way, we cannot be sure that the interests of future generations are adequately protected because all property rights belong to the present generations. Relying on market systems alone to solve the sustainability problem would therefore seem imprudent.

Either, 1. market economies will serendipitously generate the right kind of technological and other changes (broadly construed) or, 2. market economies will gradually restrict population and economic growth to conform to the limitations of the world's resources or, 3. the human experiment will be an essentially 'Hobbesian' one, i.e. nasty, brutish and short. Of course, there is always option 4: all of the above.

In order to adopt sustainability as a goal, one must be able to tell when society *is* sustainable. One approach to solving this problem is to develop '...a broadly accepted set of indicators and benchmarks to measure and monitor progress'. towards sustainability (OECD, 1997, p. 12; EC, 1997). This approach has the advantage of recognizing the complexity of the sustainability issue. On the other hand, it begs the question of what those indicators might be, which returns one to the problem of developing a scientific (in the sense of being measurable and verifiable) definition of sustainability. At the risk of oversimplification, I suggest that at the heart of this definition is the rate and direction of technological change (Greene, 1997b).

Daly (1991) defined sustainable development by three conditions: 1. rates of use of renewable resources do not exceed their rates of regeneration, 2. rates of use of non-renewable resources do not exceed the rate at which sustainable renewable substitutes are developed and 3. rates of pollution emission do not exceed the assimilative capacity of the environment. The most interesting feature of this definition of sustainability is its emphasis on rates. Rates of resource use and environmental impacts are especially critical for the growing economies of today's free market societies. Pearce and Warford (1996) introduced the concept of a 'coefficient of environmental intensity' to make the point that economic development can only be sustainable if the environmental and resource consumption of a unit of economic activity decreases as fast or faster than the rate of economic growth. The very clear implication of these insights is that sustainability is not an equilibrium but a steady state.

How can the consumption of finite fossil energy resources possibly be sustainable? If economies can expand the boundaries of exploitable fossil reserves by, for example, enhanced oil recovery or improved drilling methods, if the amount of useful work that can be obtained from a Btu of fossil fuel can be increased and it's environmental impacts decreased and if alternative sources of energy can be developed *at the appropriate rates*, then fossil fuel consumption could be considered sustainable. But how does society ensure the right kinds of technological change at the right rates? This is a difficult question indeed, because of the limitations of market systems in addressing public good externalities and sustainability itself.

The transportation energy problems of today are what economists characterize as 'market failures' (as if markets were inherently capable of solving any and all problems, if only they were perfected). Perhaps a more useful way to characterize externalities and other market failures is Papandreou's (1994) assertion that they are really all institutional failures. In his view, an institutional failure arises when society perceives that its institutions are not performing adequately and envisions a better institutional system. The beauty of Papandreou's concept is that it recognizes on the one hand that markets are human institutions (can they operate without property rights, contracts, etc. and the enforcement thereof?) and are therefore capable of improvement and at the same time allows that markets are not the only human institutions and thus do not necessarily have a monopoly on solving (or creating) problems. Papandreou's insight advises that institutional innovation will be an essential part of solving the energy problems of the future.

Towards a Sustainable Energy Policy for Transportation

The key to solving today's transportation's energy problems is finding ways to achieve the right kinds and rates of technological change.[6] The task is made especially difficult by the fact that technological changes are needed in areas that markets generally ignore or only partially address (i.e., environmental pollution, oil market power, sustainability). Furthermore, the concept of technological change must be interpreted broadly to include the development of knowledge and institutions, as well as the development of new propulsions system, alternative fuels, etc.

Technological change is critical to solving the oil dependence problem because only technological change can dramatically change the price elasticities of world oil supply and demand. In fact, those who argue that oil dependence is no longer a serious threat to the US economy and foresee smooth sailing in future petroleum markets generally cite the technological advances in oil exploration and development (3-D seismic imaging, horizontal drilling, improved offshore drilling technology) as principle reasons why the supply of oil from non-OPEC nations will undermine OPEC's market power (U.S. DOE/EIA, 1997b; Smith and Robinson, 1997).

Technological change is crucial to solving motor vehicle emissions problems, as well. No other action could have cut new vehicle emissions by an order of magnitude and on-road vehicle emissions by factors of 2 to 4. And new developments in vehicles and fuels hold the promise of virtually emissions-free transportation in the future (e.g. Reuters, 1997; U.S. DOE, 1997; Toyota, 1997).

Finally, technological change will be essential if the world is to deal successfully with global climate change by cutting greenhouse gas emissions. Developing cost-effective alternatives to carbon-based fuels and dramatically improving the efficiency of fossil fuel use demand sweeping technological innovations (Interlaboratory Working Group, 1997).

Governments in market societies have four basic strategies available for influencing the nature and rate technological change (e.g. see Kemp, 1997):

1. Regulation: setting standards for the performance of technology in order to induce suppliers to make use of existing technology and develop more cost-effective advanced technology.
2. Direct government investment in research, development and demonstration of new technologies, whether the research is performed by the government, sponsored by the government or done cooperatively with other institutions, including private firms.

3. Creation of market incentives, such as taxes on externalities or subsidies of technologies that produce public goods, in order to stimulate the use of and research into such technologies by the private sector.
4. Investment in developing human capital (education) and institutional capital, in order to increase the ability to innovate or to influence behavior. This includes investing in education, from funding basic research to providing financial incentives to encourage students to pursue studies in science and technology. It also includes public education about the nature of transportation energy problems and alternative means of solving them.

Which of these strategies is most effective? This is a natural question to ask, but probably not a constructive one. In one sense, each strategy can be thought of as a tool that may be best suited to particular situations and less well suited to others. But there are also complementarities among strategies. For example, the effectiveness of regulatory strategies may be enhanced when externality taxes are in place to send reinforcing price signals. Indeed, for regulatory standards to be economically efficient, a complementary tax is generally essential. Freeman (1997) showed how a regulatory standard for pollutant emissions, combined with a tax on vehicle miles can, under simplified assumptions, achieve the same result as a direct externality tax on emissions. Although either one alone is more efficient than doing nothing, the combination of the two provides the greatest social welfare. This result is very important, since it demonstrates that regulation is not inherently inefficient or inherently efficient and that regulation and taxation can together accomplish what each individually cannot. The economic efficiency or inefficiency of regulations depends on the situation to which they are applied and how they are implemented. The same applies to externality taxes. It has long been recognized that efficient externality taxes on motor vehicle emissions are too costly and complex to implement unless and until the technology of measuring emissions and the science of predicting their impacts advance well beyond their current state (e.g. Vickery, 1992). Emissions simply vary too widely according to how vehicles are operated and their impacts depend too strongly on environmental factors. Thus, an infeasible efficient externality tax on emissions can be replaced by a combination of regulation and motor vehicle taxation to approximate the same outcome (Innes, 1996).

Regulatory standards *can* be effective for reducing environmental pollution from transportation and for promoting energy efficiency. The impacts of motor vehicle emissions regulations on total transportation emisssions and on air quality were reviewed above. The US automotive fuel economy standards (a.k.a., CAFE standards) have also been remarkably successful (Greene, 1997c), despite considerable criticism to the contrary (e.g. Nivola and Crandall, 1995). Threats to the success of the standards, such as the 'rebound' effect of improved MPG on vehicle travel, shortfalls between test fuel economy values and those achieved in actual use, potential distortions of vehicle type, make and model purchasing patterns, possible loss of market share for domestically manufactured automobiles and impacts on public safety due to vehicle downsizing, have either failed to materialize or have been sufficiently small that they have not significantly reduced the expected benefits of the program (Greene, 1997c, provides a review of each of these factors, as well as others). Regulatory standards can work in theory, have worked in practice and are therefore likely to continue to be an important policy tool for achieving sustainable transportation.

Societies may also directly invest in technological change through government funding of research and development. Regulations and externality taxes provide economic incentives for technological change. In the case of regulations, manufacturers seek less costly and more marketable technologies that still allow them to meet environmental or energy efficiency standards. But governments can conduct their own research at national laboratories, sponsor research at universities or other institutions and fund or co-fund private sector research efforts.

The US government funds the majority of national research in four broad areas: 1. military technology, 2. medicine (not counting pharmaceuticals), 3. aerospace and 4. agriculture. While it is difficult, if not impossible to measure the cost-effectiveness of these investments, one may note that these are not areas in which US technology lags behind the rest of the world.

Greene (1997a) has estimated that the value to the US economy of R&D to reduce oil dependence ranges from billions to tens of billions of dollars annually. Edmonds et al. (1994) has estimated that the value of advanced technology to solving the greenhouse gas problem is easily of the same magnitude. This is not to mention the potential benefits in terms of cleaner air or achieving sustainable development. The approximately $250 million the US government spends each year to develop a 'new generation' of motor vehicles seems very small in comparison (U.S. Congress, OTA, 1995).

This is not to say that expenditures on R&D should necessarily equal the expected value of their outcomes. Economic efficiency dictates that the marginal expenditure should equal the marginal value of the outcome. Unfortunately, we know relatively little about the productivity of research expenditures (let alone the productivity of indirectly induced R&D expenditures such as taxes and standards). The point of citing the admittedly rough estimates of the potential value of transportation energy R&D is that it is well worth our while to make a serious effort to find out just how much effort is appropriate.

Finally, there is the need for education and institutional innovation. It has long been recognized that external costs of motor vehicle use, for example, justify externality taxes on vehicle travel and motor fuels (e.g. Nivola and Crandall, 1995). Yet there is also a general consensus among politicians that the public will not accept such taxes. On the one hand, there is a need for education and persuasion so that the public will understand the societal benefits of such taxes. On the other, there is a need for improving institutions, so that the public can have confidence that the revenues raised will be put to good use (e.g. recycled to reduce payroll taxes). It is easy to be pessimistic about the chances of achieving such changes. Yet the recent changes in public attitudes toward smoking (in which property rights to the air were taken from smokers and given to nonsmokers) and recycling (in which the willingness of individuals to act in the public interest without coercion or private incentive has created an industry) suggest that creating public awareness of the need for sustainability and a willingness to take action are far from impossible.

Pursuit of sustainability will require that we learn more about the effectiveness of all of these strategies, alone or in combination, in promoting technological changes that foster sustainable development. It will also require that we formulate effective national and global strategies for promoting the kinds and rates of technological change necessary to achieve steady-state sustainability for the world's economy.

Notes

1 The Energy Information Administration counts all gasoline, including blending components such as ethanol or MTBE as petroleum. Taking the non-petroleum constituents of these blending stocks into account results in a petroleum content estimate closer to 95 per cent (U.S. DOT/BTS, 1997, Ch. 4).

2 Miles per gallon is obviously an imperfect measure of energy efficiency, since it neglects payload, the composition of traffic and the composition of fuel use. It is used here as a gross indicator of efficiency improvement.

3 Greene and Leiby (1993) estimated the costs to the US economy over the 1972 to 1991 period at approximately $4 trillion 1990 dollars. Some argue that much of this cost was avoidable, for example through more appropriate monetary policy (e.g. Bohi and Toman, 1996). However, the vast majority of scholarly studies is in agreement on the nature and size of the impacts of oil price shocks on the US economy (e.g. see Greene et al., 1995 for a literature review).

4 This does not include particulate emissions from road dust, which comprise another 40 per cent of anthropogenic particulate emissions (U.S. DOT/BTS, 1996, p. 139). Road dust produces mainly larger diameter fine particulates, >2.5 microns and is thus believed to be less harmful to human health than the particulates generated by energy combustion in vehicles.

5 Linking sustainability and economic development is a natural pairing since without continued economic growth the inevitability of ever-increasing stress on environmental resources is lost.

6 Technological change alone cannot solve all of transportation's problems. Especially non-energy problems like traffic congestion, safety and impacts on habitats will require other kinds of solutions. Solutions to these problems and to energy problems will inevitably interact.

References

Baumol, W.J. and Oates, W.E. (1988), *The Theory of Environmental Policy*, 2nd ed., Cambridge University Press, Cambridge.

Berg, E., Kverndokk, S. and Rosendahl, K.E. (1997), 'Market Power, International CO_2 Taxation and Oil Wealth', *The Energy Journal*, vol. 18 (4), pp. 33–71.

Bohi, D.R. and Toman, M.A. (1996), *The Economics of Energy Security*, Kluwer Academic Publishers, Boston.

Daly, H.E. (1991), *Steady State Economics*, Island Press, Washington, DC.

Davis, S.C. (1997), *Transportation Energy Data Book: Edition 17*, ORNL-6919, Oak Ridge National Laboratory, Oak Ridge, TN.

Edmonds, J.A., Wise, M., Pitcher, H., Richels, R., Wigley, T. and MacCracken, C. (1994), *The Accelerated Introduction of Advanced Energy Technologies and Climate Change: An Analysis Using the Global Change Assessment Model (GCAM)*, Battelle Pacific Northwest Laboratories, draft, Washington, DC.

European Communities, Statistical Office (1997), *Indicators of Sustainable Development*, Office for Official Publications of the European Communities, Luxembourg.

Fagan, M.N. (1997), 'Resource Depletion and Technical Change: Effects on U.S. Crude Oil Finding Costs from 1977 to 1994', *The Energy Journal*, vol. 18 (4), pp. 91–106.

Freeman, A.M. (1997), 'Externalities, Prices and Taxes: Second Best Issues in Transportation', in D.L. Greene, D.W. Jones and M.A. Delucchi (eds), *The Full Costs and Benefits of Transportation*, Springer-Verlag, Heidelberg.

Gately, D. and Rappaport, P. (1988), 'The Adjustment of U.S. Oil Demand to the Price Increases of the 1970s', *The Energy Journal*, vol. 9 (2), pp. 93–107.

Greene, D.L. (1997a), 'Oil Dependence: The Value of R&D', *Proceedings of the Thirty Second Intersociety Energy Conversion Conference*, vol. 3, pp. 2148–53, American Institute of Chemical Engineers, New York.

Greene, D.L. (1997b), 'Energy and Environmental Consequences of Transportation: Indicators of Sustainability', pp. 321–4 in the *Bulletin of the International Statistical Institute*, Proceedings of the 51st Session, Istanbul, Turkey.

Greene, D.L. (1997c), 'Why CAFE Worked', *Energy Policy*, vol. 26 (8), pp. 595–614.

Greene, D.L. and Leiby, P.N. (1993), *The Social Costs to the U.S. of Monopolization of the World Oil Market, 1972–1991*, ORNL-6744, Oak Ridge National Laboratory, Oak Ridge, TN.

Greene, D.L., Jones, D.W. and Leiby, P.N. (1995), *The Outlook for Oil Dependence*, ORNL-6873, Oak Ridge National Laboratory, Oak Ridge, TN.

Greene, D.L. and Jones, D.W. (1997), 'The Full Costs and Benefits of Transportation: Conceptual and Theoretical Issues', in D.L. Greene, D.W. Jones and M.A. Delucchi (eds), *The Full Costs and Benefits of Transportation*, Springer-Verlag, Heidelberg, pp. 4–5.

Innes, R. (1996), 'Regulating Automobile Pollution under Certainty, Competition and Imperfect Information', *Journal of Environmental Economics and Management*, vol. 31, pp. 219–39.

Intergovernmental Panel on Climate Change (1996), *Climate Change 1995: Impacts, Adaptations and Mitigation of Climate Change: Scientific and Technical Analyses*, Cambridge University Press, Cambridge.

Interlaboratory Working Group on Energy-Efficient and Low-Carbon Technologies (1997), *Scenarios of U.S. Carbon Reductions*, Office of Energy Efficiency and Renewable Energy, U.S. Department of Energy, Washington, DC.

Kemp, R. (1997), *Environmental Policy and Technical Change: A Comparison of the Technological Impact of Policy Instruments*, Edward Elgar, Cheltenham, U.K.

Masters, C., Attanasi, E. and Root, D. (U.S. Geological Survey) (1994), 'World Petroleum Assessment and Analysis', *Proceedings of the Fourteenth World Petroleum Congress*, John Wiley and Sons, New York.

National Research Council, Energy Engineering Board (1990), *Confronting Climate Change: Strategies for Energy Research and Development*, National Academy Press, Washington, DC.

Nivola, P.S. and Crandall, R.W. (1995), *The Extra Mile*, The Brookings Institution, Washington, DC.

Organization for Economic Cooperation and Development (1997), *Sustainable Consumption and Production*, OECD, Paris.

Papandreou, A.A. (1994), *Externality and Institutions*, Clarendon Press, Oxford.

Pearce, D.W., Atkinson, G.D. and Dubourg, W.R. (1994), 'The Economics of Sustainable Development', *Annual Review of Energy and Environment*, vol. 19, pp. 457–74.

Pearce, D.W. and Warford, J.J. (1996), *World Without End*, The International Bank for Reconstruction and Development, Washington, DC.

Reuters Limited (1997), *Honda Claims New Engine Cleans Smoggy Air*, CNN interactive, http://cnn.com/us/9710/20/enviro.honda.reut/index.html, October 20, cyberspace.

Salameh, M.G. (1995), 'Can Technology Provide the Answer to Future Oil Crises?', *OPEC Review*, Winter 1995, pp. 293–305.

Smith, N.J. and Robinson, G.H. (1997), 'Technology Pushes Reserves 'Crunch' Date Back in Time', *Oil and Gas Journal*, April 7, pp. 43–50.

Toman, M.A., Pezzey, J. and Kraukraemer, J. (1994), 'Neoclassical Economic Growth Theory and 'Sustainability'', forthcoming in D. Bromley (ed.), *Handbook of Environmental Economics*, Blackwell, London.

Toyota Motor Corporation, International Public Affairs (1997), *Toyota Launches the Revolutionary PRIUS Hybrid Passenger Vehicle*, Press Information, October 14, Tokyo.

U.S. Congress, Office of Technology Assessment (1995), *Advanced Automotive Technology: Visions of a Super-Efficient Family Car*, OTA-ETI-638, U.S. Government Printing Office, Washington, DC.

U.S. Department of Energy, Energy Information Administration (1996), *Emissions of Greenhouse Gases in the United States 1995*, DOE/EIA-0573(95), Washington, DC.

U.S. Department of Energy, Energy Information Administration (1997a), *Monthly Energy Review, October 1997*, DOE/EIA-0035(97/10), Washington, DC.

U.S. Department of Energy, Energy Information Administration (1997b), *International Energy Outlook 1997*, DOE/EIA-0484(97), Washington, DC.

U.S. Department of Energy, Office of the Press Secretary (1997), 'Major Breakthrough in Automobile Technology', *DOE NEWS*, October 21, Washington, DC.

U.S. Department of Transportation, Bureau of Transportation Statistics (1996), *Transportation Statistics Annual Report 1996*, Washington, DC.

U.S. Department of Transportation, Bureau of Transportation Statistics (1997), *Transportation Statistics Annual Report 1997*, BTS97-S-01, Washington, DC.

Vickery, W.S. (1992), 'Theoretical and Practical Possibilities and Limitations of a Market Mechanism Approach to Air Pollution Control', *Land Economics*, vol. 68 (1), pp. 1–6, reprinted from a talk given in 1967.

World Commission on Environment and Development (1987), *Our Common Future*, Oxford University Press, Oxford.

Chapter 14

Plan Evaluation Methodologies: Some Aspects of Decision Requirements and Analytical Response

Wilbur A. Steger and T.R. Lakshmanan

Overview and Summary[1]

We have chosen to analyze the past, present and probable future status of the 'evaluation and choice' phase of the overall planning process (our pre-conference assignment) by, first, placing it in the context of the overall process and, then, suggesting methods for achieving what evaluators of public choices would like to see accomplished in this phase. Thus, this chapter can be viewed as a primitive form of 'gap analysis' of the evaluation phase, taking as its primary focus urban developmental and transportation planning and the metropolitan studies which serve as their analytic framework. In so doing, emphasis is also paid to other related parts of this overall framework which have received scant attention, i.e. the contextual (goal setting) and synthetic (alternative plan development) phases.

The chapter addresses a set of crucial questions. What are the issues and policy 'space' in current urban and regional planning? What are the emerging concerns and their dimensions? What philosophical views exist of the planning process (and its dimensions) in which to frame these issues and arrive at appropriate instrumentalities? What is the context, scope and nature of current methodologies of plan evaluation and the related plan design technology? How are control or policy variables identified and expressed? How are the effects of impacts identified and estimated in terms of magnitude and the different dimensions of incidence stratification? When these have been reviewed, the focus is then placed on plan evaluation technology and the 'gap' discernible between currently the most sophisticated expression of plan, evaluation technology and the more generally prevalent practices. The chapter concludes with what appear to be promising research strategies for 'closing' the gap between requirements and the technological and institutional determinants of supply.

This attempt to be comprehensive, at least in the planning and socio-economic dimension, has also prevented us from analyzing in detail any of a number of very interesting issues about 'evaluation'. Our choice to 'locate' the evaluation phase in the planning process was the superior strategy for this conference because a proper view of evaluation calls for a thorough restructuring of many elements of the process which, in turn, would substantially influence the methods used in the evaluation phase – and, thus, how we self-evaluate our performance during this phase.

To place urban and regional planning in context, the heritage of issues and methods are initially traced through a brief description of National Transportation and Urban Policy. Since evaluation methodology has to contend with *trends* in issues which emerge from these initial policy sets, the dimensions of a variety of metropolitan planning issues are discussed, as well as what planners are now contributing toward a resolution of these issues. The three dimensions examined are:

- Public investment and geographic hierarchy issues.
- Public vs. private sector issues.
- Incidence issues.

For a variety of reasons, planning participation in many of these areas ranges from sporadic to non-existent. The correspondence between these and classical economic issues is clarified, these becoming the issues' 'middle-bridge' between planning and normative economics.

Next, several philosophical views of how the planning process contends with the issues it chooses to resolve are contrasted. A goal oriented forward-seeking version of the planning process (representing the generally prevalent practice) is presented first. Another version, perhaps not as different as appearances make it, is presented to describe the 'incremental problem-solving' process. The 'battleground' set by these two helps set the stage for a discussion of the many different dimensions emphasized by practitioners and theorists regarding views of the process.

Evaluation methodologies are next discussed, within a framework set by the requirements for evaluation and some previous attempts at grappling with this problem. Evaluation methods are seen to set certain requirements for each of the Goal identification, Plan and Policy Design and Impact Estimation phases. Thus, this review focuses briefly on the requirements suggested by identified goals, the identification and taxonomy of control or policy variables and the definition and measurement of effect variables in terms of magnitude and dimensions of incidence stratification. A discussion of the problem of transforming effect vectors of plans to explicit preference vectors follows nest.

The stage is, thus, set for a discussion of the gaps in the state-of-the-art of evaluation, revealed by a matching of the results of analysis of 'demand' for, and 'supply' of, evaluation methodologies. These gaps, and suggestions addressed to strategies for initial investigation, are presented in terms of:

- The expansion of the 'issues' space'.
- Improved models of decision processes.
- Impact modeling strategy, as it relates to evaluation needs.
- Public preference structure estimation.

Finally, strategic directions of analytical improvements – for the long and short run – are presented. While no explicit priority structure for implementing this strategy is presented, it is anticipated that a careful examination of the future issues' space would greatly facilitate the development of such an ordering.

Thus, this chapter evidences a preoccupation with basic conceptual problems in plan evaluation, such as issue relevance, process context, plan design and identification of impacts and preference vectors. The neglect of technical issues, such as a choice of an appropriate discount rate, that loom large in water resource program evaluation discussions, is a measure of the novelty and youth of the field of urban plan evaluation and the challenges that lie ahead for its development.

From this perspective, we have resisted the temptations of a too innocently positivist approach. The search for feasible techniques in an area with a perplexing multiplicity, fluidity and conflict of values, the 'quicksand' complexity of control and effect variable dimensions and shifting criteria, has the quality of a mirage. Consequently, we resolved to thread our way through the network of premature generalizations abounding in the field with the intent on a preliminary identification of broad strategies of analytical development. It has been a very sobering experience.

Introduction

Context of this Chapter

In recent years, urban developmental and transportation planning has been in a flux: as policy-makers and planners come to grips with the problems posed by planning for complex urban systems open to change in many directions, they have become aware of new and broader sets of issues. The analytical framework for posing these planning issues are also trending away from simplistic 'end state' orientations to more appropriate 'functionalist' foundations. Thus the issue and policy 'space' in physical planning is broadening beyond earlier focus on efficient arrangements among activities in space, having close functional links, to policy issues of varying dimensions at different levels of government oriented to assuring appropriate levels of public service and harmonious relations among spatially juxtaposed, if functionally unrelated, activities.

At the same time, planning analysts who have emphasized a desired future state, are focusing on the processes by which that state is reached, combining thereby an interest in process and a desire for goals. Transportation planners have also moved away from narrow notions of transportation system efficiency to an evaluation of 'externalities' of transportation investments in considering the feedback effects of transportation on development patterns.

The legislative and institutional response and to some extent initiation of these changing trends has been the various Highway Acts, Mass Transit Act, the Community Renewal program, model Cities and Metropolitan Development Act and the creation of the US Department of Housing and urban Development. The full impact of these decisions has yet to be realized, though a basis for a continuing, comprehensive and cooperative land use and transportation planning process has emerged. In the same period, several metropolitan studies carried out under the auspices of these legislative decisions have pioneered the development of certain aspects of the analytical and computational technology addressed to urban land use and transportation planning. However, in the prevalent four-fold view[2] of the planning process as a Goal Identification – Policy and Plan Design – Impact Estimation (plan testing or simulation) – Evaluation and Choice – these new techniques have been almost solely addressed to the impact estimation phase.

The contextual (goal setting), synthetic (alternative plan development) and evaluation phases have received scant attention, partly in view of their inherent complexities. In the evaluation area, there have been parallel developments in the areas of water resources (benefit cost) and Defense analysis (cost-effectiveness). Some attempts have been made recently to apply these concepts and techniques in developmental and transportation planning.[3] Exploratory attempts have been also evident to perceive in full the relationships between plan design, plan evaluation and goal setting and identify the conceptual and technical problems therein.[4]

At this stage, a set of crucial questions are in order. What are the issues and policy 'space' in current urban and regional planning? What are the emerging concerns and their dimensions? What philosophical views exist of the planning process (and its dimensions) in which to frame these issues and arrive at appropriate instrumentalities? What is the content, scope and nature of current methodologies of plan evaluation and the related plan design technology? How are control or policy variables identified and expressed? How are the effects or impacts identified and estimated in terms of magnitude and the different dimensions of incidence stratification?

Focusing on plan evaluation technology, what 'gap' is discernible between currently the most sophisticated expression of plan evaluation technology and the more generally prevalent practice? In other words, what is the gap between the best current 'supply' of evaluation technology and prevalent practice? What measures or procedures would most effectively bridge this gap? In another sense, what is the gap between the *requirements* (conceptually satisfactory) for plan evaluation and the capability of our public institutions *and* technology to meet these requirements? What would be the most promising research strategies to close this gap and what priorities can be discerned in this future research?

These are some of the challenging and complex questions before this Conference. They serve as a backdrop to this chapter which is addressed to the problem of evaluation. It attempts to 'locate' the evaluation phase (or 'decision modeling') in the planning process, derive *requirements* for evaluation, identify 'gaps' between these requirements and capabilities and suggest appropriate long-run and short-run analytical devices addressed to these gaps.

The Objective of this Discussion

Since 'evaluation' is the ultimate objective of the entire process, it is sensible for this book to set the stage by an initial exploration of requirements and capabilities.

Of the four facets of the overall process it is perhaps the least amenable to objective professional investigation. All citizens of a democracy have views – both descriptive and normative – of the public evaluation process. The disciplines with the most professional expertise to describe this process – the public administrators, political scientists, sociologists and urban historians – usefully provide us with some needed insights to abstract the necessary ingredients for our book's analytical needs.[5] But their views are decidedly still in this very formative stage. We, obviously, should know a good deal more about the 'muddling through' process than we presently do, including a greater internalization – within the groups who manage and develop our evaluation resources – of what is already known by the students of our metropolitan public decision processes.

But the subject matter does not lend itself to simplification. At a very general level, metropolitan plan alternatives must be evaluated in terms of the human ends (or benefits) they will serve, the other ends forgone (opportunity costs) and the differing means (or costs) required to achieve these ends. Each of the alternatives of an urban area is a bundle of goods with an associated set of values and life styles and a specific price tag. But as Wurster points out, it is a hypothetical package and in the present state-of-the-art evaluation, it is very difficult to know what exactly the goods are or what the cost may be.

The objectives or ends can be compared in proximate goal statements such as housing choice, job accessibility, income or racial distribution. But the deeper indirect socio-economic benefits are not easy to identify or assess: individual opportunity, productive efficiency, family welfare, privacy, security, cosmopolitan character and stimulus, flexibility to further change, etc. Attitudinal research informs us that we know very little about peoples' tastes and needs and we need conceptual frameworks to pose relationships between attitudes, tastes, needs and behavior.

Appropriate cost comparisons among plan alternatives may deal with private and public expenditures for major items such as transportation, housing, open space and redevelopment. Again, the forms and degrees of public power, institutions needed and social costs of dislocation and plan enforcement have all to be assessed. In general and rough manner, some of these cost differences among plans are estimated, while others do not lend themselves to quantitative evaluation.

If we wish to be able to progress in the assistance we provide to public decision-makers – or planners who advise decision-makers – we require a 'manipulable' abstract view of this process, while at the same time acknowledging the breadth and variety of types of public decisions and methods to deal with them. We propose to structure our view of this evaluation process around the nature of 'gaps' between what we want to achieve and can achieve in the 'evaluation' area.[6]

No one can really hope, at least not in the near future, to evaluate the evaluation methodologies, in theory and practice, with the precision demanded for 'gap-unit' measures.[7] This would require imposing one region's set of evaluation criteria upon another. However, it is not without precedent that an attempt be made: planners, themselves, have recently taken to be self-evaluative,[8] and the analogy of this attempt to the problem at hand – as well as its potential levels of success – is apparent.

The Scope of this Discussion

First, the planning and decision process under investigation is that practiced by and with urban and regional planning agencies and transportation and land use planning agencies. The sophistication and relative openness of this process is somewhat unique in the public sector, but is already enlarging its scope of responsibilities rapidly and thus covers a wide range of public actions. Secondly, the view of this process in this chapter – and of the 'gaps' we discuss – is that representing several, but by no means all, of the disciplines involved in this process. An attempt has been made to represent the views of the planner, economist and information technologist. If any single term applies, it is that of 'systems analysis', at least as a way to organize the framework developed here.

Third, the discussion is meant to be rather broad and general. Specific plans, planning approaches, evaluation methods and criteria are not discussed individually, but are used to provide a larger framework.

Fourth, an important caveat is in order throughout. Whatever we can see today, in summary form, as *the* process is, obviously, only at the intersection of the relevant supply and demand functions. We do not *know* the entire set of 'demand for evaluation' functions. Or the complete (present and potential) set of information and analytic aids, forthcoming at different real prices. Even if it were possible to 'measure' the inputs and outputs of the decision process on either a cross-sectional or time series basis, the statistician's 'identification' problem is very much with us. It is even more difficult when our lack of sophistication prevents this measurement. This is primarily important, not for a description, *per se*, but for an *understanding* of the process sufficient for the information technologists to shape their methodologies for improved use and sufficient also for planners and decision-makers to better state requirements to the technologists. Obviously, as complete and understanding as possible is desirable before we can define the realistic implications of recent analytic and information systems methodology for the 'equilibrium' decision-making processes of the future.

Organization of the Chapter

The various sections of this chapter are structured, developed and sequenced in a manner that will most efficiently set forth the 'gaps' between evaluation requirements and capabilities and identify appropriate analytical devices.

Thus, the second section of this chapter attempts to place urban and regional planning in context through a description of the current heritage of planning in terms of issues, concerns and policy tools and a scanning of the emerging policy issues. The third section provides contrasting philosophical views of the planning process used to pose these issues and identify and evaluate appropriate policy variables. The fourth section is addressed to a description of the framework for articulation of the evaluation problem, the requirements of the evaluation problem and a review of current abilities through analytic and systematic methods to meet these requirements. This review focuses on the attainment, promise and potential of these methodologies and concludes with a discussion of 'evaluation strategy' where issue, policy, technological and resource choices are set against one another.

These set the stage for the last section, a discussion of the gaps in the state-of-the-art of evaluation, revealed by a matching of the results of analyses of 'demand' and 'supply' of evaluation methodologies in the previous sections. A variety of long-run and short-run analytical procedures addressed to these 'gaps' are presented and the role of a priority system in their development is discussed.

Metropolitan and Urban Planning in Context

Two major interrelated trends in the last decade or so have been crucial in the evolution of the demand for metropolitan and urban planning. They are:

- Evolution of National Transportation Policy.
- Evolution of National Urban Policy.

The planning issues and frameworks resulting from these trends are briefly surveyed in this section. A discussion of the emerging major issues confronting metropolitan planners and public decision-makers today follows next. These emerging issues are posed in terms of their relevance, dimensions and implications for the planning process.

National Transportation Policy

In the area of national transportation legislation, there are two major milestones, the 1956 National Defense Highway Act and the 1962 Federal Highway Act. The National Defense Highway Act brought to a close the era in which planning and highway planning in particular could be based on the aggregation of small locally based decisions. The planning of a large highway system required greater knowledge of urban structure and processes and required planners to become more concerned with benefits and costs of highways. The techniques of economic analysis were deployed to select a transportation plan alternative that involved the lowest transportation cost and the highest ratio of user benefits to costs.[9] Minimizing costs became the most important objective in transportation planning. The process of obtaining individual, institutional or societal goals did not explicitly enter the planning process. Further, the indirect effects of transportation in terms of improved spatial organization or social dislocation were not considered in the evaluation of plans. Simple projections of demand coupled with a reliance on cost minimization placed the planner in the position of following trends rather than leading them.

The disaffection with the planner's function as projecting rather than planning[10] were sought to be alleviated by the 1962 Highway Act and the associated executive memoranda.[11] The establishment of an explicit metropolitan planning process intended to be continuing, comprehensive and cooperative was required. The plans envisioned are to be characterized by consideration of all transportation modes, comprehensive interaction of transportation factors with demographic, social and economic factors, transportation system characteristics, a need for large-scale gathering of data to support the planning process and the representation of communities in the area on the plan evaluation aspects. Public policy makers are becoming cognizant of the fact that transportation systems serve as key controllable variables in guiding future desired economic and social postures of the region. This new approach to transportation planning has stimulated the efforts to the development of alternative policies to be derived from the goals of society. Emphasis is shifting from a projection of impacts of transportation policies to an evaluation in a broad framework of those impacts.[12] Thus, if a shorthand description of the emphasis in planning process in the 50s was *projection*, in the 60s the corresponding term would be *evaluation*.[13]

Evolution of National Urban Policy

The traditional approach to metropolitan planning, borrowed from planning at lesser (i.e., architectural and urban) scales and focusing on the master plan as a product (a discrete guide to future development), has been undergoing substantial modification among planners and governmental practitioners. In part, this is a recognition of the urban community as a complex web of diverse and functionally interdependent interacting parts, with the parts evolving over time as they attempt to adapt to constantly changing contexts around them. An increasing emphasis on processes by which changes are introduced that will affect future character of the city and the effectiveness with which persons and activities will be able to interact in the future has become evident. The metropolitan transportation studies, concerned with interactional flows among activities, played no mean part in this evolution.[14] About the same time the enactment of legislation for Community Renewal programs, though not explicitly concerned with metropolitan planning, vastly expanded the functional scope of urban land use planning and set the stage for identifying alternative policies whose consequences could be estimated and evaluated.[15] The recent establishment of the Department of Housing and Urban Development has provided a further impetus to metropolitan planning.

Thus, in summary, metropolitan planning today has both an interest in process and a desire for identifying goals. Alternative policies and plans are derived from these goals and their impacts estimated and evaluated. An emphasis on a broad range of impacts (magnitude and several dimensions of impact stratification) of alternative policies and a focus on a multidimensional evaluation of these impacts are emerging in urban planning today.

Emerging Metropolitan Policy Issues

Emerging metropolitan issues, naturally, assume many forms: to Wilbur Thompson, 'Urban-regional economics is just now coming into its own…(having) more than its share of the gut-issues of the day'.[16] To Wingo, the issue is primarily a problem engaging 'the whole institutional machinery for land allocation', so as to rationally consider 'the spatial dimension of the accelerating urban revolution'.[17] It assumes many forms, the clichés carrying their share of the objective truth: 'quality of the environment', 'slums and suburbs', the 'white noose', 'high central densities and amenities', 'magnetic vibrant downtowns', 'chaotic urban responsibility', 'total (national) responsibility for the ghettos and public welfare', 'no quick cures for congestion', 'the neighborly life', etc.

For a significant part, the issues revolve about the costs, benefits and incidence of public investments and/or private investments affected by public actions in urban areas. These include the short and long-term effects of these investments on the stability, growth and well-being of the combined private and public sectors.[18]

That we are speaking of enormous magnitudes is obvious. A recent study by TEMPO for the Executive Committee of the national League of Cities estimated that the total revenue needs for local governments in the decade to 1975 would exceed one-trillion dollars, or an implied revenue *gap*, even extrapolating today's sources, of more than one-quarter of this total. The *Nation's City* special report, 'What Kind of City Do We Want?' (April, 1967) estimated that, between now and the year 2000, in real terms, 'the money needed to build and rebuild our cities twice as big and twice as good will average out to over $100 billion a year': almost one-third would be for all new and better community facilities of all types. Estimates of public service investment for each new household in the New York region is anticipated to be $16,800 in real terms.[19]

Viewing metropolitan issues in a framework of public investment concerns, at least three dimensions of issues are apparent:

- Public Investment and Geographic Hierarchy Issues.
- Public vs. Private Sector Issues.
- Incidence Issues.

Each of these dimensions may be articulated in some detail:

1. Public Investment and Geographic Hierarchy Issues

Public investments in urban regions of a mature developed nation play a many-faceted role in the pursuit of development and distributional objectives. A direct impact of public investments is their income generation role through their stimulation of demand for goods and services.[20] These projects also have effects on human capital, improving its productivity and thus augmenting the regional production of goods in the long run. Again, by reducing factor costs, these projects generate internal economies for many sectors, thereby fostering external economies for all sectors. Further, public investments in certain regions, by generating growth in new sectors, may result in larger urban functions and upgrading of the centers in the urban hierarchy and consequent urbanization economies that spur further growth.

Thus, the public investments generate a wide range of benefits, other effects and incur attendant costs. An identification and measurement of these consequences and costs must be done through an overall appreciation of the economic panorama in the affected metropolitan areas, among regions and the nation. Such an analytical framework, following Hoover, would investigate the impacts of public investments from:

- The *locational* viewpoint: the role of public investments in improving the comparative advantage for specific industries, population groups, etc.
- *Regional* view: the interrelations among projects in terms of their impacts within the region over time.
- The *interregional* view: the economic interrelationships among sectors, between regions, over time, resulting from these projects.

This specifies one dimension of the 'issues' space, the geographical hierarchy: the Federal, interregional, subregional, urban and intraurban. This spatial hierarchy can be used to exhaust a wide variety of issues: the growth and cyclical stability, in relevant economic and social activities, at different levels of the geographical hierarchy. Similarly, 'comparative advantage' theory can be applied to study the relative impacts of alternative mixes and quantities of public investment at different areal levels. Most of the spatial (e.g. external effects of location) can be isolated within the spatial dimension.

2. Public vs. Private Sector Issues
Another very important issues' dimension is that of the public vs. private nature of infrastructure investment. If the geographical hierarchy issue is directed to 'what' is to be done, this issue's area raises basic questions of 'how' it is to be done.

There is nothing, per se, inviolate about the private nature of existing private sector investments. The line can, and has recently, moved across the spectrum of infrastructure investment types, as has the role of the various levels of government within the public sector. The latter involves the choice of revenue and expenditure incidence and thus, 'client group' redistribution, which is, of course, another important issues' dimension (see below).

The 'public-naturedness', to coin a term, of an investment is rarely a planning issue – at the urban or regional level – although it almost certainly *should* be a major one. The parameters of this dimension include:

- *The presence or absence of externalities,*[21] and the degree to which these can be measured, their incidence discovered and redistributions accomplished or explicitly denied.[22] (This latter possibility should be of particular interest to the urban-regional planners, since his expanding tool kit of analytic methods and information availability could substantially alter the previous 'externalities' determining' equilibrium point.)
- *The presence of absence of structural effects*, due to 'the response in parameter changes in the technological, social and economic organization of the metropolitan region'.[23] At the very least, improved knowledge of the structural processes in the private sector can improve the planning and development achieved for public sector investment. At the other extreme, the structure can

be manipulated by public investment and/or by converting previously private investments into the public category.

- *The feasibility and desirability of introducing, for external cost or net social benefit reasons, regulatory and/or pricing mechanisms.*[24] This is a major policy issue and yet it is rarely the subject of the planner's choice space. This is surprising because the choice frequently depends on the comprehensiveness, interrelatedness and complexity of the urban-regional system under consideration, a subject matter quite familiar and important to the planner.
- *The feasibility and desirability of determining public demand, in the absence of a price system.* Interpretation of voting statistics, budget-constrained time preference surveys, sociological and cultural interpretation, price-system proxies and other methods: these have all been suggested as methods for estimating present and future public demand. These are recommended as short cuts for the difficulties (impossibilities?) of (a) interpreting individual preference function, (b) aggregating them, or (c) predicting what they will be. Planners, rarely, systematically enter this issues' area, although they do attempt to help communities explicitly state their competing goal structures.
- *The presence and extent of scale economies.* This should be a major dimension structuring the planner's view of the urban management functional systems, by area and subarea. Certainly, at the regional level, the system of cities and supporting areas should be highly sensitive to the presence and extent of these economies. Furthermore, these economies can assume many forms, e.g.: transportation effects (intercity, intracity, parking, etc); public sector goods and services effects (utilities and other); private sector goods and services effects; and other effects (land values, design potential, information and coordination potential, etc.). Nevertheless, planning information systems have not been geared to assist in this most important determinant of 'public-naturedness', our costing systems being totally inadequate for even Planning-Programming-Budgeting Systems, let alone the determination of 'total systems costs' (capital plus operating, properly discounted).

This geared lack of entrance by planners into the arena of public-private sector debate is particularly unfortunate because the following trends toward increased rationalization of planning activities[25] call for an intelligent, informed view of this issues' area:

- With immense changes of real income, per capita anticipated, e.g. a fivefold increase in 70 years, there is great need for responsible, long-run planning for change in the tastes of the public, both for public and private goods.[26]
- With the intensification of jurisdictional interdependence, there is increasing need for an appropriate multiple hierarchy (in an areal sense) pricing system, or other relatively automatic and impersonal rationing devices.[27]
- With the decline of blue-collar workers, the urban environment will exist almost exclusively for decision-making, information processing and communication functions,[28] and with the increasing socialization of problem

solving,[29] the *productivity* of decision-making and private and public planning will become increasingly recognizable and measurable.

- With the increasing cost of defining alternatives to examine and collecting and processing the relevant information, there is recognition that a major role of planning is to choose those issues to which planning and study resources are to be allocated.[30]
- With planning, design and architectural inputs so labor intensive, productivity is not likely to increase in these sectors at the same rate as other urban-oriented sectors and planning will have to assume a vocal role to ensure that 'savings' generated from the productivity increasing sectors are passed on to the 'planning' sector.[31]
- With increasing emphasis upon the economies and productivity due to concentrating human capital in dense urban areas, there will be greatly increasing attention paid to the allocation of scarce land resources – 'space' being the major 'urban-peculiar' intensively utilized factor of production.

All of these offer reasons for the planning profession to be engaged more actively in important public-private area controversies, in addition to the spatial, physical, economic and social consequences of alternative public investment plans.

3. Incidence Issues

The final issues' dimension, briefly alluded to, above, is that of the *incidence* of the effects of public and/or private investment choices, i.e. the distribution and redistribution consequences.[32] This is the 'who' set of issues.

A major weakness of planning studies is their scant attention to the question of incidence of benefits. Public investment projects are often prepared for different client groups and may be also incident on a variety of other client groups in an indirect manner. For many planning projects, a basic focus is the effect that public investments may have, directly or indirectly, on low income or high unemployment subgroups of the population.

Several issues are important here. The characteristics of the local community where the public investments are located influence to a great degree the incidence of the benefits. Thus, the employment status, occupational or industrial affiliation, of the persons in the community may be highly relevant to them capturing the benefits occurring from a public investment project.

Again, there are spread effects of public investments from the locales which receive the investments to a few areas in the 'vicinity'. No empirical evidence is available to infer these spread effects. However, public investments in some urban areas or urban growth poles improve their comparative advantage vis-à-vis other places, thereby resulting in spread effects from that growth pole to adjacent areas – suburban or otherwise. Such spread effects may not be incident to a great degree in lagging regions. An investigation of these differential spread effects involves explorations of different characteristics of the communities in growth poles versus lagging regions. On the other hand, the spread effects may be understood in terms of inter-industry linkages among different regions.

The delineation of these types of incidence is no easy matter. One set of estimates required is the change in number of families in different income groups in areas where public investment projects are made. However, certain aspects of incidence (for instance the temporal aspect) are even more difficult to discover. For these, what is required is the development of a framework of posing the problem of incidence of project benefits. These frameworks may then suggest further analytical work into this problem. An example of this formulation may be a three-dimensional array of benefit incidence, the dimensions being:

- The different income groups.
- Types of public investments.
- Temporal – temporary or permanent-benefits.

This concludes our discussion of metropolitan policy issues requiring in depth 'planning' consideration and evaluation. All are concerned with infrastructure investment: the first, the geographical distribution, for growth, stability and comparative advantage reasons; the second, the responsibility of the public sector; and, third, the distribution effects. There are the classical economic issues of efficiency, equity and non-competitive system effects.

In the next section, the analytic views of planning process that serve to pose these issues are described.

Views of the Planning Process

This section is addressed to a description of the planning process in some detail, to help locate the role of evaluation in this process. A goal oriented forward seeking version of the planning process (representing the generally prevalent practice) is presented first. Another version, perhaps not as different as appearances make it, is presented to describe the 'incremental problem-solving' process. The 'battleground' set by these two helps set the stage for a discussion of the many different dimensions emphasized by practitioners and theorists regarding views of the process.

The Goal Oriented Planning Process

In general, the metropolitan planning program reflected in Figure 14.1 is one in which: (a) future regional needs and challenges are anticipated, (b) alternative strategies addressed to these issues forced, (c) the crucial impacts or outcomes of each of the alternative planning strategies stated above (in b) estimated and (d) the evaluation of alternative plans or designs based on more or less general criteria applied to the delineated impacts.[33]

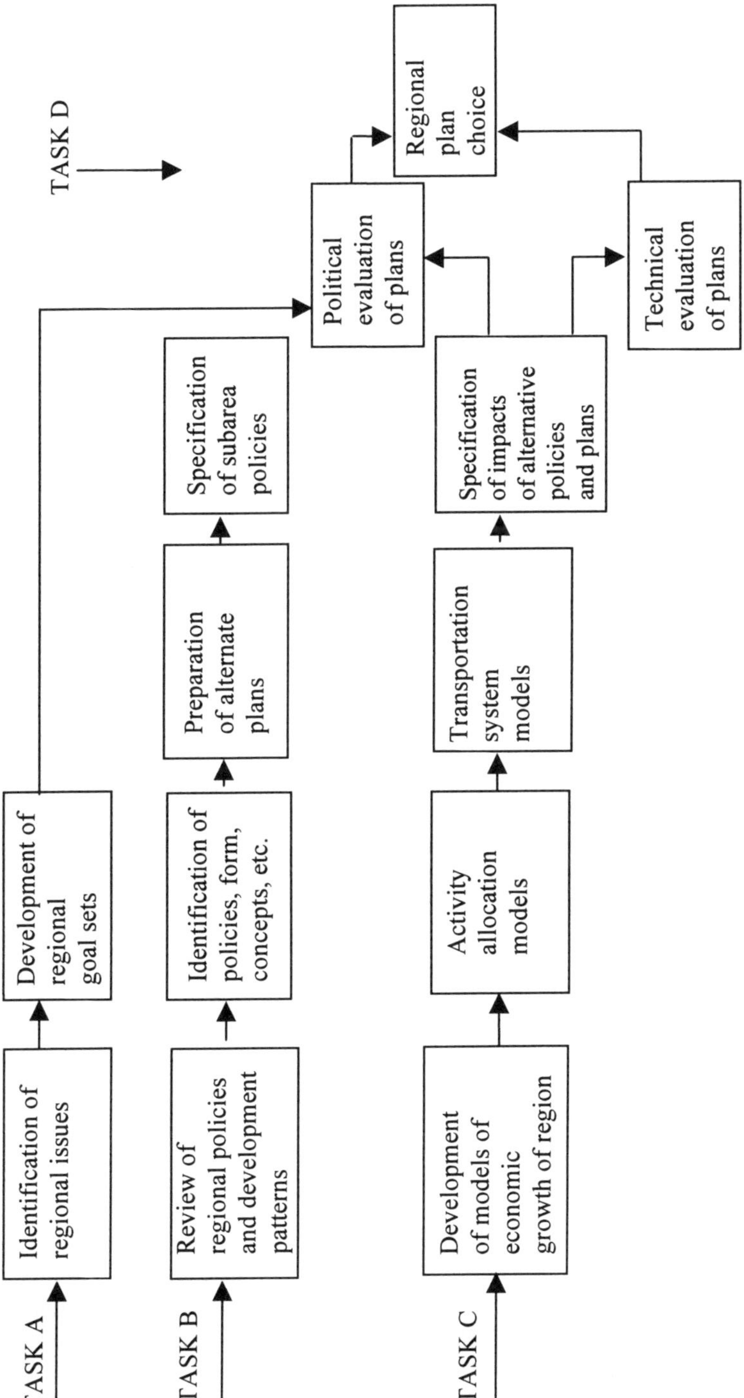

Figure 14.1 A simplified model of a regional planning work program

This process is largely to be regarded as cyclic and continuous. The impacts and evaluation of one set of metropolitan plans may well suggest a return to the process of synthesis (b, above) for fresh generation of alternatives. Again, the evaluation criteria themselves derive from regional goals that influence the development of alternative plans and indeed may guide the choice of the policy or instrumental variables appearing in these alternatives. Further, as future regional needs are reassessed, the process feeds back into itself. Thus, planning must be viewed truly as a continuing comprehensive process.

Such a process by its nature calls into play a creative, subjective and synthetic thought process on the one hand and an analytic and objective effort on the other. Thus, in contextual (goal setting – a, above) and synthetic (development of plan alternatives – b, above) phases of planning, a great deal of imagination and subjectivity are called for in identifying what goal sets are desired and how existing or new structural and form elements can be combined to produce desired metropolitan futures. However, in the phase of 'plan testing' or estimating the impacts of outcomes of alternative policy bundles (c, above), analytical techniques play a crucial part.

The last statement needs some elaboration. The impact estimation phase involves essentially the establishment of the functional relationship between t he control or instrumental or policy variables which are crucial to plan selection. These interrelationships are often very complex and difficult to trace and understanding of these underlying relationships is the focus of many land use or regional growth models.

The process of evaluation ideally involves the establishment of an overall criterion for evaluation and selection from among alternative plans in terms of their impacts (benefits and costs). This implies that various types of impacts would have to have 'weights' attached to them relative to one another to help in this grand choice. It must be obvious that a sophisticated knowledge of the value system and its dynamics is called for if such a task is to be fruitfully undertaken. Such knowledge should embrace estimates of tradeoffs among values and the degree of satisfaction of these values in a commensurate fashion. Here one deals in the area of unmeasurables, intangibles and the non-comparables.

The planners can hope to elucidate this problem in cooperation with social scientists in developing over time a greatly enriched and multidimensional benefit cost analysis that explores peoples goals and desires in their plurality and communality. The set of interacting values that are mediated by societal and technical relationships (determining the rates of tradeoff) are expected over time to be exposed for the public consideration and decision making. In this way, decision making is anticipated to be assured considerable objectivity and a broader participation.

Such are the theoretical underpinnings of the planning process of the more sophisticated metropolitan studies. They suggest techniques that are in many respects futuristic and non-operational. Consequently, as mission oriented agencies, the work program describes the essentials of an operational strategy to plan development and evaluation from the complex (and at places intractable) planning methodology, outlined above. Such strategies are designed to reflect the resolution of the tradeoffs among various complex aspects of goal definition, design and evaluation of the future regional plans.

Incremental View of the Planning Process

The planning process described above poses a number of very imposing demands for the policy maker. Such requirements include a specification of goals and values and agreement in advance, wide canvassing of plan alternatives addressed to these objectives, a similarly systematic analyses of consequences of each alternative and for policy choices to be evaluated against the selected goals. In practice, the selection of goals is a very tricky and difficult political process, complete information on relevant measures of all consequences not always possible to develop and, when developed, difficult to comprehend and, finally, the requirements of evaluation pose conceptual and technical problems. These considerations have persuaded some theorists, including Braybrooke and Lindblom, to suggest a strategy of 'disjointed incrementalism' such as the following:[34]

- Describe the metropolitan system.
- Identify problems in the system.
- Establish short term objectives.
- Generate alternative plans for problem solution.
- Evaluate plans in terms of short term objectives.

It is believed that decision makers focus on incremental alterations of existing social states rather than an erection of a rationalist deductive long run metropolitan system.

In this process one begins by using a descriptive model of the metropolitan system without making long run predictions because it is assumed that decision makers in the political milieu will tend to seek solutions which ameliorate existing problems rather than allow an approach to a set of predetermined goals. For this reason, although one wishes to use the most comprehensive, most accurate and most precise descriptive models available, almost any incremental description is suitable for getting to the next step provided that it is generally believed to be a reasonable description of reality.

This next step is the step in which we identify problems in the system. Identification of problems implies value structures and goals, but here one is able to side-step the problem of goal setting because very often two individuals or groups with conflicting goals will agree to the existence of a problem and call for its solution or eradication. Problems will appear as misallocations, gaps and functional misfits. Most problems lend themselves also to be broken down to smaller problems.

Having identified problems, it is necessary to establish some very short-term objectives for problem solution. These objectives would be problem avoidance or problem amelioration objectives rather than positive goals.

Then one generates alternative plans to meet these objectives. Since an incremental approach is being taken to generally agreed upon problems, plans can be developed problem by problem and interdependencies between problems can be considered *after* solutions are found. The important thing is to generate plans which cover the full range of feasible choices open to decision-makers.

In the evaluation stage a more limited view of the scope of evaluation is adopted. Again, plans must be evaluated in terms of the problem-oriented objectives for the comparison between plans. The evaluation of the plans can then continue by applying the rather less sophisticated costing evaluation techniques less demanding than the social welfare functions implied in the previous model.

Having completed one cycle of the incremental planning process, the process is intended for some of the problems which have been identified for which the relevant variables in the process can be forecast. This portion can be performed on a limited and selective basis.

Relevant Dimensions of the Process: Recent Trends

These two 'models' obscure many of the underlying dimensions of the metropolitan planning-decision process. Identifying those 'dimensions' should help in clarifying the choices planners and analysts have already made in establishing the process as described. It should also indicate choices which remain to be made in improving this process.

The nature of this process, in each instance, is conditioned by the relative emphasis that a planning effort places upon each of the following approaches:[35]

1. Forward vs. Backward-Seeking Processes[36]

Backward-seeking processes automatically precalculate, in a time-phased manner all that is required to achieve an end-state, optimally. The appropriate land use forms, socio-economic changes and transportation links are staged 'endogenously' within the process. If models are involved, these analytically create, for instance, the set of networks which produce alternative 'desired' regional configurations for any given multiple-goal objective function.[37] Most current studies are 'forward-seeking', where alternative for manipulating the modeled environment toward an implicitly or explicitly stated set of goals are carefully chosen for test.[38]

2. Multiple vs. Single Goals

With the advent of the writings and thinking of Carroll,[39] Holmes,[40] Garrison,[41] Fagin,[42] and a number of Bureau of Public Road manuals and other publications,[43] a number of transportation-related, economic, social, regional planning, aesthetic-design and 'general' criteria are now essential parts of the overall process. Various measures are recommended (e.g. benefit-cost ratios and rates of return for transportation efficiency, a number of qualitative measures for performance and design, accessibility and measures for economic efficiency, cost and accessibility measures for social criteria, etc.).[44] Arbitrary, but explicit, weighting schemes are then applied to these multiple measures. The trend in existing studies is, of course, towards the *multiple* criteria and *multiple* measures.[45]

3. Planning vs. Policy Making

While, at one time, it was generally accepted that urban and metropolitan planning should be non-political, there is increasing communication between the professional planner and the policy-makers of governmental units. The criticism of their non-political role and responsibility has led to a number of proposals, including a variety of new political forms. The preparation and review of metropolitan issues; the development of goal sets; the development of alternatives; the review of regional policies and development patterns; the generation of policies, form concepts and structural aspects; and the preparation of alternative plans and sub-area policies: these will all be affected by the subtle changes already taking place in the planner-politician relationship.[46]

4. Planning vs. Functional Control Operations

In contrast to most planning problems, which are concerned with determining whether or not feasible solutions exist, governmental control and control theory concerns itself mainly with findings and optimal solution, assuming that feasible solutions exist. Thus, to the degree that planning assumes a more backward-seeking theoretical base, the more control aspects it will assume as responsibilities. Furthermore, planning is becoming more concerned with *changing* (or advocating changes in) goals and restrictions which make certain plans 'unfeasible', which is a complement to the control process. Other dimensions related to 'planning vs. control' are: feasibility vs. optimality, where the objective function can or cannot be defensibly constructed, acceptable to 'all members' of society; and the duration over which the plans are to be effective. Most transportation and land use plans are designed to be effective over a medium to long-range; however, there is increasing emphasis placed on short-term planning requirements, with advocates calling for explicit requirements for short-term programs and concrete provisions for short-term action, such as is imposed (or proposed) for urban mass transportation, water and sewer facilities and open space land program planning. Another related dimension is that of planning vs. functional management decisions: clearly, most planning has not (and clearly will not be) been involved with the operational aspects of managing currently operating metropolitan service facilities. Nevertheless, there is increasing realization that much of the cost, benefit, effects and incidence data is an important by-product of current functional agency operations and planning familiarity is necessary for planning to make correct operational and control assumptions. One consequence is that the transportation and land use planning process has, frequently, literally ignored important and relevant functional areas, such as housing, where the operational and current management decisions are so crucial and frequent as to overshadow the true merits of longer-range planning. Increasingly, functional areas such as housing and recreation are being considered as detailed subject matter for regional planning studies, along with transportation and land use.

5. Comprehensive vs. Particular Problem-Solving

The first four dimensions are aspects of the overall 'degree of comprehensiveness' dimension. This takes many forms, all of which are tied to the planner's concept of the metropolitan region as a complex social system, for which public resource allocation has to be performed 'as a whole'. Nevertheless, the degree of 'wholeness' – the number of functions to be viewed as interacting simultaneously and relevant to a specific problem – is, itself, increasingly viewed as a subject for cost-effectiveness analysis. The lack of intensive use of the largest of the models – the Pittsburgh model and the San Francisco model – is partially due to the large cost (computer time for the San Francisco model) or, in the view of the current head of Pittsburgh City Planning, the over-ambitious nature of the Pittsburgh model which seeks to account for so many individual decisions.[47] Problem-solving efficiency is increasingly being seen as a process to be rationalized, itself and planning agencies are learning to better 'package' problems and problem-solving mechanisms to take advantage of joint costs and benefits.

6. Physical vs. Social Planning

This is an important enough subset of the 'multiple vs. single' goal dimension to be mentioned separately. Planning has learned to extend interests beyond physical locational arrangements so as to avoid the imposition of disproportionate costs upon one 'client group' in order to benefit another unless suitable compensation is (or can be) made. Increasingly, planning – particularly Housing and Urban Development 701 Programs – are subject to criticisms if they lack substantial reference to the social or economic impacts the plans might have and the incidence of these impacts.[48] The obsolescence of merely locational planning is particularly relevant to transportation planning in a developed economy, since several recent studies[49] confirm the earlier observation that 'today highway improvements are effected in a developed economy which has an extensive transportation system and where improvements continue to whittle away at spatial imperfections and further reduce the value of situs … one should no longer expect gargantuan dislocations because of improvements providing access to land of greater productive capacity … nonspatial relationships appear to be of even greater importance'.[50] Analogous reasoning has extended to critical evaluation of the use of quantitative cost-benefit indices in social planning; e.g. planning resource allocation for the poverty program.[51]

7. Automation vs. Manual Operations

Naturally, the trend is toward increasing use of computers in the entire process. It is possible to characterize their role in a forward-seeking process by examination of the shaded areas of Figure 14.2.[52] Here, much of the estimated impact and incidence information is calculated for each alternative investigated by the use of a computerized land use-transportation systems simulation effort, drawing upon a partially or wholly automated stored information source. Much of the process is manual in this forward-seeking version. However, development of methods for calculating efficient sets of choice possibilities,[53] estimating community needs and values,[54] and determining 'optimal' project-program mixes[55] are all within the targets of analytic methods of the next decade but are clearly not yet available for practical application, across the board, in forward-seeking processes. The backward-seeking process, on the other hand, will lend itself to automation of these

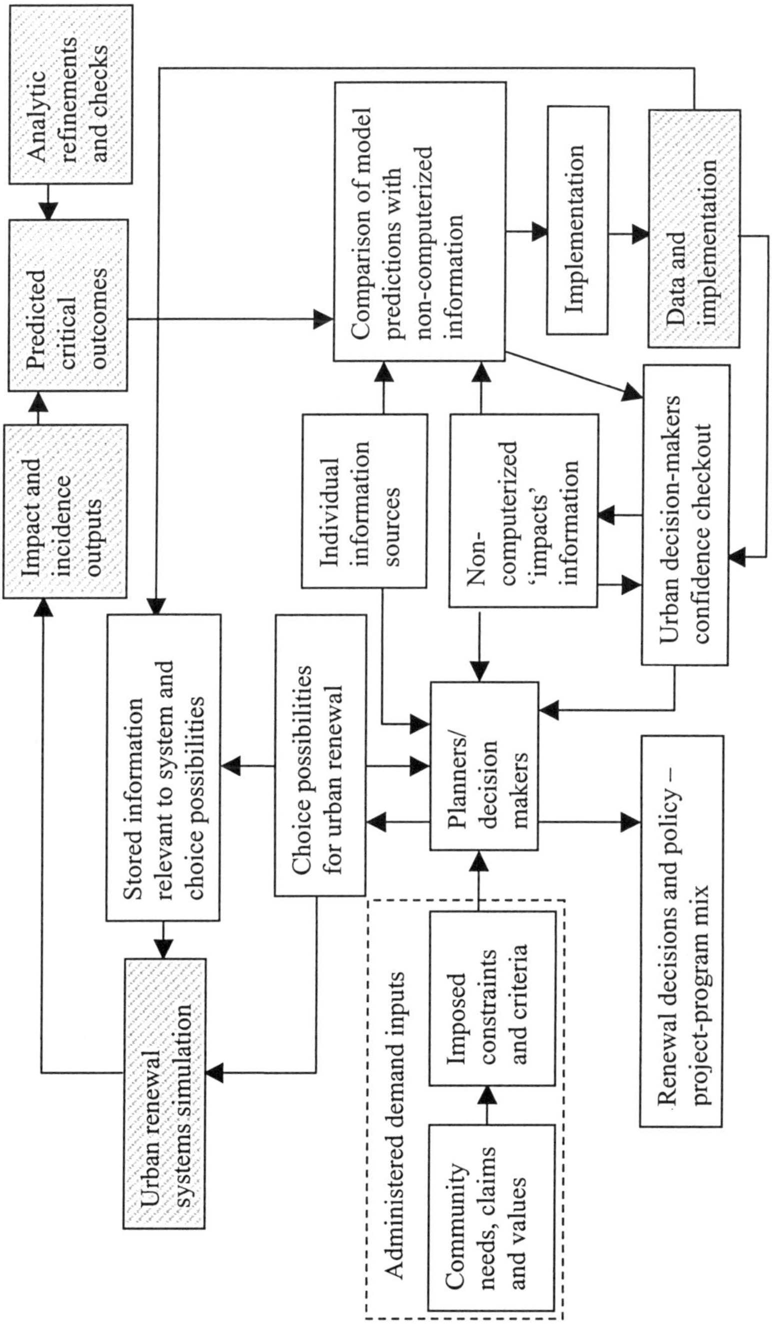

Figure 14.2 Automation vs. manual operations

features, also, leaving only the decision-makers' *ad hoc* information sources and confidence checkout techniques (of Figure 14.2) free from the influence of automation.

These, then, are the major dimensions of the transportation and land-use process just discussed, to recapitulate:

- Forward vs. backward seeking processes.
- Multiple vs. single goals.
- Planning vs. policy-making.
- Planning vs. functional control operations.
- Comprehensive vs. particular problem solving.
- Physical vs. social planning.
- Automation vs. manual operations.

They represent choices the planning processes must make, have made and will continue to make. The 'gaps' between where these studies are today – or will be in the near future – and where they should be, is, clearly, a function of what they are attempting to do.

Evaluation Methodologies

This section is intended to provide a description of the framework for articulation of the valuation problem, the requirements for evaluation and some previous attempts at grappling with this problem. This discussion essentially focuses on conceptual and fundamental issues in evaluation and turns to questions of detailed method and technique only minimally. This preoccupation with conceptual issues is a measure of the novelty and progress of the field of plan evaluation and the challenges lying ahead for its development. Thus the discussion opens with a brief review of the first three stages of the generally prevalent goal oriented planning process – Goal Identification, Plan and Policy Design and Impact Estimation. The scope of this review is to outline the nature of requirements that an effective evaluation process poses for the activities in each of the three 'earlier' stages of the planning process. Thus this review focuses briefly on the requirements suggested by identified goals, the identification and taxonomy of control or policy variables and the definition and measurement of effect variables in terms of magnitude and dimensions of incidence stratification. A discussion of the problem of transforming effect vectors of plans to explicit preference vectors follows next. The conceptual and technical problems in such an endeavor are posed in the concluding part of this section.

Goal Identification

Crucial to the process of successful regional planning is a clear understanding of regional goals. Far too often, planning has been beset with difficulties resulting from a failure to be based on an explicit consensus of goals and objectives. The more sophisticated studies are extremely conscious of this and engage in the task of delineating *realizable* goals. The opportunities and challenges for developing the region are viewed in the aggregate and a broad set of general region-wide goals developed. Some goals of the region are implicitly understood by each citizen and by the community forces that comprise the functional economic, social and political groups within the region. Implicit goals, however, must be explicitly set forth in the agency so as to develop a framework for programs of action that do in a democratic society represent the synthesis of collective need. These goals also provide a basis for identifying the leverage for alternative development patterns.

Many agencies conduct substantial analysis of data on socio-economic variables and physical variables such as housing, land use and transportation of all modes. From such informational bases, an attempt is made to identify to the extent possible the *requirements* suggested by the goals. Further, a general interpretation of the association between what is desired and the sort of 'control (or instrumental policy) variables' to 'bring them about' is often attempted. In addition to these formal and semiformal attempts, informal inquiries with key persons and groups have been helpful in identifying general development goals in the region. These regional goals may be specified over time and refer to various dimensions such as transportation, land use arrangements, economic growth, etc.

In the identification of goals, it may be conceptually satisfying to recognize two broad categories of goals:

- Performance goals.
- Contextual goals.

Performance goals and associated outputs are directly related to the performance of the system under review. In the case of a transportation system they refer to performance characteristics of the system. The *contextual* goals arise because of the way performance goals are realized. In the case of an urban area, visual beauty, pollution abatement, noise reduction are examples of contextual goals that may be expressed in terms of threshold levels to be assured. It may be that a contextual goal of an earlier period, once recognized, may be incorporated into the performance goal structure at a later point in time of a region.[56]

Another point to recognize is that an urban system has multiple goals and the planner might want to specify an explicit utility (or trade-off) function that transforms all goals into a single compound goal. Different goals in the urban area are often hopelessly incommensurable (in the sense that no general consensus exists as to the trade-off among them). In such a ca se, a spurious trade-off function suppresses information about alternative plans rather than simplifying the selection process.[57]

Sometimes, the global objectives of a large system such as an urban region, can be *factored* into a hierarchy of more manageable sub-objectives.[58] This is done through a means-end analysis that relates the desired end results – goal objectives – to the means of accomplishing them. However, it must be clear that the goals generated in this manner at each level – regional, jurisdictional or subarea – are normally multidimensional. This is because:

- Compression of incommensurables reduces the information content.
- Multiple goals are often used as an approximation for a single 'real' goal that cannot be measured in practice.
- Multiple goals are often generated as a means of coping with interactions among different areas in the same level in the hierarchy.

A final point often made is that Goal Identification is not concerned with ultimate values, but with *proximate* values on which people can often agree who disagree on ultimate values.

In summary terms, the role of this process of scanning the region for issues and goals is not only to provide a point of entry into the planning continuum but also to provide a basis for testing the acceptability of proposed plans. It is designed to assure that issues are formulated and plan solutions developed with constant references to the totality of requirements, values and constraints imposed by the regional and larger environment. Further, it addresses itself to the requirement that land use and transportation prognoses over the planning period be formalized, made explicit, communicable and hence subject to criticism and reappraisal. In this process, it may help identify goal conflicts and institutional constraints. At the end of this task, a set of goals relevant to the land use and transportation study and recognized on a functional basis will emerge. A set of tentative criteria reflecting the *requirements imposed by the selected goal* set may also be developed to be helpful in the evaluation phase.

Plan or Policy Design

This phase is concerned with the development of alternative plans or future 'end states' and the policies that are 'suggested' by the goal set chosen. The goal set may suggest a variety of desirable attributes which may conflict or be available at excessive costs (broadly conceived). Thus, as Harris points out, all locators in a metropolis cannot be given space, choice and convenience – surely not at acceptable levels of cost and safety. Some balance is struck on the assumption that one can manipulate in principal the balance of these desired goals in alternative ways by postulating various levels of density of residential development and the location of employment.

Alternative sets of general policies and regional development patterns are prepared in conjunction with the goal statements. Such a review must be posed in a context that helps the sketch planning process, which may be defined as the preparation in a preliminary fashion of a number of alternative plans at an appropriate level of detail. The preparation of these alternatives permits the planning staff to explore the possibilities in the situation, set forth new ideas and devise a basis for comparison among plans. Such imaginative views are often qualified by the awareness of the significant stability and conservatism inherent in current policies and development patterns. The ability to innovate is often thus in a narrow planning range. The recognition of this leverage for planned action is an essential preamble to the development of alternative plans.

In the light of the overall goals, a range of policies, form concepts, interaction concepts and structural relationships that may be implied in the goal sets and the devised 'end state' spatial patterns are generated. It is easy to imagine that the resulting combinations of policies, form concepts and interaction arrangements can be a very large number. Care must be taken to assure that a few sets that include a wide range of possibilities which in terms of *generic capability* merit incorporation in plans be developed. A few preliminary analytic procedures must be employed to array and screen major combinations of policies, form concepts, etc. Such procedures related to performance aspects of physical environment may be relatively simple in concept but can yet be a useful adjunct to the combinational problem referred to above. It is in this manner that plan design and evaluations are highly interconnected.

The identification of each 'lever' or control variable that can respond to public policy is therefore of strategic importance for goal achievement. This aspect of policy design can be illustrated in the context of a public investment program addressed to the economic development of an urban region.

In such a context, one must emphasize the importance of identifying all relevant control variables available to public influence, whether they be attached to the public or private sector of the economy. The first important analytical task is that of classifying public (investment) activities so as to identify all control variables that are relevant for achieving economic and social development goals and of defining or classifying public (investment) activities in terms of these control variables. The significance of this type of classification scheme is that it relates existing public (investment) alternatives directly to their role in influencing the economy toward goal achievement in the same terms that may be employed in the analytic framework. In addition, it would suggest areas of public activity for which policies have been inadequately addressed.

A preliminary set of control variables into which public projects and programs may be classified include:

- A. Indirect controls (goal achievement through private sectors)
    1. Primary Resource Development
        a. land orientation (including natural resources)
        b. labor orientation (manpower development)
        c. capital supply
        d. entrepreneurship

    2. Social overhead capital
        a. water supply
        b. power orientation (i.e. electrification)
        c. transportation
        d. education
        e. communication

3. Amenity orientation
    a. park and recreational development
    b. residential investments
    c. cultural development
    d. pollution reduction

4. Urbanization and localization economies (market-orientation and growth pole effects)
    a. sewage treatment and disposal
    b. health facilities
    c. industrial complex development (industrial states)
    d. mass transit

- B. Direct control
    a. expenditure impacts (i.e. government purchasing)
    b. employment in public works projects
    c. employment in local, State and Federal government

The public policy instruments listed under Section A, Indirect controls, essentially affect performance variables, such as per capita income in area (g), in time period (r), by upgrading internal and external locational advantages with respect to some specific industrial sector or population class for the purpose of effecting private capital or human investment in that region. On the other hand, Section B, Direct controls, affect performance variables with full control (e.g. unemployment in area (g) is reduced through jobs created in water resource development project). Both types of controls, however, further indirectly impact goals through various economic and social relationships.

The metropolitan plan incorporating many dimensions of physical economic and social development goals offers definitely a broader and more complex set of control variables then presented above. Thus, the list of control variables presented above must be viewed as illustrative. However, it does represent many types of alternative opportunities that exist for the application of urban and regional public investments in attaining a variety of development goals.

Finally, the preparation of candidate plans that incorporate the results of all previous work is carried out. Such plans express in cartographic form land uses – their types, densities and disposition – transportation facilities, natural features and form concepts. These plans are the alternatives for testing through the models.

In summary, the process of plan design consists of specifying various decisions, or control variables (or policies) addressed to the planning objectives (in the estimation phase) and their expressions in plans. Independence does not obviously exist among all the variables and relationships that could be used to describe a plan. The choice of some variables as decision variables is somewhat arbitrary and depends to a considerable extent on the planner's view of the goal structure and ease of expression. In this judgement, the planner is considerably influenced by the outcome to which we turn next, or impact measures and criteria used in the evaluation phase.

Estimation of Impacts of Alternate Control Variables

The impact estimation phase involves essentially the development of functional relationships between control or policy variables and the impact or effect variables identified as crucial to plan selection.

To identify the scope of this phase, one can begin by considering what information would be desired in an infinitely informed analytical climate. The fundamental dependent variable is, ideally, not only the magnitude of each type of effect but also the distribution of such overall magnitudes with respect to several important dimensions of incidence stratification: the time period, areal unit and economic sector or population group which occasions any given effect. This broadly defined dependent variable is influenced by the fundamental characteristics of each hypothesized policy or project and the particular combination of such projects. The fundamental characteristics of any given project include its magnitude, project type, the time period of implementation and its geographic location. The consequent effect depends upon the location characteristics of the respective areas in which each benefit type is occasioned. An ideal analysis of effect would trace the influences of such a complete characterization of projects and the local characteristics of the incident area(s), including interdependence effects between areal units and between projects.

For the sake of convenient exposition, it is helpful to cast this 'impacts' problem into mathematical language. Assuming that all impacts of a set of public investment projects can be determined in reference to the project as a fundamental analytical unit, there are two distinct types of effects which must be considered. Some projects are mutually exclusive, while others entail joint effects. Accordingly, all relevant information about the effects accruing from any proposed set of projects, together with any hypothesized schedule for implementing any such projects over time, can be summarized by the following two descriptors:

$A^{r}_{g,s,j}{}^{(t_k)}$ = the magnitude of effort type r accruing during time period s incident upon population group j (or, alternatively, upon industrial sector i) in areal unit g, associated with the implementation of project k during time period t_k (for all g, j, r, s and k).

$B^{r}_{g,s,j}{}^{(t_k,t_l)}$ = the incremental magnitude of effect type r occurring during time period s incident upon population group j (or industrial sector i) in areal unit g, associated with the joint implementation of both project k during time period t_k and project 1 during time period t_l (for all g, j, r, s, k and 1).[59]

The parenthetical notation is employed to depict the three descriptors 'as a function of' the choice variable t_k (and t_l). Given such a complete description of each project's potential effects the general evaluation problem is to describe which specific projects should be implemented and how they should be staged over time. This problem is tantamount to choosing values for the t_k (and t_l) which are, in at least a crude sense, 'optimal' or at least 'preferred' over the range of projects considered.[60]

Given these descriptors of effects, it is further necessary to establish the 'cause effect' functional relationships by which the effects descriptors depend upon individual projects' characteristics, the combination of projects and local characteristics.

I^k_{h,t_k} = the magnitude of investment prescribed for project type k in areal unit h, implemented during time period t_k.

$X^r_{g,s}$ = the magnitude of local characteristics type r in areal unit g at time period s.

Given these definitions, two types of functional relationships are of interest, expressed as f and g in the following mathematical statements:

$$A^{r}_{g,s,j}{}^{(t_k)} = f\left(I^k_{h,t_k}, X^r_{g,s-1}\right)$$

$$B^{r}_{g,s,j}{}^{(t_k,t_l)} = g\left(I^k_{h,t_k}, X^r_{g,s-1}\right)$$

Note that, as the notation implies, effects may be defined as temporal increments (or decrements) in the local characteristics variable.

In summary, there are at least three issues in the determination of impacts:

- First is the matter of identifying relevant variables and the operational definitions of incidence characteristics.
- Then, there is the task of developing meaningful measures of those relevant effects.
- Finally, there is the task of developing an analytical scheme for estimating future effects.

Utilizing the Impact Vectors: Transformation to Preference Vectors

The difficulties of transforming impact vectors to explicit preference vectors should not prevent the metropolitan planning agencies from attempting this task in one way or another. A decision must be made and – while that decision is the responsibility of policy-makers – the planning effort must assist that decision-making process to the extent possible.

The first point to be realized in this context is that this sort of public investment decision *has* been made many times in the past. That is, various types of effects for which no obvious 'value' exists have in fact had 'weights' attached to them, be they entirely subjective weights implicit to the thought processes of policy-makers.[61] Whether these decisions have been correct cannot be determined by any means; value judgments of policy-makers represent the 'final word', so to speak. On the other hand, there may be legitimate cause to question whether those decisions have been made (or even can be made) by sound method. More to the relevant point, the planning effort must address the question: given the communication of all relevant consequence information, how might the planner assist the policy-maker insofar as the latter's comprehension and comparison of these consequences are concerned?

It is most convenient to approach this matter in reference to a general abstraction of the decision-making process, which is borrowed from Holt:[62]

> Any brief summary of the process by which the President, the Congress and the electorate of the United States reach decisions on national economic policy is necessarily a crude caricature. Nevertheless, if we are to discuss some of the basic elements in the process, some such simplified picture as the following is needed: first, a problem is recognized which requires attention; second, alternative courses of action are formulated; third, the outcome associated with each of the alternatives is predicted; fourth, the outcomes are evaluated to determine their relative desirabilities; fifth, a choice is made in the context of conflicting political and constituency interests. The actual process is, of course, a complicated successive approximation procedure: for example, one of the political choices may be to redefine the problem – thereby starting the whole process from the beginning again.

The concern here, of course, is with the last two elements of the decision process. Implicit to those elements is the formulation of a criterion function and the assignment of a weight to each outcome type, by each policy-maker individually in the first instance. The point to be realized here is that decisions on social investment, by the very fact that they are made, implicitly involve 'benefit calculations' and therefore 'weights'.

The discussion is of course extremely academic, but serves as a convenient point of departure as well, making the problem more explicit: how might the planner assist the policy-maker in assigning relative weights to effect variables? This is perhaps the most difficult aspect of the entire evaluation process, arousing considerable debate.

One finds many endorsements in the literature of both extremes of this debate, as well as the less staunch positions. A variety of intellectually appealing but mostly untried techniques for estimating relative weights for multiple-objective decision situations have been advanced, hypothesizing that the preference functions of policy-makers can be identified in objective terms through opportunistic interrogation.[63] Others argue that utility, but its very definition, cannot be measured, but that these methods attempt to do so. Still others suggest that, while utility-conversion-factors are too nebulous to probe into, it is sensible to pursue, where possible, the development of dollar-conversion-factors. The use of rating schemes for evaluating preferences has also been a rapidly developing technique, including the important consideration that individual factors on which the items are being assessed interact in producing an overall result.[64]

From the bare fact that a decision is made by a policy-maker, it is incontestable that, through the intricate workings of his mind he is implicitly not only attaching weights to each outcome type (or effect variable) but also reducing these incommensurate variables to some common unit. Moreover, the nature of his criterion function is also incontestable: he is maximizing these units in a manner which is similar to the algebraic sum, over all effect variables (referring also to capital costs), of the units which he attributes to each effect, be it positive or negative.

This criterion is nothing different from the maximization of a 'welfare function' or, it referenced to the existing situation and thereby formulated in terms of temporal changes in effect variables rather than end-states *per se*, the maximization of consumer's surplus. 'Benefit-cost analysis', 'economic efficiency', 'general equilibrium analysis' and 'cost-benefit analysis' have been employed in evaluation efforts referring to tangible and valuable effects.[65] In reality, these 'techniques' differ only in the types of effect variables they deal with. The policy-maker's criterion, be it an extremely implicit one, is no different in concept from these techniques. The 'weights' are merely hypothetical 'prices' and the criterion represents a sum of individual price-quantity calculations.[66] This is true, also, for non-market effects, by reference to observed phenomenological tradeoffs between such effects and some other effect for which a market exists.

It is hardly necessary to point out that, in view of the variety of effect variables (of which the economic and demographic impact variables are only a subset) defined as relevant, metropolitan planners cannot feasibly present to policy-makers one aggregate number for each system modification alternative. They would in all probability reject the concept, particularly if interaction between planners and decision-makers were concentrated toward the end of a study. It is far less easy, however, to dismiss entirely the idea of applying (i.e. 'testing') one or more of the available scaling techniques to a subset of effect variables. As Holt argues, such a trial may be justified on the basis of sound forecasting.[67] To the extent that metropolitan plan evaluation involves the role of testing untried planning methodology which might lead to significant payoffs in the future, it should seriously consider testing such valuation techniques, at least on a group of planners and other professionals, not on policy-makers themselves.

Holt's argument might be extended along still another dimension, moreover. One of the strongest sources of skepticism toward employing such techniques refers to the transitivity requirement common to all of these methods.[68] That is, the claim of some skeptics is that policy-makers may not exhibit transitivity when subject to such methods, particularly if many effect variables are included. Indeed, this may well be the case, even if only a few variables are included. The implication of such a result, of course, would be that perhaps many public policy decisions made in the past on a purely subjective basis have also been characterized by intransitivity. Were this the case, the immediate failure of a valuation technique in itself offers justification for continued use of such techniques to help improve future decisions, even if they remain subjective, merely by helping policy-makers to be aware of the transitivity problem.

In the final analysis, whether to try such techniques rests upon the extent to which policy-makers deem it worthwhile to participate in such a trial endeavor. If nothing else, the observations of the last few paragraphs emphasize the mutual benefits to be derived from relatively continuous interaction between planners and policy-makers.

There are several alternatives to such scaling techniques, none of which is claimed to come any closer to solving the evaluation problem *in toto* but all of which may be more practical. The most pessimistic approach, though not necessarily an unwise one, derives from the extreme point of view that so many effect variables must be dealt with in a real-world decision that it is impossible to attach explicit weights to all of them. Furthermore, the argument proceeds to conclude that, since only a few variables can be weighted in dollar terms and even these must be converted to some units of psychological value for a decision (subjective or objective) to be made, any effort to measure 'weights' for *any* variables is ridiculous. This, alternative, then, favors the strategy of leaving everything up to the policy-makers. Assistance could be offered, in a limited sense, by a cogent taxonomical design.

A more reasonable approach has been at least to attempt to clarify to policy-makers the phenomenological (as opposed to the psychological) tradeoffs between selected effect variables. The modeling systems purport to be capable of representing the real world, within the limitations of available data. A limited but well-designed sensitivity analysis of this modeling system portrays at least, in a crude fashion the substitution or complimentarity relationships between selected effect variables without attempting to attach any sort of 'price' to such variables.

Finally, some effort has been directed to examining in depth the tradeoffs between selected non-market effect variables and one or more variables for which a market not only exists but indicates dollar value reliably. This approach derives from the point of view that, to the extent possible, all effects which can be expressed in dollar terms should be measured and summed as well as being identified separately.

The valuation of travel time savings has been pursued along these lines with some success and other variables might be amenable to analysis. Such in-depth exploration of trade-off are distinguished from the suggestion of the previous paragraph not only because a monetary valuation or 'price' is involved, but more importantly because such research must concentrate on situations where only two variables – the non-market variable being 'priced' and the market variable referred to as an indicator – vary significantly, so that all other variables are held constant or nearly so. In general, such explorations will at best reveal upper and lower bounds, but such information would be well worth any reasonably proportionate effort.

State-of-the-Art Gaps in Evaluation Methodology: Decision-Making Requirements and the Analytic Capability to meet these Requirements

We have attempted to describe a relatively complete spectrum of planning and decision-making requirements – issues and dimensions – and to weigh against these the potential capabilities of analytic methods to meet these requirements.

Unfortunately, while substantial 'gaps' appear to exist, it is difficult to estimate how important these are (or could be) to successful and improved decision-making. No one has yet developed adequate measures of the outputs of planning and decision-making. No substantial set of analytic, empirical case studies of cost effectiveness of planning and decision-making – with and without alternative planning and decision-making resources and operations – has been made. Therefore, these evaluation 'gaps' should be interpreted more as 'requirements' than as an unambiguous 'preferred' or optimal set.

In our endeavor to outline these gaps, we begin by developing criteria for the evaluation of plans (and the evaluation of the planning process itself). Against the backdrop of these criteria, 'gaps' between requirements and capability are outlined though not in any quantitative terms or in any priority order. These gaps and some suggestions addressed to them are presented as they pertain to:

- Issues 'space'.
- Improved models of decision processes.
- Impact modeling strategy.
- Public preference structure estimation.

Finally, strategic directions of analytical improvements – in the long run and short run – aimed at the current deficiencies in the state-of-the-art of evaluation methodology, are presented.

Role and Key Factors in Evaluation

There are two major emphases for the role of evaluation in planning:

- The evaluation of the plans which have been generated.
- The evaluation of the planning process itself including the process of designing alternative plans.

These emphases must necessarily be linked closely. However, this chapter focuses on the first – evaluation of metropolitan plans. The following factors, at least, are important in the evaluation of plans which are generated by the metropolitan planning process.

- Issue space under review. Has a comprehensive range of issues been posed? Or is there just the traditional focus on spatial aspects of phenomena? Are the

'spatial' – normative and functional organizational – aspects of metropolitan issues under consideration?
- Scope of the decision process. To what extent are the goals and functions considered capable of incorporating the salient features of the metropolis and the decision-making process? To what extent do the plan design and evaluation phases capture the essentials of the decision-processes of planning?
- Range of alternatives. Is there an inclusive set (in the generic sense) of alternatives? Or is there really a basic alternative and a bunch of 'straw men'? To what extent is alternative design influenced by the evaluation methodology?
- Impact groups and incidence dimensions. Have the plans identified the social and economic groups to be impacted by them and the magnitude and dimensions of incidence to facilitate the evaluation process in terms of preset goals and benefit groups?
- Evaluation framework. What is the framework of evaluation methodology? To what extent are the decision process, the concern for impact incidence, the preference structures of the populace and other issues reflected in the methodology selected? How adequate is the informational base for the evaluation methodology selected?[69]

The above list is quite clearly illustrative. However, it is indicative of the set of criteria that could be used in evaluating the plans generated in metropolitan planning. In any case, these criteria have been used to structure the discussion of the 'gaps' that follow next.

Enlarging the Planners' Issues Space

While both the planner and analytic technician talk of global assistance to decision-makers, their resource limitations, biases and technology have caused them, by and large, to ignore much of the 'issues' space', in urban and regional matters. When metropolitan planners seek to guide physical development, it is really the spatial organization of activities and use that is the focus of concern. Such a view ignores a whole range of 'aspatial' issues relating to community values and functional organization that can be concerned without regard for spatial arrangement. If the planners' issue space enlarges to include both the spatial and 'aspatial' urban issues, he will be encouraged to take into account the ways in which the physical environment he recommends facilitates or impedes various activity systems that are accommodated by environment.[70]

Further, with few exceptions, the planners have left the two major issues of a) t he preferred public role for urban functions and b) the incidence (redistribution consequences) of alternatives, almost exclusively to more aggregative echelons and/or the political sector. This is unfortunate, because their role places them in an excellent position for defining urban and regional functions, for sensing (and thus measuring and communicating) externalities and scale economies. Furthermore, the technologies for attacking these problem areas are no less available than that for the issues with which we primarily do concern ourselves.

Improving Descriptive Models of Decision-Making

While this decade has been described as the 'golden age' of decision-making studies,[71] there have been very few studies identifying the changing goal structures, the planning issues, the alternatives examined, the impact measures and the evaluative methods.[72] One study has described the heuristics of budget decision-making in the cities of Detroit, Cleveland and Pittsburgh and has utilized the results of the simulation for partially successful 'forecasting' of these decisions.[73] Improved studies for systematically capturing the decision-making processes of 'planning' are required, before normative 'models' can be designed. Too much is being assumed today about the planner's information availability and processing requirements. Even acknowledging the likely changes analytic methods should make to and for the process, much of the current process will remain relatively undisturbed and, thus, should be better understood. Operationally, this requires a more explicit understanding and explication of planning processes, such as that 'modeled' in the two earlier sections above.

Impact Modeling Strategy

The overall strategy of impact modeling is arrived at – and should be, for each study – by tradeoffs between:

- The diversity of impact types to be estimated.
- The dimensions of impact incidence – areal, sectoral, population class and temporal.
- The state-of-the-art of analytical techniques.
- The richness of the information base.

Other chapters in the book are addressed to an articulation of the difficult choices in this process. The scope of our discussion is limited to one aspect – the geographic hierarchy issue – in impact estimation. It illustrates an impact estimation strategy – the 'top down' approach – found convenient in expressing location, comparative advantage and growth consequences of public policies at different geographical levels.

Figure 14.3 is an attempt to relate an illustrative set of policy issues to the process 'dimensions' of which alternative planning programs are composed. Alternative planning issues of major importance[74] are indicated on the left side of Figure 14.3; the effect types, which are the consequences of the alternative choices, are next shown; then, classes of relevant economic and spatial concepts are shown, ranging from growth considerations to local 'comparative advantage' (as these are modified by access, facilities and agglomeration effects) concepts; next, various types of models are indicated; and, finally, the alternative data requirements for the concepts and the models are broadly indicated, with the feedback to models resulting from the feasibility and cost of the 'data-model' system, combined.

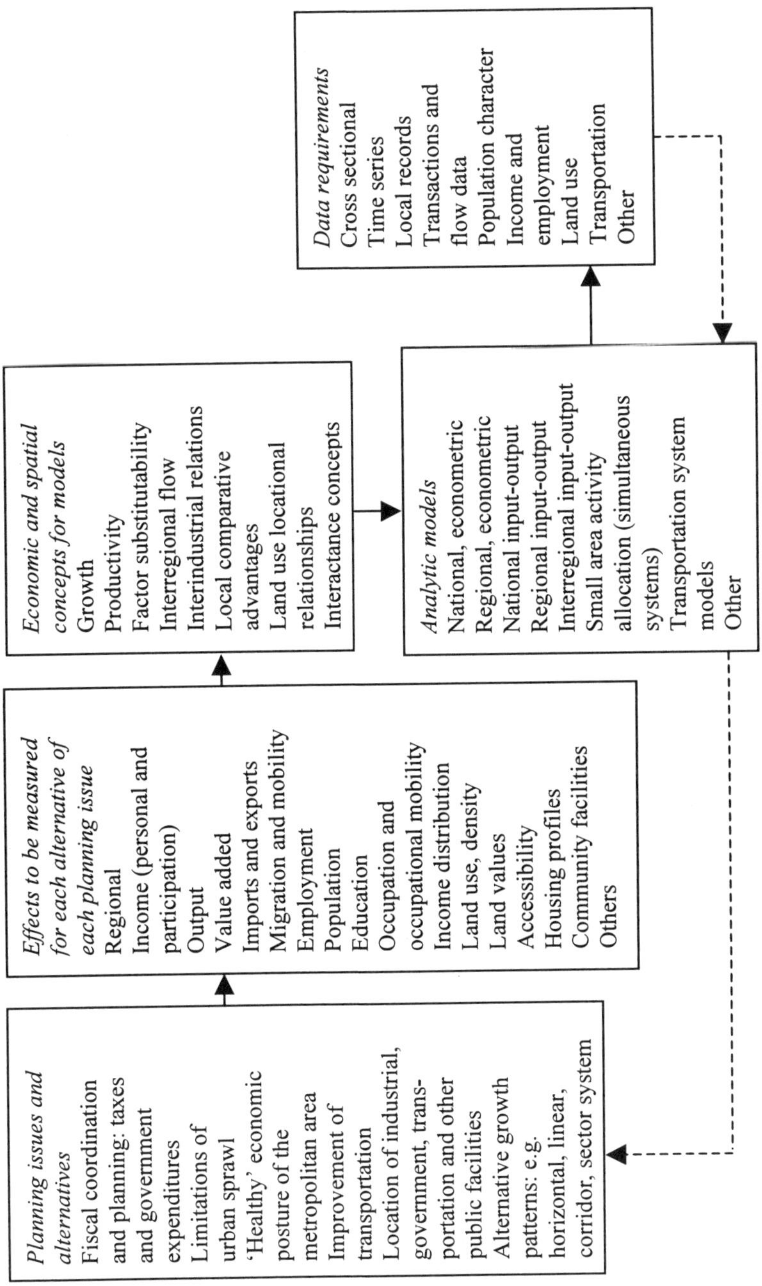

Figure 14.3 Regional policy issues and the role of impact models (e.g. Puerto Rico)

The purpose underlying the general sequence of effect estimation in the illustrative case of Puerto Rico set forth in Figure 14.3 is quite simple: to be able to estimate the consequences of impacts (in terms of income, output, population and its characteristics, employment, land use) of alternate policies addressed to the crucial planning issues at different geographical levels, nation, region, metropolitan area, subareas in an urban area, etc. As alternative policies are forged in response to planning issues and goals, mathematical models are used to make 'conditional forecasts', i.e. if a particular land use growth policy or tax policy is envisaged, what growth or distribution consequences might occur?

The development of quantitative forecasting methods addressed to such sets of impact measures can be attempted through a theoretical framework embracing regional economic theory, comparative advantage and location theory. No single analytical method, however, is likely to accomplish the forecasting requirements for evaluation of urban/regional public investments. The various analytical models, furthermore, would have to rest heavily on empirical bases that attempt to capture most of the changing patterns of economic and social growth in response to public investments.

Comparison of alternative sets of procedures strongly indicates that impacts can be best arrived at by a series of successively finer geographical approximations. For example, first, what changes might occur at the level of the region which is most 'open' to the 'outside world'; then, the various subregional levels (metropolitan, urban, etc.); and, finally, individual subareas within an urban area? This type of framework of a multilevel impact estimation is envisaged in view of the different forces, in fine detail, that appear to operate at these different levels.

Various modeling schemes may be devised so that the results of the immediately broader (geographically) scale model can constrain the solutions at the best level. The multimodel 'top down' approach can produce a maximum amount of valid information. It can serve as a very necessary and valuable link between the economic planning at the island level and the physical planning at urban and subarea levels.

The choice of modeling schema (i.e. the mix of models) appropriate to this approach is a function of the potential benefits, tied to all the uses to which the modeling outputs would be put and the total cost of producing these: the data, manpower requirements, computers, etc.

Developing Superior Methods for Estimating Public Preference Structure

Aside from the obvious benefits for conditional forecasting methods, better understanding of underlying present and future preference patterns of individuals and client groups is fundamental for evaluation, also. The methods of classifying and reducing effects' categories; of choosing effects to forecast; and for weighting effects classes: these can no longer fall back on impractical schemes for measuring consumer surplus.[75] The translation of *effects*' vectors into *preference* vectors strains the confines of traditional cost-benefit frameworks, or, for that matter, even the most sophisticated general equilibrium framework.[76]

More attention will have to be paid to other routes for assessing preference functions:

- To the historian, architect, ecologist and anthropologist, for what articulate human beings have said, and say, about the quality of their environment.
- To sociologists for the application of content analysis.
- To opinion pollsters for what people claim they want, directly.
- To the econometrician and statistician for measuring what has and is actually chosen by consumers.
- To the social scientist for descriptive and normative models of consumer behavior.
- To the social psychologist, for structural and constrained methods for conducting 'decision-free' interviews.
- To system analysts, for structured experimental situations (e.g. games).
- To the political scientist and statistician, for intensive analysis of voting behavior and for methods to simulate voting behavior.
- To public administrators, for improved ways to ascertain the tradeoffs between 'effects measures' desired by community leadership.

Operationally, within existing regional planning studies, this would call for intensive review and use of 'home interview' techniques and the enlarging of the view as to which resources might be helpful in ascertaining present and future preferences and future preference functions.

Development of Output/Performance Measures

Operational measures of the *output* of urban areas and regions; i.e. the contribution of the metropolitan environment to the public welfare are also, ultimately, required. Much can be said about the 'need to improve the social infrastructure so as to maximize human potential through increased access to opportunities of all varieties'. But what actually *do* agglomerated environments add to social and economic productivity? Without a fuller description of the functions of agglomeration and an appreciation of the preferences toward the products of these functions, we can never achieve these output measures. And without an agreed-upon set of output measures, we can never really fully achieve rational resource allocation to the policy issues of regional and urban public investments, let alone to planning for these. Clearly, this is a high-order need, similar in importance to a rekindling of interest in 'land' (i.e. spatial allocation) as a factor of production, commensurate in importance to 'labor' and 'capital'.

Making Analytic Methods More Useful in the Planning Process: Short-Run

Without dwelling at length on any of these topics, each of which itself would deserve its own chapter, experience with developing planning models has convinced us that the following improvements are required:

- More emphasis on total system costing of projects and programs.
- More use of games and man-machine simulations, not just for pedagogical purposes, but for the development of alternatives for testing and 'goal-goal' tradeoff functions.
- More intensive use of 'case studies' of the effects of public investments, if the data collection schemes can be made appropriate to the detection of the system effects.
- More explicit attention paid to the analyst-planner, communications and mutual education relationships.[77]
- More advance attention paid to the relationship between analytic outputs and specific design needs of the planners.[78]
- Better definition and mutual acceptance of definitions of 'analytic validity', including specification of validation criteria.[79]
- More attention paid to the incidence of effects.

Making Analytic Methods More Useful in the Planning Process: Long-Run

New technology users – and model-builders are no exception – frequently begin to construct their second-generation models before they are prepared to analyze the value of their first-generation efforts. Given the availability of resources this may be desirable; the second generation work can serve beneficial 'incentive' feedbacks upon the first-generation work, given proper communications between them. This work is proceeding, and should proceed, along several points:

- Improved capabilities to link models at different areal and functional hierarchies, to use and automatically revise control totals, so as to efficiently exhaust a total information space.[80]
- Better methods for utilizing comprehensive problem-solving models for 'smaller' problems, or for building on 'smaller' problem-solving models to fit better into a larger scheme (i.e. the global vs. piecemeal approaches).
- Better explicit strategic and tactical planning in the use of *all* systems research techniques, including the types of tradeoffs between technique attributes and techniques.
- Improved measures of externalities and social costs as outputs of analytic methods.
- Explicit incorporation within urban and regional models of 'states of the system', described through historical stages of growth,[81] or in terms of decision-making capabilities.[82]
- More explicit incorporation of the structure of behavior and decision-making, even if this requires new combinations of heuristic and normative submodels within a larger framework.

Concluding Remarks

We have attempted to describe public sector decision-making needs in such a way that gaps could be revealed between requirements and the capabilities of analysts to meet these needs. We have not attempted to 'quantify' these gaps, or even to arrange them in some priority order.

To some extent, the problem is similar to trying to arrange for priorities within 'basic research' by linking this research to all potential uses, probabilistically. To a larger extent, however, it is more similar to managing resource allocation for *applied* research and science programs. Here, the basic urban and regional issues of the future would be arrayed in some order of importance and the (feasible) contribution, at the margin, of decision-aiding techniques would be related to each of these issues and the informational needs represented by these issues.

Nobody, apparently, can yet do the long-term priority ordering which would be needed to accomplish this management task. Until that time, our resource allocations will be based on more pragmatic grounds – near-in 'supply' aspects, more vocal demanders and non-military budgets.

At the very least, a better record of what *is* happening in this field, as well as more uniformally accepted set of definitions – and perhaps, criteria – is needed.

Notes

1 Many of the thoughts and concepts expressed in this chapter have been developed out of conversations and interaction with many CONSAD colleagues, in particular, Gale Bach, Joseph Drake and Arthur Silvers, to whom we express much appreciation. Naturally, all opinions rendered and errors made are strictly the responsibility of the authors.

2 This adds one to the trichotomy cited by Britton Harris in 'The City of the Future: The problem of Urban Design', paper presented at the Thirteenth US Annual Meeting, Regional Science Association, November 1966.

3 For example, see Robert Dortman (ed.), *Measuring Benefits of Government Investments*, The Brookings Institution 1965, in particular the papers by Herbert Mohring and Jerome Rothenberg; CONSAD Research Corporation, *Design for Impact Studies*, prepared for the Office of High Speed Ground Transportation, 1965. James, C.T., Mao, 'Efficiency in Public Renewal Expenditures Through Benefit-Cost Analysis', *Journal of the A.I.P.*, March, 1966.

4 See Britton Harris, 'The City of the Future: The Problem of Optimal Design', paper presented at Regional Science Association Meeting at St. Louis, November 1966. CONSAD Research Corporation, *Impact Studies*, Prepared for Northeast Corridor transportation Study, January 1967, Chapter IV. Marvin Manheim, *Highway Route Location as a Hierarchically Structured Sequential Decision Process*, Ph.D. Dissertation, M.I.T., Cambridge, 1964. Edwin N. Thomas and Joseph L. Schofer, *Toward the Development of More Responsive Urban and Transportation System Models*, Research Report, The Transportation Center, Northwestern University, April 1967.

5 Nathan D. Grundstein, 'Urban Information Systems and Urban Management Decisions and Control', paper prepared for the Third Annual Conference on urban Planning Systems and programs, Chicago, 1965; Alan Altshuler, 'Rationality and Influence in Public Service', *Public Administration Review*, September 1965; Wilbur R. Thompson, 'Toward a Framework for Urban public Management', in *Planning for a Nation of Cities*, edited by S.B. Warner, Jr., M.I.T. Press, 1966; Gilbert F. White, 'Formation and Role of Public Attitudes', in *Environmental Quality in a Growing Economy*, edited by

Henry Jarrett, Johns Hopkins Press, 1966; Norton E. Long, 'New Tasks for All Levels of Government', in *Environmental Quality in a Growing Economy*, *ibid*; Charles E. Lindblom, *The Intelligence of Democracy*, Free Press, 1965; Morton L. Isler, 'Selecting Data for Community Renewal programming', *Journal of the American Institute of Planners*, March, 1967; David A. Grossman, 'The Community Renewal program: Policy Development, Progress and problems', *Journal of the American of Planners*, November 1963; 'Process Planning: Symposium on Programming and the New Urban Planning', entire issue, *Journal of the American Institute of Planners*, November, 1965; N. Beckman, 'The Planner as a Bureaucrat', *Journal of the American Institute of Planners*, November 1964.

6 R.M. Rauner defines 'gaps' as 'the mediate goals against which mudgets can be assigned and performance measures computed', p.16 in 'Regional and Area Planning: The EDA Experience', prepared for presentation at the Institute of Management Science Annual Meeting, April 1965; see also, R.A. Levine, 'Program Budgeting for an Interagency program', Program of the Thirty-Sixth Conference of Southern Economic Association, November 1966.

7 Except on rather particular grounds; e.g. a test of statistical validity. See D.E. Boyce and R.W. Cote, 'Verification of Land Use Forecasting Models: Procedures and Data Requirements', Forty-fifth Annual Meeting of the Highway Research Board, January 1966: W.A. Steger, 'Review of Analytic Techniques for the C.R.P.', *Journal of the American Institute of Planners*, May 1965; Traffic Research Corporation, 'Review of Existing Land Use Forecasting Techniques', Boston Regional Planning Project, Massachusetts Transportation Commission, July 1963; and Donald D. Lamb, 'Research on Existing Land Use Models', Southwestern Pennsylvania Regional Planning Commission, March 1967.

8 The recent National Meetings of the American Institute of Planners has established the current period as one of introspective criticism and review.

9 See Chicago Area transportation Study *First Report*, vol. II and IV, Chicago, 1962.

10 See Britton Harris, 'Plan or Projection', *Journal of American Institute of Planners*, vol. 27, November 1960, pp. 265–72.

11 Bureau of Public Roads, Instructional Memoranda, 50-2-63(1), dated September 13, 1963, on Urban Transportation Planning (10 basic elements); HHFA, 'Guidelines for Five Critical Points in Transportation Planning', dated December 29, 1964. (Five 'Critical Points.')

12 This development has been accompanied by the development of 'backward seeking' policy evaluation model framework (see below).

13 See J.L. Schofer and F.J. Wegman, *A Transportation System Plan Design Model*, Northwestern Technical Institute, March, 1966, Chart I.

14 Penn Jersey (Delaware Valley) Transportation study was among the earliest to perceive this evolution.

15 See Wilbur A. Steger, 'Review of Analytic Techniques for the CRP', *Journal of the American Institute of Planners*, May, 1965.

16 Wilbur R. Thompson, 'Programs for Metropolitan Area Economic Growth', a paper prepared for the Third Regional Accounts Conference, November, 1964.

17 Lowden Wingo, Jr., 'The Uses of Urban Land: Past, Present, and Future', *Resources for the Future*, Reprint No. 39, July, 1963.

18 No suggestion is being made, here, that these issues are entirely novel. Concern with improving the quality of our environment associated with the benefits of compact habitation is cited in literature of the eighteenth and nineteenth century. See O.C. Herfindahl and Allen V. Kneese, *Quality of the Environment*, Resources for the Future, 1965, pp. 53–4. Also, nineteenth and early twentieth century public concern for the slums, the poor, the market for low income housing, and the role of inferior uses of land, are cited by Lowden Wingo, Jr., 'Urban Renewal: Objectives, Analysis and Information Systems', a paper prepared for the Third Regional Accounts Conference, November, 1964, pp. 7–8. Nevertheless, what is novel is the scale of public investment and the concern that the costs and benefits have an explicit and agreeable incidence. Also novel is concern with the *total* environment: 'The formulation of an ideal environment should take into consideration all aspects of man's life including his emotional needs and the

development of his civilizations'. René Dubos, 'Promises and Hazards of Man's Adaptability', p. 37, in Jarrett, ed., *Environmental Quality in a Growing Economy, op. cit.*

19 Regional Plan Association (New York), Bulletin 100, 'Spread City', September, 1962; see, also, the National Planning Association Study on national goals by Louis Lecht.

20 These effects are relatively easier to trace at the national level as payments for domestic factors of production. At the regional level, they are a function of interregional interindustry linkages that determine the proportion of local productive inputs in the region.

21 O.A. Davis and A.S. Whinston, 'The Economics of Complex Systems: The Case of Municipal Zoning', *Kylos*, 1964, pp. 419–46; James W. Buchanan and William Craig Stubblebine, 'Externality', *Economica*, 1962; Ralpha Turvey, 'On Divergences Between Social Cost and Private Cost', *Economica*, August, 1963; A. Breton, 'Towards An Economic Theory of Pollution Control and Abatement', London School of Economics, *Background Paper*, D29-1, 1966; O.A. Davis and A.B. Whinston, 'Some Notes on Equating Private and Social Cost', *The Southern Economic Journal*, October, 1965; J.M. Buchanan, 'Joint Supply, Esternality, and Optimality', *Economica*, November, 1966.

22 G.M. Neutze, *Economic Policy and the Size of Cities*, The Australian National University of Canberra, 1965; J.A. Stockfish, 'Esternal Economies, Investment and Foresight', *Journal of Political Economy*, 1955, pp. 446–9; R.N. McKean, 'Some Problems of Criteria and Acquiring Information', in H. Jarrett, ed., *Environmental Quality, op. cit.*, pp. 63–5.

23 L.Wingo, Jr., 'Urban Renewal: Objectives, Analysis, and Information Systems', p. 14, *op. cit.*; also, W. Thompson, 'Programs for Metropolitan Area Economic Growth', p. 12.

24 Davis & Whinston, 'The Economics of Complex Systems', *op. cit.*, pp. 442–43; Allen V. K neese, 'Research Goals and Progress Toward Them', in H. Jarrett, *Environmental Quality, op. cit.*, pp. 72, 87.

25 Donald N. Michael, 'Urban Policy in the Rationalized Society', *Journal of the American Institute of Planners*, November, 1965.

26 W.A. Steger, 'The Management Sciences: The Future Users', a paper presented at the Institute of Management Sciences Annual Meeting, Boston, April, 1967.

27 Willian Wheaton, 'Metro.Allocation Planning', *Journal of American Institute of Planners*, March, 1967, pp. 103–7.

28 R.L. Meier, *Communications Theory of Urban Growth*, M.I.T. Press, MA, 1962.

29 H.G. Johnson, 'The Social Sciences in the Era of Opulence', *Canadian Journal of Economics and Statistics*, November, 1966.

30 M. Webber, 'Comprehensive Planning and Social Responsibility', *op. cit.*; L. Wingo, Jr., 'Urban Renewal: Objectives, Analysis and Information Systems', *op. cit.*, pp. 5–6.

31 This argument is due to William Baumol's discussion of planning for urban growth in an 'unbalanced' economy.

32 See H. Liebenstein, 'Long-Run Welfare Criteria' in Julius Margolis, ed., *The Public Economy of Urban Communities*, Resources for the Future, 1965.

33 We borrow most heavily, here, from knowledge of the following studies: Detroit Land Use and Transportation; Bay Area Transportation; Penn-Jersey (now Delaware Valley) Transportation; Southwestern Pennsylvania; and Southeastern Wisconsin; Baltimore Regional Planning Council; and several (previous and existing) Community Renewal (and Analysis) Programs, in particular, Los Angeles, New York City, Pittsburgh, San Francisco and St. Louis.

34 David Braybrooke and Charles E. Lindblom, *A Strategy for Decision: Policy Evaluation as a Social Process* (New York: The Free Press of Glencoe, 1963).

35 These dimensions are not completely orthogonal with respect to one another, nor are they listed in order of importance.

36 See H.W. Bruck, 'Problems of Planning for the Future: The Marriage of the White Queen and Tiresias', paper presented at the National Transportation and Railroad Symposium, San Francisco, May, 1966.

37 H.W. Bruck, S.H. Putman and W.A. Steger, 'Evaluation of Alternative Transportation Proposals: The northeast Corridor', *Journal of the American Institute of Planners*, November, 1966.

38 A notable exception, with its emphasis on transportation and land use design optimization, is the Southeastern Wisconsin Study. See Southeastern Wisconsin Regional Planning Commission, Planning Report No. 7, *Forecasts and Alternative Plans*, 1990, June, 1966.
39 J. Douglas Carroll, Jr., 'Urban Transportation Research', HRB Special Report 69, 1962.
40 E.H. Holmes, 'Why Transportation Planning?', Bureau of Public Roads, May, 1964.
41 W. Garrison, et al., *Studies of Highway Development and Geographic Change*, University of Washington Press, 1959. See, also, N. Irwin, 'Criteria for Evaluating Alternative Transportation Systems', a paper prepared for Highway Research Board, Forty-Fifth Annual Meeting, January, 1966.
42 H. Fagin, 'Urban Transportation planning Criteria', The Annals of the American Academy of Political and Social Sciences, March, 1964.
43 *Guide for Highway Impact Studies*, 1959; *Manual 9, Social and Community Value Factors*, prepared for the Ohio Department of Highways by Vogt-Ivers and Associates, 1966; Jacob Silver and Joseph R. Stowers, 'Population, Economic and Land Use Studies in Urban Transportation Planning', July, 1964.
44 See Southeastern Wisconsin, *Volume II, op. cit.*; also, Bureau of Public Roads, *Manual 9, Social and Community Value Factors, op. cit.*
45 Alan A. Altshuler, 'Rationality and Influence in Public Service', *op. cit.*; also, Altshuler, 'The Goals of Comprehensive Planning', *Journal of the American Institute of Planners*, August, 1965.
46 Bernard J. Frieden, 'Toward Equality of Urban Opportunity', *Journal of the American Institute of Planners*, November, 1965; Melvin M. Webber, 'Comprehensive Planning and Social Responsibility', *Journal of the American Institute of Planners*, November, 1963; Paul Davidoff, 'Advocacy and Pluralism in Planning', *Journal of American Institute of Planners*, November, 1965; Subcommittee on Intergovernmental Relations, *The Effectiveness of Metropolitan Planning*, U.S. Senate Committee on Government Operations, June, 1964.
47 The Planning Commission apparently also believes that relatively 'narrow objectives', such as developing a strategy for racial balance in the school system, or extensive clearance in one area, could be assisted through the use of the model and that, eventually, a large scale testing of numerous alternatives could ultimately be achieved. Bernard Fuchs, 'Federal Comprehensive Urban Planning Grants', U.S. Bureau of the Budget memorandum, November, 1966.
48 See, particularly, the contributions by Ira M. Robinson and Harvey S. Perloff in the *Journal of American Institute of Planners*, November, 1965, issue on this topic, *op. cit.*
49 In particular, the Penn-Jersey land use models.
50 Robert H. Stroup and Louis A. Vargha, 'Reflections on Concepts for Impact Research', a paper presented at the 40th Annual Meeting of the Highway Research Board, January, 1961.
51 Martin Rein, 'Social Science and the Elimination of Poverty', *Journal of the American Institute of Planners*, May, 1967.
52 This is a modification of a figure developed by nathan Grundstein for the Pittsburgh simulation effort. See Grundstein, 'Urban Information Systems and Urban Management Decisions and Control', *op. cit.*, p. 5.
53 Marvin L. Manheim, *Hierarchical Structure: A Model of Design and Planning Processes*, M.I.T Report No. 7, M.I.T Press, 1966.
54 William C. Birdsall, 'A Study of the Demand for Public Goods'.
55 W.A. Steger, 'Analytic Techniques to Determine the Needs and Resources for Urban Renewal Action', Proceedings of the IBM Scientific Computing Symposium on Simulation Models and Gaming, December, 1964; Robert C. Meier, 'The Application of Optimum Seeking Techniques to Simulation Studies: A Preliminary Evaluation', *Journal of Financial and Quantitative Analysis*, March, 1967.
56 See Edwin Thomas and Joseph Schofer, *op. cit.*
57 See Hitch and McKean, *The Economics of Defence in a Nuclear Age*, Harvard University Press, Cambridge, 1960.
58 See March and Simon, *Organizations*, Wiley, New York, 1958.
59 Inherent to this conceptualization of the 'joint' descriptor is the assumption that third-

order effects (second-order interproject externalities) are negligible. This involves questions of project complementarity below.

60 We have already seen that much planning is of the 'feasibility' or 'satisficing', rather than the optimizing variety. J.W. Dyckman cites Herbert Simon's views as most descriptive of long-range social planning methods in 'Planning and Decision Theory', *Journal of the American Institute of Planners*, November, 1961, p. 339. Dyckman cites as reasons the difficulty of formulating objective functions, the difficulty of mathematically optimizing one, even if it exists, and the large cost (in time or money) – even if one *could* achieve a solution.

61 This observation requires some qualification since practically all of the decision processes in which such 'weights' have been attached have involved only a few effect variables, often times only two (efficiency and income distribution). On the other hand, it may be argued that, whether or not a policy-maker has dealt with only a few variables for which explicit information has been quoted, the question of what other (unmeasured) effects he *perceives* is purely speculative.

62 Holt, C.C., 'Quantitative Decision Analysis and National Policy: How can we bridge the gap?' in Hickman, B.G. ed., *Quantitative Planning of Economic Policy*, The Brookings Institution, Washington, D.C., 1965, p. 253.

63 See, for example, McNemar, O., 'Opinion-Attitude Methodology', *Psychological Bulletin*, vol. 43, pp. 289–374 (July, 1946); Von Neumann, J. and Morgenstern, O., *Theory of Games and Economic Behavior*, Princeton University Press, 1953; Fishburn, P.C., 'Evaluation of Multiple-Criteria Alternatives Using Additive Utility Measures', Research Analysis Corporation, published as AD 633 595, US Department of Commerce, National Bureau of Standards, Washington, March, 1966; Marshall Freimer and Leonard S. Singer, 'The Evaluation of Potential New Product Alternatives', *Management Science*, February, 1967.

64 Discriminant analysis and Bayesian theory have been applied here. See Freimer and Simon, ibid; also, Herbert Terry, 'Comparative Evaluation of Performance Using Multiple Criteria', *Management Science*, April 1963; also Philip Kitler, 'Competitive Strategies for New Product Marketing over the Life Cycle', *Management Science*, December 1965.

65 H.W. Bruck, S.H. Putman, and W.A. Steger, 'Evaluation of Alternative Transportation Proposals: The Northeast Corridor', *op. cit.*

66 Arrow, K.J., 'Criteria for Social Investment', *Water Resources Research*, vol. 1, no. 1, p. 4, (1965).

67 Holt, C.C., *op. cit.*, pp. 255–256.

68 By example, transitivity exists if a subject prefers A over C given that he has independently claimed to prefer A over B and B over C.

69 Some key factors in the evaluation of the planning process (not detailed here) are: a) the comprehensiveness or scope of the approach, b) view of the planning process, c) organizational structure of the process, d) impact estimation techniques, and e) relevance of evaluative criteria.

70 See Donald L. Foley, 'An Approach to Metropolitan Spatial Structure', in M.M. Webber et. al., *Explorations into Urban Structure*, University of Pennsylvania Press, 1964.

71 Kent Mathewson, 'Planning and Decision-Making in the Detroit Metropolitan Area', *Highway Research Board*, No. 137, 1966, p. 14.

72 A. Altshuler, *The City Planning Process: A Political Analysis*, Cornell University Press, 1965, is an excellent case study of the planning process. Another is Frieden, *op. cit.*

73 J.P. Crecine, doctoral dissertation, Carnegie Institute of Technology, 1966.

74 Note that planning issues and alternatives are grouped in the same box, just to simplify the graphic presentation.

75 M. Ahmed, 'The Development of the Concept of Consumers' Surplus in Economic Theory and Policy', *Indian Economic Journal*, April-June 1966; P.M. Gutmann, 'Neoclassical Utility and Inter-temporal Consumer Decisions', *Economia Internazionale*, August 1966.

76 For a summary and comparison of these many methods used in evaluating transportation and land use systems, see Bruck, Putman and Steger, 'Evaluation of Alternative Transportation Proposals: The North-east Corridor', *op. cit.*, pp. 330–3.

77 W.A. Steger, 'Review of Analytic Techniques for the CRP', *op. cit.*, pp. 170–1; N. Grundstein, 'Urban Information Systems', *op. cit.*

78 The Bureau of Public Roads and the Department of Housing and Urban Development are both supporting research in this important area, currently.

79 Charles F. Hermann defines several kinds of model-building validation including: internal validity; face validity; variable-parameter validity; event validity; and hypothesis validity. See 'Validation problems in Games and Simulations with Special Reference to Models of International Politics', *Behavioral Science*, May 1967, pp. 220-4.

80 Some people refer to this as a 'top-down vs. bottoms-up' problem: can urban areas make choices so efficiently that macro-income and wealth totals should be formed by summing regional data rather than allocating macro totals to regions?

81 Eric E. Lampard, 'American Historians and the Study of Urbanization', *American Historical Review*, October 1961; Ray Lubove, 'The Urbanization process: An Approach to Historical Research', *Journal of the American Institute of Planners*, January 1967; Sam Bass Warner, Jr, 'If All the World Were Philadelphia: A Framework for Urban History, 1774–1930', Institute for Urban and Regional Studies, Washington University, Working Paper INS No 1, 1967.

82 Nathan D. Grundstein, 'Some Conceptual Problems in the Simulation of Public Social Systems', in Allen G. Feldt, ed., 'Selected Papers in Operational Gaming', *op. cit.*, pp. 51–53.

Literature

CONSAD Research Corporation (1981), *The New Economics: Implications for Economic Forecasting and Policy Analysis*, prepared for the U.S. Department of Energy, Office of Policy Planning and Analysis, Washington, DC.

CONSAD Research Corporation (1988), *Methodology for Estimating Unintended Health Effects of Regulation*, Pittsburgh, PA, prepared for the U.S. Environmental Protection Agency.

CONSAD Research Corporation (1990a), *Jobs at Risk: Updating the Economic Effects of Proposed Clean Air Act Amendments*, Pittsburgh, PA, prepared for The Business Roundtable and the Clean Air Working Group.

CONSAD Research Corporation (1990b), *Estimating the Changed Consumption of Energy Tied to Clean Air Act Options*, prepared for the Clean Air Working Group.

CONSAD Research Corporation (1990c), *Analysis of the Air Toxics Provisions Contained in the Proposed Clean Air Act Amendments*, Pittsburgh, PA.

CONSAD Research Corporation (1990d), *Analysis of Small Facility Job Impacts Resulting from the Permitting Provisions Contained in the Proposed Clean Air Act Amendments*, Pittsburgh, PA.

CONSAD Research Corporation (1992), *Jobs-at-Risk: Short-Term and Transitional Employment Impacts of Global Climate Policy Options*, May, and *Appendices*, June.

CONSAD Research Corporation (1993a), *Economic Evaluation of Energy Efficient and Pollution Control/Prevention Technologies*, prepared for the U.S. Department of Energy.

CONSAD Research Corporation (1993b), *The Design and Pilot Application of a Jobs Forecasting System for DOE Policy Options*, prepared for the U.S. Department of Energy.

CONSAD Research Corporation (1993c), *DOEs Industrial Waste Reduction Program: 'Made in California' Initiative*, prepared for the Los Alamos National Laboratory.

CONSAD Research Corporation (1993d), *Industrial Waste Reduction Program Economic Evaluation*, prepared for the U.S. Department of Energy.

CONSAD Research Corporation (1993e), *Employment Impacts Associated with Proposed Employer Health Insurance Options*, prepared for Health Care Financing Administration.

CONSAD Research Corporation (1994a), *Case Study Analysis of NIST/ATP Two Millimeter Project*, prepared for the U.S. Department of Commerce.

CONSAD Research Corporation (1994b), *Preliminary Results of CONSADs Economic, Environmental and Energy Impact Assessment of Selected NDCEE Activities*, prepared for the U.S. Department of Defense, National Defense Center for Environmental Excellence.

Index